The
Greenwood Library
of
American Folktales

The Greenwood Library of American Folktales

VOLUME II

The South,
The Caribbean

Edited by Thomas A. Green

GREENWOOD PRESS
Westport, Connecticut • London

Library of Congress Cataloging-in-Publication Data

The Greenwood Library of American folktales / edited by Thomas A. Green.
     p. cm.
   Includes bibliographical references and index.
   ISBN 0-313-33772-1 (set : alk. paper)—ISBN 0-313-33773-X (vol. 1 : alk. paper)—ISBN 0-313-
33774-8 (vol. 2 : alk. paper)—ISBN 0-313-33775-6 (vol. 3 : alk. paper)—ISBN 0-313-33776-4 (vol.
4 : alk. paper)   1. Tales—United States—History and criticism. 2. Legends—United States—
History and criticism. 3. United States—Folklore. I. Green, Thomas A., 1944–
   GR105.G75 2006
   398.20973—dc22   2006022952

British Library Cataloguing in Publication Data is available.

Library of Congress Catalog Card Number: 2006022952
ISBN: 0-313-33772-1 (set)
         0-313-33773-X (vol. I)
         0-313-33774-8 (vol. II)
         0-313-33775-6 (vol. III)
         0-313-33776-4 (vol. IV)

First published in 2006

Greenwood Press, 88 Post Road West, Westport, CT 06881
An imprint of Greenwood Publishing Group, Inc.
www.greenwood.com

Printed in the United States of America

Every reasonable effort has been made to trace the owners of copyright materials in this book,
but in some instances that has proven impossible. The author and publisher will be glad to
receive information leading to more complete acknowledgments in subsequent prints of the
book and in the meantime extend their apologies for any omissions.

Contents

Contents

Contents

derived. A combination of military action beginning in the late fifteenth century and diseases brought first from Europe and later from Africa via the slave trade decimated the native population of the islands. As a result, the impact of Native Caribbean oral traditions on the folktale corpus was minimal.

In contrast, the Native North American cultures made a lasting imprint on the folk narratives of the southern United States. Among the major native cultures in the area under consideration during the early period of contact was the Natchez—a culture of such complexity that it was unrivaled north of Mexico. By the middle of the eighteenth century, however, the Natchez, who had settled along the eastern bank of the Mississippi River, had been destroyed as a distinct cultural entity. However, individuals survived, passing along oral traditions such as those contained in this volume. Influences from neighboring non-Native cultures are readily apparent in tales such as "The Tarbaby" (p. 52).

The Cherokee, along with the Chickasaw, Choctaw, Creek, and Seminoles, were one of the "Five Civilized Tribes." Of these groups, the influence of the Choctaw and the Chickasaw declined during the historical period following European contact. The Creek Confederation was an alliance of various groups including the Alabama, Coushatta, and Hitchitee, whose traditions are represented in the present collection of tales. The Seminole emerged in historical times as a splinter group of the Creek Confederation that went on to absorb smaller indigenous groups in its territory and a considerable number of fugitive slaves of African descent. The impact of the African-descended population is apparent in many of the tales from Native Americans in this region.

Cherokee influence merits particular notice. At various points in their history they resided in Alabama, Georgia, Kentucky, North and South Carolina, Tennessee, Virginia, and West Virginia. The Cherokee were the most numerous culture in the Southeastern United States and ultimately the most influential throughout the period of European contact. In 1827, they approved a constitution that created a government with three distinct branches (executive, legislative, and judicial) modeled on the governmental structure of the United States and adopted a syllabary created by the Sequoia for writing their language. By the late 1820s, the Cherokee would seem to serve as a model for adaptation and accommodation. In 1830, however, Congress passed the Indian Removal Act, which called for the relocation of the Cherokee and other Native Americans of the Southeast to Indian Territory (now Oklahoma). In 1838, the Cherokees, with the exception of a small band who had taken refuge in the North Carolina mountains, were forcibly removed from Georgia and driven to Oklahoma. The North Carolina Cherokees, who came to be known as the Eastern Band of the Cherokee, were eventually allowed to remain. They maintained many of their oral traditions, often preserving them in manuscript form by means of the Sequoia syllabary. The traditional narratives of the "Five Civilized Tribes" contained in this volume range from indigenous myths to tales that represent obvious adaptations of the narratives of those African American and European communities with whom Native Americans shared territory.

European footholds were established early on by explorers. Spanish influence entered into the Caribbean in the late fifteenth century and into the southern United States in the early sixteenth century. The British established colonies in the Carolinas and the Caribbean in the late-sixteenth and early seventeenth centuries. The French became a factor in the Caribbean in the middle of the seventeenth century and in the southern United States by the end of the century.

While all these European contacts made an impact on the South, in the coastal states, French heritage, and to a lesser degree Spanish heritage, is strikingly represented in Creole traditions. Some have contended that the term used to designate New World traditions entails the meanings of the Spanish term *criollo* (a resident of the New World of European ancestry). The academic usage of the term "creole," however, refers to a language that began as a "pidgin," a language that arises from contact between groups who share no common language. The pidgin is created from elements of the languages of the groups in contact as a linguistic compromise to serve temporary communication needs. If a pidgin goes on to become a group's native language and, as a result, develops the capacity to serve the needs of that group of native speakers, it comes to be called a creole. Used in reference to culture, a creole or creolization describes the convergence—in any sphere—of distinctive cultural traits that results in a new form. The term has been commonly used as a label for the cultural mix of traits found in Louisiana and the West Indies.

In Louisiana, the definition of creole has fluctuated with social changes. In its earliest usage, it included colonists of European descent born in the Americas, slaves of African descent, and free people of color. After Spain's assumption of control over the Louisiana Territory in 1768 and the subsequent immigration of French aristocrats fleeing the revolution at home, Acadians from Canada, and elites from St. Domingue (modern Haiti), French ancestry became the major criterion for defining "creole" along with the association of high socioeconomic status. After the Louisiana Purchase in 1803 and throughout the "American period," French ancestry, French creole dialect, and racial difference developed as the defining features of creole identity (Dubois and Melançon 2000). The tales in this volume that have been labeled as creole, either by tradition bearers or collectors, stress European as distinct from African roots. This is the case with both tales from the southern United States (see *"La Graisse,"* p.

312, and "The Talking Eggs," p. 224) and the Caribbean (see "The Night Beauty," p. 281, and "Dayday Agastin," p. 295).

As noted, Cajuns are the descendents of Europeans of French ancestry who were exiled from Acadia (now Nova Scotia, Canada) by the British, who began a systematic program of deportation in 1755. Some Acadians deported from Canada found refuge in the French Caribbean; others found their way to territory inhabited primarily by Native Americans, which may account for the shared tales among the Cajun corpus and the repertoires of Native Americans in the southeastern United States. See, for example, "The Rabbit and the Frenchman" (p. 54), and compare the tale "On Horseback" (p. 61) to "Rabbit Rides Wolf" (p. 58).

The largest, and historically the most identifiable, Cajun population settled in what was then the Louisiana Territory. Maintaining a separate identity, these southern Cajuns held on to French narratives featuring Jean Sot (Foolish John), featured in "Jean Sot Feeds Cows Needles" (p. 110) and "Jean Sot Kills the Duck" (p. 111). However, the preservation of identity does not entail insulation from neighbors occupying the same region or ossification of the tale repertoire. The tales of Lapin and Bouqui provide particularly useful examples of borrowing between the Cajun and the African American communities. Particular tales, such as "The Wine, the Farm, the Princess, and the Tarbaby" (p. 49), survived in both ethnic traditions. Moreover, the name Bouqui, the comic foil for the **trickster** Lapin (Rabbit) in the Cajun cycle of **trickster** tales, means "hyena," a word borrowed from a West African language called Wolof. Bouqui, under a variety of spellings, is found not only in the United States but in the Caribbean as well (see "Brother Rabbit, Brother Booky, and Brother Cow," p. 255). Moreover, ample evidence of sharing among Cajun, African American, and Native Americans is provided by a comparison of the Cajun tale "On Horseback" (p. 61) to "Rabbit Rides Wolf" (p. 58) and the African American "Mr. Deer's My Riding Horse" (p. 56).

The folktales in this collection demonstrate the early and profound influence of African cultures—especially in the coastal South and the Caribbean. The African influence appears in the vast corpus of the African American community as well as in the European and Native American repertoires. The enslavement and importation of Africans into the Caribbean (beginning in the late sixteenth century) and colonial America (beginning with the Jamestown, Virginia, colony in 1619) eventually provided a major source of African influence. This was especially true in the coastal states of the South with the development of a plantation economy following the explosive growth of the cotton-farming industry caused by the invention of the cotton gin in 1793. A similar expansion of the commerce in African slaves in the Caribbean had attended the switch from tobacco to production.

Although the enactment of legislation in 1808 banned the importation of slaves into the United States, the American South did not become a sealed environment. Around this period, refugees from the Haitian Revolution—some of African ancestry—made their way to areas of the coastal United States. Even earlier, the historical record shows that in the wake of the colonial Revolution against the British "United Empire Loyalists" (Tories) emigrated to the British Caribbean from the Carolinas, taking with them their household slaves. This immigration, Elsie Clews Parsons argues (1917), provides at least part of the explanation for the continuities between the Southern and Caribbean repertoires a century after the official U.S. ban on African slave commerce.

Other than their labor, these captive Africans also brought their indigenous traditions. In the past, the issue of the eventual impact of these African traditions on African America was hotly contested, with one side contending that they had been destroyed by the repressive institution of slavery and the other arguing for the survival of Africanisms in the Western Hemisphere. Late in the twentieth century a compromise was reached. The solution proposed that African American culture was neither a simple reaction to the slavery encountered in the Americas nor an equally unmediated relocation of Old World forms into new contexts. The notion of creolization was adopted to describe the convergence in any sphere of distinctive cultural traits that results in a new form. Thus, African and European expressive culture met and produced new products that bore the marks of both worlds—see, for example, "How Brer Rabbit Bring Dust Out of the Rock" (p. 149), a tale in which European and European American Jack tale **motifs** and plot structures converge with the African American **trickster** Brer Rabbit.

The Appalachian region is also relevant to this volume. The southern Appalachian region encompasses West Virginia as well as large areas of North and South Carolina, Kentucky, Tennessee, and Virginia and portions of Alabama, Georgia, and Mississippi. The European ethnic makeup of the region is historically composed of northern English and Scots-Irish who had been settled in Ulster during the early seventeenth century. A century later, many had immigrated to the American colonies and pushed westward into the Appalachian region between 1718 and 1775. Later, settlers from the southern Appalachian region moved on to the Ozarks, limited here to the northern Arkansas and southern Missouri area. These immigrants, though not the first of European descent to settle there, eventually became the largest faction. As a result, they became the dominant influence on traditional narratives in the area. The relative isolation of the rural communities in the southern highlands encouraged the preservation of archaic British dialect features as well as various **genres** of folklore and folklife. For example, localized versions of English folktales such as "Jack and the Beanstalk" (see "Jack and the Beanstalk," p. 134, and "Jack the Giant Killer," p. 79) were collected in the early decades of the twentieth century along with **personal experience narratives** and **legends** of witchcraft and hauntings, as in "A Bewitched Gun" (p. 179) and "Miller's Witch Wife" (p. 171).

Despite the diversity of these regions, unifying factors may be seen within the tales of this volume. Shared cultural concerns derived from a common origin stimulated by continued contact between the coastal south and the Caribbean were at work to mobilize continuities within the New World African traditions. Social tensions between the empowered and the misused encouraged the sharing of **trickster** narratives across cultural boundaries. Living in close proximity in a common environment promotes similarities in lifestyles and material culture and commonalities in the expression of sentiments regarding the shared way of life. The following narratives are driven by the historical, social, and environmental features particular to the region. As in the other volumes in this series, although efforts have been made to preserve the flavor of the original transcriptions of these tales, when necessary, tales have been modified for readability by contemporary, nonspecialist readers. Unedited versions of many of the tales are included in the Appendix to this volume to illustrate the nature of their original renderings.

SUGGESTED READINGS

Abrahams, Roger D., ed. *African American Folktales: Stories from Black Traditions in the New World.* New York: Pantheon, 1985.

———. *The Man-of-Words in the West Indies.* Baltimore: Johns Hopkins University Press, 1983.

Ancelet, Barry Jean. *Cajun and Creole Folktales: The French Oral Tradition of South Louisiana.* Jackson: The University Press of Mississippi, 1994.

Bascom, William. *African Folktales in the New World.* Bloomington: Indiana University Press, 1992.

Beckwith, Martha Warren. *Jamaica Anansi Stories.* Memoirs of the American Folklore Society 17. New York: American Folklore Society, 1924.

Botkin, Benjamin A. *A Treasury of Southern Folklore: Stories, Ballads, Traditions and Folkways of the People of the South.* New York: Crown, 1949.

Campbell, Marie. *Tales from the Cloud Walking Country.* Bloomington: Indiana University Press, 1958.

Claudel, Calvin Andre. *Fools and Rascals: Folktales of Louisiana and Their Backgrounds.* Baton Rouge, LA: Legacy, 1978.

Courlander, Harold. *Afro-American Folklore.* New York: Crown, 1976.

Crowley, Daniel. *I Could Talk Old Story Good.* Berkeley: University of California Press, 1966.

Dance, Daryl. *Folklore from Contemporary Jamaicans.* Knoxville: University of Tennessee Press, 1985.

Dorson, Richard. *American Negro Folktales.* Greenwich, CT: Fawcett, 1967.

Harris, Joel Chandler. *The Complete Tales of Uncle Remus.* Compiled by Richard Chase. Boston: Houghton Mifflin, 1953.

Hurston, Zora Neale. *Mules and Men.* Philadelphia: Lippincott, 1936.

Martin, Howard N. *Myths and Folktales of the Alabama-Coashatta Indians.* Austin, TX: Encino Press, 1987.

Mooney, James. *James Mooney's History, Myths, and Sacred Formulas of the Cherokees.* Asheville, NC: Historical Images, 1992.

———. *Myths of the Cherokee.* New York: Dover, 1995.

Randolph, Vance. *The Devil's Pretty Daughter, and Other Ozark Folktales.* New York: Columbia University Press, 1955.

———. *We Always Lie to Strangers: Tall Tales from the Ozarks.* New York: Columbia University Press, 1951.

Roberts, Leonard W. *South from Hell-fer-Sartin: Kentucky Mountain Folktales.* Lexington: University of Kentucky Press, 1988.

Swanton, John R. *Myths and Tales of the Southeastern Indians.* Smithsonian Institution Bureau of American Ethnology Bulletin 88. Washington, DC: U.S. Government Printing Office, 1929.

THE SOUTH

ORIGINS

KANATI AND SELU: THE ORIGIN OF CORN AND GAME

Tradition Bearer: Unavailable

Source: Mooney, James. "Myths of the Cherokees." *Journal of American Folklore* 1 (1888): 98–106.

Date: 1887

Original Source: Cherokee

National Origin: Native American

The following **myth** required anyone who heard it to fast and take a ritual bath presided over by a holy man. Connected to this **myth** is a series of events occurring later in the first age of the Cherokee in which the people, starving from a lack of game, sent for the brothers who returned and gave them the rituals to use for calling game. This **myth** alludes to a range of esoteric knowledge shared by the traditional Cherokee. For example, the **myth** establishes the intimate relationship between Kanati (representative of hunters in general) and the wolf, thus establishing the animal's protected status among any Cherokee desiring a successful hunt. Similar narratives focused on two brothers—one of whom is "tame" while the other is "wild" and lives on the margins of society and at the edge of the social order—are distributed widely in Native American tradition. "The Story of Lodge Boy, After-Birth Boy and Double-Face" among the Omaha is one such closely related example. For another example of the "twin motif," see also "Origin of Acoma" (Vol. III, p. 7) and

"The Two Boys Who Slew the Monsters and Became Stars" (Vol. III, p. 212) in the present collection.

When I was a boy, this is what the old men told me they had heard when they were boys.

Long ages ago, soon after the world was made, a hunter and his wife lived at Looking-glass Mountain, with their only child, a little boy. The father's name was Kanati, "The Lucky Hunter," and his wife was called Selu, "Corn." No matter when Kanati went into the woods, he never failed to bring back a load of game, which his wife cut up and prepared, washing the blood from the meat in the river near the house. The little boy used to play down by the river every day, and one morning the old people thought they heard laughing and talking in the bushes, as though there were two children there. When the boy came home at night, his parents asked who had been playing with him all day. "He comes out of the water," said the boy, "and he calls himself my elder brother. He says his mother was cruel to him, and threw him into the river." Then they knew that the strange boy had sprung from the blood of the game which Selu had washed off at the river's edge.

Every day, when the little boy went out to play, the other would join him; but, as he always went back into the water, the old people never had a chance to see him. At last, one evening, Kanati said to his son, "To-morrow, when the other boy comes to play with you, get him to wrestle with you, and when you have your arms around him hold on to him and call for us." The boy promised to do as he was told; so the next day, as soon as his playmate appeared, he challenged him to a wrestling-match. The other agreed at once, but as soon as they had their arms around each other Kanati's boy began to scream for his father. The old folks at once came running down, and when the wild boy saw them he struggled to free himself, and cried out, "Let me go! You threw me away!" But his brother held on until his parents reached the spot, when they seized the wild boy and took him home with them. They kept him in the house until they had tamed him, but he was always wild and artful in his disposition, and was the leader of his brother in every mischief. Before long the old people discovered that he was one of those persons endowed with magic powers, and they called him, "He who grew up Wild."

Whenever Kanati went into the mountains he always brought back a fat buck or doe, or maybe a couple of turkeys. One day the wild boy said to his brother, "I wonder where our father gets all that game; let's follow him next time, and find out." A few days afterward, Kanati took a bow and some feathers in his hand, and started off. The boys waited a little while, and then started after him, keeping out of sight, until they saw their father go into a swamp where there were a great many of the reeds that hunters use to make arrow-shafts. Then the wild boy changed himself into a puff of bird's down, which the wind took up and carried until it alighted upon Kanati's shoulder just as he entered the swamp, but Kanati knew nothing about it. The hunter then cut reeds, fitted the feathers to them, and made some arrows, and the wild boy—in his other shape—thought, "I wonder what those things are for." When Kanati had his arrows finished, he came out of the swamp and went on again. The wind blew the down from his shoulder; it fell in the woods, when the wild boy took his right shape again, and went back and told his brother what he had seen. Keeping out of sight of their father, they followed him up the mountain until he stopped at a certain place and lifted up a large rock. At once a buck came running out, which Kanati shot, and then, lifting it upon his back, he started home again.

"Oho!" said the boys, "he keeps all the deer shut up in that hole, and whenever he wants venison he just lets one out, and kills it with those things he made in the swamp." They hurried and reached home before their father, who had the heavy deer to carry, so that he did not know they had followed him.

A few days after, the boys went back to the swamp, cut some reeds and made seven arrows, and then started up the mountain to where their father kept the game. When they got to the place they lifted up the rock, and a deer came running out. Just as they drew back to shoot it, another came out, and then another, and another, until the boys got confused and forgot what they were about. In those days all the deer had their tails hanging down, like other animals, but, as a buck was running past, the wild boy struck its tail with his arrow so that it stood straight out behind. This pleased the boys, and when the next one ran by, the other brother struck his tail so that it pointed upward. The boys thought this was good sport, and when the next one ran past, the wild boy struck his tail so that it stood straight up, and his brother struck the next one so hard with his arrow that the deer's tail was curled over his back. The boys thought this was very pretty, and ever since the deer has carried his tail over his back.

The deer continued to pass until the last one had come out of the hole and escaped into the forest. Then followed droves of raccoons, rabbits, and all the other four-footed animals. Last came great flocks of turkeys, pigeons, and partridges that darkened the air like a cloud, and made such a noise with their wings that Kanati, sitting at home, heard the sound like distant thunder on the

13

mountains, and said to himself, "My bad boys have got into trouble. I must go and see what they are doing."

So Kanati went up the mountain, and when he came to the place where he kept the game he found the two boys standing by the rock, and all the birds and animals were gone. He was furious, but, without saying a word, he went down into the cave and kicked the covers off four jars in one corner, when out swarmed bed-bugs, fleas, lice, and gnats, and got all over the boys. They screamed with pain and terror, and tried to beat off the insects; but the thousands of insects crawled over them, and bit and stung them, until both dropped down nearly dead from exhaustion. Kanati stood looking on until he thought they had been punished enough, when be brushed off the vermin, and proceeded to give the boys a lecture.

"Now, you rascals," said he, "you have always had plenty to eat, and never had to work for it. Whenever you were hungry, all I had to do was to come up here and get a deer or a turkey, and bring it home for your mother to cook. But now you have let out all the animals, and after this, when you want a deer to eat, you will have to hunt all over the woods for it, and then maybe not find one. Go home now to your mother, while I see if I can find something to eat for supper."

When the boys reached home again they were very tired and hungry and asked their mother for something to eat.

"There is no meat," said Selu, "but wait a little while, and I will get you something."

So she took a basket and started out to the provision-house.... This provision-house was built upon poles high up from the ground, to keep it out of the reach of animals, and had a ladder to climb up by, and one door, but no other opening. Every day, when Selu got ready to cook the dinner, she would go out to the provision-house with a basket, and bring it back full of corn and beans. The boys had never been inside the provision-house, and wondered where all the corn and beans could come from, as the house was not a very large one; so, as soon as Selu went out of the door, the wild boy said to his brother, "Let's go and see what she does." They ran around and climbed up at the back of the provision-house, and pulled out a piece of clay from between the logs, so that they could look in. There they saw Selu standing in the middle of the room, with the basket in front of her on the floor. Leaning over the basket, she rubbed her stomach—so—and the basket was half-full of corn. Then she rubbed under her arm-pits—so—and the basket was full to the top with beans. The brothers looked at each other, and said, "This will never do; our mother is a witch. If we eat any of that it will poison us. We must kill her."

When the boys came back into the house, Selu knew their thoughts before they spoke.

"So you are going to kill me!" said Selu.

"Yes," said the boys; "you are a witch."

"Well," said their mother, "when you have killed me, clear a large piece of ground in front of the house, and drag my body seven times around the circle. Then drag me seven times over the ground inside the circle, and stay up all night and watch, and in the morning you will have plenty of corn."

Then the boys killed her with their clubs, and cut off her head, and put it up on the roof of the house, and told it to look for her husband. Then they set to work to clear the ground in front of the house, but, instead of clearing the whole piece, they cleared only seven little spots. This is the reason why corn now grows only in a few places instead of over the whole world. Then they dragged the body of Selu around the circles, and wherever her blood fell on the ground the corn sprang up. But, instead of dragging her body seven times across the ground, they did this only twice, which is the reason why the Indians still work their crop but twice. The two brothers sat up and watched their corn all night, and in the morning it was fully grown and ripe.

When Kanati came home at last, he looked around, but could not see Selu anywhere, so he asked the boys where their mother was.

"She was a witch, and we killed her," said the boys; "there is her head up there on top of the house."

When Kanati saw his wife's head on the roof he was very angry, and said, "I won't stay with you any longer. I am going to the…[Wolf] people." So he started off, but, before he had gone far, the wild boy changed himself again to a tuft of down, which fell on Kanati's shoulder. When Kanati reached the settlement of the Wolf people, they were holding a council in the town-house…. He went in and sat down, with the tuft of bird's down on his shoulder. When the Wolf chief asked him his business, he said, "I have two bad boys at home, and I want you to go in seven days from now and play against them." Kanati spoke as though he wanted them to play a game of ball, but the wolves knew that he meant for them to come and kill the two boys. The wolves promised to go. Then the bird's down blew off from Kanati's shoulder, and the smoke carried it up through the hole in the roof of the town-house. When it came down on the ground outside, the wild boy took his right shape again, and went home and told his brother all that he had heard in the town-house. When Kanati left the Wolf people, he did not return home, but went on farther.

The boys then began to get ready for the wolves, and the wild boy—the magician—told his brother what to do. They ran around the house in a wide circle until they had made a trail all around it, excepting on the side from which the wolves would come, where they left a small open space. Then they made four large bundles of arrows, and placed them at four different points on the outside of the circle, after which they hid themselves in the woods and waited for the wolves. On the appointed day a whole army of wolves came and surrounded the house, to kill the boys. The wolves did not notice the trail around the house, because they came in where the boys had left the opening, but the moment they were inside the circle the trail changed to a high fence, and shut them in. Then the boys on the outside took their arrows and began shooting them down, and, as the wolves could not jump over the fence, they were all killed excepting a few, which escaped through the opening into a great swamp close by. Then the boys ran around the swamp, and a circle of fire sprang up in their tracks, and set fire to the grass and bushes, and burned up nearly all the other wolves. Only two or three got away, and these were all the wolves which were left in the whole world.

Soon afterward some strangers from a distance, who heard that the brothers had a wonderful grain from which they made bread, came to ask for some; for none but Selu and her family had ever known corn before. The boys gave them seven grains of corn, which they told them to plant the next night on their way home, sitting up all night to watch the corn, which would have seven ripe ears in the morning. These they were to plant the next night, and watch in the same way; and so on every night until they reached home, when they would have corn enough to supply the whole people. The strangers lived seven days' journey away. They took the seven grains of corn, and started home again. That night they planted the seven grains, and watched all through the darkness until morning, when they saw seven tall stalks, each stalk bearing a ripened ear. They gathered the ears with gladness, and went on their way. The next night they planted all their corn, and guarded it with wakeful care until daybreak, when they found an abundant increase. But the way was long and the sun was hot, and the people grew tired. On the last night before reaching home they fell asleep, and in the morning the corn they had planted had not even sprouted. They brought with them to their settlement what corn they had left, and planted it, and with care and attention were able to raise a crop. But ever since the corn must be watched and tended through half the year, which before would grow and ripen in a night.

As Kanati did not return, the boys at last concluded to go and see if they could find him. The wild boy got a wheel and rolled it toward the direction where it is always night. In a little while the wheel came rolling back, and the boys knew their father was not there. Then the wild boy rolled it to the south and to the north, and each time the wheel came back to him, and they knew their father was not there. Then he rolled it toward the Sun Land, and it did not return.

"Our father is there," said the wild boy, "let us go and find him."

So the two brothers set off toward the east, and after traveling a long time they came upon Kanati, walking along, with a little dog by his side.

"You bad boys," said their father, "have you come here?"

"Yes," they answered; "we always accomplish what we start out to do—we are men!"

"This dog overtook me four days ago," then said Kanati; but the boys knew that the dog was the wheel which they had sent after him to find him.

"Well," said Kanati, "as you have found me, we may as well travel together, but I will take the lead."

Soon they came to a swamp, and Kanati told them there was a dangerous thing there, and they must keep away from it. Then he went on ahead, but as soon as he was out of sight the wild boy said to his brother, "Come and let us see what is in the swamp." They went in together, and in the middle of the swamp they found a large panther, asleep. The wild boy got out an arrow, and shot the panther in the side of the head. The panther turned his head, and the other boy shot him on that side. He turned his head away again, and the two brothers shot together, but the panther was not hurt by the arrows, and paid no more attention to the boys. They came out of the swamp, and soon overtook Kanati, waiting for them. "Did you find it?" asked Kanati.

"Yes," said the boys, "we found it, but it never hurt us. We are men." Kanati was surprised, but said nothing, and they went on again.

After a while Kanati turned to them, and said, "Now you must be careful. We are coming to a tribe called the 'Cookers' [i.e., Cannibals], and if they get you they will put you in a pot and feast on you." Then he went on ahead. Soon the boys came to a tree which had been struck by lightning, and the wild boy directed his brother to gather some of the splinters from the tree, and told him what to do with them. In a little while they came to the settlement of the cannibals, who, as soon as they saw the boys, came running out, crying, "Good! Here are two nice, fat strangers. Now we'll have a grand feast!" They caught the boys and dragged them into the town-house, and sent word to all the people of the settlement to come to the feast. They made up a great fire, filled a large pot with water and set it to boiling, and then seized the wild boy and threw him into the pot, and put the lid on it. His brother was not frightened in the least, and made no attempt to escape, but quietly knelt down and began putting the splinters into the fire, as if to make it burn better. When the cannibals thought the meat was about ready, they lifted the lid from the pot, and that instant a blinding light filled the town-house, and the lightning began to dart from one side to the other, beating down the cannibals until not one of them was left alive. Then the lightning went up through the smoke-hole, and the next moment there were the two boys standing outside the town-house as though nothing had happened. They went on, and soon met Kanati, who seemed much surprised to see them, and said, "What! Are you here again?"

"Oh, yes, we never give up. We are great men!"

"What did the cannibals do to you?"

"We met them, and they brought us to their town-house, but they never hurt us."

Kanati said nothing more, and they went on.

Kanati soon got out of sight of the boys, but they kept on until they came to the end of the world, where the sun comes out. The sky was just coming down when they got there, but they waited until it went up again, and then they went through and climbed up on the other side. There they found Kanati and Selu sitting together. The old folks received them kindly, and were glad to see them, and told them they might stay there a while, but then they must go to live where the sun goes down. The boys stayed with their parents seven days, and then went on toward the sunset land, where they are still living.

THE ORIGIN OF CORN

Tradition Bearer: Unavailable

Source: Swanton, John R. Page 230 in *Myths and Tales of the Southeastern Indians.* Smithsonian Institution Bureau of American Ethnology Bulletin 88. Washington, DC: U.S. Government Printing Office, 1929.

Date: 1929

Original Source: Natchez

National Origin: Native American

The three primary food crops for Native American gardening cultures were corn, beans, and squash, and the importance of these plant foods is highlighted in the myths of these groups. The following **myth** performs this function and goes on to underscore the consequences of directing disrespectful behavior to the supernatural powers that control food sources. The "fall from grace" due to curiosity provides interesting parallels to Judaeo-Christian beliefs and may have been a later modification of the **myth** as it existed prior to European contact.

Corn-woman lived at a certain place in company with twin girls. When the corn was all gone she went into the corn house, taking two baskets, and came out with the baskets full. They lived on the hominy which she made from this.

One time the girls looked into this corn house and saw nothing there. They said to each other, "Where does she get it? Next time she goes in there we will creep up and watch her."

When the corn was all gone she started to go in and they saw her. So they crept after her and when she entered and closed the door they peeped through a crack. They saw her set down the basket, stand astride of it and rub and shake herself, and there was a noise, as if something fell off. In this way she filled one basket with corn. Then she stood over the other, rubbed herself and shook, the noise was heard and that basket was full of beans. After that the girls ran away.

"Let us not eat it," they said. "She defecates and then feeds us with the excrement." So when the hominy was cooked they did not eat it, and from that she knew they had seen her. "Since you think it is filthy, you will have to help yourselves from now on. Kill me and burn my body. When summer comes things will spring up on the place where it was burned and you must cultivate them, and when they are matured they will be your food."

They killed Corn-woman and burned her body and when summer came corn, beans, and pumpkins sprang up. They kept cultivating these and every day, when they stopped, stuck their hoes up in the ground and went away. But on their return more ground would be hoed and the hoes would be sticking up in different places.

They said, "Let us creep up and find out who is hoeing for us," and they did so. When they looked they saw that the hoes were doing it of themselves and they laughed. Immediately the hoes fell down and did not work for them any more. They did not know that it was just those two hoes which were helping them and they themselves spoiled it.

THE MAN WHO INVENTED FIRE

Tradition Bearer: Unavailable

Source: Fauset, Arthur Huff. "Negro Folk Tales from the South (Alabama, Mississippi, Louisiana)." *Journal of American Folklore* 40 (1927): 273.

Date: 1925

Original Source: Alabama

National Origin: African American

The following tale is a straightforward narrative of a **culture hero** acquiring fire, an event that led to the dominion of man over nature and the animal world. The fact that the **culture hero**, "the inventor of fire," is a blacksmith is significant. In both Africa and the Americas the blacksmith has supernatural significance. The profession in West Africa is surrounded with a supernatural aura. Moreover, in West African Yoruba and Yoruba-influenced traditions in the New World (Santeria and candomble, for example), Ogun is a powerful supernatural figure who is associated, among other things, with the blacksmith and with the realm of technology in general.

Once upon a time men didn't have fire. It was a long time before fire ever been invented.

Man lived in another part of the country an' didn't know anything about fire. He was a blacksmith and made swords. When it was cold he piled leaves around the feets of his wife and baby to keep them warm. Fire jumped from his anvil and lit the leaves. He knew then he had invented fire.

He called all his friends and told them he had invented fire. Then one day Bear came and took the baby. Bear doesn't like fire.

Mother came back from the woods and she didn't know what to do. So she got some fire, put it in her hands and hunted Bear. Bear got frightened and dropped the baby.

So he came across where Zebra lived telling about his invention of fire. He sold fire by coals. He killed deer and bees and hung these up in his cave. With the fire he learned to cook meat in his cave.

So he invited his friends to a dinner. He showed how fire cooked meat. He told them all about how he had did. He told them about fishing and hunting and they came and stayed a long time with him and lived with him.

Then they selected him as king and ruler.

ORIGIN OF THE ALABAMA INDIANS

Tradition Bearer: Unavailable

Source: Swanton, John R. Pages 118–21 in *Myths and Tales of the Southeastern Indians.* Smithsonian Institution Bureau of American Ethnology Bulletin 88. Washington, DC: U.S. Government Printing Office, 1929.

Date: 1929

Original Source: Alabama

National Origin: Native American

Initially the following narrative displays traits of **myth** in its **motif**s of migration across a great ocean and the invention of weapons and the means to make fire. For the most part, however, plausible events are set in the historical past, leading to the tale's classification as a **legend**. Actual events and names are used in the narrative. The Alabama and the Cousatti, with whom they eventually became affiliated, were members of the Creek Confederacy in what eventually became Alabama. At this time in their history, they fought the Choctaw mentioned in the "Origin of the Alabama Indians." The berdache mentioned in the narrative was a male transvestite who acted socially as a woman; the role was neither uncommon nor maligned in many Native American cultures. By the early nineteenth century they had moved to Texas and established several villages; the most prominent was Peach Tree Village, where they relied primarily on hunting and gathering and horticulture. The episode in which the Alabama befriended and fed white refugees seems based on the "Runaway Scrape" and other events of the Texas Revolution of 1836.

Formerly the ocean was not as large as it is today, and at that time the Alabama Indians, who lived upon the other side, came westward across it in canoes. When they had gotten about halfway over they came upon an island where they rested and fished. Then they resumed their journey and presently reached this land.

At first they lived upon acorns, and they also roasted and ate cane sprouts. Later they made bows and arrows with which to kill deer, and having nothing with which to cut up the meat they used sharp rocks. They also had to learn how to kindle a fire. To accomplish this they used as a drill the stem of a weed called "plant-with-which-to-make-fire" which is like sassafras and the wood of a tree called bass for a base stick.

Traveling inland, they established their village near a river and lived there for a long time. Presently they came in contact with the Choctaw and warred against them, almost destroying one Choctaw town, so that the Choctaw became disheartened and wanted to make peace. For this purpose they selected a poor man, promising that, if he were successful, they would give him the two daughters of a certain prominent woman. They gave him a white deerskin shirt and white deerskin leggings and moccasins, put a string of white beads about his neck and a rattle in his hand.

Thus provided, the man crossed to the first Alabama village shaking his rattle and singing as he went. When the Alabama heard him they came out, took hold of him, and accompanied him back. On coming near the town they raised him on their backs and entered the place in this manner, singing continually. They set him down and he talked to them for a long time, laying down one string of white beads as he did so. Then he set out for another village, accompanied as before. On the way one of them seized a gun and shot under him. Another ran toward him and discharged a gun near his ear. At the next village he made another long talk and laid out a second string of white beads. He did the same at the third village. Then he returned to his people and they gave him the girls as they had promised, but soon afterwards he lay down and died.

One summer a man said he wanted to go west and several wished to accompany him, but a berdache ("half-man") tried to stop them. "Why are you going?" he said. "I am going in order to kill and eat turkey, deer, and other game animals; after that I will return." "There are plenty of turkey and deer here," said the berdache, but the other persisted in his plan and after they had disputed for some time the berdache said, "You are a man but you want to run away. I will not run. I will not run, although my grandfather used to say that the English, Ålåta, and French are all hard fighters. When they come, I will take a knife, lie down under the bed, and keep striking at them until they kill me."

Nevertheless the man and his friends started off. They came to a river, made canoes, and proceeded along it a great distance until they finally reached a Choctaw settlement. They stopped for a while, thinking that these people were friends, but presently they observed that they were making arrows, so they became frightened and reentered their canoes.

Following the river, they came upon many bears swimming across and some wanted to kill them, but others said, "Don't shoot," and they kept on. Presently they heard the sound of firearms behind and said to one another, "People are following us." Not long afterwards they came upon a creek emptying into the river, its mouth almost obscured by canes, and they shoved their canoes into it and waited. After a while they heard the Choctaw canoes pass on up, so they remained where they were all that night. When it was nearly day they heard the sound of returning paddles and after they had died away they continued their journey.

After they had gone on for some time the Alabama came to the house of a white man. He exchanged corn for venison and told them that the route by the river which they had intended to take was very long, so he tied oxen to their canoes and dragged them across a narrow place.

Then they paddled along for some time and reached a trading house belonging to a white blacksmith. They procured from him old knives and axes in exchange for venison. Some Choctaw lived there who said to them, "There is no war here. There is peace. We are friends of the Alabama." Afterwards, however, some of both tribes got drunk on whisky obtained at the store and wanted to fight. But the Alabama who had remained sober took their friends down to the canoes, put them in, and started along.

As they pushed off the Choctaw stood near the shore and shot at them until they got out into the middle of the river. Later they went back to the store and found that the Choctaw were all gone, so they had the blacksmith make knives for them and sharpen their old axes.

The white people came from the other side of the ocean long after the Alabama had crossed and tried to buy land from them. They would get the Indians drunk, and when they had become sober they would find bags of money hung to their necks in payment for land. It was after they had sold their lands in this way that they came westward.

After leaving the blacksmith the Alabama came to Bayou Boeuf. Later they moved to Opelousas, La., and still later to Tyler County, Tex. Afterwards they settled Peach-tree village. There were many Alabama at that time and they separated into a number of villages. One was north of North Woodville and was called "Cane Island" and afterwards simply island, because some canes were found near the creek. They were living in these towns when the Mexican War broke out.

When the Mexicans were here the white men came and built a town, putting up stores. After a while they heard that the Mexicans and whites were coming to fight with each other, and the people all ran off. They left their stores and went away. While they were moving on without stopping, it rained and the white girls walked along with their dresses half soaked. Some were weeping. Continuing on in this way they passed through Peach-tree village. Some of them were perishing with hunger and asked the Indians for food. Then they gave them milk, but instead of drinking it they gave it to the children.

Just after the whites had left, the Mexicans came to this town, and their soldiers opened the stores which they had abandoned and used the goods. By and by they wanted to cross a big river there and threw bales of cotton into the water and crossed upon them. When they got over they found that the Indians had a camp on this side. They did not like them and wanted to kill them. But instead of killing them they drove them back and made them stay on the other side of the river. The Indians walked while two Mexicans rode on each horse.

After that the white people came to fight. Some of them went round the town and broke down a bridge over a bad creek, so that when the Mexicans arrived they could not cross and all were killed.

Their general Santa Anna, escaped alone on his horse. He fell down in a swampy place but got up and ran on and lay down in a thicket. While he lay there two deer whistled, and the whites came up and captured him. Then they demanded his land of him, and he left the people, got into a boat, and went away.

Another party of whites reached that town and the Mexicans all ran off. Some Mexicans who were drunk remained walking about holding each other up, and the whites threw them down and stabbed them. When the Mexicans ran off they had just been cooking and left earthen pots full of peas mixed with red peppers on the fire. When the white men saw the Indians there they recognized them and had them recross the river. "Hang up something white and stay by it," they said, "lest those coming after us make trouble." So they hung up a white cloth and remained by it.

WHEN MR. PINE TREE AND MR. OAK TREE FALL OUT

Tradition Bearer:

Source: Backus, Emma M. "Folk-Tales from Georgia." *Journal of American Folklore* 13 (1900): 29–30.

Date: 1900

Original Source: Georgia

National Origin: African American

Beyond illustrating how jealousy can lead to a permanent rift between friends, the following tale presents an example of minding someone else's business. Gossip, backbiting, and rumor are particularly destructive in small traditional communities such as the ones in which this tale arose and was perpetuated. "When Mr. Pine Tree and Mr. Oak Tree Fall Out," like most origin tales, goes beyond ecological explanations to present a social message.

Mr. Pine Tree and Mr. Oak Tree used to be great friends and live in peace side by side, until Mr. Oak Tree he get jealous of Mr. Pine Tree 'cause Mr. Pine Tree he keep his fine green clothes on all winter; but jest as sure as cold weather come Mr. Oak Tree's clothes they fade out a most ugly sort of color and fall off, and that make Mr. Oak Tree jealous to see hisself and his family with just few faded old clothes on their backs, while his neighbor, Mr. Pine Tree and his family, stand up proudful with all their fine green clothes on.

Mr. Oak Tree he grow more jealous year by year, but he keep it all to hisself, 'cause Mr. Oak Tree he don't know just what he going do about it.

One year the people was looking for a place to have the camp-meeting. Now they always have the camp-meeting on big grove hill, where Mr. Oak Tree and Mr. Pine Tree grow side by side, and Mr. Oak Tree and Mr. Pine Tree, both powerful prideful, 'cause they have the camp-meeting there.

But one time the people come, and instead of placing round the seats and breshin' up the grounds, they go 'bout tearing everything up and toting them over in the big pine grove, where Mr. Pine Tree live all by hisself.

Mr. Oak Tree he hear the people talking, and they say it am much nicer in Mr. Pine Tree's house, 'cause he have a nice carpet on the ground, while Mr. Oak Tree's house all covered with dirty old leaves.

Well, it nigh 'bout break Mr. Oak Tree's heart, that it do, 'deed and double 'deed it do; and Mr. Wind, he done see how Mr. Oak Tree drooping and mourning, and Mr. Wind he ask Mr. Oak Tree what his trouble.

Mr. Oak Tree he tell Mr. Wind all 'bout it, and Mr. Wind he say to Mr. Oak Tree, "Cheer up, cheer up!" and Mr. Wind he tell Mr. Oak Tree how he going help him get the best of Mr. Pine Tree. So all winter Mr. Wind, every day, and all enduring the night, he take the dirty old leaves from Mr. Oak Tree's floor and carry them all over and spread them all over Mr. Pine Tree's fine carpet. Mr. Pine Tree he don't like it, but he can't help hisself 'cause what Mr. Wind want to do he going to do it, Mr. Wind is.

But when camp-meeting time come, Mr. Oak Tree he stand there, and he see the people come and rake off all his leaves, what Mr. Wind done carry on Mr. Pine Tree's carpet.

Then Mr. Oak Tree he say he can't bear it no more, and Mr. Oak Tree he tell Mr. Pine Tree how they can't live together no more; and Mr. Oak Tree he say, he will go to the plains and Mr. Pine Tree can go to the mountain; or he say, will Mr. Pine Tree take the plains and let Mr. Oak Tree go to the mountains? Mr. Pine Tree he 'low how he will take the plains and let Mr. Oak Tree go to the mountains; and Mr. Pine Tree he go to the plains, and Mr. Oak Tree he take the up country, and they don' live together no more. But they still on the watch-out; for when Mr. Oak Tree leave a field, directly here come Mr. Pine Tree, and when Mr. Pine Tree leave a field, sure enough up come Mr. Oak Tree; but they don't live together friendly like no more.

WHY THE PEOPLE TOTE BRER RABBIT FOOT IN THEIR POCKET

Tradition Bearer: Unavailable

Source: Backus, Emma M. "Tales of the Rabbit from Georgia Negroes." *Journal of American Folklore* 12 (1899): 109–11.

Date: 1900

Original Source: Georgia

National Origin: African American

Rabbit, as a **trickster** figure in African American folklore, at times acts in the community's interest. In this tale, Brer Rabbit uses more than his wits to overcome Ole Mammy Witch Wise; he turns to his knowledge of the occult practices of the shape-shifting witches who slip off their skins in order to cause nocturnal mischief, thus revealing himself to be "wise" as well. In other tales, Brer Rabbit displays his skill in conjuration and hoodoo. This knowledge allows him to save the community from Mammy Wise Witch and marks his foot as a powerful protective amulet.

Why do people tote Brer Rabbit's foot in their pocket? Well, sir, that's cause Ole Brer Rabbit done killed the last witch what ever live.

They tells how they done hang some of 'em, and burn some, till they get mighty scarce, but there was one ole witch what was risin' on five hundred years old, and 'cause she keep clear of all the folks what try to catch her, they done name her Ole Mammy Witch Wise.

Well, she do carry on to beat all them times, she 'witch all the folks, and she 'witch all the animals, and when they go to get their meal out some of the gardens, she just 'witch them animals, and they can't get in to save 'em, and they all nigh 'bout starved out, that they was, and they all hold a big consultation and talk over what they gwine do.

They was a mighty ornery lookin' set, just nigh 'bout skin an' bone, but when Ole Brer Rabbit come in, they observe how he mighty plump and in fine order, and they ask him, however he so mighty prosp'rous and they all in such powerful trouble. And then he allow, Brer Rabbit did, dat Ole Mammy Witch Wise can't 'witch him, and he go in the gardens more same as ever.

Why, Ole Mammy Wise don't 'low the animals get in the garden, she just want the pick of 'em herself, cause she don't have no garden that year; but when she set her mind on some Major Brayton's peas, she just put the pot on the fire, an' when the water bile smart, she just talk in the pot and say, "Bile peas, bile peas," and there they come, sure 'nough, for dinner; but you see if the animals done been troubling them peas, and there ain't no peas on the vine, then she call 'em in the pot.

So she just keep the creeters out till they nigh 'bout broke down, and they ask Brer Rabbit, can't he help 'em? Brer Rabbit scratch he head, but he don't say nothin', 'cause I tell you, when Ole Brer Rabbit tell what he gwine do, then you just well know that just what he ain' gwine do, 'cause he's a man what don't tell what he mind set on.

So he don't make no promise, but he study constant how he gwine kill Ole Mammy Witch Wise. He know all 'bout how the old woman slip her skin every night, and all the folks done try all the plans to keep her out till the rooster crow in the morning, 'cause every witch, what's out the skin when the roosters crow, can't never get in the skin no mo'; but they never get the best of the Ole Mammy Witch Wise, and she rising five hundred years old. Brer Rabbit he go off hisself, and set in the sun on the sand bed and rum'nate. And you may be sure, when you see the old man set all to hisself on the sand bed, he mind just working. Well, sir, that night, he go in the garden and take a good turn of peppers, and tote them up to Ole Mammy Witch Wise house, and just he 'spect, there he find her skin in the porch, just where she slip it off to go on her tricks, and what you 'spect he do? Well, sir, he just mash them peppers to a mush, and rub 'em all inside the Ole Mammy Witch Wise skin, and then he set hisself under the porch for to watch.

Just 'fore crowing time, sure 'nough, there come the ole woman, sailing along in a hurry, 'cause she know she ain't got long, but when she go for to put on her skin, it certainly do bite her, and she say, "Skinnie, skinnie, don't you know me, skinnie?" But it bite more same than before, and while she fooling with it, sure 'nough the rooster done crow, and the ole woman just fall over in a fit. And in the morning Brer Rabbit notify the animals, and they gravel a place and burn her. And the people, they find out how Brer Rabbit get the best of the Mammy Witch Wise, and then they tell the white folks, and that why nigh 'bout all the rich white folks totes a rabbit foot in their pocket, 'cause it keeps off all the bad luck, and it do that, sure's yo' born.

ORIGIN OF THE BEAR: THE BEAR SONGS

Tradition Bearer: A`yûn'inï ("Swimmer")

Source: Mooney, James. "Myths of the Cherokee." Pages 325–26 in *Nineteenth Annual Report of the Bureau of American Ethnology 1897–1898, Part I.* Washington, DC: U.S. Government Printing Office, 1900.

Date: 1897–1898

Original Source: Cherokee

National Origin: Native American

In the Cherokee worldview, Bear maintained a kinship to humans because he was descended from one of their clans during the mythic period. The widely held Native American belief that animals grant success to hunters who follow the proper rituals of respect is apparent in this **myth** of the origin of bears and the songs used to call them forth to be hunted. Like Cherokee sung incantations in general, the Bear Songs, when repeated precisely, have an ability to focus supernatural power and bring about a desired end. This **myth** is especially valuable because it was transcribed by Cherokee ritual expert Swimmer himself using the syllabary invented by Sequoia discussed in the "Introduction" (p. 1). Thus, there is far less of an opportunity for "interference" (extrapolation and reinterpretation) from the collector than was usually the case in the context of fieldwork.

Long ago there was a Cherokee clan called the Ani'-Tsâ'gûhï, and in one family of this clan was a boy who used to leave home and be gone all day in the mountains. After a while he went oftener and stayed longer, until at last he would not eat in the house at all, but started off at daybreak and did not come back until night. His parents scolded, but that did no good, and the boy, still went every day until they noticed that long brown hair was beginning to grow out all over his body. Then they wondered and asked him why it was that he wanted to be so much in the woods that he would not even eat at home. Said the boy, "I find plenty to eat there, and it is better than the corn and beans we have in the settlements, and pretty soon I am going into the woods to stay all the time." His parents were worried and begged him not to leave them, but he said, "It is better there than here, and you see I am beginning to be different already, so that I can not live here any longer. If you will come with me, there is plenty for all of us and you will never have to work for it; but if you want to come you must first fast seven days."

The father and mother talked it over and then told the headmen of the clan. They held a council about the matter and after everything had been said they decided: "Here we must work hard and have not always enough. There he says there is always plenty without work. We will go with him." So they fasted seven days, and on the seventh morning all the Ani'-Tsâ'gûhï left the settlement and started for the mountains as the boy led the way.

When the people of the other towns heard of it they were very sorry and sent their headmen to persuade the Ani'-Tsâ'gûhï to stay at home and not go into the woods to live. The messengers found them already on the way, and were surprised to notice that their bodies were beginning to be covered with hair like that of animals, because for seven days they had not taken human food and their nature was changing. The Ani'-Tsâ'gûhï would not come back, but said, "We are going where there is always plenty to eat. Hereafter we shall be called bears, and when you yourselves are hungry come into the woods and call us and we shall come to give you our own flesh. You need not be afraid to kill us, for we shall live always." Then they taught the messengers the songs with which to call them, and the bear hunters have these songs still. When they had finished the songs the Ani'-Tsâ'gûhï started on again and the messengers turned back to the settlements, but after going a little way they looked back and saw a drove of bears going into the woods.

First Bear Song

He-e! Ani'-Tsâ'gûhï, Ani'-Tsâ'gûhï, akwandu'li e'lanti' ginûn'ti,
Ani'-Tsâ'gûhï, Ani'-Tsâ'gûhï, akwandu'li e'lanti' ginûn'ti—Yû!
He-e! The Ani'-Tsâ'gûhï, the Ani'-Tsâ'gûhï, I want to lay them low on the ground,
The Ani'-Tsâ'gûhï, the Ani'-Tsâ'gûhï, I want to lay them low on the ground—Yû!

The bear hunter starts out each morning fasting and does not eat until near evening. He sings this song as he leaves camp, and again the next morning, but never twice the same day.

Second Bear Song

This song also is sung by the bear hunter, in order to attract the bears, while on his way from the camp to the place where he expects to hunt during the day. The melody is simple and plaintive.

He-e! Hayuya'haniwä', hayuya'haniwä', hayuya'haniwä', hayuya'haniwä',
Tsistuyi' nehandu'yanû', Tsistuyi' nehandu'yanû'—Yoho-o!
He-e! Hayuya'haniwä', hayuya'haniwä', hayuya'haniwä',
    hayuya'haniwä',
Kuwâhi' nehandu'yanû', Kuwâhi' nehandu'yanû'—Yoho-o!
He-e! Hayuya'haniwä', hayuya'haniwä', hayuya'haniwä',
    hayuya'haniwä',
Uyâhye' nehandu'yanû', Uyâhye' nehandu'yanû'—Yoho-o!
He-e! Hayuya'haniwä', hayuya'haniwä', hayuya'haniwä',
    hayuya'haniwä',
Gâte'gwâ' nehandu'yanû', Gâte'gwâ' nehandu'yanû'—Yoho-o!
(Recited) Ûlë-`nû' asëhï' tadeyâ'statakûhï' gûñ'näge astû' tsïkï'
He! Hayuya'haniwä' (four times),
In Tsistu'yï you were conceived (two times)—Yoho!
He! Hayuya'haniwä' (four times),
In Kuwâ'hï you were conceived (two times)—Yoho!
He! Hayuya'haniwä' (four times),
In Uyâ'hye you were conceived (two times)—Yoho!
He! Hayuya'haniwä' (four times),
In Gâte'gwâ you were conceived (two times)—Yoho!

And now surely we and the good black things, the best of all, shall see each other.

HOW COME BRER BEAR SLEEP IN THE WINTER

Tradition Bearer: Unavailable

Source: Backus, Emma M. "Animal Tales from North Carolina." *Journal of American Folklore* 11 (1898): 287–88.

Date: 1898

Original Source: North Carolina

National Origin: African American

The exploits of a **trickster** or **culture hero** are commonly celebrated in the animal **fables** and the origin tales that arise not only in African

American repertoires but in the traditional narratives of many of the world's cultures. Rabbit usually plays the role of master **trickster**, but this narrative deviates from that model and instead celebrates cooperation and community action. In concert, the group bands together to manage the behavior of a larger and more powerful tyrant. As such, the tale offers alternative strategies to **trickster**'s wily deviance or the outlaw hero's bold frontal attacks for dealing with a common threat. The threat is simply diminished, however, rather than eliminated because of individual frailties—"a meddlesomeness to move them rocks." Thus, the narrative simultaneously praises cooperation and warns against potential pitfalls to community action. Neither message would have been lost on the African American audiences for whom the tale originally was performed.

When the animals was young, Brer Bar, he never sleep in the winter, no more'n the rest. The way it was in them days, old man Bar was flying roun' more same than the other creeters, and he was the meanest one in the lot, and 'cause he the biggest he get in he mind that he king of the country, and the way he put on the animals was scand'lous, that it was.

Well, the animals was all crossways wid the old man a long time, but they bound to step up when he tell 'em, cause you kin see in these times old Brer Bar ain't a powerful man, but he just on the onery side, was what he was in the old times. 'Pears like all the animals is getting mighty low down these here times, 'cept old Sis Coon, and sure you born she get more heady every year.

Well, they talk it over 'twixt themselves many and many a day, how they going to take down Mr. Bar. They know he mighty fond of sleepin' in the dark, and one day Brer Rabbit 'low that they stop the old man up when he sleep in a dark tree; he take a mighty long nap, and they get a little comfort.

So they all watch out, and when the old man sleep that night in a hollow tree they all turn in and tote rocks and brush, and stop up the hole.

And sure 'nough, when morning come, Brer Bar don't know it, and he just sleep on; when he wake up he see it all dark, and he say day ain't break yet, and he turn over and go sleep, and there the old man sleep just that a way till the leaves turn out the trees, and I 'spect the old man been sleeping there to this day; but the animals, they all hold the old man dead for sure, and they just feel a meddlesomness to move them rocks; and when they let the light in, old Brer Bar he just crack he eye and stretch hisself and come out, and when he see the spring done come he say, the old man did, that he done had a mighty comfortable winter, and from that time every year, when the cold come, old Brer Bar go to sleep.

HOW COME MR. BUZZARD TO HAVE A BALD HEAD

Tradition Bearer: Unavailable

Source: Backus, Emma M. "Animal Tales from North Carolina." *Journal of American Folklore* 11 (1898): 288–89.

Date: 1898

Original Source: North Carolina
National Origin: African American

Ann Nancy, the protagonist of this tale, is a North American incarnation of Anansi, the familiar West African and Caribbean **trickster**. As a result of the process of oral transmission, in which "Anansi" is homophonous with "Ann Nancy," he is given a name that is more comprehensible in nineteenth-century North Carolina. With this transformation comes a change in gender from male to female in keeping with the name shift. These changes in the West African and West Indian tale illustrate principles of localization discussed in the Introduction. As is the case with her Caribbean and Continental African counterpart, however, Ann Nancy is an anthropomorphic spider with a penchant for pranks and an insatiable appetite. As with most other **trickster** figures, Ann Nancy lives by her wits—usually at the expense of her neighbors—employing subterfuge to gain her selfish ends and to extricate herself from the trouble which inevitably comes from her schemes. Ann Nancy, as noted by the narrator, is particularly mean-spirited and unforgiving. Her "sour" mind and temper not only fulfill her desire for revenge but also forever alter Buzzard's appearance and appetite.

One day, in the old times, Ann Nancy started out to find a good place for to build her house; she walk on till she find a break in a nice damp rock, and she set down to rest, and take 'servation of the points to throw her threads.

Presently, she hear a great floppin' of wings, and the old Mr. Buzzard come flying down and light on the rock, with a big piece of meat in he mouth. Ann Nancy, she scroon in the rock and look out, and she hear Mr. Buzzard say, "Good safe, good safe, come down, come down," and sure 'nough, when he say it three times, a safe come down, and Mr. Buzzard, he open the door and put in he meat and say, "Good safe, good safe, go up, go up," and it go up aright, and Mr. Buzzard fly away.

Then Ann Nancy, she set and study 'bout it, 'cause she done see the safe was full of all the good things she ever hear of, and it come across her mind to call it and see if it come down; so she say, like Mr. Buzzard, "Good safe, good safe, come down, come down," and sure 'nough, when she say it three times, down it come, and she open the door and step in, and she say, "Good safe, good safe, go up, go up," and up she go, and she eat her fill, and have a fine time.

Directly she hear a voice say, "Good safe, good safe, come down, come down," and the safe start down, and Ann Nancy, she so scared, she don't know what to do, but she say soft and quickly, "Good safe, go up," and it stop, and go up a little, but Mr. Buzzard say, "Good safe, come down, come down," and down it start, and poor Ann Nancy whisper quick, "Go up, good safe, go up," and it go back. And so they go for a long time, only Mr. Buzzard can't hear Ann Nancy, 'cause she whisper soft to the safe, and he cock he eye in 'stonishment to see the old safe bob up and down, like it gone 'stracted [distracted, crazy].

So they keep on, "Good safe, good safe, come down," "Good safe, good safe, go up," till poor Ann Nancy's brain get 'fused [confused], and she make a slip and say, "Good safe, come down," and down it come.

Mr. Buzzard, he open the do', and there he find Ann Nancy, and he say, "Oh you poor mis'rable creeter," and he just 'bout to eat her up, when poor Ann Nancy, she begged so hard, and compliment his fine presence, and compare how he sail in the clouds while she 'bliged [is obliged] to crawl in the dirt, till he that proudful and set up he feel mighty pardoning spirit, and he let her go.

But Ann Nancy ain't got no gratitude in her mind; she feel she looked down on by all the creeters, and it sour her mind and temper. She ain't gwine forget anybody what cross her path, no, that she don't, and while she spin her house she just study constant how she gwine get the best of every creeter.

She knew Mr. Buzzard's weak point am he stomach, and one day she make it out dat she make a dining, and 'vite Mr. Buzzard and Miss Buzzard and the children. Ann Nancy, she know how to set out a-dining for sure, and when they all done got sot down to the table, and she mighty busy passing the hot coffee to Mr. Buzzard and the little Buzzards, she have a powerful big pot of scalding water ready, and she slop it all over poor old Mr. Buzzard's head, and the poor old man go bald-headed from that day. And he don't forget it on Ann Nancy, 'cause you see she de onliest creeter on the top side the earth what Mr. Buzzard don't eat.

THE RATTLESNAKE'S VENGEANCE

Tradition Bearer: Unavailable (perhaps Swimmer, see "Origin of the Bear: The Bear Songs," p. 28)

Source: Mooney, James. "Myths of the Cherokee." Page 306 in *Nineteenth Annual Report of the Bureau of American Ethnology 1897–1898, Part I.* Washington, DC: U.S. Government Printing Office, 1900.

Date: 1898

Original Source: Cherokee

National Origin: Native American

According to Cherokee tradition, snakes were supernatural beings possessing power over meteorological phenomena as well as over plant and animal life. The narrative traditions contain an extensive selection of **myths** and **legends** devoted to snakes both natural and mythic. Snakes are the focus of prayers and rituals, and rattlesnakes are invested with particular power. Although killing them is usually an invitation to disaster (as in the following **myth**), holy persons who are trained in the appropriate rites, songs, and prayers may kill them in order to obtain teeth, rattles, flesh, or oil for medicinal or religious purposes. "The Rattlesnake's Vengeance" reveals the character of this animal and relates the origin of one of the ritual songs associated with the feared and venerated rattlesnake.

One day in the old times when we could still talk with other creatures, while some children were playing about the house, their mother inside heard them scream. Running out she found that a rattlesnake had crawled from the grass, and taking up a stick she killed it. The father was out hunting in the mountains, and that evening when coming home after dark through the gap he heard a strange wailing sound. Looking about he found that he had come into the midst of a whole company of rattlesnakes, which all had their mouths open and seemed to be crying. He asked them the reason of their trouble, and they told him that his own wife had that day killed their chief, the Yellow Rattlesnake, and they were just now about to send the Black Rattlesnake to take revenge.

The hunter said he was very sorry, but they told him that if he spoke the truth he must be ready to make satisfaction and give his wife as a sacrifice for the life of their chief. Not knowing what might happen otherwise, he consented. They then told him that the Black Rattlesnake would go home with him and coil up just outside the door in the dark. He must go inside, where he would find his wife awaiting him, and ask her to get him a drink of fresh water from the spring. That was all.

He went home and knew that the Black Rattlesnake was following. It was night when he arrived and very dark, but he found his wife waiting with his supper ready. He sat down and asked for a drink of water. She handed him a gourd full from the jar, but he said he wanted it fresh from the spring, so she took a bowl and went out of the door. The next moment he heard a cry, and going out he found that the Black Rattlesnake had bitten her and that she was already dying. He stayed with her until she was dead, when the Black Rattlesnake came out from the grass again and said his tribe was now satisfied.

He then taught the hunter a prayer song, and said, "When you meet any of us hereafter sing this song and we will not hurt you; but if by accident one of us should bite one of your people then sing this song over him and he will recover." And the Cherokee have kept the song to this day.

HOW COME PIGS CAN SEE THE WIND

Tradition Bearer: Unavailable

Source: Backus, Emma M. "Animal Tales from North Carolina." *Journal of American Folklore* 11 (1898): 285–86.

Date: 1898

Original Source: North Carolina

National Origin: African American

This tale is reminiscent of the well-known "Three Little Pigs and the Big Bad Wolf," which was popular in the late nineteenth century. In fact,

Joel Chandler Harris included a wolf and pig tale in his *Nights with Uncle Remus,* published in 1883. Unlike either Chandler's version or the tales of the Big Bad Wolf familiar to American children, this is an origin narrative. Brer Wolf calls on Satan for help, and the encounter ends badly for Sis Pig. The collector provided no contextual information nor commentary along with the folktale, but several features of the tale invite further speculation. For instance, Brer Wolf claims that he is "the master," leading to Sis Pig's surrender of four of her five offspring. This action reflects the bondsperson's plight and also casts light on the master's character. In addition, Brer Wolf enlists Satan's aid only to find himself frightened out of his wits by his pact. Similar pacts throughout African American tradition elicit similar consequences; perhaps the best known is the **legend** of blues musician Robert Johnson (1911–1938) selling his soul to the Devil at the crossroads.

Did you done hear how come that old Sis Pig can see the wind? Well, to be sure, ain't you never hear that? Well, don't you take noticement, many and many a time, how unrestful, and 'stracted like, the pigs is, when the wind blows, and how they squeal, and run this here way and that here way, like they's 'stracted? Well, sir, all dat gwine on is along of the fact that they can see the wind.

One time the old sow, she have five little pigs—four black and one white one.

Now old Brer Wolf, he have a mighty good mouth for pig meat, and he go every night and walk round and round Miss Pig's house, but Sis Pig, she have the door lock fast.

One night, he dress up just like he was a man, and he put a tall hat on he head, and shoes on he foots; he take a sack of corn, and he walk hard, and make a mighty fuss on the brick walk, right up to the door, and he knock loud on the door in a great haste, and Sis Pig, she say, "Who there?" and Brer Wolf say up, loud and powerful, Brer Wolf did, "Quit your fooling, old woman, I is the master, come for to put my mark on the new pigs; turn 'em loose here lively."

And old Sis Pig, she mighty skeered, but she feared not to turn 'em out; so she crack the door, and turn out the four black pigs, but the little white pig, he am her eyeballs, the little white pig was, and when he turn come, she just shut the door and hold it fast.

And Brer Wolf, he put down the corn, and just pick up the four little pigs and tote 'em off home; but when they done gone, he mouth hone for the little

37

pig, but Sis Pig, she keep him mighty close. One night Brer Wolf was wandering up and down the woods, and he meet up with old Satan, and he ask Brer Wolf, old Satan did, can he help him, and Brer Wolf he just tell him what on he mind, and old Satan told him to lead on to Miss Pig's house, and he help him out.

So Brer Wolf he lead on, and directly there Sis Pig's house, and old Satan, he 'gin to puff and blow, and puff and blow, till Brer Wolf he that skeered, Brer Wolf is, that he hair fairly stand on end; and Miss Pig she done hear the mighty wind, and the house a-cracking, and they hear her inside down on her knees, just calling on God A'mighty for mercy; but old Satan, he puff and blow, and puff and blow, and the house crack and tremble, and he say, old Satan did, "You hear this here mighty wind, Sis Pig, but if you look this here way you can see it."

And Sis Pig, she that skeered, she crack the door and look out, and there she see old Satan's breath, like red smoke, blowing on the house, and from that day the pigs can see the wind, and it look red, the wind look red, sir. How we know that? I tell you how we know that, sir: if anybody miss a pig and take the milk, then they can see the wind, and they done tell it was red.

WHY MR. OWL CAN'T SING

Tradition Bearer: Unavailable

Source: Backus, Emma M., and Ethel Hatton Leitner. "Negro Tales from Georgia." *Journal of American Folklore* 25 (1912): 134–35.

Date: 1912

Original Source: Georgia

National Origin: African American

This tale, along with explaining the origin of the owl's cry and current habitat, underscores the value of responsibility and respectability—qualities needed to preserve one's social standing in the traditional communities in which this and similar tales circulate. Choosing the frivolous activities of singing and fiddling over his domestic responsibilities of staying home to mind the children, Mr. Owl falls victim to the trifling of Miss Cuckoo—the very image of irresponsibility and disrespectability. As a result, his family is fragmented, his previous social status is undermined, and he loses the fine singing voice that led to his downfall. All in all, Mr. Owl illustrates the dangers of nonsensical behavior and the ways in which it can stand in opposition to respectability and domesticity. See Roger Abrahams 1983 and 1985 works for discussions of these central concepts in African American culture.

When Mr. Owl was young, he could sing to beat all the birds in the woods. This ole man what you see flying about calling "whoo, whoo!" In the ole time, he could sing so fine that he teach the singing-school. In them days Mr. Owl he never wander round, like he do in these here times, 'cause he have a happy home, and he stay home with his wife and children, like a 'spectable man.

But that poor ole man done see a heap of trouble in he time, he shore has; and it all come along 'cause of that trifling no count Miss Cuckoo, what too sorry to build her nest fer herself, but go about laying her eggs in her neighbors' nests.

In the old time, Mr. and Miss Owl they belong to the quality; and they have a shore 'nuff quality house, not like these little houses what you see these here times, what secondary people live in.

One night Miss Owl she go out to pay a visit, and she leave Mr. Owl at home to mind the children; but directly she gone, Mr. Owl he take he fiddle under he arm, and go off to he singing-school. Then that trifling no count Miss Cuckoo come sailing along calling "Cuckoo, cuckoo!" And she leave her eggs in Miss Owl's fine nest, and then she go sailing off, calling, "Cuckoo, cuckoo!"

Now, presently Miss Owl she come home; and when she find that egg in her nest, she rare end charge on the poor ole man to beat all; and she tell him she never live with him no more til he tell her who lay that egg; but the poor ole man can't tell her, 'cause he don't know hisself. But Miss Owl she be mighty proud-spirited; and what she done say, she done say.

So the ole man he leave he fine home, and he go wandering through the woods looking for the one what lay that egg and make all he trouble. And the ole man he that sorrowful he can't sing no more, but jest go sailing 'bout, asking, "Whoo, whoo!" But Mr. Owl he never find out to this day who lay that egg, and so Miss Owl never live with him no more; but he keep on asking, "Whoo, whoo?" And now it done been that long, the poor ole man plum forgot how to sing, and he don't play he fiddle no more, and can't say nothing but "Whoo, whoo!"

WHEN BRER RABBIT SAW BRER DOG'S MOUTH SO BRER DOG CAN WHISTLE

Tradition Bearer: Unknown

Source: Backus, Emma M., and Ethel Hatton Leitner. "Negro Tales from Georgia." *Journal of American Folklore* 25 (1912): 125–26.

Date: 1912

Original Source: Georgia

National Origin: African American

The behavior of Brer Rabbit in the following tale is more representative of his usual nature in the African American tradition than was his altruism in "Why the People Tote Brer Rabbit Foot in their Pocket." Brer Rabbit, despite "know[ing] in his own mind Brer Dog ain' going to whistle," saws Brer Dog's mouth anyway. As in many of his escapades, the **trickster**'s motivation is simply to stir up trouble. Also typical is the fact that both Brer Rabbit and the butt of his trick, Brer Dog, suffer injuries that mark them and set up their social relationship from that day forward.

In the ole times, when Brer Dog a-roaming through the woods, he come up with Brer Rabbit, Brer Dog do. Brer Rabbit he set on the sand just a-whistling, and a-picking of the banjo.

Now, in them times Brer Rabbit was a master-hand with the banjo. These here hard times 'pears like Brer Rabbit done forget how to whistle, and you don' hear him pick the banjo no more; but in the ole times Brer Rabbit he whistle and frolic, and frolic and whistle, from morning til night.

Well, Brer Dog he mighty envious of Brer Rabbit, 'cause Brer Dog he can't whistle, and he can't sing, Brer Dog can't. Brer Dog he think he give anything in reason if he could whistle like Brer Rabbit, so Brer Dog he beg Brer Rabbit to learn hisself to whistle.

Now, Brer Dog he called the most reliable man in the county; and he have some standing, Brer Dog do; and he have right smart of sense, Brer Dog have;

but bless you, Sir, Brer Dog he can't conjure 'longside that Ole Brer Rabbit, that he can't.

Well, when Brer Dog beg Brer Rabbit will he learn hisself to whistle, Brer Rabbit he say, "Brer Dog, your mouth ain't shape for whistling." Brer Rabbit he say, "Name of goodness, Brer Dog, how come you studying 'bout whistling with that mouth? Now, Brer Dog, you just watch my mouth and try youself"; and Brer Rabbit he just corner up his mouth and whistle to beat all.

Brer Dog he try his best to corner up his mouth like Brer Rabbit; but he can't do it, Brer Dog can't. But the more Brer Dog watch Brer Rabbit whistle, the more envious Brer Dog get to whistle hisself.

Now, Brer Dog he know how Brer Rabbit are a doctor; so Brer Dog he ask Brer Rabbit can he fix his mouth so he can whistle?

Brer Rabbit, he 'low as how he might fix Brer Dog's mouth so he can whistle just tolerable, but Brer Rabbit he 'low how he have to saw the corners of Brer Dog's mouth right smart; and he 'low, Brer Rabbit do, how "it be mighty worrisome for Brer Dog."

Now, Brer Dog, he that envious to whistle like Brer Rabbit, Brer Dog he 'clare he let Brer Rabbit saw his mouth.

Brer Rabbit he say as how he don' want deceive Brer Dog; and he say, Brer Rabbit do, as how he ain' gwine promise to make Brer Dog whistle more same as hisself, but he say he "make Brer Dog whistle tolerable."

So Brer Rabbit he get his saw, and he saw a slit in the corners Brer Dog's mouth. It nateraly just nigh 'bout kill Ole Brer Dog; but Brer Dog he are a thorough-going man, and what Brer Dog say he going to do, he going to do, he sure is.

So Brer Dog he just hold hisself together, and let Brer Rabbit saw his mouth.

Now, Brer Rabbit he know in his own mind Brer Dog ain' going to whistle sure 'nough, but Brer Rabbit he don' know just what Brer Dog going to say; so when Brer Rabbit get through a-sawing of Brer Dog's mouth, Brer Rabbit he say, "Now try if you can whistle!" Brer Dog he open his mouth, and he try to whistle; and he say, "Bow, wow, wow!" Brer Dog do say that for a fact.

Well, when Brer Rabbit hear Brer Dog whistle that there way, Brer Rabbit he that scared he just turn and fly for home; but Brer Dog he that mad, when he hears hisself whistle that there way, he say he going to finish Ole Brer Rabbit: so Brer Dog he put out after Brer Rabbit just a-hollering, "Bow wow, bow wow, bow wow!"

Now, in them times, Brer Rabbit he have a long bushy tail. Brer Rabbit he mighty proud of his tail in the ole times.

Well, Brer Rabbit he do his best, and he just burn the wind through the woods; but Brer Dog he just going on the jump, "Bow wow, bow wow!"

Presently Brer Dog he see Brer Rabbit, and he think he got him; and Brer Dog he open his mouth and jump for Brer Rabbit, and Brer Dog he just bite Brer Rabbit's fine tail plum off.

That how come Brer Rabbit have such little no-count tail these here times; and Brer Dog he that mad with ole Brer Rabbit 'cause he saw his mouth, when he run Brer Rabbit through the woods, he still holler, "Bow wow, bow wow!" And you take noticement how, when Brer Rabbit hear Brer Dog say that, Brer Rabbit he just pick up his foots and fly, 'cause Brer Rabbit done remember how he done saw Brer Dog's mouth.

OL' RABBIT AN' DE DAWG HE STOLE

Tradition Bearer: Unavailable

Source: Owen, Mary A. "Ol' Rabbit an' de Dawg He Stole." *Journal of American Folklore* 9 (1890): 135–38.

Date: 1890

Original Source: Missouri

National Origin: African American

The **animal tale** of "Ol' Rabbit an' de Dawg He Stole" offers an elaborate explanation of the reason dogs chase rabbits. In this case, Rabbit's powers as a conjure man (practitioner of folk magic) bring him more attention than he intends. Along the way, the tradition bearer develops stock derisive images of European Americans and Native Americans. A major portion of the original attempt at rendering the rural African American Southern dialect has been modified. The original version is included in the Appendix to this volume.

I n de good ole times, Ole Rabbit he wasn't bothered none by de neighbors. It was miles to de corner of any one of hims fiel'.

After awhile, Mister Injun an' he folkses set 'em up a settlement, but dat ain' nothin', 'cause Injun folks was always a-paradin' aroun' an' a-catchin up dey baggage an' a-movin' it here an' yonder.

By an' by, though, de white men come 'long a-choppin' down de trees an' a-diggin' up de earth. Den all de critters pack dey go-to-meetin' clothes in their pillow-case an' get ready to start, 'cause dey know dat Mister White Man come for to stay, an' he ain' one o' de kind dat want to sleep three in de bed an' dey ain' ne'er. Dat is all of 'em 'cept Ole Chuffy Rabbit an' de Squirrel family set out. Dey two allow dey goin' to tough it out awhile longer.

What pester Ole Chuffy mo' den all de res' was dat white man's dawg. It wasn't like dem Injun dawgs, dat's a-scatterin' roun' de country today an' in de pot tomorrow (i.e., get eaten tomorrow). It was one o' dem sharp-nosed houn' dawgs dat hunt all day an' howl all night. It was as still as a fox on a turkey-hunt from de mawnin' til candle-light, but jess wait til de sun go down an' de moon come up an' Oh Lawd! Ah, oo-oo-oo-wow, ow, ow! Ah oo-oo-oo, wow, ow, ow! Ah oo-oo-oo, wow, ow, ow! Hear it go from mos' sun-down to mos' sun-up, an' dat was de mos' aggravatingest soun' dat de Ole Boy e'er put in de throat of a livin' critter. It distracted Ole Rabbit. He flounce roun' in de bed like a cat-fish on de hook. He groan an' he grunt, an' he turn an' roll, an' he jus' can't get no good res'.

Ole Miss Rabbit she obliged to roll de bed-covers roun' her ears, she dat scandalized.

"Why don't yo' get outen de bed an' turn yo' shoe wid de bottom-side up an' set your bare foot onto it?" she say. "Dat make any dawg stop he yowlin'."

"Well! ain' I done it forty-eleven time?" say Ole Man Rabbit jus' a-foamin' an' a-snortin'. "Ain' I been a-hoppin' in an' out de bed all de lib-long night? 'Cause it stop 'em for a half a jiff an' den it tune up agin 'for I jus' kin get de bed warm under me."

Ah oo-oo-oo, wow, ow, ow! Ah oo-oo-oo, wow, ow, OW! Dat ole houn' fetch a yowl dat far make de man in de moon blink.

"Cuss dat ole dawg! Cuss him say I! Why don't dat ole fool dat own him stuff a corn-cob down he throat, or chop him into sausage meat?" says Ole Rabbit, says 'e. "I givin' up on de sleepin' question tonight," says 'e, "but I lay I ain' disturbed like dis in my res' tomorrer," says 'e.

Wid dat he bounce out on de floor an' haul on he britches an' light a candle; an' he take dat candle in he han' an' he go pokin' round' amongst de shadows like he a-huntin' for sumpin'.

Scratch, scratch! Scuffle, scuffle! He go in de corners of de cupboard.

"Ah oo-oo-oo! Wow, ow, ow!" go de houn' outside.

Scratch, scratch! scuffle, scuffle! Ah oo-oo-oo! Wow, ow, ow! Scratch, scratch! Scuffle, scuffle! Ah oo-oo-oo! Wow, ow, ow!

An' so dey keep it up, til ole Miss Rabbit is as mad at one as the other.

"What is you doin', Mister Rabbit?" she say aging an' aging, but Ole Chuff ain' satisfy 'bout dat.

Directly, though, when he get through an' blow out de candle an' de day goin' to broke, she been noticin' dat he step sorta lop-side.

"What is de matter, Mister Rabbit?" she ask. "Is you run a brier into yo' foot?"

"No," says 'e, mighty short, "I ain' got no brier in my foot dat I knows of, but I gotta brier in my mine 'bout de size of a snipe-bill, of I ain' mistookened."

At dat she let fly a swam o' questions, but he jus' grin dry an' say—

"Ask me no questions an' I tell yo' no lies. Don't bother me, ole woman (old woman, wife). I ain' feel very strong in de head dis mornin', an' I might have to answer questions wid my fist if I gets pestered."

Dat shut 'er up, in due course, an' she set in to gettin' breakfast. Pretty soon she holler out—

"Who been touchin' de bread? Somebody been a-cuttin' de bread! I lay I got to trounce greedy chilluns for dat. Appear like I can't set down nothin' dese days but dey got to muss in it! I goin' to cut me a big hick'ry limb' dis mornin' an' see if I can't lick some manners into de whole kit an' caboodle of 'em! In de mean-whiles o' gettin' dat limb' I goin' to smack de jaws of de whole crowd."

"No yo' ain'," says Ole Rabbit, says 'e. "Jus' left dem young uns o' mine 'lone. Dey ain' done nuttin'. I cut dat bread, an' I got dat bread, an' I ain' goin' to eat 'er up."

Pretty soon ole Miss Rabbit sing out agin.

"Who been cuttin' de bakin (bacon) fat?" says she, "an' cuttin' it crooked too," says she. "I lay I jus' leave de breakfast an' set out 'n' get dat limb' right now," says she.

"No, yo' won't," says Ole Rabbit, says 'e. "I ain' goin' to have de sense beat outten dem young uns o' mine. I took dat fat an' I got dat fat, an' if I haggle de slice (cut the slice crooked) dat my look out," says 'e. "I paid for it, an' I goin' to cut it wid de saw or de scissor, if I feel like it," says 'e.

Wid dat he get up an' walk off, lim-petty-limp.

Miss Rabbit ain' see no mo' of 'im 'til sundown. Den he come in lookin' mighty tuckered out, but jus' a-grinnin' like a baked skunk. He set down he did, an' et like he been holler clear to he toes, but he won't say nuttin'. When he get through he sorter stretch hissef an' say, "I goin' to go to bed. I got a heap o' sleep to make up, an' I lay no dawg ain' goin' to 'sturb my res' dis night."

An' dey don't. Dey wasn't a soun', an' Miss Rabbit make a great admiration at dat in her mind, but she ain' got nobody to talk it over with til de nex' mornin', when Ole Rabbit get up as gay an' sassy as a yearlin'. Den 'e have de big tale to tell, an' dis was what he tell 'er—

When he was a-foolin' in de cupboard he get 'im a piece o' bread, an' he tie dat on he foot. Den he cut 'im a slice o' bakin', an' he put dat on top de bread. Den he slip on he shoe an' he start out. Dat he do 'cause he goin' to fix 'im some shoe-bread for feed to dat dawg, 'cause if yo' wear bread in yo' shoe an' den give it to a dawg, an he eat it, dat dawg your'n. He goin' to foller yo' to de ends o' de Earth, dat he am. De bakin he put against dat bread give it a good taste, an' to fool de folks what see 'im, 'cause he goin' to let on like he run a brier in he foot an' tuck 'n' putt on dat bakin for to draw out de soreness an' keep 'im from a-gettin' de lock-jaw.

Well, he tromp roun' til de white man go to de fiel', an' den he sorter slip up easy-like, an' he fling dat shoe-bread afront o' dat ole houn' dawg. It gulp it down in jus' one swaller. Yo' know dem houn' dawgs jus' always been hongry sense de minute dey was barn, an' yo' can't fill him up no mo' 'n if dey got holes in him de same es a collander.

De minute dat shoe-bread been swaller, dat Ole houn'-dawg jus' naturally long after Ole Rabbit. He tuck out after 'im through' de brush so swif' dat it sorter scare Ole Chuffy. He was jus' a-studyin' 'bout a-leadin' dat houn' to de creek, an' a-tyin' a rock roun' he neck an' a-drownin' him, but dis here terrible hurry surprise 'im so dat he jus' run like de Ole Boy was a-tryin' to catch 'im. Here dey had it! Up hill an' down holler, across de fiel' an' roun' de stump, over an' under, roun' an' roun', catch if yo' kin an' follow if yo' can't. O sirs, dat was a race!

No tellin' how it might have come out of Ole Rab hadn't run across an Injun man wid a bow an' arrow.

De Injun gun to fit de arrow to de string for to shoot dat Chuffy Rabbit, when he holler out loud as he could holler for de shortness of he breath,

"Oh! Hold on, Mister Injun Man, hole on a minute. I'm a-fetchin' yo' a present," says 'e, "a mighty nice present," says 'e.

"What yo' fetch?" says de Injun Man, kind o' suspicious-like.

"It's a dawg," says Ole Rabbit, a-working he ears an' a-flinchin' he nose, 'cause he here dat dawn a-cracklin' through' de brush, "a mighty nice fat dawg, Mister Injun Man. I here tell dat yo' ole woman was poorly, an' I was a-bringin' dies here houn' dawg so yo' could make a stew oaten him," says 'e. "I'd a-fetch him ready cook," says 'e, "but my ole woman jus' nowhere 'long o' yon in de makin' o' stews," says 'e. "I was for fetchin' have string o' onions for seas' in an' den I don't know if yo' like him wid onions," says 'e.

De Injun certainly was tickle wid dat lollygag, but he don't say much. He jus' sorter grunt an' look towards de brush.

"Dat him! Dat my houn'-dawg a-comin'!" say Ole Rabbit a-flinchin' mo' an' mo' as de cracklin' come nearer. "Yo' bettah shoot him, jus' as 'e bounce outen de brush, 'cause dat a monstrous shy dawg, monstrous shy! He won't foller nobody but me, an' I can't go 'long home wid yo' an' take him, 'cause I'm lame. Las' night I couldn't sleep my lef' behin' foot hurt so, an' now I got him tie up in bakin fat. Shoot him right here, Mister Injun! Dat de bes' an' de safes', come on!"

Jus' dat minute out jump de dawg, an'—zim!—Mister Injun jus' shoot him an' pin him to de groun'.

Den Ole Man Rabbit mop de sweat offen he face an' lope off home, leas' dat de tale he tell de family, an' if it ain't true nobody ain't a-denyin' it dese days, an' as he say to he ole woman, bit a good laughin' tale today, but twas monstrous solemn yesterday.

Since dat time all de houn' dawgs is surely conjure, 'cause if dey catch a glimpse of a rabbit tail out dey take out after it.

ALLEN CHESSER'S INITIATION: THE BEAR FIGHT

Tradition Bearer: Allen Chesser

Source: Harper, Francis. "Tales of the Okefinoke." *American Speech* 1 (1926): 409–10.

Date: ca. 1914

Original Source: Georgia

National Origin: European American

Allen Chesser's **personal experience narrative** focuses on the dangers of life in the Georgia swamps during his boyhood in the late nineteenth century. While some elements seem to border on fiction, the story never slips into **tall tale** mode.

Now I'll tell yet about that Bear fight, if you'll get your book.

"I must tell yet how come we come to go. I was a boy; I reckon ten or twelve years old, an' the other boys 'uz older. I 'uz off with my bow an' arrow some'eres, an' they went off an' lef' me; took the gun an' the dogs.

"They lef' one gun, an' hit was an of flint-an'-steel. As true a shootin' gun as I ever shot, too. I taken that gun, an' went to Hurst Island. Wal, when I walked out on the island, I didn't have to look, there was the Bear *right there.* An' I, yet know, could 'a' killed with all ease of I had a mind to-if I'd had the sense I have now-but I thought I had to be right close on to 'im.

"An' while I was a-slippin' to get close to 'im, he jumped up a tree. He went about two jumps up the tree (I could hear 'is paws hit the tree), an' slung 'is head off on each side, *thisaway* an' *thataway,* an' then 'e come down. He took 'is time, an' went noselin' about, feedin' on palmetto buds. An' 'e drifted off in the bay, an' me along after 'im, tryin' to get a chance to shoot. Pokin' along an' feedin' along. As fur as he went, I went. An' I got, I reckon, in about ten steps from 'im. Lost all my good chances to kill 'im out on the island, an' had 'im there in that bay. I couldn't see nothin' of 'im but 'is head. When I decided to shoot (I got a notion to shoot then), I aimed through the bushes to strike 'is body, an' I shot. Of course, them kind of ball is easy turned. An' of course I missed 'imp clear— never touched 'imp. So I stood still, an' so did the Bear. An' 'e stood there, I reckon, somethin' like a quarter of a minute, somethin' like a few breaths. An' 'e commenced grumblin', growlin'; I could hear 'imp jest as plain, in 'is manner. An' the notion struck me; I had *better get out of that bay.* So I went, an' I went in a hurry, too. I didn't look for a Bear of nothin', only for a way to get out of that bay, *quick.* I got out to the island. The island was burnt off, an' the grass 'uz only about that high [stretching out his hand a foot above the ground]; looked pretty an' green. So I went out about, I reckon, seventy-five yards on the island. The notion struck me I better load my gun. An' I sot my gun down jest like that [butt touching the ground, barrel at a slant], an' I was a-pourin' my charge of powder in. An' I raised my head an' looked back to see of I could see anything of the Bear; an' shore enough he come right on my trail. So I pulled out my knife an' opened it, an' stuck it in the ground right down beside me, so of I come in close contact, I'd have a chance to use it. So I kep' on loadin' then jest as fast as I could (kep' the balls aroun' loose in my pocket), an' a-lookin' for the Bear, an' he kep' a-comin', too.

"So there 'us an ol' log that had fell, lyin' jest like that, an' 'e come to the top of the log (some of rotten limbs), an' he 'uz a-gnawin' on them limbs, poppin' the limbs an' throwin' the bark off'n 'em.'

"Wha'd he do that for?" I ventured to ask.

"He 'uz mad. He walked jest like a billy goat (you've seen 'em when they're mad—feel bigitty), an' 'e had 'is ears hugged right close to 'is head, jest *thataway*, an' I was settin' about four er five steps from the stump of that tree. An' 'e got through gnawin' there (at the other end of the log). He raised 'is head up, jest looked right at me, jest as straight as he could do it. An' 'e grinned. An' I could see 'is teeth a-shinin', jest as pretty an' white. Didn't open 'is mouth, jest there with 'is ears laid back.

"He started to walk then, right aside of the log, till 'e got to the stump. An' then 'e put in to gnaw on it, jest like 'e had on the top, an' jest like he'd be gnawin' on me in a minute, I thought, an' me a-loadin' all that time. I 'uz about done loadin' then. I'd turned the gun down then to put the primin' in the pan. Wal, I 'uz down on my knees. I jest squatted down thataway. I took deliberate aim at 'im, too, an' shot. I knowed it had to be a dead shot, or me catched one or another. *Spang* said the rifle, an' at the crack of the gun the Bear dashed. An' I rise an' took right after 'im. Now there was a chase, shore as you're livin'. Wal, it 'uz about a hunderd yards, I reckon, to the swamp on the other side. I made a brave run that far. I thought I'd see 'im fall any minute, an' I wanted to see that sight.

"So when 'e landed inter the bushes, I stopped. I reckon I 'uz about thirty steps behind 'im. The next thing occurred to my mind 'uz to get out of that place. So I went an' got my knife an' my gun-stick. An' I had a bay, I reckon, about three-quarters of a mile through, an' the water about up to here [indicating his waist-line] on me. So your better know I 'uz makin' all the railroad time I could.

"Now all this [that follows] is imagination, I know it wuzn't so, but I'm goin' to tell you. I could hear that Bear come a-sousin' right in behind me.

"So that's about all of it. I come back home. That's jest about how near I come to gettin' Bear-catched. The next stump he'd 'a' gnawed on, I reckon 'u'd a' been me.

"I've had lots of contests with Bears an' Alligators an' things, but that's about as near as I ever come to gettin' Bear catched.

"It took me from about one o'clock in the day to about sundown.

"When the Bear 'uz up that tree, it 'uz only about sixty yards; I could 'a' broke a ten-cent piece on 'im—a dollar anyhow. Them kind of guns shore shot true.

"That 'uz my initiation, an' it 'uz a pretty bad un, too. Like George Stokes said that time he got catched in the storm, with the timber fallin' all about 'im, I wouldn't 'a' given ten cents fer my chances."

HEROES, HEROINES, TRICKSTERS, AND FOOLS

THE WINE, THE FARM, THE PRINCESS, AND THE TARBABY

Tradition Bearer: Aneus Guerin

Source: Claudel, Calvin. "Louisiana Tales of Jean Sot and Boqui and Lapin." *Southern Folklore Quarterly* 8 (1944): 288–91.

Date: 1931

Original Source: Aneus Guerin, Pointe Coupee Parish, Louisiana. Recorded by Lafayette Jarreau, "Creole Folklore of Pointe Coupee Parish." MA thesis, Louisiana State University, 1931.

National Origin: Cajun

The Cajun cycle of Lapin and Bouqui tales casts Lapin (French, "Rabbit") in his common role of **trickster** and Bouqui (apparently derived from the Wolof word for "hyena," as noted on p. 4) as Lapin's foil and the butt of all his jokes. The Lapin and Bouqui cycle in general and "The Wine, the Farm, the Princess, and the Tarbaby" in particular show the influence of African American tradition. In this regard, this tale should be compared to the two Native American tales that follow: "The Tarbaby" (p. 52) and "The Rabbit and the Frenchman" (p. 54). Cross-cultural borrowing and adaptation to the Southern environment are striking in these three tales. In addition, this tale, composed of several narratives that are capable of standing alone, should be compared to other **trickster** narratives in this collection, especially "How Brer

Rabbit Practice Medicine" (p. 66) and "Brother Rabbit an' Brother Tar-Baby" (p. 232).

One day Comrade Lapin was working with Comrade Bouqui on a farm. They were cropping together that year, and they had arranged to divide the crop equally at the end of the year. It was very hot that day, and Comrade Lapin wanted to fool Comrade Bouqui in some way or other.

"What do you say if we buy a jug of wine today?" suggested Lapin.

"Fine!" agreed Bouqui. "You will go get it yourself."

Comrade Lapin went to fetch the wine. When he returned, he put it in a ditch where there was shade. He went to work again, but did not try to keep up with Bouqui. He took his time, cheating on his comrade. Bouqui was working fast to get finished, and Lapin was far behind. Suddenly Lapin exclaimed:

"Ooh!"

"What's the matter?" requested Bouqui.

"There's someone calling me," explained Lapin.

"Go see who it is," suggested Bouqui.

Lapin left, went toward the jug and took a drink. When he returned, Bouqui asked him why he had stayed so long.

"I was called for a christening," explained Lapin.

"Is that so?" questioned Bouqui. "What did you name the baby?"

"I named him First-One," continued Lapin.

They started working, and soon Comrade Lapin was called again. He went to take another big drink. When he returned, he told Bouqui it was another christening and he had called the baby Second-One.

Next he went to perform a third christening and named this baby Third-One. This time he finished drinking all the wine, turning the jug over before he returned to his work.

"Ah now!" exclaimed Bouqui when it was time to quit, "let's go drink us some wine now."

They went to the jug and saw it was turned over. There was not a drop of wine left in the jug.

"Too bad!" declared Lapin. "Our wine is all lost."

Bouqui was sad, disappointed and tired. Comrade Lapin felt good as he returned to his cabin.

A little while after that Bouqui and Lapin went into the field to see their potatoes. There was a good crop. The potato plants were big and full of flowers. They stayed there a long time, talking and admiring their labor.

"It's almost time to dig our potatoes," said Lapin "How are we going to divide our crop? Do you want to take the roots, and I'll take the plant?"

"Oh no!" replied Bouqui, "myself I want the pretty plant."

"As you wish," agreed Lapin.

When they took in the potato crop, Bouqui brought all the pretty plants into his storeroom. He had nothing at all. Lapin took the roots, and he had food for the whole year.

Later on it was time to harvest the crop of corn. Bouqui made up his mind that Lapin would not fool him on the corn. He said he wanted the roots this time, and Lapin told him to choose as he wanted again. Bouqui took the roots, taking them to his storeroom, and he had nothing. Lapin took the stalks, and he had a lot to eat for the whole year.

During the winter Bouqui went to ask Lapin for something to eat. Lapin refused him. Bouqui almost died from hunger that year, and he decided not to work on shares with Comrade Lapin anymore.

Comrade Bouqui was very dissatisfied, but he was to be still more unhappy yet before he would be done with Lapin.

They were courting the same girl, a princess. She was a pretty girl, and she liked Lapin better. Bouqui was jealous, and he wanted to know whether he or Lapin would marry the girl.

"I'll tell you what we'll do," suggested Comrade Bouqui to Lapin one day. "We'll have a race. We'll leave here together tomorrow morning. He who gets at the girl's place first will marry her."

"Fine!" agreed Lapin. "We shall run a race."

As they had planned, the following morning they started the race. Comrade Lapin beat him by a long distance. When Bouqui got there, he asked Lapin to give him another chance.

"What do you want to do this time, Comrade Bouqui?" asked Lapin.

"Let's see," thought Bouqui, scratching his head. "Oh yes! Let's boil a big pot of water, and he who jumps over it wins the girl. Do you want to try that?"

"As for me, I'll do whatever you want," replied Lapin.

They boiled some water until it was boiling over. They placed it in the yard by the house, and it was decided that Lapin should jump first. Lapin started running to make his jump; but when he got up to the big pot, fear seized him and he did not jump.

"It's high, yes!" exclaimed Lapin.

He tried again. This time he jumped it.

"It's your turn now, Bouqui," said Lapin.

Bouqui started running. When he jumped, he fell into the middle of the pot. The water was so hot, he was cooked before he could count to four.

After that Bouqui's family had a grudge against Lapin. They blamed Lapin for the death of their son, Bouqui; and they watched for the chance to pay him back in the same way.

Comrade Lapin would come to steal water from their well every night. Now old man Bouqui knew it was Lapin who was stealing his water. When Lapin came for water that night, he saw a little tarbaby. He could not make out who it was. He walked all around it, looking closely. Finally he got up enough courage to talk to it.

"Get away from that well!" cried Lapin.

But it did not act as if it heard. Lapin advanced more closely, crying out:

"Go away! Go away, before I hit you a blow with my foot." But it did not pay any attention at all. Comrade Lapin struck a blow with his foot, and his foot stayed stuck.

"Let my foot go!" cried Lapin. "Let me go, or I'll strike you with my other foot."

As he struck, the other foot stayed stuck, too. Lapin struck with his other two, and they stayed stuck, too. Then he struck with his head, his body, all staying stuck on the tarbaby. Lapin was well caught.

The following morning old Bouqui found Lapin in his trap. "Now I have you!" exclaimed he. "I will go kill you, and I think I'll burn you."

"Burn me if you will!" cried Lapin, "But I beg of you not to throw me into the briars behind the fence there. That would be too mean a death."

"I am going to give you the worst death I know," added old man Bouqui, "and it's into the briars you go."

He went off with Lapin, to throw him into the briars. When he got by the fence, he threw him over. Lapin fell into the middle of the briar patch. Old Bouqui looked through a crack to see him die, but Lapin only laughed at him. Bouqui realized his mistake, but too late.

"You threw me exactly into my home here," shouted back Lapin, running quickly toward his place.

"He's a bad fellow, yes, that Lapin!" exclaimed old Bouqui to himself, turning homeward very regretful.

THE TARBABY

Tradition Bearer: Unavailable

Source: Swanton, John R. Pages 258–59 in *Myths and Tales of the Southeastern Indians*. Smithsonian Institution Bureau of American Ethnology Bulletin 88. Washington, DC: U.S. Government Printing Office, 1929.

Date: 1929

Original Source: Natchez

National Origin: Native American

The following narrative offers another version of the widespread Tarbaby **tale type** (AT175), known not only in the Americas but also in the Old World. There are many similarities, such as the "Briar patch punishment for Rabbit" (AT1310 A), but unlike the Cajun example of "The Wine, the Farm, the Princess, and the Tarbaby" (p. 49) and the Caribbean "Brother Rabbit an' Brother Tar-Baby" (p. 232), the **trickster** hero Rabbit plays the role of shapeshifter by literally donning the skin of gray squirrel to gain initial access to the well. This disguise is also used in "Tasks of Rabbit," which is collected among the neighboring Hitchiti; however, the change of species is magical rather than mechanical in their tale. Taking on the shape of another being by donning its skin is commonly associated with witchcraft—but not in this case, it seems. Also, no apparent significance can be found for Rabbit's decision to adopt gray squirrel's shape. Therefore, the similarity may indicate an exchange of **motifs** among neighboring groups sharing a common environment and way of life in the same region. It is ironic that Rabbit, who is seen to be the master of disguise in most narratives, is trapped by a similarly false image.

All of the wild animals appointed a time to dig for water and when the time came assembled and began digging. But presently Rabbit gave up digging, and the others went on digging without him. They found water. Then they stationed two people to watch it. But Rabbit became very thirsty. He killed a gray squirrel, stripped off its hide, got into it, and came to the watchers. It was Rabbit who did it, but in the form of the gray squirrel he said that he had become very thirsty for lack of water. "You may drink water because you are just a gray squirrel," they said to him, and he drank. He drank all he wanted and went away. Then he pulled off the hide.

But when he thought of going back to drink again the hide had become hard and he could not get it on, so when he became thirsty he dipped up the water at night. But when he set out water for his visitors they said to him, "Where did you find it?" and he answered, "I got it from the dew." Then, following the tracks by the water, they saw signs of Rabbit, made an image of a person out of pitch and set it up near the place where they had dug the well.

The next night Rabbit came and stood there. "Who are you?" he said. There was no reply and he continued, "If you do not speak I will strike you." Rabbit struck it with one hand and his hand stuck to it. "Let me go. If you do not let me go I will strike you with my other hand," he said, and he struck it with that hand. When he hit it that hand also stuck. "Let me go. Stop holding me. If you do not let me go I will kick you," he said, and he kicked it. When he kicked it his foot stuck. "If you do not let go I will kick you with my other foot," he said, and he kicked it with that foot. When he did so his other foot stuck. "Let me go," he said, "I have my head left, and if you do not let me go I will butt you." He pulled back and forth to get free and butted it with his head and his head stuck. Then he hung there all doubled up.

While he was hanging there day came. And when it was light the water watchers came and found Rabbit hanging there. They picked him up, made a prisoner of him, and carried him off. They assembled together to kill him. "Let us throw him into the fire," they said, but Rabbit laughed and replied, "Nothing can happen to me there. That is where I travel around." "If that is the case we must kill him some other way," they said, and after they had debated a long time concluded, "Let us tie a rock around his neck and throw him into the water," but Rabbit laughed and called out, "I live all the time in water. Nothing can happen to me there." "Well," they said, "he will be hard to kill. How can we kill him?" After all had conferred for a while, they said, "I wonder what would become of him if we threw him into a brier patch?" At that Rabbit cried out loudly. "Now you have killed me," he said. "Now we have killed him," they replied. "If we had known that at first we would have had him killed already," so they carried him to a brier thicket, Rabbit weeping unceasingly as he was dragged along. Then they threw him into the brier thicket with all their strength, and he fell down, got up, and ran off at once, whooping.

THE RABBIT AND THE FRENCHMAN

Tradition Bearer: Unavailable

Source: Dorsey, J. Owen. "Two Biloxi Tales." *Journal of American Folklore* 6 (1893): 48–49.

Date: 1892

Original Source: Biloxi

National Origin: Native American

The following **trickster** tale was collected in central Louisiana from an elderly woman who was a "survivor of the Biloxi tribe." The narrator told the tale in her native language, and the text was translated during performances by her daughter and son-in-law. The tale is an obvious borrowing; it bears striking resemblance to the Lapin and Bouqui tale, "The Wine, the Farm, the Princess, and the Tarbaby" (p. 49) as well as the tarbaby **motif** found in neighboring African American traditions. The substitution of "Frenchman" for Bouqui as the butt of Rabbit's tricks likely signifies enduring Native American enmity toward the historical incursions of the French.

The Rabbit and the Frenchman were two friends. The Rabbit aided the Frenchman, agreeing to work a piece of land on shares. The first season they planted potatoes. The Rabbit, having been told to select his share of the crop, chose the potato vines, and devoured them all. The next season they planted corn. This year the Rabbit said, "I will eat the roots." So he pulled up all the corn by the roots, but he found nothing to satisfy his hunger.

Then the Frenchman said, "Let us dig a well." But the Rabbit did not wish to work any longer with his friend.

Said he to the Frenchman, "If you wish to dig a well, I shall not help you."

"Oho," said the Frenchman, "you shall not drink any of the water from the well."

"That does not matter," replied the Rabbit, "I am accustomed to licking the dew from the ground."

The Frenchman, suspecting mischief, made a tarbaby, which he stood up close to the well. The Rabbit approached the well, carrying a long piece of cane and a tin bucket. On reaching the well he addressed the tarbaby, who remained silent. "Friend, what is the matter? Are you angry?" said the Rabbit. Still the tarbaby said nothing. So the Rabbit hit him with one forepaw, which stuck there. "Let me go or I will hit you on the other side," exclaimed the Rabbit. And when he found that the tarbaby paid no attention to him, he hit him with his other forepaw, which stuck to the tarbaby. "I will kick you," said the Rabbit. But when he kicked the tarbaby, the hind foot stuck. "I will kick you with the other foot," said the Rabbit. And when he did so, that foot, too, stuck to the tarbaby. Then the Rabbit resembled a ball, because his feet were sticking to the tarbaby, and he could neither stand nor recline.

Just at this time the Frenchman approached. He tied the legs of the Rabbit together, laid him down and scolded him. Then the Rabbit pretended to be in great fear of a brier patch.

"As you are in such fear of a brier patch," said the Frenchman, "I will throw you into one."

"Oh, no," replied the Rabbit.

"I will throw you into the brier patch," responded the Frenchman.

"I am much afraid of it," said the Rabbit.

"As you are in such dread of it," said the Frenchman, "I will throw you into it." So he seized the Rabbit, and threw him into the brier patch. The Rabbit fell at some distance from the Frenchman. But instead of being injured, he sprang up and ran off laughing at the trick which he had played on the Frenchman.

MR. DEER'S MY RIDING HORSE

Tradition Bearer: Unavailable

Source: Johnston, Mrs. William Preston. "Two Negro Folktales." *Journal of American Folklore* 9 (1896): 195–96.

Date: 1896

Original Source: Louisiana

National Origin: African American

The following tale of Rabbit feigning illness in order to humiliate a gullible romantic rival enjoys wide distribution throughout the South. In some versions, Fox or an animal other than Deer becomes Rabbit's steed and, thus, the butt of his joke. The tale is not limited to African American communities; extensive borrowing occurs between the various ethnic groups inhabiting the region. For example, see the Louisiana French tale of Lapin and Bouqui, "On Horseback" (p. 61) for a **variant** of "Mr. Deer's My Riding Horse" and the narrative "Rabbit Rides Wolf" (p. 58) for the Native American take on the same plot. In all versions, however, Rabbit exploits a personality trait, such as Deer's kind heart, to defeat a romantic rival and, in the process, humiliate him.

Well, once upon a time, when Mr. Rabbit was young and frisky, he went a courting Miss Fox, who lived way far back in the thick woods. Mr. Fox an' his family was very skeery, an' they very seldom come outer the wood 'cept for a little walk in the clearin' near the big house, sometimes when the moon shine bright; so they did n' know many people 'sides Mr. Rabbit and Mr. Deer.

Mr. Deer he had his eyes set on Miss Fox, too. But he didn't suspicion Mr. Rabbit was a lookin' that way, but kep' on being jus' as friendly with Mr. Rabbit as he ever been.

One day Mr. Rabbit call on Miss Fox, and wile they was talkin', Miss Fox she tells him what a fine gentleman she thinks Mr. Deer is. Mr. Rabbit jes threw back his head and he laugh and he laugh.

"What you laughing 'bout?" Miss Fox says; and Mr. Rabbit he jes laugh on an' won't tell her, an' Miss Fox she jes kept' on pestering Mr. Rabbit to tell her what he's laughing 'bout, an' at las' Mr. Rabbit stop laughing an' say, "Miss Fox, you bear me witness I didn't want to tell you, but you jes made me. Miss Fox, you call Mr. Deer a fine gentleman; Miss Fox, Mr. Deer is my riding horse!"

Miss Fox she nearly fell over in a faintin' fit, and she say she don't believe it, and she will not till Mr. Rabbit give her the proof.

An' Mr. Rabbit he says, "Will you believe it if you sees me riding pass yo' door?" and Miss Fox says she will, and she won't have nothin' to do with Mr. Deer if the story is true. Now, Mr. Rabbit is been fixing up a plan for some time to git Mr. Deer outer his way; so he says good evenin' to Miss Fox, and clips it off to Mr. Deer's house, and Mr. Rabbit he so friendly with Mr. Deer he don't suspec' nothin'. Presently Mr. Rabbit jes fall over double in his chair and groan and moan, and Mr. Deer he says, "What's the matter, Mr. Rabbit, is you sick?" But Mr. Rabbit he jes groan; then Mr. Rabbit fall off the cheer and roll on the floor, and Mr. Deer says, "What ails you, Mr. Rabbit, is you sick?"

And Mr. Rabbit he jes groans out, "Oh, Mr. Deer, I'm dying; take me home, take me home."

An' Mr. Deer he's mighty kindhearted, and he says, "Get up on my back, and I'll tote you home"; but Mr. Rabbit says, "Oh, Mr. Deer, I'm so sick, I can't set on your back 'less you put a saddle on." So Mr. Deer put on a saddle.

Mr. Rabbit says, "can't steady myself 'less you put my feets in the stirrups." So he put his feets in the stirrups.

"Oh, Mr. Deer, I can't hold on 'less you put on a bridle." So he put on a bridle.

"Oh, Mr. Deer, I don't feel all right 'less I had a whip in my hand." So Mr. Deer puts the whip in his hand.

"Now I'm ready, Mr. Deer," says Mr. Rabbit, "but go mighty easy, for I'm likely to die any minute. Please take the shortcut through the wood, Mr. Deer, so I kin get home soon."

So Mr. Deer took the short cut, an' forgot that it took him pass Miss Fox's house. Jes as he 'membered it, an' was 'bout to turn back, Mr. Rabbit, who had slipped a pair of spurs on unbeknownst to him, stuck 'em into his sides, and at the same time laid the whip on so that po' Mr. Deer was crazy with the pain, and ran as fas' as his legs could carry him right by where Miss Fox was standin' on the gallery, and Mr. Rabbit a standin' up in his stirrups and hollerin', "Didn't I tell you Mr. Deer was my riding horse!"

But after a while Miss Fox she found out 'bout Mr. Rabbit's trick on Mr. Deer, and she wouldn't have nothin' more to do with him.

RABBIT RIDES WOLF

Tradition Bearer: Unavailable

Source: Swanton, John R. Pages 64–66 in *Myths and Tales of the Southeastern Indians.* Smithsonian Institution Bureau of American Ethnology Bulletin 88. Washington, DC: U.S. Government Printing Office, 1929.

Date: 1929

Original Source: Creek

National Origin: Native American

This is another impressive example of the ways in which neighboring cultures influence one another's folktale repertoires. This tale appears in Cajun tradition as "On Horseback" (p. 61) and in the African American corpus as "Mr. Deer's My Riding Horse" (p. 56). Such cross-fertilization should come as no surprise; the Creek Confederacy had extensive contact, including intermarriage, with the French from at least the early eighteenth century and with Africans and African Americans since the beginning of the Southern slave trade. Compared to Lapin in "On Horseback," the Rabbit's motivation for humiliating Wolf in this narrative and Brer Rabbit's similar treatment of Deer in "Brer Rabbit Deer" are far more reasonable. Notice the similarities between the dead horse **motif** here and in "The Fox and the Wolf" (p. 76).

Some girls lived not far from Rabbit and Wolf, and Rabbit thought he would like to visit them. So one time he called upon Wolf and said, "Let us go visiting." Wolf said, "All right," and they started off. When they got to the place the girls told them to sit down and they took a great liking to Wolf, who had a good time with them while Rabbit had to sit by and look on. Of course he was not pleased at this turn of affairs and said presently, "We had better be going back." But Wolf replied, "Let us wait a while longer," and they remained until it was late.

Before they left Rabbit got a chance to speak to one of the girls so that Wolf would not overhear and he said, "The one you are having so much sport with is my old horse." "I think you are lying," said the girl. "I am not. You shall see me ride him up here to-morrow." "If we see you ride him up we'll believe you."

When they started off the girls said, "Well, call again." Wolf was anxious to do so and early next morning be called upon Rabbit, whose house was much nearer, and said, "Are we going?" "I was sick all night," Rabbit answered, "and I hardly feel able to go." Wolf urged him, but he said at first that be really wasn't able to. Finally, however, he said, "If you will let me ride you I might go along just for company." So Wolf agreed to carry him astride of his back. But then Rabbit said, "I would like to put a saddle on you so as to brace myself," and Wolf agreed to it. "I believe it would be better," added Rabbit, "if I should bridle you." Wolf did not like this idea but Rabbit said, "Then I could hold on better and manage to get there," so Wolf finally consented to be bridled. Finally Rabbit wanted to put on spurs. Wolf replied, "I am too ticklish," but Rabbit said, "I will not spur you with them. I will hold them away from you but it would be nicer to have them on," so Wolf finally agreed, saying only, "I am very ticklish; you must not spur me." "When we get near the house," said Rabbit, "we will take everything off of you and walk the rest of the way."

So Rabbit and Wolf started on, but when they were nearly in sight of the house Rabbit plunged the spurs into Wolf and before he knew it they had passed right by the house. Then Rabbit said, "They have seen you now. I will tie you here and go up to see them and come back after a while and let you go." So Rabbit went to the house and said to the girls, "You all saw it, did you not?" "Yes," they answered, and he sat down and had a good time with them.

After a while Rabbit thought he ought to let Wolf go and started back to the place where he was fastened. He knew that Wolf was angry with him and thought up a way by which he could loose him with safety to himself. First he found a thin hollow log which he beat upon as if it were a drum. Then he ran up to Wolf as fast as he could go and cried out, "Do you know they are hunting for you? You heard the drum just now. The soldiers are after you." Wolf was very much frightened and said "Let me go." Rabbit was purposely a little slow in untying him and he had barely gotten him freed when Wolf broke away and went off as fast as he could run. Then Rabbit returned to the house and remained there as if he were already a married man.

Near this house was a large peach orchard and one day Rabbit said to the girls, "I will shake the peaches off for you." So they all went to the orchard together and he climbed up into a tree to shake the peaches off. While he was there Wolf came toward them and called out, "Old fellow, I am not going to let you alone." By that time he was almost under the tree. Then Rabbit shouted out loud as if to people at a distance, "Here is that fellow for whom you are always hunting," and Wolf ran away again.

Some time after this, while Rabbit was lying close under a tree bent over near the ground, he saw Wolf coming. Then he stood up with the tree extended over his shoulder as if he were trying to hold it up. When Wolf saw him he said, "I have you now." Rabbit, however, called out, "They told me to hold this tree up all day with the great power I have and for it they would give me four hogs. I don't like hog meat but you do, so you might get it if you take my place." Wolf's greed was excited by this and he was willing to hold up the tree. Then Rabbit said, "If you yield only a little it will give way, so you must hold it tight." And he ran off. Wolf stood under the tree so long that finally he felt he could stand it no longer and he jumped away quickly so that it would not fall upon him. Then he saw that it was a growing tree rooted in the earth. "That Rabbit is the biggest liar," he exclaimed, "if I can catch him I will certainly fix him."

After that Wolf hunted about for Rabbit once more and finally came upon him in a nice grassy place. He was about to spring upon him when Rabbit said, "My friend, don't punish me. I have food for you. There is a horse lying out yonder." Wolf's appetite was again moved at the prospect and he decided to go along. Then Rabbit said, "It is pretty close to a house, therefore it would be well for me to tie your tail to the horse's tail so that you can drag it off to a place where you can feast at leisure." So Rabbit tied the two tails together. But the horse was only asleep, not dead, as Wolf supposed, and Rabbit ran around to its head and kicked it. At once the horse jumped up and was so frightened that it kicked and kicked until it kicked Wolf to death.

ON HORSEBACK

Tradition Bearer: Aneus Guerin

Source: Claudel, Calvin. "Louisiana Tales of Jean Sot and Boqui and Lapin." *Southern Folklore Quarterly* 8 (1944): 294–95.

Date: 1931

Original Source: Pointe Coupee Parish, Louisiana. Recorded by Lafayette Jarreau, "Creole Folklore of Pointe Coupee Parish." MA thesis, Louisiana State University, 1931.

National Origin: Cajun

This tale, in which Lapin chooses to humiliate Bouqui in front of some female friends, is very similar to "Mr. Deer's My Riding Horse" (p. 307). However, unlike Rabbit, whose motive is to eliminate a romantic competitor, Lapin demonstrates no motive beyond the **trickster**'s standard desire to stir up trouble.

One day Comrade Lapin and Comrade Bouqui planned to go see some girls together. Bouqui was to come to meet Lapin at his house at four o'clock Sunday afternoon, and they would go together. At four o'clock Bouqui arrived.

"Well now, let's go," he called to Lapin.

"I don't think I can go," replied Lapin. "I was coming down my steps yesterday, and I fell down. I really believe I broke my foot, because I can't walk."

"Can't you walk just a little bit?" asked Bouqui very disappointedly.

"The only way I can go with you is if you carry me," suggested Lapin.

"I'll carry you until we get to the big-gate," agreed Bouqui. "But I'll put you down there, and you will have to walk the rest of the way, because the girls will laugh at me if they see that you ride me like a horse."

Lapin put on a pair of spurs and mounted Bouqui. When they got to the big-gate, Lapin got down but could not make a single step, his foot hurt him so much.

"I can't make it," complained Lapin. "If you want me to go all the way, you will be obliged to carry me a little farther."

"Oh well! Get upon my back again," agreed Bouqui.

Bouqui did not want to leave his friend there and would do anything to help him. When they passed the house, the girls were all upon the gallery. Seeing Lapin seated upon Bouqui, they wanted to laugh, but they did not laugh, because they did not want to hurt Bouqui's feelings.

Poor Bouqui placed himself next to the steps, and Lapin bounded upon the gallery, completely well. Lapin then turned toward the girls, saying: "Didn't I always tell you Bouqui was my horse!"

The girls could no longer withhold themselves. They almost burst with laughter at Bouqui, right in front of him. He was so ashamed he was all miserable. So he excused himself right away and left.

INCRIMINATING THE OTHER FELLOW

Tradition Bearer: Unavailable

Source: Smiley, Portia. "Folk-Lore from Virginia, South Carolina, Georgia, Alabama, and Florida." *Journal of American Folklore* 32 (1919): 366–67.

Date: 1919

Original Source: South Carolina

National Origin: African American

Wolf attempts to trick his rival Rabbit into a false confession by leading him into singing a chorus that incriminates him. As usual in this pairing, Rabbit triumphs over Wolf and his clumsy scheme.

Miss Kingdeer of Coon Swamp had two da'ghters, and Brer Wolf and Brer Rabbit was in love with the young Miss Kingdeer. Young Miss Kingdeer allowed she loved Brer Rabbit better than she did Brer Wolf.

Brer Wolf he got jealous, and say he's goin' to git even with Brer Rabbit by killing Miss Kingdeer's goat, cause she say anybody who'd kill that goat, her father would horn 'im.

So Brer Rabbit and Brer Wolf went to call on Miss Kingdeer; and when dey was goin' back home, Brer Wolf said to Brer Rabbit, "Ye must excuse me for not going home all de way wid you, 'cause I promised to call on Brer 'Possum wife, who is mighty sick." Brer Rabbit allowed, "I'd go along wid you, but I'm mighty feeble myself tonight."

So Brer Wolf left Brer Rabbit, an' went back in the field an' kill Miss Kingdeer's goat. Next day he went callin' on Miss Kingdeer to see what dey'd say, like he know nothin' about it.

"Good-mornin', Miss Kingdeer!" says Brer Wolf, "how's your ma?"

"She's between de gate-posts an' de hinges dis mornin', Brer Wolf, how is you?"

"Well, I'm kind of hucckumso."

"Brer Wolf, has you heard about our goat? Someone killed her last night."

Brer Wolf he made out he's so 'stonished. "Miss Kingdeer, I think I know who killed dat dere goat, nobody but Brer Rabbit, 'cause I saw him amblin' across de field after he left de house last night!"

Miss Kingdeer is very sorry 'cause she loved Brer Rabbit an' didn't want Brer Rabbit killed. "I don't t'ink he'd do dat, 'cause he done loved dat goat," says she.

"Well, I'll make him tell you himself dat he killed dat goat."

An' he went, an' he went 'round to Brer Rabbit's house. "Mornin', Brer Rabbit! How is you today?"

"Kinder poorly, Brer Wolf, kinder poorly. How's you?"

"Well, I'm between de hawk an' de break-down, ain't much myself today. Brer Rabbit, I got a scheme on foot; I thought we'd serenade de girls tonight. I done told dem what a good bass-singer you is; we'll practice de song. I'll play de fiddle, and den we'll go under de window an' sing, an' den de ladies'll come out an' invite us in!" Brer Rabbit agreed, an' same night dey went up to Miss Kingdeer's house an' stood under de window. Brer Wolf chumin de fiddle— plum, plum, plum! Chan, chan, chan!

> Brer Rab-bit is a trick-y man, and ev-ery-bod-y know.
> Did you kill Miss King-deer's goat and ev-ery-bod-y know?
> Yes, yes, yes, yes, yes, yes, yes, and ev-ery-bod-y know.
> Chorus.
> Rio Brer Rab-bit, Pop-eyed rab-bit,
> Buck-eye rab-bit.

"Ladies," said Brer Wolf, "I told you Brer Rabbit killed Miss Kingdeer's goat, 'cause he done tell you."

Den Brer Rabbit threw up his hands, an' said, "Brer Wolf got this game up on me, 'cause he's jealous!" Miss Kingdeer says she didn't believe Brer Rabbit killed de goat, and Brer Wolf is de fox dat is de finder, an' he's done killed dat goat, an' she called for her pa. Den Brer Wolf licked out an' tore down de road at such a rate, you couldn't see him running for de sand. Miss Kingdeer an' Brer Rabbit got so tickled, dey had to hold their sides to keep from poppin'. Brer Wolf is runnin' yet from Kingdeer.

PLAYING GODFATHER

Tradition Bearer: Unavailable

Source: Fauset, Arthur Huff. "Negro Folk Tales from the South (Alabama, Mississippi, Louisiana)." *Journal of American Folklore* 40 (1927): 237–38.

Date: 1927

Original Source: Mississippi

National Origin: African American

This **tale type**—AT 15 or "Theft of Butter (Honey) by Playing Godfather"—is distributed widely throughout the South and the Caribbean. For example, compare this tale to "The Wine, the Farm, the Princess, and the Tarbaby" (p. 49) and "Playing Mourner" (p. 240). Typically the **trickster**, Rabbit, shifts the blame for the theft onto one of the dupes. The slow-witted Possum also appears as Rabbit's victim in "How Brer Fox Dream He Eat Brer 'Possum" (p. 83) and "When Brer 'Possum Attend Miss Fox's House-Party" (p. 91).

Rabbit an' Fox make a proposition once to start farmin'. Dey bought lot of groceries for the year, butter, coffee, everything you could mention. So the butter was the most important. So they all went out in the field to work.

Rabbit studied a plan to leave Possum an' Fox in the field an' make believe that someone was callin' him away. So he let on someone callin' him, "Yoo-hoo-yoo-hoo-yoo-hoo!" So Fox an' Possum said, "What's that?"

Rabbit said, "Aw, I can't work here for bein' bothered by these people. I'm goin' this time but I won't go no more." So Rabbit goes to the house an' sees the bucket o' butter. He ate some of the butter. Pretty soon he come back.

Pretty soon somebody callin', "Yoo-hoo-yoo-hoo-yoo-hoo!"

So they all said, "What's the matter, Brother Rabbit?"

Rabbit said, "Aw, they want me to christen another baby. These people are botherin' me too much. I'm not goin'."

So they all said, "You better go ahead. Hurry on." So he went an' got another stomach full o' butter. So when he come back they said, "Well, what did you name the baby?"

He said, "Just begun." So pretty soon they heard somebody callin', "Yoo-hoo-yoo-hoo-yoo-hoo."

So they all said, "What's the matter, Brother Rabbit?"

Rabbit said, "Aw, those people just won't let me alone. They want me to christen another child. I'm not goin' this time, tho', deed I'm not."

But they all said, "You better go ahead." So he went an' got some more butter. So he come back an' they asked him what name the baby had. He said, "Pretty Well On The Way." He comes back an' works a little while an' somebody yells, "Yoo-hoo-yoo-hoo-yoo-hoo."

They all said, "What's that?"

So Rabbit said, "Aw, it's them same people want me to come christen another baby. I'm not goin', I tell you."

They said, "You better go ahead." So he went off an' eat some more butter. When he come back they asked him what the baby's name was.

He said, "About Quarter Gone." So he went on workin' some more an' somebody yelled, "Yoo-hoo-yoo-hoo-yoo-hoo."

They said, "What's that?"

He said, "It's those same people again. I tell you I just won't go an' christen any more of their children."

But they said, "You better go on ahead." So he went off an' eat some more of the butter. When he returned they asked him what was the child's name.

He said, "Half Gone." So he went on back to work. This time somebody yelled, "Yoo-hoo-yoo-hoo-yoo-hoo."

So they all said, "What's that?"

He said, "Doggone the luck, you know that's rotten. A fellow can't work here for those people callin' on you to christen their children."

So they all said, "You better go on ahead." He went on an' eat some more of the butter.

When he come back he said, "Well I christened another child."

They said, "What you name him?"

He said, "Quarter Left." So he come on back, work awhile, an' pretty soon somebody cry, "Heh-h-h-h-h-h-h." Rabbit say, "Doggone the luck. I ain't goin' this time. By God they want to run a fellow to death."

So they all said, "You better go on ahead." So he went this time an' eat all the butter.

When he come back they said, "What happened this time?"

He said, "I had another child to christen."

They said, "What did you name him?"

He said "All Gone." Well about the middle o' June they was gonna open the keg of butter. The crops were half grown. So when they got there the butter was all gone.

They all said, "Who stole the butter?" Rabbit didn't know; Fox didn't know; Possum didn't know.

So Rabbit say, "I tell you, Possum, he been layin' around dat house all time. I believe he must o' done it." So he said, "Let's build a big fire. Then all three of us will lay aroun' the fire, an' whoever et the butter the grease will come out o' his stomach." So they made a big fire an' everybody went to sleep but Rabbit. So he peeped. Everybody sound asleep. So Rabbit say, "All right, I got him now." So he took his tail an' greased it an' his belly right good. He oiled Fox up too. So pretty soon Fox woke up.

He spied Possum an' cried, "Dah, dah, I tot' you, Possum done it!" Possum woke up an' looked aroun'. He say, "Hey there, Fox, you had some too; look at your belly." Fox made for Rabbit but Rabbit got away. So Fox struck Possum a lick an' Possum went through the blaze of fire. That's why his tail is bare of hair today.

HOW BRER RABBIT PRACTICE MEDICINE

Tradition Bearer: Unavailable

Source: Backus, Emma M. "Tales of the Rabbit from Georgia Negroes." *Journal of American Folklore* 12 (1899): 108–9.

Date: 1899

Original Source: Georgia

National Origin: African American

At its heart, the following tale of Brer Rabbit contains messages concerning why Rabbit (and perhaps all con men, for that matter) can make his way so successfully in society. Poor judgment leads Brer Wolf to take him on as a partner despite his "bad name for a partner." Then, gullibility and avarice set Wolf up for the "fool's bargain" Rabbit proposes. When Brer Rabbit's ploy is discovered and a jury is being selected to decide the disposition of the money from their venture, Sheriff Coon is given the job of finding bigger fools than the plaintiff and defendant to sit on the jury. When Coon is successful, the judge, plaintiff, jury, and spectators become so caught up in the courtroom drama that Rabbit is able to win the day by keeping his wits about him and putting his ethics on hold. Compare this to "Playing Godfather" (p. 64).

Ole Brer Rabbit had a bad name for a partner, but one time he get Mr. Wolf to work a crop on shares with him, and they have a 'greement writ out on paper, how in the harvest they goin' to divide half and half. Mr. Rabbit know Ole Mr. Wolf mighty good hand in the field, and sure to make a good crop. But when Ole Brer Rabbit set in to work, he get mighty tired, and the corn rows, they look so mighty long, and he 'gin to lag behind and work he brain.

Presen'ly he jump to the work, and make he hoe cut the air, and soon catch up with Mr. Wolf, and he open the subject of the education in medicine, and he tell how he am a reg'lar doctor, and got his 'plomy in a frame to home, but he say he don't know how all the patients goin' get on now he turn over the farming, and Ole Mr. Wolf ask how much money he get for he doctoring, and when he hear so much, he tell Mr. Rabbit to go when he have a call, and put by the money, and in the fall put in the crop money and then divide. So that night Mr. Rabbit, he instruct his children how they got for to run and call him frequent, and how they got to tell Mr. Wolf they wants the doctor.

And sure 'nough, Mr. Rabbit ain't more'n in the front row next day, when here come little Rab all out of breath and say, "Somebody send in great 'stress for the doctor." Mr. Rabbit make out like he can't go and leave Mr. Wolf to do all the work, but Mr. Wolf studying 'bout that big fee Brer Rabbit goin' turn in to the company, and he tell him, "Go 'long, he can get on with the work."

So Mr. Rabbit clips off in great haste, and he just go down on the edge of the woods, and what you 'spect he do? Well, sir, he just stretch hisself out in the shade of a swamp maple and take a nap, while Ole Mr. Wolf was working in the corn rows in the hot sun. When Mr. Rabbit sleep he nap out, he set up and rub he eyes, then he mosey off down by the spring for a drink, then he come running and puffing like he been running a mile, and tell Mr. Wolf what a mighty sick patient he got, and make out like he that wore out he can't more'n move the hoe.

Well, when they come back from dinner, Mr. Rabbit, he strike and make he hoe fly, but directly here come little Rab for the doctor, and Ole Mr. Rabbit, he take hisself off for 'nother nap, and matters goes on just dis here way all summer. Ole Mr. Wolf, he have to do all the work, but he comfort himself with the reflection, that he have half them big fees what Brer Rabbit turning in to the company money.

Well, when the fodder done pulled, and all the crop done sold, and they go for to count the money, Mr. Wolf ask Brer Rabbit where the doctor's fees what he goin' turn in. Brer Rabbit say they all such slow pay, he can't collect it. Then they fell out, and Mr. Wolf that mad, he say he goin' eat Brer Rabbit right there, and make an end of he tricks. But Mr. Rabbit beg that they take the trouble up to the court-house to Judge Bar.

So they mosey off to the court-house, and the old judge say it were a jury case, and he send Sheriff Coon out to fetch the jurymans, and he say, "Don' you fetch no mans here, 'cepter they be more fool than the parties in the case." But Sheriff Coon 'low he don' know where he goin' find any man what's more fool than Brer Wolf's in dis here case, but he take out down the county, and by and by he seed a man rolling a wheelbarrow what ain't got nothing in it round the house and round the house, and he ask him what he doing that for? And he say, he trying to wheel some sunshine in the house. Sheriff Coon say, "You is the man I wants to come with me and sot on the jury."

They go 'long, and directly they see a man pulling a long rope up a tall tree that stand 'longside a house; they ask him what he goin' do? He say he goin' to haul a bull up on top of the house to eat the moss off the roof, and Sheriff Coon say, "I'll be bound you is my man for the jury, and you must go long with we all to the court." So they take their way back to the court-house, then they have a great time taking evidence and argufying.

Ole Brer Wolf, he set up there, and 'sider every word of the evidence, but Ole Brer Rabbit he lean back and shut he eye, and work he brain on he own account. He settin' right close to the door; when the lawyer done get everybody worked up so they take no noticement, Brer Rabbit just slip softly out the back door, and he creep 'round the side of the cabin back to where Ole Judge Bar set wid de bag of money on the floor, and what you 'spect? When they all talking,

Ole Brer Rabbit just slide he hand in the crack, and softly slip out the bag of money, and take out home, and leave the case in the care of the court. That just like Ole man Rabbit.

WHEN BRER WOLF HAVE HIS CORN SHUCKING

Tradition Bearer:

Source: Backus, Emma M. "Folk-Tales from Georgia." *Journal of American Folklore* 13 (1900): 21–22.

Date: 1912

Original Source: Georgia

National Origin: African American

"When Brer Wolf Have His Corn Shucking" details another of Brer Rabbit's clever turns to gain the upper hand over his romantic rivals. In this case, Brer Rabbit must win a contest to remove the most shucks from fresh corn in an allotted time. Aware of his limitations (aversion to work) and his advantages (charm and dancing ability), he connives to confuse the outcome of the shucking contest and to put the decision in the hands of Miss Wolf, whose affections he courts while his competitors devote themselves to the original, but ultimately irrelevant, shucking contest.

Brer Wolf he make a powerful crop of corn one year, and he turn it over in his mind how he going to get all that corn shucked, cause Brer Wolf mighty unpopular man with his neighbors, and when Brer Wolf have a corn shucking the creeters don't turn out, like they do when Sis Coon have a corn shucking.

But Brer Wolf he have a powerful handsome daughter on the carpet. All the chaps about the county has their heads set to step up to Brer Wolf's daughter. So Brer Wolf he send out word how the chap what shucks the most corn at his shucking shall have his handsome daughter.

Well, the chaps they come from the fur end of Columbia County, and some come over from Richmond County, and they set to work, and they make the shucks fly, and each chap have a pile to hisself. Brer Coon he mighty set on Brer Wolf's daughter, and Brer Coon he know hisself are powerful likely corn shucker, and Brer Coon he 'low to hisself how he have a right smart chance to get the gal.

Brer Fox his head done plum turned when Miss Wolf roll her handsome eyes at hisself; and so Brer Fox he get a pile to hisself and fall to work.

Now old Brer Rabbit his heart set on the gal, but Brer Rabbit he are a mighty poor corn shucker. Brer Rabbit he jest naturally know he don' stand no chance shucking a pile of corn and making time against Brer Coon.

So Brer Rabbit he don't waste hisself, Brer Rabbit don't, but Brer Rabbit he take his hat off and he go up to Brer Wolf, and he make his bow, and he ask Brer Wolf, if he learn his daughter to dance, can he have her?

But Brer Wolf he say, "What I said I said." Well, Brer Rabbit he feel terrible put down, but he fall to, and he act most survigorous [to survive with vigor]. He sing and he dance, and he dance and he sing, and he amuse the company most 'greeable like; and he sing before the gals, and he dance before the gals, and he show them the new step and the new shuffle, Brer Rabbit do. Brer Coon he just turn his eye on Brer Rabbit 'casionly, but he don't pay no 'tention to his acting and frolicking. Brer Coon he just make time with his corn shucking, 'til Brer Coon's pile it make three times the pile of the other chaps.

When it come time for Brer Wolf to come round and count his piles, Brer Rabbit he set down long side Brer Coon, and he fall to shucking corn to beat all. When Brer Wolf come round, Brer Rabbit he certainly do make the shucks fly powerful, 'cause the old rascal just been cutting up and acting all the evening, and he ain't tired like the other chaps.

When Brer Wolf see the great pile so much bigger than what all the other chaps got, Brer Wolf he say, "What for both you chaps shuck on one pile?" Brer Coon he 'low that all his pile. He 'low, Brer Coon do, how Brer Rabbit been cutting up and frolicking all the evening, and he just now come and set down 'longside his pile.

Brer Rabbit he say he swear and kiss the book, this my pile. Brer Coon he just been frolickin' and going on all the evening to beat all; he make us laugh nigh 'bout fit to kill ourselves, while I done work my hands plum to the bone. Now he set hisself down here and say it his pile.

Brer Wolf he say he leave it out to the company. But the chaps they don't want Brer Rabbit to have the gal, and they don't want Brer Coon to have the gal, so they won't take sides; they 'low they been working so powerful hard, they don't take noticement of Brer Coon or Brer Rabbit. Then Brer Wolf he 'low he leave it out to the gals.

Now. Miss Wolf she been favoring Brer Rabbit all the evening. Brer Rabbit dancing and singing plum turned Miss Wolf's head, so Miss Wolf she say, "It most surely are Brer Rabbit's pile." Miss Wolf she say she "plum 'stonished how Brer Coon can story so." Brer Rabbit he take the gal and go off home clipity, clipity. Poor old Brer Coon he take hisself off home, he so tired he can scarcely hold hisself together.

THE SACK OF PEAS AND THE MULE

Tradition Bearer: Aneus Guerin

Source: Claudel, Calvin. "Louisiana Tales of Jean Sot and Boqui and Lapin." *Southern Folklore Quarterly* 8 (1944): 292–94.

Date: 1931

Original Source: Pointe Coupee Parish, Louisiana. Recorded by Lafayette Jarreau, "Creole Folklore of Pointe Coupee Parish." MA thesis, Louisiana State University, 1931.

National Origin: Cajun

In the following narrative, Lapin takes advantage of Bouqui's appetite in order to acquire a free mule by very indirect means. Considering Bouqui easier prey than the farmer who owns the mule he covets, Lapin manipulates his victim into trading his beautiful wife for the mule and a sack of peas to start a vegetable farm. Much of the tale hangs on Bouqui's poor powers of observation. He does not appreciate how beautiful his wife is until he has initiated the trade and alienated her. He is unable to recognize the dearly bought mule after its tail has been bobbed, and at last, he is deceived into seeing a drowning mule in a bundle of floating hair.

One day Bouqui went to visit Lapin. While at the dinner table Bouqui noticed what fine vegetables Lapin's wife served—squash, pumpkin and fine celery salad.

"What fine food you have, Lapin!" remarked Bouqui. "I wish I had such wonderful vegetables for my household."

"I raise them on my farm," replied Lapin. "Why don't you start a vegetable farm yourself and farm the way I do?"

"That's a good idea," ventured Bouqui. "But I have no mule or seed to start such a farm."

After they had all eaten a while, Lapin said to Bouqui:

"I know just the thing for you, Bouqui. A farmer nearby has a mule and a sack of peas. You can probably make a bargain with him to get them. You can use the peas to start a crop."

"But what can I offer him, Lapin?" questioned Bouqui. "I have no money. My wife is all I've got."

"I'll tell you what," proposed Lapin. "Trade your wife for his mule and the peas.... I'm sure he'll accept. I'll talk to him and fix it up for you.... Tomorrow I'll come to see you."

After Bouqui had returned home, he pondered over Lapin's proposition. Finally he said to his wife, who was indeed very pretty:

"My wife, I have been thinking about swapping you for a mule and a sack of peas. We can't live in this poverty. So I really need a mule more than I need you."

Next day Bouqui heard Lapin knock at the door.

"I have brought the mule and sack of peas," explained Lapin. "All you have to do now is get your wife over to the farmer's place. He has agreed to the bargain."

At first Bouqui was reluctant, for he had noticed how his wife was pretty, and he really wanted to keep her. However, his wife came up just then with her clothes all bundled and packed ready to leave and said:

"No, Bouqui, I shall go.... You were stupid enough to want to trade me for a mule and a sack of peas. So I'm going to leave you now for the farmer.... Goodbye."

This settled the bargain. Bouqui's wife left, carrying her bundle. Bouqui kept the mule and the sack of peas, and Lapin went home.

Now it happened that Lapin really wanted the mule for himself. So he began to devise a trick to get the mule away from Bouqui. That night he went to Bouqui's barn, unlocked the door and started to lead the mule to his own place. While on his way home, he clipped off the end of the mule's tail and threw it into a pond nearby, where there was a very deep hole. Next day Bouqui came to Lapin's house and knocked at the door.

"Lapin," began Bouqui, "someone must have stolen my mule. Have you seen him?"

"Why no," replied Lapin.

Just then Bouqui noticed his mule in Lapin's barn, and he exclaimed: "That looks very much like my mule!"

"Of course not," added Lapin. "That mule has a bobbed tail. Your mule has a long tail."

That's true enough," answered Bouqui, shaking his head, however, in a puzzled fashion.

"I'll go help you to look for your mule, Bouqui," offered Lapin, feigning sympathy. So the two started off together. Finally Lapin reached the pond and exclaimed: "There! Your mule slipped into the deep hole of the pond. I see his tail sticking out of the water."

Lapin walked out over the water on a fallen tree to the place where the piece of tail was floating. He reached down and pulled and pulled on the tail, making out as if he was trying to pull up the mule on the other end of the tail. Finally he flew backwards out of the water, holding the tail in his hands.

"You see, Bouqui," explained Lapin. "Your mule fell in here and drowned. I pulled so hard, his tail came off.... It's no use; he is lost under the water."

"Yes, that's too bad," replied Bouqui, as he left with a look of despair.

THE IRISHMAN AND THE PUMPKIN

Tradition Bearer: Unavailable

Source: "The Irishman and the Pumpkin." *Journal of American Folklore* 12 (1899): 226.

Date: 1899

Original Source: *Southern Workman*, May 1899.

National Origin: African American

The following ethnic joke, which casts "the Irishman" in the role of **numskull**, is representative of the tales about a character whose actions are typified by "rustic simplicity." Such tales comprised a significant segment of the African American folktale corpus in the nineteenth century. This particular tale (AT 1319, "Pumpkin Sold as an Ass's Egg") appears in a number of variants throughout the American South.

Once there was a man driving along the road with a pair of mules and a load of pumpkins, when an Irishman stopped him and wanted to know what those things were that he had in his cart. The man replied they were mule's eggs, and told the Irishman that, if he would put one on the south side of a hill and sit on it, it would hatch out a mule.

So the Irishman bought one, and carried it up on the south side of a hill and sat down on it and soon went to sleep. Of course he fell off, and the pumpkin went rolling over and over down the hill and into the brush; out jumped a rabbit and went running off. "Koop, colie! Koop, colie! Here's your mammy," called the Irishman, but the rabbit wouldn't stop. So the Irishman went back to the other man and said he wanted another mule's egg; the first one hatched into a mighty fine colt, but it ran so fast he couldn't catch it, and he would like to buy another.

THE SEA TICK AND THE IRISHMAN

Tradition Bearer: Unavailable

Source: "The Sea Tick and the Irishman." *Journal of American Folklore* 12 (1899): 226.

Date: 1899

Original Source: *Southern Workman*, May 1899.

National Origin: African American

In this pair of ethnic jokes, the Irishman is cast again as the **numskull** figure. The first narrative depends on a pun: tick is both an insect and an onomapoetic rendering of the sound a timepiece makes. The second reveals the Irishman to be a "tenderfoot," uninitiated to life outside the city and too primitive to recognize a pocket watch. As a result, he mistakes the shape and sounds of a watch and chain for a rattlesnake.

An Irishman had heard of sea ticks but had never seen one, though he wanted to very much. Once he was walking along the beach, and found a watch, dropped by someone who had gone on ahead of him.

The Irishman had never seen a watch before; so when he heard it ticking he said, "Be Jasus, it's a long time I've been hearing of sea ticks, and here I've got one." Then he got a stick and beat the watch until it stopped ticking.

* * *

In the other version the Irishman is walking in the woods, and sees a watch with a long chain lying in his path. When he hears it ticking he says, "Faith, there's a rattlesnake!" and gets a rock and smashes it all to pieces.

SHOOTING GRASSHOPPERS

Tradition Bearer: Unavailable

Source: Fauset, Arthur Huff. "Negro Folk Tales from the South (Alabama, Mississippi, Louisiana)." *Journal of American Folklore* 40 (1927): 267.

Date: 1925

Original Source: Mississippi

National Origin: African American

In this ethnic joke from the Irish Pat and Mike cycle, the ignorance of a "tenderfoot" with no knowledge of woodcraft or common devices is used to create the **numskull** image. Qualities of the **tall tale** appear in the first person conclusion of the joke and the treatment of the hindquarter of a grasshopper as game to be borne home over the hunter's shoulder. **Formulaic** closing statements in which the narrator becomes part of the concluding action are not uncommon in traditional tales.

Pat an' Mike seen a man with a shotgun on his shoulder in the woods, an' they asked him what was that he had. He told 'em dat was a gun.

So the Irishman said, "A gun, I think you say gun, didn't you? I never have heard the name of a gun. What do you do with it?"

So de man said, "I shoot game wid it."

The Irishman say, "Faith, Mike, what do you call game?"

He said, "Birds or anything like that."

So de man shot a bird an' showed what he was talking about, an' den dey wanted to buy de gun.

Pat said, "How much you want fo' de gun?"

De man said, "One hundred dollars."

So each one paid fifty dollars apiece an' got it. So one taken de gun an' de other one walk behind huntin' the game. So dey got where some grasshoppers flew on his chest. Mike said, "I would shoot dem off," but he beckoned to Pat wid his fingers.

Mike said, "Pat, I'm gonna shoot."

So Pat shot an' killed de grasshopper an' Pat too. But he found de thigh of de grasshopper an' hung him on his shoulder an' left, an' I left too.

THE FOX AND THE WOLF

Tradition Bearer: Josiah Mikey (Ca`bi'tci, "clearing")

Source: Speck, Frank G. "European Tales among the Chickasaw Indians." *Journal of American Folklore* 26 (1913): 292.

Date: 1913

Original Source: Chickasaw

National Origin: Native American

Originally residing in the Mississippi Valley region, the Chickasaw were one of the Five Civilized Tribes discussed in the Introduction. The other four were the Cherokee, Choctaw, Creek, and Seminole. In the 1830s they were relocated to Indian Territory (now Oklahoma). The Chickasaw divided themselves into two moieties ("halves"), each composed of several exogamous clans. According to the narrator, this tale was "told by the Fox band to make fun of the wolf, and get the Wolf band to hurrah for the Fox band." Although this explains what seems to be an unmotivated prank by Fox, the collector does not note the existence of either a Fox or Wolf band among the Chickasaw. A narrative collected by John R. Swanton, however, accounts for the origin of the Fox clan, and among the Cherokee, the Wolf clan is prominent. The fact that the tale was collected almost a century after relocation may account for such discrepancies. These stories that are set in a period when animals and men spoke the same language are regarded as a distinct **genre**, but interestingly this particular tale seems to be one of European origin (AT47A, "The Fox [Wolf] Hangs by his Teeth to the Horse's Tail") borrowed and adapted to suit the needs of the Chickasaw.

The Fox and the Wolf were friends. One time they agreed to go hunting. The Fox went off in one direction, and so did the Wolf in another direction. The Fox traveled in a circle, and by and by ran across the Wolf. He asked him what luck he had had. The Wolf told him that he had met with a Dog, and asked the Dog why he liked to stay around human beings. Said the Dog, "I like them because they defend me." Then he asked the Dog how they defended him. Said he, "Look behind that tree!" Now, there stood a man with a gun. Then the Wolf was terrified, ran off, and forgot about hunting until he met the Fox.

Now, the Fox told what luck he had had. He had had good luck. He told the Wolf that he found a dead horse; but the horse was lying very near a road, and he was afraid to tackle him alone. He told the Wolf, however, that if he would help him carry the horse off, they would have a feast. The Wolf agreed, and they went to where the dead horse was. They stopped nearby. The Wolf wouldn't believe the horse was dead. He told the Fox to bring him a handful of hair. The Fox brought him a handful of hair, and the Wolf smelled it. Said he, "Yes, he's been dead quite a while."

So now the Wolf and Fox consulted how to carry the dead horse away. The Wolf allowed the Fox to tie his tail to the dead horse's tail, and the Fox took hold of his head to pull him off. When the Wolf was securely tied to the horse's tail, the Fox went over to his place near the head to get hold. Then suddenly he scratched the horse on the nose; and being, in truth, only asleep, the horse woke up, and dashed away, dragging the Wolf. Then the Fox shouted to the Wolf, "Hurrah for me, my friend!" but the Wolf cried in despair, "How can I hurrah, when I'm up in the air?"

WHEN BRER RABBIT WAS PRESIDIN' ELDER

Tradition Bearer: Unavailable

Source: Backus, Emma M. "Folk-Tales from Georgia." *Journal of American Folklore* 13 (1900): 20–21.

Date: 1900

Original Source: Georgia

National Origin: African American

In the African American folktale corpus, the **stock character** of "Preacher," like "Rabbit," appears as a figure who creates a façade to exploit gullible members of the community with the power of wit and words. This critique of "Preacher" puts Brer Rabbit in the role of self-appointed presiding elder (in this case, a traveling preacher). At first offended to the point of "churching" (evicting from membership) Brer Rabbit, the congregation demonstrates similar greed by finally taking such a "good paying member" back into the fold.

Now Brer Rabbit he never get to be no sure 'nough presidin' elder. Brer Rabbit he always been a meeting going man, but it all along [alongside] of his trifling ways that he never get no higher than a steward in the church. Brer Rabbit he never get to be a preacher, not to say a sure 'nough presidin' elder.

But one year Brer Rabbit he get powerful ambitious. He see all his neighbors building fine houses, and Brer Rabbit he say to hisself he going to have a fine house. So Brer Rabbit he study and he study how he going get the money for his house, and one day he say to Miss Rabbit, "You bresh up my meeting clothes."

So Miss Rabbit she get out Brer Rabbit's meeting clothes, and bresh 'em up, and take a few stitches, and make the buttons fast.

One Saturday Brer Rabbit he put on all his meeting clothes, and his church hat, and take his bible and hymn-book, and cut hisself a fine walking cane, and Brer Rabbit he start off.

Brer Rabbit he take the circuit, and he preach in every church, and Brer Rabbit he say how he be the presidin' elder of the district, and how he taking up a collection to build a new parsonage; and being as Brer Rabbit am a powerful preacher when he aim to try hisself, and preach in the spirit, the people they give with a free hand.

Brer Rabbit he know what he doing, Brer Rabbit do, and he ride the circuit just before Christmas, and they tells how nigh 'bout the lastest one enduring the whole circuit done rob his Christmas for Brer Rabbit's parsonage.

Well, when they see Brer Rabbit's fine house going up and hear how Brer Rabbit done used they alls money, well, there was a time, you may be sure, and they church Brer Rabbit; but Brer Rabbit he don't trouble hisself, he just go on and build his fine house. But bless you, the last shingle ain't laid before here they come begging Brer Rabbit to come back in the church, 'cause Brer Rabbit be a good paying member. So Brer Rabbit he go back in the church and he live in his fine house and hold his head powerful high, and what the people done say they done say, but you may be sure they don' say a word when Brer Rabbit listen.

JACK THE GIANT KILLER

Tradition Bearer: Jane Gentry

Source: Carter, Isabel Gordon. "Mountain White Folk-Lore: Tales from the Southern Blue Ridge." *Journal of American Folklore* 38 (1925): 351–54.

Date: 1923

Original Source: North Carolina

National Origin: Anglo American

The following tale is an American version of the English *märchen* "Jack the Giant-Killer" (AT 328), in which the protagonist uses his wits to trick and eliminate a family of giants. In his European American incarnation, the **trickster** turns the tables on his more powerful adversaries not by his own powers of shape-shifting, conjuring, or other supernatural means but by sleight of hand, folk psychology, and, at last, lying. The American tale shares familiar **motifs** with its European variants, for example, "ogres duped into fighting each other" (K771), "squeezing the stone" (K62), and "**trickster** shouts to warn people" at a distance (K18.1).

One time they was a fine wealthy man lived way out in the forest. But he couldn't have nothing, hogs and sheep and cows and such like because the giants killed 'em. So he went out and put him up an ad-ver-tisement (Put up a board or hew out the side of a tree and write what he want to.) So he put up one for someone to clear land. Little old boy Jack saw hit and he tramped and tramped until he got away out in the forest and he called, "Hello."

Old man hollered, "What'll ye have?"

Jack says, "I've come to clear yer land."

"All right," says the man. It was Sunday evenin' un they 'uz havin' supper.

The old lady says, "What'll ye have for supper, Jack?" He said mush and milk. While they was makin' the supper a preacher come in an' they sit the mush away and they fried him a chicken and fixed some coffee and fixed a good supper. After supper Jack tol' 'em he wanted a piece of leather so he made him a pouch, a sort of haversack thing to tie around his waist.

Next morning they got up, asked Jack what he'd have for breakfast. Said, "Jest give me that cold mush and milk." He'd take a spoonful and then poke one in a hole in his pouch. So he got it full. Then he said he was ready to go to work.

So man says, now he says, "Jack, I don't want you to back out, but I'm no a wantin' any land cleared. I want to kill them giants over there and I'll give a thousand dollars a head for them—some of 'em has two heads, and I'll give you five hundred dollars down, and five hundred dollars when you come back."

Jack says, "Give me a tomihawk (that's a thing like a hatchet 'cept it has two heads to hit. They used hit in olden times. Indians use to use hit to scalp with.) and I may be in for dinner, and hit may be night when I git in." So they give him a tomihawk and he went over in the forest and climb a great long pine.

Along about one o'clock he looked way down in the holler and saw a great old giant a comin' up with two heads. So he says to himself, "Land I'm gone."

So the old giant come up, and he says, "What are you doin' up there?"

Jack says, "I'm a clearin' timber."

Giant says, "Come down from there, you ain't got sense enough to clear timber, you have to have an ax and chop down timber." So Jack come down a little way. "Have ye had yer dinner?" says the Giant. Jack says, "I've had my dinner." Giant says, "I'm sorry, I jest come to ask you to come down and take dinner with me. Come down, let's wrestle and play a while." Jack says, "All right, bedads, I'll be down." So Jack come down and down, till he got right on a limb a top the giant. He had no idea of comin' down when he started, jest tryin' to bluff the giant. Jack says to the giant, "I can do somethin' you can't do." Giant says, "What is hit?" Jack says, "I can squeeze milk out of a flint rock." Giant says, "Oh ye can't do hit?" Jack says, "Yes I can, you hand me up one and I'll show you." So Giant handed him up one, and Jack gits hit right close to his little old pouch and squeezes milk out on the rock and drapped the milk on the giant. Giant says, "Hand me down that rock; if you can squeeze milk out of hit, I can." Jack handed it down to the giant. The giant was so stout that when he put his hands to hit, he just crushed it into powder. Jack says, "I told you you couldn't squeeze milk out of hit. I can do something else you can't do."

"What's that?"

"I kin take a knife and cut my belly open and sew hit up again." Giant says, "Oh you can't neither."

"Yes, I can," says Jack. "I'll show you, hand me your knife." So the giant hands him up his knife and Jack cut that pouch open and sewed hit up again. "Now didn't I tell you I could?"

Giant says, "Hand me down that knife," and he just rip his belly open and fell over dead. So Jack crawled back down and took his tomihawk and cut off his head. And that evening late he come waggin' him in a giant's head. That jest tickled the forest man and he paid Jack a heap of money and says, "Now Jack, if you kin jest get the rest of 'em; they's a whole family of 'em."

So next morning Jack took his tomihawk (or Tommy hatchet) and went over and climb the big old pine agin. So long about noon he looked down the holler and he saw two giants a comin' each with two heads on. So they begin to get closter and closter. Jack climb down and took out down the holler and as he went he filled his shirt tail with rocks. After a while he come to a big old holler log and he climb in hit with his shirt tail plumb full of rocks. So the giants went up and mourned over their brother. And they went down past Jack sayin', "Poor brother, if we jest knew who it was a murdered him, we'd shore fix him." Jack was a layin' in there with his heart jest a beatin'. They past the log and said, "Let's pick up this log and carry hit down to poor old mother for some kindlin." So they each took an end and carried hit a little ways. Jack thought he'd try his rocks on 'em. So he crawled up pretty close to the end and throwed a rock and hit one of the giants. Giant says to other one, "What you hit me for?"

Giant says, "I didn't hit you."

"Yes, you did too." Then Jack crawled back and throwed a rock at the other giant. "What you hit me for? I never hit you."

"I didn't hit you."

"Yes you did too." So they fit and they fit and fit and directly they killed each other; one fell one side of the log dead and the other on the other side. So Jack crawled out and cut their heads off and went on back home.

So he was gettin' him a pretty good load of money and was gettin' awfully tickled. The forest man were plumb tickled too and said, "Jack, if you jest can get the rest. But watch out they don't get you."

"Bedads they won't git me," says Jack.

So next morning he says, "Give me my tomihawk," and he went on out. So along in the evenin' he looked down the holler and saw a little old giant comin' up about his size. "Well," says Jack, "I've about got 'em from the looks of this one." This little giant come up a talkin' to hisself. Looked up in the tree and saw Jack sittin' there. "Stranger, can you tell me who has killed my poor old brothers?"

"Yes, I killed your brothers, and bedad, I'll come down and kill you if you fool with me."

"Oh please, Jack, please Jack, I'm all the child my mother's got left, and you kill me there won't be nobody to git her wood this winter and she'll freeze to death. If you'll come down I'll take you home with me and we'll have the best dinner." So Jack went on down. Giant went to his mother and says, "Jack come home with me, and he says he's the one who killed brothers but he's not much."

So Giant's mother says, "Well, come on in Jack, you'uns go out and play pitch crowbar awhile." Jack couldn't lift it. Little old giant pick hit up and throwed hit about one hundred yards. Jack went over and picked up one end and begin to holler, "Hey, uncle. Hey, uncle."

Giant says, "Hey, Jack, what you hollerin' about?"

"I've got an uncle in the Illinois who is a blacksmith and I thought I'd jes' pitch hit to him."

"Oh don't do that Jack, hit's all we have."

"Well if I can't pitch hit to Illinois, I won't pitch hit at all." Little old giant slipped back to the house, "Mother, I don't believe Jack is much stout."

"Well, we'll see," says the mother. "Here boys, take these pails down to the river." Little old giant took the buckets and when he got to the river he stove in his bucket and put hit up full and then he stove Jack's in and put hit up full. Jack begun to roll up his sleeves. Little old giant says, "What you goin' to do Jack?"

"Oh thought I'd carry up the river."

"Oh don't Jack, mother might walk in her sleep and fall in."

"All right," says Jack, "but I wouldn't be ketched a carryin' that little old bucket." So they went on back. The mother had a big hot oven sittin' in front of the fire with a plank across hit. "Get on this plank Jack and I'll ride ye," says she. So Jack got up un she shuck him and shuck him trying to shake him into the oven but he fell off on the wrong side.

"Let me show you," says old mother giant, and she got on and Jack give her a shake and popped her in the oven, and he had him a baked giant in a minute.

Little old giant came in, says, "Mother, mother, I smell Jack."

Jack says, "No you don't, that's your mother ye smell." When little old giant sees Jack, he begin to holler, "Oh Jack, I'll give ye anything if you won't kill me."

"All right, give me a suit of invisible clothes." So he give him invisible suit and Jack just went over the house and took what he wanted, all that was any account, because the giant couldn't see him. And Jack took a sword and walked up to the little old giant and stuck hit in him and went and got him some silver and when I left there, Jack was plumb rich.

HOW BRER FOX DREAM HE EAT BRER 'POSSUM

Tradition Bearer: Unavailable

Source: Backus, Emma M., and Ethel Hatton Leitner. "Negro Tales from Georgia." *Journal of American Folklore* 25 (1912): 132–33.

Date: 1912

Original Source: Georgia

National Origin: African American

This narrative pairs two traditional adversaries, Brer Fox (the clever) and Brer Rabbit (the tricky), in an uneasy alliance. Although the tale does deal with the origins of Brer 'Possum's hairless tail, the major focus is on the fragile nature of the social bonds between members of the community. Brer Rabbit, as usual, is ruled by his appetites, and Brer Fox is betrayed by a "fatal" flaw. Given the number of loopholes in the social contract, vigilance must be the order of the day. Trust may be betrayed by self-interest, and even the power of the law is no match for the guile of the **trickster**.

In the old times Brer 'Possum he have a long, wide, bushy tail like Brer Fox. Well, one day Brer Rabbit and Brer Fox get a mighty honein' to set er tooth in some fresh meat, and they both start off for to find some, and directly they find Brer 'Possum up a black gum-tree.

Now, in them times Brer Rabbit he can climb well as any other of the creatures, 'case he has sharp claws like a cat; and he don't set down to nobody on climbing, Brer Rabbit don't. So when they find Brer 'Possum way up in the top of the gum-tree, Brer Rabbit he jest climb up after Brer 'Possum, Brer Rabbit do; and jest before he reach him, Brer 'Possum he wind his tail on the limb, an' hang wid he head down, an' swing hisself out.

Brer Rabbit he standing on the limb; an' he reach out, and he grab Brer 'Possum's tail nigh the stump, Brer Rabbit do; and Brer 'Possum he swing hisself out, and try to reach another limb with he hand; and every time Brer 'Possum swing out, Brer Rabbit's hand slip a little on Brer 'Possum's tail; and next time Brer 'Possum swing and reach out, Brer Rabbit he hand slip a little more, til Brer Rabbit he done skin the whole of Brer 'Possum's tail; an' Brer 'Possum fall to the ground where Brer Fox done wait for him, and Brer Fox done caught him and kill him but since that day Brer 'Possum he never have no hair on his tail. Then Brer Rabbit he come down, Brer Rabbit did, and they study how's der bestest and soonest way to cook Brer 'Possum, 'cause dey both jes a-droolin' for some fresh meat.

Brer Fox he say, "he take Brer 'Possum home and cook him," and he invite Brer Rabbit to come and dine with him. Brer Rabbit agrees to that, so Brer Fox he takes Brer 'Possum home and he fly round to beat all, Brer Fox do; and he get some nice fat bacon and yams, and he just cooks dat 'Possum up fine and brown.

Then Brer Fox he get mighty tired, and he say, "I 'clare, I plum too tired out to eat. I don't know if I better eat that 'Possum now, and go to sleep and dream about him, or whether I better go to sleep and dream about him first, and then wake up and eat him"; and he lay down on the bed to study a minute, and first thing Brer Fox knowed he fast asleep.

Directly here come Brer Rabbit, he knock on the door, but he ain't get no answer; but he smell dat 'Possum, and the bacon and the yams, and the sage and he most 'stracted [distracted] to set he tooth in it. He crack the door softly and he find Brer Fox fast asleep on the bed, an' the nice dinner all smoking hot on the table.

Brer Rabbit he just draw up and set to, Brer Rabbit do. He eat one hind-leg and it so fine, he say to hisself he bound to try a fore-leg, and then Brer Rabbit 'low [allows] he bound to try the other hind-leg.

Well, sir, dat old man Rabbit he set there and eat til the lastest mouthful of that 'Possum done gone.

Then he just turn to wonderin', Brer Rabbit did, what Brer Fox gwine to say when he done wake up and find the bestest bits of that 'Possum gone.

Brer Rabbit he find hisself in a right delicate situation, and was disturbed, Brer Rabbit was; but he say to hisself he gwine fool Brer Fox; and Brer Rabbit he take all the bones, and he put them on the floor in a row round Brer Fox's head; and he take the marrow-grease, and he rub it softly on the whiskers round Brer Fox' mouth; then he go out softly and close the door, and put he eye to the key-hole.

Directly Brer Fox he yawn and stretch hisself and wake up; and course his mind turn to that 'Possum, and he rise up; and shorely he most powerful astonished when he see the dish empty, and the bones all 'bout hisself on the floor.

Directly here come Brer Rabbit's knock. Brer Fox say, "Come in!" and Brer Rabbit say, "Brer Fox, I come for my share of that 'Possum." Brer Fox say, "Fore he Lord, Brer Rabbit, where that 'Possum gone?" and he fling he hand at the bones on the floor.

Brer Rabbit he snap he eye, like he most mighty got a way with [upset]; and he say, "Brer Fox, I heard the creatures tell heap a powerful hard tales on yourself, but I 'clare, I never think you treat a friend dis here way."

Then Brer Fox he swear and kiss the book [swear on the Bible] he ain't set a tooth in that 'Possum. Then Brer Rabbit he look most mighty puzzled; and at last he say, "Brer Fox, I tell you what you done done, you just eat the lastest mouthful of that 'Possum in your sleep." Brer Fox he rare and charge, and swear he ain't "even got the taste of 'Possum in he mouth."

Then Brer Rabbit he take Brer Fox to the glass, and make Brer Fox look at hisself; and he say, Brer Rabbit did, "Brer Fox, how come all that fresh marrow-grease on your whiskers?" and Brer Fox he look mighty set down on; and he say, "Well, all I 'low dat the most unsatisfying 'Possum I ever set a tooth in."

BRER RABBIT'S COOL AIR SWING

Tradition Bearer: Unavailable

Source: Backus, Emma M. "Folk-Tales from Georgia." *Journal of American Folklore* 13 (1900): 22–24.

Date: 1900

Original Source: Georgia

National Origin: African American

In this narrative, Brer Rabbit plays the role of the **trickster** to its fullest extent. He deceives the powerful Brer Wolf with an outright lie. In order to get Brer Squirrel to release him from the knots tied by Mr. Man, he uses the African American rhetorical device of "signifying," or indirect persuasion. In describing his situation to Brer Squirrel, Brer Rabbit is not a bound captive seeking a means of escape—he is enjoying a "cool air swing." The deception is so convincing that Squirrel begs to take a turn in the "swing," unties the knots, and takes Rabbit's place. There is even the **motif** of **trickster** as shapeshifter in Mr. Man's observation that, "I done hear of many and many your fine tricks, but I never done hear you turn yourself into a squirrel before."

Mr. Man he have a fine garden. Brer Rabbit he visit Mr. Man's garden every day and destroy the everything in it, 'til Mr. Man plum wore out with old Brer Rabbit. Mr. Man he set a trap for old Brer Rabbit down 'longside the big road.

One day when Mr. Man going down to the cross-roads, he look in his trap and sure 'nough, there old Brer Rabbit. Mr. Man he say, "Oh, so old man, here you is. Now I'll have you for my dinner."

Mr. Man he take a cord from his pocket, and tie Brer Rabbit high on a limb of a sweet gum tree, and he leave Brer Rabbit swinging there 'til he come back from the cross-roads, when he aim to fetch Brer Rabbit home and cook him for his dinner.

Brer Rabbit he swing this away in the wind and that away in the wind, and he swing this away in the wind and that away in the wind, and he think he time done come. Poor old Brer Rabbit don't know where he's at.

Presently here come Brer Wolf loping down the big road. When Brer Wolf see old Brer Rabbit swinging this away and that away in the wind, Brer Wolf he stop short and he say, "God a' mighty, man! What you doing up there?" Brer Rabbit he say, "This just my cool air swing. I just taking a swing this morning."

But Brer Rabbit he just know Brer Wolf going to make way with him. Brer Rabbit he just turn it over in his mind which way he going to get to. The wind it swing poor Brer Rabbit way out this away and way out that away. While Brer Rabbit swinging, he work his brain, too.

Brer Wolf he say, "Brer Rabbit, I got you fast; now I going eat you up." Brer Rabbit he say, "Brer Wolf, open your mouth and shut your eyes, and I'll jump plum in your mouth." So Brer Wolf turn his head up and shut his eyes. Brer Rabbit he feel in his pocket and take out some pepper, and Brer Rabbit he throw it plum down Brer Wolf's throat. Brer Wolf he nigh 'bout 'stracted with the misery. He cough and he roll in the dirt, and he get up and he strike out for home, coughing to beat all. And Brer Rabbit he swing this away and that away in the wind.

Presently here come Brer Squirrel. When Brer Squirrel he see the wind swing Brer Rabbit way out this away and way out that away, Brer Squirrel he that 'stonished, he stop short. Brer Squirrel he say, "Fore the Lord, Brer Rabbit what you done done to yourself this here time?"

Brer Rabbit he say, "This here is my cool air swing, Brer Squirrel. I taking a fine swing this morning." And the wind it swing Brer Rabbit way out this away and way back that away.

Brer Rabbit he fold his hands, and look mighty restful and happy, like he settin' back fanning hisself on his front porch.

Brer Squirrel he say, "Please sir, Brer Rabbit, let me try your swing one time."

Brer Rabbit he say, "Certainly, Brer Squirrel, you do me proud," and Brer Rabbit he make like he make haste to turn hisself loose. Presently Brer Rabbit he say, "Come up here, Brer Squirrel, and give me a hand with *this* knot," and Brer Squirrel he make haste to go up and turn Brer Rabbit loose, and Brer Rabbit he make Brer Squirrel fast to the cord. The wind it swing Brer Squirrel way out this away and way out that away, and Brer Squirrel he think it fine.

Brer Rabbit he say, "I go down to the spring to get a fresh drink. You can swing 'til I come back."

Brer Squirrel he say, "Take your time, Brer Rabbit, take your time." Brer Rabbit he take his time, and scratch out for home fast as he can go, and he ain't caring how long Brer Squirrel swing.

Brer Squirrel he swing this away and he swing that away, and he think it fine.

Presently here come Mr. Man. When Mr. Man he see Brer Squirrel, he plum 'stonished. He say, "Oh, so old man, I done hear of many and many your fine tricks, but I never done hear you turn yourself into a squirrel before. Powerful kind of you, Brer Rabbit, to give me fine squirrel dinner." Mr. Man he take Brer Squirrel home and cook him for dinner.

THE LION AND THE UNICORN

Tradition Bearers: Monroe Ward and Miles Ward

Source: Chase, Richard. "The Lion and the Unicorn." *The Southern Folklore Quarterly* 1 (1937): 16–19.

Date: 1937

Original Source: North Carolina

National Origin: European American

As in many variants of the well-known European *märchen* on which "The Lion and the Unicorn" is modeled, this Jack tale is built around the unlikely hero's inadvertent successes in defeating wild animals. His conquests are based not on hunting skill nor on cleverness but on lucky accidents. Beyond luck, Jack's primary attribute in the tale is audacity in asserting his prowess. The invariable conclusion of this tale, and the others of the cycle, is that Jack ends up rich.

Jack started out one time to try his fortune. Told his mother he couldn't do any good there at home. So he went traveling about over the country, and was going past a saw mill 'side the road, picked up a little thin piece of plank looked rather nice. He laid down under a tree to rest a while and got to shaving on that plank till finally he'd made him a paddle. He didn't know what he'd do with it, just carried it along. He struck out directly through a pasture field, come to where a bunch of flies had lit down on a cow-pile. So Jack cut loose with his paddle and come down on 'em, then he looked to see how many he'd killed. Well, he went on down the road and come to a blacksmith shop. Jack went in and got the blacksmith to make him some big letters for his belt, said:

> "Strong Man Jack
> Killed Seven at a Whack."

So Jack put that around him and went on. Pretty soon here come the King riding on his horse, says, "Hello, Jack. What's all that writing you got around you?" So the King read it, says to Jack, "You must be a pretty brave fellow."

"Not so awful. I can do some things."

"Well, if you're up to that sign on your belt, I got a job for you. How'd you like to take a chance on killing a wild boar? There's one over on the side of the mountain yonder been killing lots of sheep. I'll pay you a thousand dollars if you kill it. All my men are scared of it."

"Well," says Jack, "I'll try."

Jack got the King to pay him five hundred down, and then the King says, "Come on, Jack, I'll go with you and show you what mountain it uses on."

So Jack says, "If I can find it, King, I'll sure kill it."

Jack knew if the King's men were scared of it, it must be awful dangerous. The King took him over in the mountain a right smart piece, got to looking around kind of nervous, stopped his horse directly, says, "Now, Jack, you'll have to go on up in the mountain and find it. I got important business back home."

Then he turned his horse around and just lit out. Jack said he'd wait a little while and then he'd slip out before that wild boar smelled him. He'd got five hundred dollars, and he didn't want to get mixed up with no wild hog. But when he started back to the road, he heard it breaking brush up the mountain, making an awful racket, then he saw it coming. So Jack took out across the field, him and the boar, whippety cut! Whippety cut! And the wild hog just a-gaining. Well, Jack saw an old waste-house with no roof on it, standing down the field a ways, so he made for it, run in the door, and scrambled up the wall. The old hog was right on him and got a piece out of Jack's coat tail, Then he stood there with his forefeet up on the wall, looking for Jack. Well, Jack clumb down the outside and run around and pushed the door to and propped it with some timbers. Then he went on back to the King's house.

"Well, Jack, did you have any luck?"

"No, I couldn't find no wild hog. I hunted all over that mountain, didn't see nothing."

"Why, Jack, that wild boar just makes for anybody goes up there, time he smells 'em."

"Well, a little old boar shoat come bristling up to me, kept follering me around, I kicked it over several times, but the blame thing got playful and jerked a piece out of my coat tail. Made me a little mad then so I took it by the tail and ear, throwed it in an old waste-house up there and barred him in. You can go up and look if you want to."

When the King rode up there and saw it was that boar, he like to beat his horse to death getting back. Then he blowed his horn and fifty or sixty men come up. They took a lot of Winchester rifles and went up to that old waste-house; but they was so scared that they wouldn't go close enough to get a shoot at it. Jack said he wasn't scared so he went down with a rifle and poked it in there and shot two or three times. That old hog commenced tearing around inside and tore the house plumb down. He give one kick, knocked the chimney down and one of the rocks took him between the eyes and he keeled over dead. So the men skinned it out, and it made two wagon loads of meat. The King paid Jack the rest of the thousand dollars, said he had another job for him. Jack asked him what it was.

"They say there's a unicorn using back here on another mountain, doing a lot of damage to people's livestock. It's a lot more dangerous than that boar, but a brave feller like you, Jack, ought not to have any trouble killing it. I'll pay you another thousand dollars, too."

Well, Jack couldn't back out of it, but before he said he would try it he got the King to pay him five hundred down. When the King took Jack up there and left him, Jack watched him out of sight, then he says, "I'll just get out of here now. I'm not going to fool around and get killed. I got my money, I'll just go another way."

But Jack hadn't got out of the woods when he heard unicorn a-coming. So he started running around in among them trees as hard as he could go. He looked back and saw that horn making a lunge for the middle of his back so he grabbed hold of a little white oak and swung around behind it. The unicorn swerved at him, but he hit that oak and stove his horn plumb through it. And when Jack saw it come through, he took some nails out of his overall pocket, grabbed him up a rock, and wedged the horn in tight. Then he went on back to the King.

"What luck you have this time, Jack?"

"Why, King, I didn't see no unicorn."

"Now that's a curious thing to me. Nobody else ever went in there but what that unicorn come right after 'em."

"Well, some kind of little old yearling bull, didn't have but one horn, come down there bawling and pawing the ground. Follered me around so close it kind of aggravated me finally. So I took it by the tail and stove its horn through a tree. I reckon it's still fastened up where I left it. You can go up there and see if you want to."

So Jack took the King where it was, and when he saw it he whirled his horse and got back in a hurry. The men got their rifles but they were too scared to go close enough to get a shoot at it. So Jack went up to the unicorn, took a switch and hit it, says, "See, men, there's not a bit of harm in him."

The men finally shot it and when it fell it tore that tree plumb up by the roots. Then they skinned it and brought back the hide. The King paid Jack the other five hundred and Jack was just about to leave when the King called him, says, "Jack, they've just brought in word that a lion has come over the mountain and been using around a settlement over there killing everything it comes across, cattle and horses, and they say it's done killed several men tried to go after it. I told them about you, Jack, and they made me promise to send you."

"Well, King, that sounds like the dangerest thing of all."

"I'll pay you nother thousand dollars for it, Jack."

"I don't know as I favor working any more right now, King. I said I'd be back home tonight and they'll be looking for me in. Besides I'm tired out with all that running around I done already."

"Come on now, Jack, I'll pay you two thousand."

"Well, I don't know. I'll have to study on it a while."

"Here's a thousand dollars right now, son. I'd sure like to get shed of that lion."

"I'll do it then, I reckon."

So the King took Jack up behind him on his horse and they rode over to where they said the lion was. Then the King said he'd not venture any further, so Jack slipped off the horse, and the King says to him, "When it smells you, Jack, you'll sure hear from it," and then he put out like a streak.

Well, Jack said he had three thousand dollars and he'd go a different direction and get back home. But before he'd started hardly, that old lion smelt him and commenced roaring up in the woods, roared so he jarred the mountain.

"Lordy me!" says Jack, "I'm a goner this time."

He didn't waste no time running, he made for the closest scaly-bark sapling and skinned up it like a squirrel. The old lion jumped up on the tree a time or two and then prowled around looking up at Jack. Then the lion commenced gnawing on the tree and Jack was just about scared to death. He got it gnawed about half through, when he quit and laid down and went to sleep right against the foot of the tree. Well, Jack had heard that lions were hard to wake up, so he thought he'd better take a chance and try to slip down and get away before it woke up again. He got down about halfway all right, but he was looking so hard at the lion's eyes that he didn't see when he set his foot on a prickly snag. Well, that snag broke with him and he went scooting down and landed right straddle of the lion's back.

Well, the old lion started in roaring and jumping and humping around but Jack just held on. And directly the lion got to running and he was so scared he didn't know that he was headed right for town. All the people come out shouting and hollering and the King's men started in to shooting at it till finally they tumbled it up. When they done that Jack picked himself up out of the dirt and come over where the King was, says, "Look a-here, King, I'm mad."

"Why, how come, Jack?"

"These men have done killed your lion."

"My lion? What you mean, son?"

"Why, King, I'd a-not had him killed for three thousand dollars; I was just riding him down here to get him broke in for you a ridey horse."

So the King went over to where his men were and raised a rumpus with 'em, says, "Why, I'd a-felt big riding that lion around. Now you men will have to pay Jack three thousand dollars for killing that lion."

So Jack went home with six thousand dollars in his pocket, and the last time I was down there he was still rich.

WHEN BRER 'POSSUM ATTEND MISS FOX'S HOUSE-PARTY

Tradition Bearer: Unavailable

Source: Backus, Emma M., and Ethel Hatton Leitner. "Negro Tales from Georgia." *Journal of American Folklore* 25 (1912): 130–31.

Date: 1912

Original Source: Georgia

National Origin: African American

This tale of the disastrous end of the imposter at the house party carries a message found in many of the **animal tales** in the Southern African American corpus: "putting on airs" leads to trouble. Brer 'Possum, though rich, was just "poor white trash." In spite of help from Brer Rabbit, whose stock and trade was such subterfuge, 'Possum finds himself unable to control his true nature and is found out.

Once long before the war, when times was good, Miss Fox she set out for to give a house-party, Miss Fox did.

And Miss Fox she 'low she ain' going invite any person to her house-party 'cepting the quality; and when Brer Fox he just mention Brer 'Possum's name, Miss Fox she rare and charge, Miss Fox do. She give it to Brer Fox, and she 'low how she don't invite no poor white trash to her house-party; and she 'low, Miss Fox do, how Brer Fox must set his mind on giving a tacky party.

Brer Fox he 'low how Brer 'Possum ain't no poor white trash; but Miss Fox she 'clare Brer 'Possum ain't no more than a half-strainer, and so Miss Fox she don't invite Brer 'Possum to her house-party.

Well, Brer 'Possum he feel mighty broke up when he hear all the other creeters talking about the house-party, 'case Brer 'Possum he have plenty money. Brer 'Possum are a mighty shifty man, and always have plenty money.

Well, Brer 'Possum he tell Brer Rabbit how he feel 'bout Miss Fox house-party; and he ask Brer Rabbit, Brer 'Possum do, why he don' be invited.

Brer Rabbit he 'low it all because Brer 'Possum don't hold up his head and wear store clothes; and Brer Rabbit he advise Brer 'Possum to order hisself some real quality clothes, and a churn hat, and go to Miss Fox house-party; and he 'low, Brer Rabbit do, how they won't know Brer 'Possum, and mistake hisself sure for some man from the city.

So ole Brer 'Possum he got plenty money, and he go to the city, Brer 'Possum do; and he order just a quality suit of clothes, Brer 'Possum do; and he go to the barber, and get hisself shaved, and his hair cut, and he present hisself at Miss Fox house-party.

Well, you may be sure Brer 'Possum he receive flattering attention, he surely did; and every last one of the people asking, "Who that fine gentleman?" "Who that city gentleman?" "Who that distinguished-looking gentleman?" and Brer Rabbit he make hisself forward to introduce Brer 'Possum right and left, "My friend Mr. Potsum from Augusta!" That old Brer Rabbit he done say "Potsum," 'cause in case they find him out, that old Brer Rabbit he going swear and kiss the book [swear on the Bible] he done say 'Possum, all the time. That just exactly what that old man Rabbit going to do.

But, Lord bless you! They all that taken up with the fine gentleman, they don' spicion hisself; and he pass a mighty proudful evening, Brer 'Possum do.

But when it come retiring-time, and the gentlemans all get their candles, and 'scorted to their rooms, Brer 'Possum he look at the white bed, and he look all 'bout the room, and he feel powerful uncomfortable, Brer 'Possum do, 'case Brer 'Possum he never sleep in a bed in all his born days. Brer 'Possum he just can't sleep in a bed.

The poor old man he walk round the room, and round the room, 'til the house get asleep; and he take off all his fine clothes, and he open the door softly, and step out all to hisself, he powerful tired; and he just climb a tree what stand by the porch, and hang hisself off by his tail and fall asleep.

In the morning, when Miss Fox get up and open the door, she see Brer 'Possum hanging from the limb. She that astonished she can't believe her eyes; but Miss Fox know a fine fat 'Possum when she see him, she surely do.

Well, Miss Fox she catch hold of Brer 'Possum and kill him, and dress him, and serve him up on the breakfast-table; and the guests they compliment Miss Fox on her fine 'Possum breakfast; but when they go call the fine gentleman from the City, they just find his fine clothes, but they never suspicion where he done gone, 'til many day after, when old Brer Rabbit he done let the secret out.

THE TASKS OF RABBIT

Tradition Bearer: Unavailable

Source: Swanton, John R. Pages 104–5 in *Myths and Tales of the Southeastern Indians.* Smithsonian Institution Bureau of American Ethnology, Bulletin 88. Washington, DC: U.S. Government Printing Office, 1929.

Date: 1929

Original Source: Hitchiti

National Origin: Native American

"The Tasks of Rabbit" bears the marks of a Native American **myth**, an African **trickster** tale, an African American **animal tale**, and a European *märchen*. The episode in which Rabbit is given his physical attributes is a common mythic **motif**. Rabbit's initial encounter with a supernatural helper and the obligation to complete three tasks suggest the **motifs** and repetitive patterns of the European magic tale. The tale plot itself is found in Africa; the tale here is a **variant** of the West African tale of Zomo the Hare who must use his wits to perform three equally "impossible tasks." An African American **variant** was documented by Joel Chandler Harris. The distribution of iterations of this tale throughout the region demonstrates the continuing contact among the culture bearers regardless of ethnicity. Throughout the tale Rabbit displays his range of **trickster** attributes: he shapeshifts into a squirrel in his persona of Rabbit the conjurer, and he is able to control other characters by capitalizing on their own weaknesses in his role of master manipulator.

Rabbit asked food of an old man. Then the old man said to him, "Kill an alligator and bring it to me and when I see it I will enumerate to you all of the various kinds of food that you may eat." Rabbit started along thinking over what he should say to the Alligator in order to kill him. He got close to a river and thought, "I might tell him this." He went into the water and spoke aloud to any Alligator that was in the water, "Are you here, old person?"

"Yes, I am here," the Alligator answered. "Why have you come here?" asked the Alligator, and Rabbit said, "Because they told me to bring you to fashion a wooden spoon." "All right, I will fashion it," the Alligator answered, and he came out.

Now Rabbit started on ahead, and when he got some distance away Rabbit thought of a way to kill him. He picked up a stick and beat the Alligator repeatedly, but the latter ran back to the water and, with Rabbit still beating him, jumped into the stream and swam away. Rabbit stopped. He did not know how he was to make him believe again. Then he thought, "I might tell him this."

He turned himself into a gray squirrel. There was a tree that hung over the water and bent down toward it, and the Rabbit thus turned into a gray squirrel, sat on the top of that tree and made a chattering noise which the Alligator heard as he lay in the water. "I am getting tired of your noise," said the Alligator finally.

"Well," Rabbit answered, "the old man told Rabbit to bring you to chop out a wooden spoon for him. He went and has not returned, so he said to me, 'Go and see what is the matter.' That is why I am here."

"One was around talking like that," said the Alligator, "and beat me a lot, and in spite of what you are saying you might do the same thing."

"Rabbit is always a fool, they say. He came over and treated you so because he is just a fool. He came over because the old man wants to employ you to chop out a wooden spoon, but he treated you abominably. But come out and chop it for me and I will take it back." He came out and followed him. Both set out.

When they got near the place where he had beaten him before the Alligator said, "Right here Rabbit beat me." After he had told him, they reached the place, and, while they were going along a little beyond it, the Alligator said, "If Rabbit had known where to hit me in order to kill me he could have done so. He did not know and so I am alive." "Where does one have to hit you to kill you?" the Gray Squirrel asked the Alligator. "My hip joint is the place on which to hit me. Then when I stop and raise my head, all that is necessary is to hit me on the back of my head. One must do that in order to kill me, but Rabbit did not know it. He hit me in another place and did not kill me."

Now while they were going on Rabbit again picked up a stick he found, turned and ran back to the Alligator and hit him on the hip joint. This stopped him and when the Alligator threw his head up he hit him upon the back of it and killed him. Then he cut off his tail, impaled it on the stick and took it to the old man.

But the old man said to him, "Pick up a sackful of ants and bring them back." So Rabbit took a sack and started off. He arrived at the Ants' home and said to them, "Many people were saying that the Ants can not fill this sack, but I said it could be filled, and so I have come here to prove it."

When Rabbit told the Ants this they said, "There are many of us here. We can fill that sack." He opened the sack and all of the Ants went in, and then he closed it.

When he brought it back the old man said, "Kill a rattlesnake and bring it to me." He started off again and came to a place where he had noticed a rattlesnake was living. He sharpened a short stick at one end and carried it along. Then Rabbit said to the Rattlesnake, "People were saying, you are of about the length of this stick. 'No, he is a long fellow,' I said to them, and, when they would not believe me, I said, 'Well then, I will go and measure him,' and so I am here."

The Snake answered, "I am not a small fellow." He stretched out, and while he lay there Rabbit began measuring him from the end of his tail toward the bead. But when he got as far as the back of his head with the sharp stick, he stuck it through into the ground and killed him. He took him up and came back with him.

When he brought the body of the Rattlesnake to the old man the latter said, "I do not know what else to ask of you. Come to me." So Rabbit went up to the old man and the latter pulled his ears up and down. He stretched his long ears straight up. He slapped one cheek and made it flat. He did the same thing to both, so that both cheeks became flat.

This is how it is told.

WHEN BRER RABBIT HELP BRER TERRAPIN

Tradition Bearer: Unavailable

Source: Backus, Emma M., and Ethel Hatton Leitner. "Negro Tales from Georgia." *Journal of American Folklore* 25 (1912): 128–30.

Date: 1912

Original Source: Georgia

National Origin: African American

In this tale, Brer Rabbit relies both on his wits and on his reputation as a conjurer and a practitioner of hoodoo (traditional African-descended magical techniques used to influence events and persons or cure disease). The talents of conjurer and hoodoo practitioner appear from time to time in the traditional narratives, and Brer Rabbit may be portrayed as a genuine hoodoo doctor or may simply take on this persona to carry out his schemes. Relying on his powers to terrorize his neighbors, Brer Wolf attempts to enlist Rabbit's aid in his plan to destroy Brer Terrapin. Instead, Brer Rabbit uses his deceptive abilities to put the fear of conjuration into Wolf. The power of the left eye to enact supernatural work is an authentic touch added by the narrator.

In the ole days Brer Wolf he have a mighty grudge against Brer Terrapin, Brer Wolf do; and one day Brer Wolf come up with old Brer Terrapin in the woods; and he say, Brer Wolf do, how he just going to make a end of ole Brer Terrapin.

But Brer Terrapin he just draw in his foots and shut the door; and he draw in his arms and shut the door; and then if the ole man don't bodaciously draw in his head and shut the door right in Brer Wolf's face.

That make ole Brer Wolf mighty angry, sure it naturally do; but he bound he ain't going to be outdone that way, and he study 'bout how he going smash Brer Terrapin's house in; but there ain' no rock there, and he feared to leave the ole man, 'cause he know directly he leave him the ole chap going open the doors of his house and tote hisself off.

Well, while Brer Wolf study 'bout it, here come Brer Rabbit; but he make like he don't see Brer Wolf, 'case they ain't the bestest of friends in them days, Brer Wolf and Brer Rabbit ain't, no, that they ain't.

But Brer Wolf he call out, he do, "O Brer Rabbit, Brer Rabbit, come here!"

So Brer Rabbit he draw up, and he see Ole Brer Terrapin's house with the doors all shut; and he say, "Morning, Brer Terrapin!" But Brer Terrapin never crack his door; so Brer Wolf say, he do, "Brer Rabbit, you stay here and watch the ole man, while I go and fetch a rock to smash his house!" And Brer Wolf he take hisself off.

Directly Brer Wolf gone, ole Brer Terrapin he open his door and peek out. Now, Brer Rabbit and Brer Terrapin was the best friends in the ole time; and Brer Rabbit, he say, he do, "Now, Brer Terrapin, Brer Wolf done gone for to tote a rock to smash your house"; and Brer Terrapin say he going move on.

Then Brer Rabbit know if Brer Wolf come back and find he let Brer Terrapin make off with his house, Brer Wolf going fault hisself; and Brer Wolf are a strong man, and he are a bad man; and poor ole Brer Rabbit he take his hindermost hand and he scratch his head, and clip off right smart. Brer Rabbit was a pert man them days.

Directly he come up with ole Sis Cow, and he say, "Howdy, Sis Cow? Is you got a tick you could lend out to your friends?" and he take a tick and tote it back, and put it on the rock just where Brer Terrapin was.

Presently here come Brer Wolf back, totin' a big rock; and he see Brer Rabbit just tearing his hair and fanning his hands, and crying, "Oh, dear! oh, dear! I'se feared of my power, I'se feared of my power!" but Brer Wolf he say, "Where ole man Terrapin gone with his house? I done told you to watch." But Brer Rabbit he only cry the more, and he say, "That what I done tell you, don't you see what my power done done? There all what left of poor ole Brer Terrapin right there." And Brer Rabbit he look that sorrowful-like, he near 'bout broke down, and he point to the cow-tick.

But Brer Wolf he done live on the plantation with Brer Rabbit many a day; and Brer Wolf he say, "Quit your fooling, ole man. You done turn Brer Terrapin loose, and I just going to use this here rock to smash your head." Then Brer Rabbit he make haste to make out to Brer Wolf how that little chap surely are all what's left of poor ole Brer Terrapin.

And Brer Rabbit he make out how the power are in his left eye to make a big man perish away; and Brer Rabbit he 'low how he just happen to strike his left eye on his ole friend Brer Terrapin, and directly he get smaller and smaller, 'til that all there be left of the poor ole man. When Brer Rabbit say that, he turn and cut his left eye sharp at Brer Wolf, Brer Rabbit do.

Brer Wolf he just look once on the little tick, and he say, "Don' look at me, Brer Rabbit! Don' look at me!" and Brer Wolf he strike out, and he just burn the wind for the woods.

Then Brer Rabbit he clip it off down the road 'til he come up with ole Brer Terrapin; and they strike a fire, and make a good pot of coffee, and talk it over.

RABBIT KILLS BIG MAN-EATER

Tradition Bearer: Unavailable

Source: Swanton, John R. Page 161 in *Myths and Tales of the Southeastern Indians.* Smithsonian Institution Bureau of American Ethnology Bulletin 88. Washington, DC: U.S. Government Printing Office, 1929.

Date: 1929

Original Source: Alabama

National Origin: Native American

Big Man-eater appears in a number of traditional tales from the Native American Southeast. The cannibal figure strikes at a particularly fearful element in the human psyche and is found in such widely dispersed forms as the Windigo figure of the subarctic, the Giant at the top of Jack's beanstalk (See "Jack and the Beanstalk," p. 134 in present collection), Hansel and Gretel's witch, and "Old Foster" of the southern highlands

(p. 155). Rabbit exercises his power of deception in this narrative to play the role of culture hero, the life-enhancing persona of the **trickster**. Although the culture hero brings technology and social order in many traditions, his role as a monster slayer who cleanses the natural order and makes the universe safe for humanity also is well-represented. In typical fashion, Rabbit changes shapes and even gender to gain the advantage over his monstrous adversary.

Big Man-eater lived with his wife at a certain place and wanted to kill human beings. People heard of it and said, "They want to kill us," and all were afraid.

Then Rabbit said, "Give me an old dress," and they gave it to him. He said, "Give me an old blanket," and they gave that to him. Then he put on the dress, wrapped up his head in the old blanket, and started off.

When he reached the place and stood in the yard Big Man-eater's wife saw him and came out, and asked who he was. "I am your youngest aunt who has traveled to this place," he said. "Come in," said Big Man-eater's wife, so he started to go in. "Sit down," she said, and down he sat.

Then they gave the supposed aunt some hard deer meat to eat, but he said, "I can't eat that, because I have no teeth. I need a hatchet, for I can't eat that [as it is]." So they gave him a hatchet and he chopped the dry venison into small pieces and ate them. Then he said, "That is the way I always eat it."

Now Big Man-eater lay down but the two women sat still by the fire. Rabbit said to Big Man-eater's wife, "When your husband is asleep what kind of noise does he make?" "When he is not sleeping very soundly he makes a noise like 'sololon sololon.' When he makes a noise like 'soloñ soloñ' he is very sound asleep."

"I will stay all night with you; in the morning I will start on," said Rabbit. So Big Man-eater's wife lay down and Rabbit lay down close to the fire. As he lay there he listened to the noises Big Man-eater was making. Then he slept and made a noise like "sololon sololon." After some time he made a noise like "soloñ soloñ." Then Rabbit took the hatchet and, after he had sat close to Big Man-eater for a while listening, he struck him with it in the neck and cut his head off. Then he threw off his old dress and blanket, shouted, jumped up and down several times, went out of the house, and ran off.

RABBIT AND BIG MAN-EATER

Tradition Bearer: Unavailable

Source: Swanton, John R. Pages 159-60 in *Myths and Tales of the Southeastern Indians*. Smithsonian Institution Bureau of American Ethnology Bulletin 88. Washington, DC: U.S. Government Printing Office, 1929.

Date: 1929

Original Source: Alabama

National Origin: Native American

The following **myth** is another in the cycle of adventures of Rabbit and Big Man-eater discussed in the introductory remarks to the preceding narrative.

Big Man-eater traveled along until he came to a town where he killed and ate all of the people. On the way to another town he met Rabbit, who said, "At this town all the people have run off. I kill and eat people and here are their bones." When he met Big Man-eater he carried over his shoulder a child with a stick run through it. Then they sat down beside the trail to defecate. Both shut their eyes, and when they defecated Big Man-eater evacuated bones while Rabbit passed only grass. Rabbit opened his eyes, picked up Big Man-eater's excrement and put it under himself and took his own and placed it under Big Man-eater. When both finally opened their eyes, Big Man-eater said, "I never passed anything like this before." The next time both defecated with their eyes open and Rabbit passed nothing but grass while Big Man-eater defecated bones.

After that they struck up a friendship. Rabbit said, "Let us go to Tree-falling-down Camp." So they set out. When they arrived Rabbit said, "Wait right here while I hunt for a good camping place." He went on until he saw a tree that shook and was ready to fall, when he called his companion. "Over here there is a good place," he said and Big Man-eater went there.

When night came, both lay down, and, while Big Man-eater slept, Rabbit awoke and pushed the tree down upon him. Then he threw small limbs upon himself and made a noise as if he had been hurt. Big Man-eater pushed the tree away and woke up. "This camp is always like that," said Rabbit.

Next time Rabbit said, "Let us go to Ashes-thrown-on Camp," and they started off. When they got there and had made camp Rabbit picked up a quantity of wood, kindled it, and made a big fire. But after the two had lain down Rabbit awoke, gathered up a lot of hot ashes on some bark with which he had provided himself, and threw them on Big Man-eater. On himself he threw cold ashes. Big Man-eater was badly hurt.

In the morning Rabbit said, "Let us go to Jumping-bluff Creek," and they started on. After they had traveled for a while they reached the place and went down the creek. "Let us jump across it and back four times," said Rabbit. Rabbit jumped first four times. When Big Man-eater prepared to jump Rabbit held for him the bag he was carrying. Before Big Man-eater had jumped four times he fell from the bluff into the water. The water rose and Big Man-eater went down into it. "My friend is gone; he is going far out into the sea," said Rabbit. Rabbit, however, took Big Man-eater's bag and started home.

HOW THE DEER OBTAINED HIS HORNS

Tradition Bearer: Unavailable

Source: Mooney, James. "Myths of the Cherokees" *Journal of American Folklore* 1 (1888): 106–8.

Date: 1887

Original Source: Cherokee

National Origin: Native American

In this **myth** from the Cherokee, Rabbit plays his familiar role of **trickster**. The **myth** of "Kanati and Selu" focused on sacred features of the Cherokee world. In these **trickster** myths, however, the origins of the animals' attributes and the phenomena of the physical universe are at times overshadowed by the amusement value of the escapades of characters such as Rabbit. Therefore, the tales invite comparison to the African American tales of Brer Rabbit and the Cajun Comrade Lapin. These narrative similarities comprise an interesting continuity across the South.

In the old days the animals were fond of amusement, and were constantly getting up grand meetings and contests of various kinds, with prizes for the winner. On one occasion a prize was offered to the animal with the finest coat, and although the otter deserved to win it, the rabbit stole his coat, and nearly got the prize for himself. After a while the animals got together again, and made a large pair of horns, to be given to the best runner. The race was to be through a thicket, and the one who made the best time, with the horns on his head, was to get them. Everybody knew from the first that either the deer or the rabbit would be the winner, but bets were high on the rabbit, who was a great runner and a general favorite. But the rabbit had no tail, and always went by jumps, and his friends were afraid that the horns would make him fall over in the bushes unless he had something to balance them, so they fixed up a tail for him with a stick and some bird's down.

"Now," says the rabbit, "let me look over the ground where I am to run."

So he went into the thicket, and was gone so long that at last one of the animals went to see what had become of him, and there he found the rabbit hard at work gnawing down bushes and cutting off the hanging limbs of the trees, and making a road for himself clear through to the other side of the swamp. The messenger did not let the rabbit see him, but came back quietly and told his story to the others. Pretty soon the rabbit came out again, ready to put on the horns and begin the race, but several of the animals said that he had been gone so long that it looked as if he must have been cutting a road through the bushes. The rabbit denied it up and down, but they all went into the thicket, and there was the open road, sure enough. Then the chief got very angry, and said to the rabbit, "Since you are so fond of the business, you may spend the rest of your life gnawing twigs and bushes," and so the rabbit does to this day. The other animals would not allow the rabbit to run at all now, so they put the horns on the deer, who plunged into the worst part of the thicket, and made his way out to the other side, then turned round and came back again on a different track, in such fine style that everyone said he had won the horns. But the rabbit felt sore about it, and resolved to get even with him.

One day, soon after the contest for the horns, the rabbit stretched a large grape-vine across the trail, and gnawed it nearly in two in the middle. Then he went back a piece, took a good run, and jumped up at the vine. He kept on running and jumping up at the vine, until the deer came along and asked him what he was doing.

"Don't you see?" says the rabbit. "I'm so strong that I can bite through that grape-vine at one jump."

The deer could hardly believe this, and wanted to see it done. So the rabbit ran back, made a tremendous spring, and bit through the vine where he had gnawed it before. The deer, when he saw that, said, "Well; I can do it if you can." So the rabbit stretched a larger grape-vine across the trail, but without gnawing it in the middle. Then the deer ran back as he had seen the rabbit do, made a powerful spring, and struck the grape-vine right in the centre; but it only flew back, and threw him over on his head. He tried again and again, until he was all bruised and bleeding.

"Let me see your teeth," at last said the rabbit. So the deer showed him his teeth, which were long and sharp, like a wolf's teeth.

"No wonder you can't do it," says the rabbit; "your teeth are too blunt to bite anything. Let me sharpen them for you, like mine. My teeth are so sharp that I can cut through a stick just like a knife." And he showed him a black-locust twig, of which rabbits gnaw the young shoots, which he had shaved off as well as a knife could do it, just in rabbit fashion.

The deer thought that was just the thing. So the rabbit got a hard stone, with rough edges, and filed and filed away at the deer's teeth, until they were filed down almost to the gums.

"Now try it," says the rabbit. So the deer tried again, but this time he couldn't bite at all.

"Now you've paid for your horns," said the rabbit, as he laughed and started home through the bushes. Ever since then the deer's teeth are so blunt that he cannot chew anything but grass and leaves.

RABBIT FOOLS ALLIGATOR

Tradition Bearer: Unavailable

Source: Swanton, John R. Pages 52–53 in *Myths and Tales of the Southeastern Indians*. Smithsonian Institution Bureau of American Ethnology Bulletin 88. Washington, DC: U.S. Government Printing Office, 1929.

Date: 1929

Original Source: Creek

National Origin: Native American

In the following Creek tale, Rabbit's malicious persona exemplifies the **trickster**. The narrative is of particular interest for the variety of cultural influences it displays. The devil is an obvious European introduction to the tale, whereas Rabbit is an indigenous **trickster** in African (as hare), African American, and Native American traditions. Rabbit's strategy of asking an apparently innocent question designed to victimize Alligator by means of his own vanity, however, could be classified as "signifying," the African American rhetorical strategy of directing by indirection.

The Alligator was sunning himself on a log when the Rabbit said to him: "Mr. Alligator, did you ever see the devil?" "No, Mr. Rabbit, but I am not afraid to see him," replied the Alligator.

"Well, I saw the devil, and he said you were afraid to look at him," said the Rabbit. "I'm not afraid of him, and you tell him so," bravely responded the Alligator.

"Are you willing to crawl up the hill to-morrow and let me show you the devil?" asked the Rabbit. "Yes, I am willing," said the Alligator. The Rabbit spoke up and said, "Now Mr. Alligator, when you see smoke rising don't be afraid, the devil will be just starting out."

"You need not be so particular about me. I am not afraid," said he. "Now when you see birds flying and deer running past you don't get scared." "I shall not get scared." "When you hear fire crackling close to you and the grass burning all around you, don't get scared. The devil will come along and you can get a good look at him," and with this advice the Rabbit left.

The next day he returned and told Alligator to crawl out and lie in the high grass and wait until the devil came. So out crawled the Alligator and took his position in the grass as directed by the Rabbit.

When he saw the Alligator so far from the water the Rabbit laughed to himself. He ran across the prairie till he reached a burning stump, got a chunk of fire, and returned to a spot near his confiding friend, where he kindled the grass and soon had the pleasure of seeing a blaze all around the Alligator. Then, running to a sandy place where there was no grass, he sat down to see the fun. He had not long to wait, for when the smoke rose in clouds and the birds flew by, and the animals ran for life over the prairie, the Alligator cried out: "Oh, Mr. Rabbit, what's that?"

The Rabbit answered: "Oh, you lie still; that's nothing but the devil starting out." Soon the fire began to crackle and roar, and the flames swept over the prairie, and the Alligator called: "Oh, Mr. Rabbit, what's that?"

"Oh, that's the devil's breath. Don't be scared. You will see him directly." The Rabbit rolled over in the sand and kicked his heels in the air. The fire came nearer and nearer and began to burn the grass all around the Alligator, and under him, till he rolled and twisted in pain. "Don't be scared, Mr. Alligator. Just lie still a little longer and the devil will be right there and you can get a good look at him," cried out the Rabbit, as he saw the movements of the Alligator. But the latter could stand it no longer and started down the hill to the water through the burning grass, snapping his teeth and rolling over in pain, while the Rabbit laughed and jumped in delight, saying, "Wait, Mr. Alligator, don't be in such a hurry. You are not afraid of the devil." But the Alligator tumbled into the water to cool his roasted skin, and wondered how the Rabbit could stand such awful scenes.

RABBIT GETS A TURKEY FOR WILDCAT

Tradition Bearer: Unavailable

Source: Swanton, John R. Pages 47–48 in *Myths and Tales of the Southeastern Indians.* Smithsonian Institution Bureau of American Ethnology Bulletin 88. Washington, DC: U.S. Government Printing Office, 1929.

Date: 1929

Original Source: Creek

National Origin: Native American

The Creek Nation was a confederation of tribes in the "deep" southern states of Georgia, Alabama, and contiguous areas. Prior to their removal to "Indian Territory" (Oklahoma), the Creeks developed close ties with African Americans, offering refuge to runaway slaves. These ties undoubtedly influenced the **animal tales** that were collected from their descendants in later centuries. The following narrative is one such tale. In it, **trickster** Rabbit reveals his willingness to sacrifice his neighbors to save himself. Typically he couples his guile with the character flaws of his victims to attain his ends.

A Rabbit was overtaken by a Wildcat, who threatened to kill and eat him. The Rabbit said: "Do not kill me; I will bring you a turkey." The Wildcat consented to let Rabbit try, so he ran into the woods to find the turkey, first telling the Wildcat to lie down and pretend he was dead.

Rabbit soon found some turkeys and told them the Wildcat was dead and proposed that they all go and dance and sing around his body. The turkeys agreed and went with Rabbit and when they saw the Wildcat's body stretched on the ground and his mouth and eyes looking white as if he were flyblown (for Rabbit had rubbed rotten wood on the edges of his eyes and mouth) they were satisfied that he was really dead.

Rabbit took his place at the head of the Wildcat and began to beat his drum and to sing while the turkeys danced around him.

After the song and dance had continued a while they heard Rabbit sing:

"Jump up and catch the red leg, Jump up and catch the red leg."

"Why, he is dead and cannot jump," they said, but since they objected, he promised not to say that any more.

So Rabbit sang and drummed away and the turkeys again danced around their enemy's body; but soon Rabbit sang in a low tone:

"Jump up and catch the biggest, Jump up and catch the biggest."

The turkeys stopped their dance, but too late, for the Wildcat jumped up and caught the biggest gobbler. Rabbit ran away to the woods and the turkeys pursued him, threatening to kill him for his trickery. They chased him round and round the trees till at last one of the turkeys bit at his long tail and bit it off, and ever since that time all rabbits have had short tails.

WHEN BRER FROG GIVE A BIG DINING

Tradition Bearer: Unavailable

Source: Backus, Emma M. "Folk-Tales from Georgia." *Journal of American Folklore* 13 (1900): 25–26.

Date: 1900

Original Source: Georgia

National Origin: African American

In this tale, which demonstrates the **trickster**'s penchant for being ruled by his appetites rather than prudence, Brer Rabbit brings about his own downfall. First, by crashing a party lured by the smell of fried fish, and then by falling into a trap set with the same bait, Rabbit finds himself literally out of his element. This narrative of the **trickster** tricked pits an elder's wisdom against the brash schemes of a consummate African American con artist. In this case at least, the "spry old man" beats the young **trickster**. This triumph of the wisdom of age over the bravado of youth is echoed in "Are You Man?" (p. 220).

Brer Frog he think he give a big dining to all his friends, so he send out invitations to all his friends to come down and eat fried fish with him.

Brer Frog he invite Brer Fox and his wife, and Brer Wolf and his wife, and Brer Coon and his wife, and Brer Possum and his wife, but he don' invite Brer Rabbit, Brer Frog don', 'cause there be hard feelings between Brer Frog and Brer Rabbit from way back.

When the creeters all went past Brer Rabbit's house on their way to the dining, they ask Brer Rabbit, why he don't go to Brer Frog's dining? Brer Rabbit he say, he ain' invited, and he 'low he ain't powerful fond of fried fish nohow.

So they pass on, and when they come to the branch [creek], they find Brer Frog frying fish over twenty little fires. Brer Frog he hop round from one frying-pan to the other, like a spry old man like he is.

Directly Brer Rabbit he smell the fish frying where he set on the porch. It smell so powerful good, Brer Rabbit he just can't stand it. He take his way down to the branch, and he see Brer Frog taking off the fish from his twenty little fires, and set it on the table.

Brer Rabbit he slip into the swamp and make a big noise. The creeters they say, "What that!"

Brer Rabbit he make a big noise. Once more Brer Fox he say, "Where we going fly to?"

Brer Frog he say, "I know the best place for me to get at." He just give one jump over all the creeters' heads and go plunk into the water. Brer Terrapin he go slippin' and slidin' one side, then the other, and he go splash in the water; the other creeters, they just strike out for home.

Brer Rabbit he go up to the table and he eat his fill of fried fish.

Now Brer Frog are a mighty cold-blooded kind of a man; nobody ever see Brer Frog in a passion. Brer Frog's eyes on the top of his head. All the time while Brer Rabbit was eating that fried fish, Brer Frog he set down in the water looking straight up at Brer Rabbit, and Brer Frog he was studying; but Brer Rabbit he don't know that.

Brer Frog he take it mighty hard, 'case Brer Rabbit break up his dining, and he study to hisself how he going punish Brer Rabbit.

Sure enough, a week later, Brer Frog he send out invitations to all the other creeters to another dining.

So the creeters all set out, and as they go past Brer Rabbit's house they stop, and ask Brer Rabbit why he don' go to Brer Frog's dining? Brer Rabbit he say his mouth ain't set for fried fish, and he 'low he powerful busy anyhow, and can't leave home.

The creeters they make haste, and when they get to the branch they see the bank all covered with little fires, and a pan of fish frying on every fire, and Brer Frog hopping from one frying-pan to the other, and turning the fish; and Brer Frog he hop up and whisper in the ear of each one of his guests. Then Brer Frog he set the table.

Brer Rabbit he set upon his porch smoking his pipe, and the smell of the fish frying come up on the wind, and Brer Rabbit he just can't stand it. He say he bound to set a tooth in that fish. So Brer Rabbit he go clipity clipity down to the branch, and he find the table done set, and it certainly do look powerful tempting.

Brer Rabbit he go in the edge of the swamp and make a big noise; the creeters they just strike out and fly for home. Brer Frog he say, "I know the nighest place for me to get," and he jumped plum over the table and go in the water "Kersplash!"

Then Brer Rabbit he jump on the table. Now that just what Brer Frog know Brer Rabbit going do, and Brer Frog he done set the table on a plank, on the edge of the water, and he done put leaves and bresh all round the plank, so Brer Rabbit ain' see how it done set on the water; and when Brer Rabbit jump on the plank, over it go, and Brer Rabbit and all the fishes go "Kersplash!" down to the bottom.

Brer Frog he right down there, and Brer Frog he say, "Oho, Brer Rabbit, you is mighty kind to fetch my dinner down to me," and Brer Frog he say, "You is my master many a day on land, Brer Rabbit, but I is your master in the water." And Brer Frog he kill old Brer Rabbit and eat him up.

BOUQUI AND LAPIN: THE SMOKEHOUSE

Tradition Bearer: Leona Edwards Claudel

Source: Claudel, Calvin, and J.-M. Carrier. "Three Tales from the French Folklore of Louisiana." *Journal of American Folklore* 56 (1943): 43–44.

Date: 1943

Original Source: Louisiana
National Origin: Cajun

The following tale is unusual in that Lapin the **trickster** demonstrates uncharacteristic restraint in satisfying his appetite. The act of sharing his secret for obtaining meat with his customary foil Bouqui is out of character also. More in keeping with the plot of the Lapin and Bouqui cycle, however, is the fact that Lapin escapes unscathed with his booty while Bouqui, as a consequence of his uncontrollable greed, is left with the blame for past and present crimes and rewarded with a beating in this **variant** of "The Wolf Overeats in the Cellar" (AT 41).

Bouqui, who was very poor, went to Lapin the rabbit's house to eat supper. Bouqui said to Lapin: "Lapin, you surely make good gumbo; it has in it the best meat I've ever tasted. Where do you get such good meat?"

Now at first Lapin did not wish to tell his comrade Bouqui where he got the meat, but he finally answered: "It's smoked meat. If you can keep a secret, I'll tell you where I get it. There's a farmer nearby, an old French farmer, who has a smokehouse. In it are all sorts of hams and sausages. I got the meat from his smokehouse."

"Oh, I want to go get some of this smoked meat myself," exclaimed Bouqui. "Lapin, you must show me how you do it."

"I cannot take you there," began Lapin, "because you know how stupid you are, Bouqui. You'll tell everybody in the neighborhood, and we'll get caught. Besides you are too greedy; you'll want to go every day."

"Please, Lapin; please take me along with you," begged Bouqui.

"All right," finally gave in Lapin. "Come tomorrow and spend the night with me. We shall get up early when the roosters crow and pay the smokehouse a visit."

Bouqui arrived at Lapin's house the next night very early, carrying along with him his blanket. After they were inside, Lapin said: "Now let's go to bed, and when the roosters crow, we'll get up and go to the smokehouse."

They went to bed; Lapin fell fast asleep. At about midnight he was awakened by a noise from the henhouse; the chickens were roosting in disorder and making a noise and cackling. Lapin went out to see. Bouqui was up and pushing a pole at the chickens to make the roosters crow. He was anxious to leave for the smokehouse.

"Bouqui, let those chickens alone and come back to bed!" cried Lapin. Again Lapin fell sound asleep. Later he was awakened once more, this time by a loud cackling from the hens.

"Bouqui, O Bouqui!" called Lapin; "it's not time to go yet. I said to wait until the roosters crow. They will know when to crow. Then it will be time for us to leave."

Finally the roosters crowed. Bouqui and Lapin set out.

In the gray light of the early morning Lapin saw Bouqui was carrying something. He asked: "What are you carrying, Bouqui?"

"My blanket," answered Bouqui.

"But what are you going to do with that?" questioned Lapin.

"Why, carry out sausages and hams," said Bouqui.

Then Lapin said in anger: "You are too greedy, Bouqui. We had better be careful not to get caught."

Bouqui entered first into the hole at the back of the smokehouse, and after him came Lapin. Bouqui spread his blanket on the ground in the middle of the smokehouse and began to select and pile up the hams. Lapin had taken one sausage and was ready to leave through the hole. He whispered to Bouqui: "Hurry, Bouqui; it's time to leave."

"Yes, all right, but wait another moment," answered Bouqui. Bouqui was now piling sausages on his blanket over the hams. It was now growing late, and the sun was about to come up.

"Hurry, hurry, Bouqui," cried Lapin from the outside where he was waiting. "I hear someone coming."

The farmer was coming. Bouqui had made a bundle of the pile of smoked meat. He first went out and began to tug, to get the load through the hole. As Bouqui pulled harder and harder, the more it seemed that the blanket of hams and sausages stuck on the inside.

By then it was broad daylight; and up came the farmer, who exclaimed:

"Ho! Ho! There, so you have been entering my smokehouse and stealing my meat."

He was carrying a switch. Bouqui wanted to leave but could not seem to let go the end of the blanket. The farmer caught him. He whipped and whipped Bouqui, as Lapin ran away.

JEAN SOT FEEDS COWS NEEDLES

Tradition Bearer: Unavailable

Source: Ray, Marie. "Jean Sotte Stories." *Journal of American Folklore* 21 (1908): 364.

Date: 1908

Original Source: Louisiana

National Origin: European American

The following narrative (a **variant** of AT1345, "Stupid Stories Depending on a Pun") casts Jean Sot (French, "John the Fool") in the **numskull** role once again. In this case, his linguistic misinterpretation has no saving grace.

Jean Sot's old mother was in despair over the stupidity of her boy, but thought she would try him again, hoping he would do better. So calling him, and giving him some money, she said, "My son, I want a paper of needles, and you must go down the road to the village and buy me one, but do not lose it on the way."

Jean Sot promised to be careful and went off in high glee, for he liked to go on errands to the village. He knew just where to go; and, having counted out the money to the old dame who gave him the needles, he started down the lane which led to his home. He had not gone far when he met a number of cows, who, when they saw him, lifted their heads and cried, "A-moo, a-moo!" and turned into a barnyard. Jean Sotte, thinking they were calling him, followed; and when they continued to cry "A-moo!" he said, "Well, if it is the needles (a pun on French *aiguille*, "needle") you want, here they are!" and he sprinkled them all over the straw they were eating.

Then he went home; and when the old woman asked where the needles were she had sent him for, he said, "Mother, I obeyed you: I did not *lose* them, but, when the cows cried so for them, I was obliged to give them to them on their hay."

JEAN SOT KILLS THE DUCK

Tradition Bearer: Unavailable

Source: Ray, Marie. "Jean Sotte Stories." *Journal of American Folklore* 21 (1908): 364–65.

Date: 1908

Original Source: Louisiana

National Origin: Cajun

Jean Sot commonly reveals his stupidity when justifying the logic that motivates his unconventional actions. In this narrative, however, he attempts to conceal a minor crime by committing and then confessing to a worse one.

There was an old woman who had two sons—one so simple that he received the name of Jean Sotte, and the other so bright and intelligent that he was known as Jean Esprit.

One day the old woman said to Jean Sotte, "My son, I am old and stiff, but you are young and active and can go on my errands; so go into the storeroom and bring me a bottle of wine you will find there."

Jean Sotte went to the storeroom, and, having found the bottle, he thought he would take out the cork and make sure it was wine; and when he had smelled it, he thought he would taste it to be sure it was all right; but the wine was so good and old, he soon felt very merry, and continued to drink until the bottle was quite empty.

Now, in a corner of the room an old duck had made her nest in some straw, and when Jean Sotte began capering around, she cried out, "Quack, quack!"and flapped her wings, which so frightened him that he caught her by the neck, and wrung her head off, and seated himself on her eggs.

The old woman, having waited some time for Jean Sotte's return, determined to see what was keeping him. What was her surprise, on hobbling to the storeroom, to find her old duck dead and Jean Sotte sitting on her nest. "Silly boy!" she said, "why have you killed my duck, why are you sitting on the nest, and where is the bottle of wine you were to bring me?"

"Mother," said Jean Sotte, rolling his head and looking very sleepy, "I drank the wine; and when the old duck saw me, she cried out, and I knew she would tell you, so I killed her to keep her from telling; and, now she is dead, you will never know!"

JEAN SOT AND THE COWHIDE

Tradition Bearer: Jack Vidrine

Source: Claudel, Calvin. "Louisiana Tales of Jean Sot and Bouqui and Lapin." *The Southern Folklore Quarterly* 8 (1944): 297–98.

Date: 1944

Original Source: Louisiana

National Origin: Cajun

In the opening episode of this *Cajun* comic tale, Jean Sot kills the family's cow. In any other case, the misinterpretation of his mother's instructions leading to this act would seem a willful attempt to misconstrue. In the case of Jean Sot, however, such behavior is consistent with the **stock character**. In a later episode in the tale, due to a misinterpretation of Jean's words by a group of robbers, he turns folly to fortune. The following tale (1653F, "Numskull Talks to Himself and Frightens Robbers Away") and **motifs** from it are found throughout the South. Foolish John and his mother lived by the bayou in Louisiana and they spoke French. He was such a foolish lad he misunderstood everything he was told.

"Foolish John, go get the cow by the bayou and drive her into the lot," said his mother.

In the French they spoke, "to drive" can also mean "to push." So Foolish John went to fetch the wheelbarrow and rolled it out to where the cow was pasturing. He placed her into the wheelbarrow and rolled her home. When he reached home, he was panting and sweating like a horse.

"What in the world are you doing, Foolish John?" questioned his mother.

"Well, Mama, you told me to push the cow here, and that's what I'm doing."

"Fool! Will you ever learn anything!" exclaimed the exasperated woman. "Now take that cow out of there and go milk her."

As with many words that have double meanings, "to milk" also meant "to shoot."

While his mother was busy inside, Foolish John went to get the gun and shot the cow. When he appeared inside without the milk, his mother became worried.

"Foolish John, where is the milk for supper?" she asked.

"Why, Mama, I thought you meant for me to shoot the cow with a gun.... That's what I did," replied the lad.

"Ah, foolish son!" she cried, "killing our only cow.... Now you must go skin her and sell the hide so we can buy food, because we don't have milk.... Hurry now!"

Foolish John fetched the big butcher knife, strung the cow up to a tree by her hind legs and skinned her—head, feet and everything. He put the hide over his head and set out for town. As he walked under the hide, he looked like a strange beast.

It was getting dark and growing cold, for it was almost winter. He reached a tree that was losing its leaves. The tree groaned and shivered as the cold wind whistled through its limbs.

"That poor tree must be cold," remarked Foolish John to himself. "I'll cover it with this hide to keep it warm."

He began climbing the tree with the cowhide still on his head. When he was up in the top ready to place the hide over the tree, a band of seven men suddenly came and sat down in a circle under the tree. They were robbers with a huge sack of money. The chief began to divide the money.

"This is for me.... That's for you," counted the chief as he placed each robber's share before him.

Everytime he said this, Foolish John would pluck a hair from his cowhide and cry, "And one hair for me-eee!"

"Listen, listen, the Old Devil!" would exclaim one of the robbers, and the chief would start to divide again. The dividing and counting continued far into the night, and each time the chief would say, "This is for me.... That's for you," Foolish John would add while plucking out hair, "And one hair for me-eee!"

Finally when they had all the money spread out, and Foolish John had picked his cowhide clean, he suddenly lost his grip on the limb he was holding and crashed to the ground right into the middle of the circle of thieves. When they beheld this strange apparition with horns, they all took to their heels and fled. Foolish John gathered up the money, placed the hide over the tree and went back home.

"Well, how much did you get for the hide?" inquired his mother.

"I collected a dollar for every hair on the hide," answered Foolish John, laying down the heavy sack load of money.

"Foolish John!" exclaimed the mother with joy, "sometimes I think you are not so foolish!"

LAZY JACK AND HIS CALF SKIN

Tradition Bearer: Jane Gentry

Source: Carter, Isabel Gordon. "Mountain White Folk-Lore: Tales from the Southern Blue Ridge." *Journal of American Folklore* 38 (1925): 343–46.

Date: 1923

Original Source: North Carolina

National Origin: Anglo American

Jack inherits a calf at his parents' death, but because of his lazy disposition, he lets his calf starve to death. He is rejected by his brothers Will and Tom but becomes wealthy in spite of his laziness. Unlike the crafty Jack seen in the other Jack tales in this collection, the protagonist of this version of "The Magic Cowhide" (AT1535) virtually falls into good fortune rather than striving to make his way in the world.

They was an old man and old woman had three sons, Jack, Will and Tom. Jack was awful lazy. So they didn't give Jack anything when they see they had to die, with the exception of one little old poor calf and Jack was too lazy to feed hit.

So the other boys was over in the new ground a clearin' away and Jack's little old calf were over there a buzzin' round eatin' lin bushes and such, and they cut a tree down and killed hit. So they come on over to the house and said, "Killed your little old calf over there, Jack. You can go over and skin hit and eat hit or just let hit lay there."

"Bedads, I'll go over and skin hit," says Jack. So he went over and skinned hit and come on back and grilled the meat. He sit there in a corner and grilled and grilled hit 'til he got the meat all eat up. When he got the meat all eat up the hide was good and dry. So he got the hide down and he sewed hit all up good and he left the tail on and filled hit with old shucks and cobs so when he shuck hit he could make hit rattle good.

So he took hit by the tail and started off down the road one morning, a draggin' hit all day until late that evenin' he come to a house. He called, "Hello! Can I stop here this evenin'?"

Woman come to the door, says, "Yes, I guess ye can. My husband's gone but Mr. Passenger's here and I guess ye can stop the night." So she met Jack at the door and jest sent him on up stairs. Didn't offer him no supper or nothin'. So, instead of gettin' in bed, Jack lay down on the floor and peeked thru a knot hole to see what they all did there and he saw her fix the finest supper. They jest had everything that cud be thought of, baked pig and stuffed goose and roast chicken and pies and cakes. And her and Mr. Passenger sat down and started eatin'. So Jack was a lyin' up there jest starved to death. So they eat all they cud eat, then took and put hit all away and got out all kinds of drinks. Jack watched good where they put hit. So they was sittin' a drinkin' and they heard her husband come a whistlin'. So the old man said, "Where'll I git. Where'll I git."

She said, "Jump in that big chest and I'll lock you up." So he run jumped in the chest and she run got all the drinks put away and she run jumped in the bed. So the husband come in and said, "Old woman, got anything cooked to eat around here?"

"Yes, I guess you'll find some bread on the table," she says.

So Jack saw the man a eatin' down there so he dragged the cowhide around and old man said, "What's that?" Woman says, "Little old crazy boy stopped here to stay the night. Guess that's him makin' that noise."

Man said, "What's his name?"

"Says his name's Jack."

So the man hollered, "Jack, come down here and have some supper with me."

Jack says, "Don't care if I do." So Jack didn't eat two bites of the bread 'fore he stuck his hand back and shuck that cowhide so hit made a noise. So he fired in on the old cowhide and went to beatin' on hit. "Shut your mouth, you blabber mouthed thing," he says.

Old man says, "What's hit sayin', Jack? What's hit sayin'?"

Jack says, "Oh I don't want to tell, the big mouthed thing. I'm afraid hit will make the woman of the house mad."

Man says, "Now, you go ahead and tell me. I don't care for the woman of the house. You tell me what hit said."

Jack says, "Well, hit says over there in that buffet there's roast pig and stuffed goose and roast chicken and pies and cakes."

Man says, "Is they, old woman?"

"Yes, little bit I was a savin' fur my kinfolks."

Man says, "Jack and I er your kinfolks, you bring 'em out here."

So the old woman got up and set 'em out all the good eatings. They didn't eat long 'fore Jack reached out and shuck the little old calf ag'in. Said, "You shut your mouth, you blabber mouthed thing."

Old man says, "What's hit saying Jack? What's hit sayin?"

"Oh, I don't want to tell," says Jack, "I'm afraid hit will make the woman of the house mad."

"Now, you go ahead and tell me," says the man.

"Well, hit says over in that cabinet is whiskey and brandy and gin and all manner of drinks."

"Is they, old woman?"

"Yes, little I was savin' for my kinfolks."

"Well, Jack and me 'er your kinfolks, you bring 'em out here." So she brung 'em out.

The man begin to git a little foxy. "What'll you sell that fer?"

"Oh, I couldn't sell hit."

"I'll give you five hundred guineas for hit."

"Well," Jack says, "if you give me that chest over there and five hundred guineas you kin have hit." (My mammy always told that a five dollar bill was as much as a guinea.)

So old woman says, "You can't sell that old chest. That's a chest my poor old father give me."

Man says, "I bought that chest and I paid fer hit too, and I'm a goin' to sell hit." So the man and Jack traded and the man helped Jack git the old chest up on his shoulders.

So Jack carried the old chest a little ways. He didn't want hit 'cept to tease the Old Passenger. He said, "I'll jest drap this in the well."

Old Passenger says, "Oh don't put me in the well. I'll poke you out five hundred guineas if you'll not put me in the well." So Jack put down the chest and took the five hundred guineas that the Old Passenger poked out. Jack jest took hit and went on. Old Passenger didn't have sense enough to say if you'll let me out. So some people come along and heard the Old Passenger a hollerin' and they run back to a house and said they was a takin' chest up the road. They let the Old Passenger out.

Jack went on home and he had him a load of money. So his brothers said, "Jack, where'd you git all that money."

"Sold my cowhide, how'd you think I'd get hit?" So his brothers run out and shot some big fine horses and skun 'em. And they didn't give 'em time to dry or nothin! They jest sewed 'em up and started. So the flies just got after them and they drug 'em around and nobody wouldn't let 'em come in with old green flies. So they come home and says, "Jack, we're a-goin' to kill you. You can have your choice. You can be shot, hung, or drown."

He said, "Well, I reckon you kin jest drown me." So they sewed 'im up in a sheet and Jack walked with 'em about a mile down to the river. So when they got down there they poked Jack in but they didn't have no string to tie him. Their conscious was so guilty over killin' their brother neither one of them wanted to go back to the house to git a string. "Well, ye can both go back," says Jack, "I'll not leave." So while Jack was a layin' there a man come up the road with a big immense sheep drove.

"Stranger, what are you doin' here?"

"I'm fixin' to fly to heaven," says Jack. "In a few minutes two little angels will come and fly up to Heaven with me."

So the man said, "I'm old now and if you'll let me go to heaven in your place I'll give you my sheep drove."

So Jack says, "All right," and he jumped out and drove his sheep up the road a bit and then he come back and helped the old man git in the sheet. He saw his brothers a-comin' and he hide in the thicket. So they come on down and tied up the sheet and throwed hit in the river. So then Jack started to holler, "Sheep! Sheep! Open up the gates and let me in."

"Where'd ye git them sheep?" says his brothers.

"Got 'em in the river. Where did you think I got 'em?"

"Oh, Jack, you reckon we could git a sheep drove?"

"I reckon so, but I'm not a-goin' to fix up your sheets. You'll have to yourselves. I'll throw you in. I could have got a lot more if you'd throwed me out in the river farther." So they throwed one of the brothers and he begin to kick about.

"What's he doin' that fur?" says the other.

"Oh, he's gathering his sheep."

"Oh, Jack, hurry up and throw me in fore he gits 'em all. Throw me farther." So Jack throwed him in and then he driv his sheep drove home and when I left there Jack was rich.

TI JEAN CANNOT TELL A LIE

Tradition Bearer: Valerie Green

Source: Personal communication

Date: 2000

Original Source: Louisiana

National Origin: Cajun

Ti Jean (French, "Little John") is a **trickster** figure found throughout French-descended traditions in the Americas. Unlike many such figures, this character has successfully survived in contemporary joke repertoires. Compare this character to Boudreaux in the narrative "Boudreaux and the Cottonmouth" (p. 119).

Early one morning, Ti Jean was walking along the bank of the bayou behind his house. All of a sudden, he noticed that the family outhouse, located right on the bank, was sliding into the bayou. He decided to help it out and picked up a big tree limb and hit the outhouse til it fell into the water.

Later, when Ti Jean got home his papa met him at the door and said, "Ti Jean, did you knock that outhouse into the bayou?"

"Papa," the boy answered, "like George Washington, I cannot tell a lie. I did it."

"Ti Jean, come with me to the woodshed. You are going to get the whipping of your life!"

Ti Jean looked up at his father and said, "Papa, when George Washington told his papa that he had chopped down the cherry tree, his papa didn't give him a whipping."

"*Mais no* (French, "But no"), Ti Jean, but George Washington's papa wasn't in that cherry tree when he cut it down, either."

BOUDREAUX AND THE COTTONMOUTH

Tradition Bearer: Lisa Smalley

Source: Personal communication

Date: 1985

Original Source: Louisiana

National Origin: Cajun

The **stock character** of "Cajun" in jokes, as folklorist Barry Jean Ancelet has pointed out, can speak neither English nor French, is incapable of being educated, and is rural and stubborn. Boudreaux is far and away the supreme stock Cajun who can be a wily **trickster** or an impregnable **numskull**. In contemporary intra-group narratives, however, Boudreaux's foolishness is intended to attack the stereotype rather than the stereotyped.

Boudreaux tell this story 'bout when he been fishin' down at da bayou one night and he done run outta bait. He got ready bout to leave when he seen a big snake with a frog in his mouth, so he decide to steal dat frog from de snake.

Dat snake, he be a cottonmouth water moccasin, so he have to be real careful not to git bit. He sneak up behind dat snake and grab him round da neck. Dat snake squirm and twist tryin' to git loose from Boudreaux, and he don't let go of dat frog. No.

Now, Boudreaux need dat frog, so reach into his back pocket and pull out a little bottle of whiskey he keep in there. Den he pour a little bit o' dat whiskey in da corner o' dat snake's mouth just to make him relax a little bit.

Da snake swallow down dat whiskey and turn loose of dat frog. Boudreaux take da frog outta da snake's mouth and let da cottonmouth loose and he swim away slow and happy. Den, he put the frog on his hood and goes back to fishin'.

In a few minutes, Boudreaux hear a splashing down in the water by him and feel somethin' bumpin' against his leg. He look down, and what you t'ink he see?

It dat water moccasin an' he lookin' up at Boudreaux and got another frog in his mouth.

CAJUN COCKFIGHT

Tradition Bearer: Unavailable

Source: Personal communication

Date: 2001

Original Source: Louisiana
National Origin: Cajun

The following joke puts together two regional stereotypes: the Aggies (students and graduates of Texas A&M University who are commonly cast in the **numskull** role in the South and Southwestern regions) and the Cajuns, who (as noted in the introduction to "Boudreaux and the Cottonmouth," p. 119) have been similarly stereotyped. In this contemporary **trickster** tale, however, the Aggies, the Cajun bettors, and (one can assume) a Cajun detective turn the tables on detractors with the aid of the Mafia.

The Louisiana State Police received reports of illegal cock fights being held in the area around Lafayette, and duly dispatched the infamous Detective Desormeaux to investigate. Desormeaux reported to his sergeant the next morning.

"Dey is t'ree main groups in dis cock fightin'," Desormeaux began.

"Good work Desormeaux! Who are they?" the sergeant asked.

Desormeaux replied confidently, "De Aggies, de Cajuns, and de Mafia."

Puzzled, the sergeant asked, "How did you find that out in one night?"

"Well," said Desormeaux, "I went down and done seed dat cock fight, I knowed de Aggies was involved when a duck was entered in de fight."

The sergeant nodded. "Ok, I'll buy that, but what about the others?"

Desormeaux intoned knowingly, "Well, I knowed de Cajuns was involved when somebody bet on de duck."

"Ah," sighed the sergeant. "And how did you deduce that the Mafia was involved?"

"De duck won."

'COON IN THE BOX

Tradition Bearer: Unavailable

Source: Fauset, Arthur Huff. "Negro Folk Tales from the South (Alabama, Mississippi, Louisiana)." *Journal of American Folklore* 40 (1927): 265–66

Date: 1925

Original Source: Mississippi

National Origin: African American

In this classic example of the John and Master cycle, Jack uses his repertoire of eavesdropping, wit, and even sham fortune telling to advance and maintain his position with Master. When at last he believes his subterfuge has been found out, he significantly saves the day by his use of a racist and derogatory term for African American; thus, from weakness and apparent denigration yet another advantage emerges. The tale is commonly found as an episode of "Dr. Know-All" (AT 1641; the **motif** is N688).

White man had a slave; his name was Jack. This slave let on he knew everything. Wasn't a thing he didn't let on he knew. Every night this man would talk to his wife. He'd say, "Y'know Jack, he's a smart slave, smartest slave I ever knew." One night he was talkin' to his wife, and Jack he was eavesdroppin'. Man says, "Y'know, wife, the slaves are about done in de bottoms, I think I'll send 'em down to de new lands."

So nex' day he goes to Jack an' says, "Oh, Jack."

Jack says, "Yassir, master."

"What's on fo' t'day."

Jack says, "Well de slaves done pretty good in de bottoms, t'morrer y' goin' send us to de new lands."

So de master said to his wife, "Y'know, dat's a smart slave. I asked him today what I was gonna do, an' he tol' me jus' what I tol' you las' night. Said slaves done so good in de bottoms gonna send 'em to de new lands."

So nex' mornin' Master said to Jack, "Say, Jack, hitch up fifteen or sixteen wagons, I'm gonna send 'em to de grocery."

So Jack said, "Yassir, master, I know 'xactly what you want."

So de man said to his wife, "You know dat slave's a fortune teller." So dey goes to town, an' in town de master meets another plantation owner. So dis man had a barrel an' dere was a 'coon in dat barrel.

So Jack's master said, "Say, I bet you I kin tell you 'xactly what's in dat barrel."

De other man says, "Whut you bet?"

So de master says, "Le's bet my plantation 'gainst yours." So de other plantation owner says, "All right, my plantation 'gainst yours. Now whut's in de barrel?"

So de master says to Jack, "Come here, Jack."

Jack says, "Whut you want, master?"

Master says, "Y'got t' tell me whut's in dis man's barrel."

Jack says, "I got t' tell you whut's in dis here barrel?"

De master says, "Yes, or you're a dead man."

So Jack commenced scratchin' his head. He says, "Off it right now, cause he's wool gatherin'."

So he couldn't guess whut was in de barrel. He says to his master, "Send to town an' git me twelve deck o' cards." Dey got him de cards. He tore open a deck. He wanted to whisper. He tear open another deck. He wanted to whisper.

Den he says, "Aha, master, git me another twelve decks." So he wanted to whisper. He tore open one deck after de other.

Den he say, "Well, oh, sen' git me twelve mo'." So he looked through eleven decks, den he fell back against a tree an said, "Well, oh master," an' he shook his head, "y' caught de 'coon [derogatory term for African American] at las'."

De master won de bet an' he said to de other plantation owner, "I tol' you he could do it, I tol' you he could do it."

Ol' Jack he ups an' says, "I could ha' tell you when I fust cooked up here, but I only wanted to have some fun. I know dat was a racoon in dat barrel."

THE BUCK FIGHT

Tradition Bearer: Allen Chesser

Source: Harper, Francis. "Tales of the Okefinoke." *American Speech* 1 (1926): 414–15.

Date: ca. 1914

Original Source: Georgia

National Origin: European American

During the mating season, bucks (male deer) fight for territory and mating rights to does (female deer) by clashing antlers in the fashion described in this **personal experience narrative**. Injuries to the deer are rare, but such accounts often provide raw material for **tall tales**.

Few hunters are so fortunate as to witness the sort of affair that Allen Chesser here describes.

"I seen two of buck hitch an' fight one time, to see which one wuz the best man. I wuz in gunshot of 'em at the time. I wuz a-huntin' on Black Jack Island and it wuz soon one mornin'. I got up in gunshot of one buck. He raised 'is head up an' looked down the swamp, an' I knowed 'e seen somethin'. There wuz another buck, he'd come out an' wuz a-watchin' this un. This un wuz standin right still. I knowed 'e couldn't git away without my shootin' of 'im, an' I thought I'd watch an' wait.

"Wal, when 'e started, he come right on out. An' I soon saw he didn't see me. He wuz lookin' right at the other one. He come up within, I reckon, ten or fifteen steps of the other one, an' 'e stopped again. The other hadn't moved. He stood right there with 'is head raised up an' 'is horns a-glitterin' They stood still, I reckon, fer as much as a minute. All at once, that un that had come out of that point, begun to circle. Started 'is circle right around 'im. Went aroun', I expec', two or three times, an' ev'ry circle he'd come in closeter.

"An' 'e got 'is circle out, the last circle he made aroun'. I suppose he wuz within five or six yards. His hair wuz jest turned the wrong way, bristled back An' 'e got right in front of 'im, an' made a dash *jest like that,* an' the other one, he catched 'im. I thought I'd see a big scuffle, but I didn't. It happened so quick I couldn't tell, but one whipped, an' I don't know which one it wuz. But there wuz a poppin' of horns. The one that run, he done some runnin', too. He got away from that place.

"The one that wuz left, he stood there lookin' after 'im, *jest thataway.* An' I got 'im to tannin'. I put a ball right through 'im. He run, I reckon, fifteen or twenty steps, an' tumbled right over.

"That happened on Black Jack Island, on a point that's called Bee Tree Point, about, I reckon, three an' a half miles from the east end."

A SIGHT OF ALLIGATORS

Tradition Bearer: Allen Chesser

Source: Harper, Francis. "Tales of the Okefinoke." *American Speech* 1 (1926): 417–18.

Date: ca. 1914

Original Source: Georgia

National Origin: European American

"A Sight of Alligators" is another **personal experience narrative** that borders on the **tall tale genre**. Note the **validating devices** included, such as a willingness to admit that the story is unbelievable and calling on an eyewitness to the events.

On the following day our talk was still of reptiles, and particularly of one whose size and habits lend it distinction above all others of the swamp. There is also a melancholy interest in the present story, for such a sight as Allen Chesser here describes, harking back to days of long ago, will never again be witnessed in our day. Years before I knew him, other life-long residents of the swamp had told me how it used to seem, at times, as if one could walk across an Okefinokee lake on Gator backs. So the abundance reported here is readily comprehensible; it was before the days when hide-hunters had so greatly reduced the ranks of this interesting saurian. Later in the season I visited the exact scene of the story, and saw how accurately the spot had been described.

Even within the past ten years or so, during a single night Allen Chesser and a companion killed fifty-eight Alligators on Buzzard Roost Lake, which is scarcely a quarter of a mile in its greatest diameter.

"Now I want to tell you about a sight of Alligators I seed one time. I'm satisfied there ain't many people willin' to believe such a story as that, but it's true.

"That occurred at the Buzzard Roost Lake. Here the lake [scratching a diagram on the ground], an' here's a little run goes out about thirty yards broad. An' right here at the en' is a little round lake. These Alligators, I suppose, they must 'a' driv' all the fish out of this big lake, an' down this road [the outlet]. It was in between daylight an' sunrise. I heerd the racket before I got there. Me an' my brother Sam was together.

"I reckon there was five er six hunderd birds aroun' the edge of that lake scoggins (herons), blue an' white uns, an' all kinds.

"We heerd the racket, an' moved on cautiously. We didn't know whut it meant, but we could hear the water jest a-churnin'. Our business was to go a-huntin' on Number One Island, an' that was the only way we could go. We got in sight, an' there was a sight to look at. I never seed such a sight before in my life.

"The birds, Preachers, they're a powerful shy bird. They cared nothin' a-tall fer us. Run our boat right in the edge of the lake. The Alligators cared nothin' fer us. There must 'a' been three hunderd uv 'em. They'd catch fish that long

125

[indicating about a foot and a half]. Ef they'd catch a perch, you'd hear 'im flut-terin' in their *mouth-thrrr,* jest like a-that. An' the funny part, there'd be a Gator sometimes that high [indicating about a yard] out of the water an' ernother un on to 'is tail. He'd think it was a fish.

"When he'd catch a fish, jest stick 'is head up *thataway,* an' ernother un tryin' to git it away from 'im. They'd go right under our boat. Wouldn' pay no attention to us. We stayed there till the sun was about an hour high.

"We fell to shootin', an' it was either fourteen or sixteen we killed before they took any notice a-tall. An' when they did take a notion to git away, there was a sight to look at when they commenced smellin' the blood. They started down that road. They was that thick, I could 'a' walked down that road on Gator heads. My brother up yonder'll identify to it. It's true.

"We went on then; they give us space. The scoggins, when the Gators begun to leave, they lef' too. They was there from Salt-water Cranes right down to lit-tle fellers. They picked up the fish aroun' the edge. Them Gators had the little fish run out, an' they'd lodge aroun' the edge.

"Whenever one Gator 'u'd freeze on to ernother un's tail, it was a sight. He'd jump plumb out of the water.

"Ev'rything was agitated that mornin', the birds an' the Alligators, an' even I was amused.

"There must 'a' been five hunderd of the birds. Even the Injun Pullet (green heron) was there, a-gittin' his mess."

LIES TOO FAR APART

Tradition Bearer: Unavailable

Source: Fauset, Arthur Huff. "Negro Folk Tales from the South (Alabama, Mississippi, Louisiana)." *Journal of American Folklore* 40 (1927): 266.

Date: 1925

Original Source: Alabama

National Origin: African American

In this John and Master tale, the slave is again demonstrated to be supe-rior to the master. "Jack" rescues "Marster" by manufacturing, on the spot, a scenario to fit the latter's implausible lie. The bondsman then takes the liberty of admonishing his owner to learn to lie better in the future.

A fellow had his lady along with him n' they all went together. They prove everything by Jack.

So this fellow said to the crowd, "Today I shot a deer through the foot an' head all at the same time an' killed it, didn't I do that, Jack?"

So they asked Jack to explain how that happened. Jack scratched his head an' said, "Well, the deer was runnin' an' the hounds was chasin'. So the deer topped to listen t' see where the hound was an' just then put its foot up to its ear. That's when Marster shot him an' the bullet went through the foot an' through his head."

So when Jack an' the master was by themselves, Jack said. "Look here, Marster, I want you to get your damn lies closer together."

THE ARKANSAS SHAKES

Tradition Bearer: William D. Naylor

Source: Bowman, Earl. "Interview of William D. Naylor." *American Life Histories: Manuscripts from the Federal Writers' Project, 1936–1940.* Manuscript Division, Library of Congress. 12 October 2005. http://memory.loc.gov/ammem/wpaintro/wpahome.html.

Date: 1938

Original Source: William D. Naylor

National Origin: European American

Using a common theme for the **tall tale**, the narrator offers an exaggerated comment on the Arkansas environment through a tale describing a distinctive illness brought on by living in the state. The narrator introduces specific names and locations to establish his credibility.

Such validating devices coupled with the gradual introduction of exaggeration are the marks of the well-crafted **tall tale**.

One of Doc. Porter's most powerful and popular Kickapoo Indian medicines, that we used to sell when I was with his medicine show, was his "Chill and Ague Eliminator." It was put up in a square pint bottle and Doc guaranteed that two bottles would drive out the worst case of chills on the market. Whether it would or not I don't know. But I do know it was mighty potent and...bitter.

I think it was probably a straight "emulsion" of quinine and whiskey and the directions told the "patient" to take enough of it before his chill started to make him go to sleep.

Doc's theory was, no doubt, that if a person about to have a chill could be gotten drunk enough to go to sleep he'd sleep through his chill period and if he did have one in his sleep, he'd never know he had it when he waked up and naturally think he had missed it entirely and was cured!

Doc's medicine was strong but it wouldn't have worked on the kind of chills people got down in the Ozark country of Arkansas, South Missouri and over in the Indian Territory where I spent a lot of time in the carnival business and exhibiting "dancing turkeys" and other things at country fairs.

Down in that country people didn't call chills and ague, "chills and ague" they called it the "shakes." And that was the right name. For when a man with the "shakes" started to shake, he shook! He couldn't stop shaking till the chill was over.

There were two kinds, the "every-other-day shakes," and the "every-day shakes." I had both kinds. They started on me as the every-other-day kind and after a week or two turned into the every-day kind, then switched back and forth that way, first one sort and then the other till I finally got rid of them.

The "shakes" were so common in the Ozark country along back in the 1890s, about the time the Star [Gang?] was being busted up in the Indian Territory and Al [Jennings?] was holding up the M. K. & T. trains, that practically everybody would have them some time or other.

And people would talk about their "shakes" with a sort of pride, something like a lot of people like to talk in these later days of their "operations" after they've been to the hospital and had something cut out. The harder a man shook when he had the "shakes" the prouder he seemed to be!

That vanity of affliction, you might say, brought about one of the queerest contests that was ever pulled off, I suppose. To me, and I saw it, it had frog-jump-ing matches, horn toad races, cock-roach fights, and all that stuff beaten a mile.

It was out in the Arkansas River bottomlands country not far from Van Buren, during the fall of 1897 or 1896, if I remember right. Anyhow, I know it was in the fall for two reasons, first because the fall was when people had most of their shakes, and the pecans were ripe. Pecans, you know grow naturally on the river bottomlands down in that country and the harvest of nuts adds quite a bit to the incomes of the natives who shake them down out of the trees and sell them.

There were a couple of brothers-in-law, had married sisters, who lived on adjoining farms and like is sometimes the case among country people they suffered from a sort of mutual jealousy. Their names were Toliver Green and Hank Breckenridge. Each thought his hound dogs were better than the other's hound dogs, that his hogs grew faster and fatter, his cow gave more milk, his mule could kick harder, or he could shoot a squirrel out of a taller tree with a single ball rifle, or excel in some other way—and the result was a continual boasting when together.

They both happened to get the shakes at the same time and it happened too, that their chills ran on the same hourly schedule and would hit them at about the same time each day.

Toliver Green vowed that the chills he had were the hardest chills any man in Arkansas ever had or ever could have; Breckenridge had the same opinion and made the same boast about his own shakes.

The result was that they agreed to match "shakes" and Green challenged Breckenridge to shake it out in a pecan tree!

Each was to climb a pecan tree just as his chill was about due to start and see which shook the tree cleanest of pecans before it was over.

The shaking match took place in Toliver Green's pasture in the Arkansas River bottoms. It was well advertised and a big crowd of natives came to see it. An old Justice of the Peace (I don't recall his name) was to judge the contest.

Although it was my chill day too, I went out to see it, and it was one of the queerest contests I ever witnessed.

Green and Breckenridge picked out a couple of good tall pecan trees; each climbed his tree, straddled a limb, wrapped his legs around the trunk of the tree and started to shake...and after each started he couldn't stop till his chill had run its course.

Well, at first those darned pecans began to sort of dribble down out of the trees, like slow rain or hail, then as the chills got to work in earnest and speeded up Green and Breckenridge's shakes the pecans were coming down in a regular machine-gun tattoo as they hit the ground.

129

It lasted for an hour and then each climbed down...and there wasn't a pecan left an either tree! So, the old Justice of the Peace declared it a draw...and that's they way it ended. It was kind of funny seeing those two leather-[cheeked?] farmers up in those pecan trees with the "shakes," the pecans raining down on the ground...I was sort of glad Doc Porter's "Eliminator" wasn't too all-fired potent—in Arkansas.

VOICES IN THE FRYING PAN

Tradition Bearer: Unavailable

Source: Fauset, Arthur Huff. "Negro Folk Tales from the South (Alabama, Mississippi, Louisiana)." *Journal of American Folklore* 40 (1927): 261.

Date: 1925

Original Source: Mississippi

National Origin: African American

This **tall tale** (AT 1889F, "Frozen Words"), masquerading at first as a **personal experience narrative**, contrasts the narrator's native region, the South, with the region "far up north." The residents of the North are characterized as speaking an incomprehensible language, and the climate is indicated as being so cold that words freeze on being uttered.

I have been so far up north until I couldn't understand anything anybody said. I got a gang of fryin' pans an' everybody I would meet I would hold it in front of them an' ketch their voices. The voices froze in the fryin' pan an' said, "Good morning."

THE BENT GUN

Tradition Bearer: John Campbell

Source: Carter, Isabel Gordon. "Mountain White Folk-Lore: Tales from the Southern Blue Ridge." *Journal of American Folklore* 38 (1925): 374.

Date: 1923

Original Source: Tennessee

National Origin: European American

According to the narrator, this **tall tale** ("Gun Barrel Bent to Make Spectacular Shot,"AT1890E and **motif** X1122.3.1) is typical of those performed among men as they sat around seeing "who could tell the biggest [lie]." Hunting in this community and during this time period was not only a supplement to farming but a means of establishing status among one's peers by demonstrating woodcraft. The bent gun used to shoot around corners, trees, or, as in this case, mountains is a common **tall tale motif**.

There was a man use to hunt on a little old round mountain and they was a deer there and jest couldn't git it. He chase it and chase and it 'ud go round and round the mountain and he couldn't git clost enough to hit it. So he went on home and made the barrel of his gun jest to the curve of the mountain and he went on back to where he could see the deer and then he fired and after a while here come the deer jest a splittin' past him and then he heard the bullet jest a whistling after the deer and they went round that little old mountain two or three times that away, but after a while the bullet ketched up to the deer and kill it and he took it on home.

THE MARVELOUS POTATO

Tradition Bearer: Unavailable

Source: Fauset, Arthur Huff. "Negro Folk Tales from the South (Alabama, Mississippi, Louisiana)." *Journal of American Folklore* 40 (1927): 260.

Date: 1925

Original Source: Alabama

National Origin: African American

Tall tales often focus on the environment: its rigors, unique qualities, or bounty. Such is the case the following narrative of soil rich enough to produce a gargantuan potato. As with many of the tales of this type, it is introduced as a **personal experience narrative** in order to encourage initial belief until the borders of credibility snap with the discovery of a trail leading into the tuber. Variants of the narrative (AT 1860D, "The Marvelous Vegetable") are distributed internationally.

My daddy growed potatoes once an' he had one that was so big he said "Mama, go out an' see the potato." So they got plowin' up around tha potato, they took two mules an' run up to dat potato. It was rough on the mules. So they got a big whup to whup those mules.

They thought it might be a root. No, it wasn't no root. They kept on an kept on. Pretty soon they found a trail. There was a hole in the groun'.

Then they come to some pig tracks. They was another hole an' they wa: hogs up there in that hole way up in that tater. Them hogs wouldn't never ge' hungry. It was a sow an' twenty-four pigs.

THE KING AND OLD GEORGE BUCHANAN

Tradition Bearer: Susie Wilkenson

Source: Carter, Isabel Gordon. "Mountain White Folk-Lore: Tales from the Southern Blue Ridge." *Journal of American Folklore* 38 (1925): 370–71.

Date: 1923

Original Source: Tennessee

National Origin: Anglo American

The historical George Buchanan (1506–1582) was a man of letters: a poet, politician, and tutor to James VI of Scotland. Buchanan was a notorious social critic of high Catholic officials and Mary Queen of Scots, as well as an early supporter of the Reformation. The **anecdotes** of Buchanan that captured the folk imagination, however, are more likely to have circulated orally and to have been influenced by "The Witty and Entertaining Exploits of George Buchanan, Commonly Called the King's Fool," which is found in an original London manuscript dated 1725 and another British edition probably printed in 1850. There is also "The Witty Exploits of Mr. George Buchanan, the King's Fool," included in Sir George Douglas' 1901 *Scottish Fairy and Folktales* published in the United States. In both his folk and official biographies, however, George Buchanan gains fame for exposing and defeating folly by recourse to wit.

In olden times they was a king (jest a king of the United States, I reckon— that's jest the way they told hit) and they was old George Buchanan, he was called the king's fool, and he didn't like the way the king made the rules. The king made a law that anyone come in and asked him to pardon 'em he'd pardon 'em and not law 'em. George Buchanan didn't like this law, so he kept a doin' things and then askin' the king to pardon him. Finally at last he come in and told the king to pardon him fer knockin' a man's hat off the bridge and the king did and then George said, "His head was in hit." But the king had done pardoned him and couldn't do nothing. The king told him he'd behead him if he didn't come to the king's house to-morrow at noon, "Clothed and onclothed, riding and walking." So George tore one breech leg, one shoe and one sock, one half his shirt. He bridled his old ram sheep and put a saddle on hit and throwed one leg over hit and time of day come he went hoppin' up to the king's door. So the king says, "I thought I told you to come clothed and onclothed and a ridin' and a walkin' both."

"I did, sir," says George. "Part of me's clothed, part of me's onclothed, one of my legs rode and one walked."

So the king took him to be his fool but before he took him he went to George's house; wasn't anyone there but George's sister who was in back room. King says, "Where's your mammy?" and George says, "She took some honey to go to town to buy some sweetenin'." (Took some honey and went to git some sugar.) He headed the king that way.

"Where's your poppy?"

"He's gone to the woods. What he kills he'll throw away and what he don't kill he'll bring back." (He uz picking off lice.)

"What's your sister doin'?"

"She's in the back room mournin' fer what she did last year." (She uz hav ing a baby.) You see George headed (out-witted) the king every time.

So George, he was called the king's fool. So he tried to do one thing and another to make the king make good laws. The king had a law that a man could burn his own house down anytime he had a mind to. So George built a house next to the king's and filled hit with shavin's. King says, "George, what er you doin'?"

George says, "I'm fixin' to burn my house."

King says, "George, you can't do that, hit'll ketch my house."

George says, "Hit's the law."

So king says, "If you won't burn hit I'll pay you a good price."

George says, "All right, if you make a law that you can't burn a house without you tear hit down and pile hit up." That's the law now.

The king keep a pardonin' George fer things he'd do, and after awhile he told him that whatever George wished he could have. So George wished to be the king and the king his fool. So the king says, "George, you headed me all the time, now you got my seat." So George sat up there a while and then give hit back to the king if the king 'ud promise not to grant nothing until he seed what he was a grantin'. So the king told him, "Now, George, you leave here and don't you show yourself on Scotland land anymore." So George he left and put England dirt in the bottom of his shoes and got England dirt and put in his hat and he come where they was havin' court, and the king said, "Fetch him here I told him I'd behead him if he ever stood on Scotland land anymore." And they went and fetched him and he says, "I'm standing on England land and livin under England land." So he headed the king agin. And the king never could head George and George never would let the king make no bad laws.

JACK AND THE BEANSTALK

Tradition Bearer: Jane Gentry

Source: Carter, Isabel Gordon. "Mountain White Folk-Lore: Tales from the Southern Blue Ridge." *Journal of American Folklore* 38 (1925): 365–66.

Date: 1923

Original Source: North Carolina

National Origin: European American

In this version of "The Boy Steals the Giant's Treasure" (AT 328), best known in English-speaking tradition as "Jack and the Beanstalk," the protagonist is not the victim of an apparently foolish trade. Instead, an abusive grandmother sets the plot into action. As with the other European tales adopted into the repertoires of the southern highlands, the circumstances of the tale are localized to an American rural setting rather than the vaguely medieval one of European variants.

Once there was a little boy and he didn't have no mother or no father and his grandmother was a raising him and she 'uz awfully mean to him. So she whipped him one morning and she whipped him awfully hard and he was cryin'. So she was sweepin' the house and she swept up a bean and she says, "Here, take this bean and go out and plant hit and make you a bean tree." He went out and planted hit and he played around all day and was very good after that.

So next morning he got up and ran out early to see about his bean tree and hit had growed to the top of the house. So he run and said, "Grandmother, my bean tree is as high as the house." So she slapped his face and said, "Go on out of here, you know hit's not up yet." When she went out, sure enough hit was high as the house. So hit made her kind a sorry and she give him a piece of bread and butter.

So next morning he jumped up and ran out and says, "Granny, my bean tree's as high as the sky." So she slapped him again and says, "Son, don't come in here telling such lies as that, you know hits not as high as the sky." So after a while when she got thru cleanin' up she went out and sure enough hit did look like the bean tree had growed up thru the sky. So Jack played around all that day and looked at his bean tree and next day he decided he'd climb hit.

So he started and he told his grandmother, "I'll hack you off a mess of beans as I go up." So he clumb and clumb and throwed her down the beans. After a while he come to a big field. So he got out and got to wandering around in that field and he saw a house.

So he went to this house and then he saw the old giant's wife was a sittin' thar and she says, "Law, little boy, what you doin' here? Don't you know the giant will be in directly?"

"Oh, hide me, do please hide me," says Jack. And after a while she hid him under the bed. So directly the old giant come in and says, "Fi fo fiddledy fun, I smell the blood of an Englishman. Dead or alive I'll have his bones to eat with my bread and butter."

His wife says, "Aw now, Poppy, don't talk that way, that was just a little old boy that was here this evenin' and he's gone now." So the giant et his supper and Jack lay there under the bed and he looked out at the giant's boots and a gun. Fastened to the bed cords they was the prettiest china bells. So he wanted the china bells and he wanted the boots and he wanted the giant's gun. So he laid there 'til they was all asleepin' and he eased out and got the giant's gun and down the bean stalk he went.

So he laid around all next day, he rested and next morning he started to climb the bean stalk again. So he clumb back up the field and went back to the giant's house. "Law, Jack, what you come back for? The giant thinks you stole his gun and he'll sure eat you up."

"No, no, he won't, jest let me crawl under the bed one more night." So she let him crawl under the bed. So the old giant come in says, "Fi fo fiddledy fun, I smell the blood of an Englishman. Dead or alive I'll have his bones to eat with my bread and butter."

"Aw, Poppy, don't talk that way, hit's jest that little old poor boy comin' back here everyday." So Jack, he laid there and studied what he'd get next, so way in the night he got out and got the giant's boots and went down the bean tree. So after he got down he laid around two or three days, but he wanted them bells so he decided he'd go again.

So he clumb up the bean tree and went to the giant's house and when the giant's wife saw him she says, "Law, Jack, the giant's awfully mad at you, he thinks you stole his boots. You better go way before he ketches you."

"Aw, he wont ketch me, jest let me come in one more time." So he crawled under the bed. So the giant come home and says, "Fi fo fiddledy fun, I smell the blood of an Englishman. Dead or alive I'll have his bones to eat with my bread and butter."

"Law now, Poppy," says his wife, "that little old boy's been here but he ain't comin' back again." So Jack laid there under the bed and he begun untying the bells and every now and then one ud make a noise and the old giant ud say, "Fi fo fiddledy fun, I smell the blood of an Englishman. Dead or alive I'll have his bones to eat with my bread and butter." Then another bell ud go "dingle" and he'd say, "Fi fo fiddledy fun, I smell the blood of an Englishman. Dead or alive I'll have his bones to eat with my bread and butter." So finally at last Jack, he got 'em all untied from the bed cords and got 'em down. And he started out for the bean stalk and they begun to go "dingle." And the giant says, "Fi fo fiddledy fun, I smell the blood of an Englishman. Dead or alive I'll have his bones to eat with my bread and butter." And took out after Jack. And when they got to the bean stalk, Jack clumb down and then he looked up and here come the giant right after him. And Jack hollers, "Give me a hand ax, granny, give me a hand ax." And he begun to hack and hack and down come the bean tree and down come the giant too.

OLD BLUEBEARD

Variant A: Old Bluebeard

Tradition Bearer: Jane Gentry

Source: Carter, Isabel Gordon. "Mountain White Folk-Lore: Tales from the Southern Blue Ridge." *Journal of American Folklore* 38 (1925): 341–43.

Date: 1923

Original Source: North Carolina

National Origin: Anglo American

Although the following narrative—with its relatively complex plot, monstrous antagonist, and descent into a magical realm—resembles the European *märchen*, its setting, characters, and occupations are localized to the rural southern highlands of the United States. Featuring the exploits of a clever hero Jack, who is often the youngest of three brothers, the tale is one of a widely distributed cycle derived from European models. Jack, unlike his brothers, offers hospitality to the ogre, and this may be the reason for his successes in the tale. Despite the name differences—Variant A, "Old Bluebeard," and Variant B, "Jack and the Fire Dragaman"—there seems to be no difference between attributes and behavior of the antagonists in the two narratives.

One time they was an old man and woman had three sons, Jack, Will and Tom. Will was the oldest one, Tom he was next and Jack was the least one. The old woman and the old man died and left Jack, Will and Tom to look after the place. They was workin' away over in the field and each took his time goin' to git dinner. Tom, he was the oldest, was first and he tried to see what a good dinner he could git up. He hung the meat up afore the fire to boil and he fixed some turnips and some potatoes and fixed everything nice for his brothers and when hit was ready he went out to blow the horn—they didn't have no dinner bell in them days—and when he blowed the horn down the holler he saw an old man comin' with his beard as blue as indigo, his teeth as long as pipe stems and his thumbs tucked behind him.

And the man says, "Have ye anything to eat?"

Will says, "No," cuz he didn't want the old man to come in and eat up the nice dinner he'd fixed up for his brothers.

Old Bluebeard says, "Well, I'll see about hit!" And he went in and eat up everything Will had cooked up. And Will had to fly around and fix up something for his brothers. He fixed up what he could, but he couldn't fix much cuz he didn't have time. Then he went out and blowed down the holler and when his brothers come in they says, "What in the world took you so long to fix up such a shabby dinner?"

And Will says, "Well, I fixed ye up a good dinner, but when I went out to blow for ye to come in an old man come up the holler with his beard as blue as indigo, his teeth as long as pipe stems and his thumbs tucked behind him and he walked in and ate up everything I'd fixed. So I had to fly around and fix you something else."

Tom says, "Well, I knowed he wouldn't have eat it all up if I'd been here."

Will says, "All right tomorrow is your day and we'll see what he does to you." So next morning Tom put him on some meat to boil in front the fire and when he come in from the new ground he got him some turnips and potatoes and pumpkin and baked him some bread and fixed him up a good dinner. And when he went out to blow the horn he saw an old man comin' up the holler with his beard as blue as indigo, his teeth as long as pipe stems and his thumbs tucked behind him and he said, "Have ye anything to eat?"

And Tom says, "No."

Old Blue-beard says, "Well, we'll see about that." And he went in and eat up everything Tom had fixed except jest a little bit of pumpkin. And Tom had to fly around and git up something for his brothers and when they come in Jack says, "Why didn't you keep him from eatin' hit up?"

Tom says, "Tomorrow is your time to git dinner and see if you can keep him from hit."

And Jack says, "Bedad, I will."

So next day Jack put him some meat to boil in the fireplace and got some turnips and potatoes and fixed 'em and when he went out to blow the horn for his brothers to come in, Old Bluebeard was a comin' up the holler with his beard as blue as indigo, his teeth as long as pipe stems and his thumbs tucked behind him. Jack says, "Now, uncle, you jest come in and have something to eat."

Old Bluebeard says, "No, I don't want anything."

Jack says, "Yes, but you must come in and have dinner with us."

Old Bluebeard says, "No, I don't want to," and he took around the house and took out down the holler. Jack took out down the holler after him and saw him git down a den—a hole in the ground—and when the brothers come home and Jack was gone they thought Old Bluebeard had eat Jack up 'stead of his dinner but after a while Jack come in and they says, "Jack, where you bin?"

Jack says, "I been watchin' Old Bluebeard, watchin' where he went to, and I watched him go down a hole in the ground and I'm goin' to foller him." So Jack took a big old bushel basket out and put a strop on hit and him and his brothers went to Old Bluebeard's hole. Will says he was a-goin' down. Jack says, "We'll take turns. Will, go first." So Will he climbed in the basket and they let him down in the hole and when he shuck the rope they pulled him up and asked him what he found. Will says, "Well, I went until I saw a house and then I shuck the rope."

"Oh pshaw, Will, what did you shake the rope then fer? Why didn't you find out what was in the house?"

Will says, "Well, you go in and find out."

Tom says, "All right I will." So he clumb in the basket and went down 'til he was on top the house and then he shuck the rope and they pulled him up. When he told 'em he shuck the rope when he was on top of the house, Jack says, "You're nary one no account but me." So he went down and looked in the room and there sat the prettiest woman he ever saw in his life. And Jack says, "Oh! You're the prettiest woman I ever saw in my life and you're goin' to be my wife."

"No," she said, "Old Bluebeard will git you. You better git out of here."

"Oh no, he won't," says Jack. "He's a good friend of mine and I'm goin' to take you up and marry you."

"No," she said, "you wait 'til you get down to the next house. You won't think nothin' of me when you see her." So Jack put her in the basket and shuck the rope. And when she come out, Will says, "Oh! You're the prettiest woman I ever saw in my life!" and Tom said, "Oh! You're the prettiest woman I ever saw in my life."

Jack went on down to the next house and looked in and there the prettiest woman he ever did see, the other wasn't nothing along side this one. Jack says,

"You're prettiest woman I ever saw and you're goin' to be my wife. My brothers can have the other one but I'm goin' to have you."

She says, "Oh no, Jack, when you go down to the other house you won't think nothin' of me."

"Yes, I will too," says Jack. "You jest come git in this basket." So he put her in the basket and shuck the rope. Then he went down to the next house and there was the prettiest woman. Jack says, "Oh! You're jest the prettiest woman I ever did see and you're goin' to be my wife. My brother's kin have the other two but you're goin' to be my wife. Come git in this basket." But afore she was pulled up she give him a red ribbon and told him to plait it in her hair so he'd know her when she come out and she give him a wishin' ring. Jack put her in the basket and shuck the rope. When the brothers saw her they stopped talkin' to the other two and fell in love with her right away. Tom says, "You're goin' to be my wife,"

Will says, "No, she's goin' to be mine." And they started fight-in'.

She says, "I won't have nary one. I'm goin' to marry Jack."

They said, "No, you won't fer we'll leave Jack down there." So they pulled up the basket and they commenced to fight and left Jack down there.

Jack jest sit there and Old Bluebeard come in and walked around but he didn't give Jack nothin' to eat. Jack jest sit there and after a while he turned the ring on his finger seein' how he'd fell away and said, "I wish I was in my old corner beside the fire smokin' my old chunky pipe."

And there he was and there was the woman with red ribbon plaited in her hair and she said, "Oh Jack!"

And they was married and they uz rich when I left there.

Variant B: Jack and the Fire Dragaman

Tradition Bearer: Monroe Ward and Miles Ward

Source: Chase, Richard. "Jack and the Fire Dragaman." *The Southern Folklore Quarterly* 5 (1941): 151–55.

Date: 1941

Original Source: North Carolina

National Origin: European American

Well, hit's said that one time Jack and his two brothers, Will and Tom, wuz a-layin' around home; wuzn't none of 'em doin' no good, so their daddy decided he'd set 'em to work. He had him a tract of land out in a wilderness of a place back up on the mountain. Told the boys they could go up there and work it. Said he'd give it to 'em. It wuz a right far ways from where anybody lived at, so they fixed 'em up a wagon load of rations and stuff for housekeepin' and pulled out.

There wuzn't no house up there, so they cut poles and notched 'em up a shack. They had to go to work in a hurry to git out any crop and they set right in to clearin' 'em a new ground. They decided one boy'd have to stay to the house till twelve and do the cookin'.

First day Tom and Jack left Will there. Will went to fixin' around and got dinner ready, went out and blowed the horn to call Tom and Jack, looked down the holler and seed a giant a-comin'. Had him a pipe about four foot long, and his long old blue beard drug the ground.

When Will seed the old giant wuz headed right for the house, he run and got behind the door, pulled it back on him and scrouged back ag'inst the wall jest a-shakin' like a leaf. Old Bluebeard come on in the house, threwed the cloth back off the dishes, eat ever' bite on the table and sopped the plates. Went to the fire and lit his pipe; the smoke jest come a-bilin' out. Then he went on back down the holler.

Tom and Jack come on in directly, says, "Why in the world ain't ye got us no dinner, Will?"

"Law me!" says Will, "If you'd 'a seed what I seed, you'd a not thought about no dinner. Old Fire Dragaman come up here, eat ever' bite on the table, and sopped the plates."

Tom and Jack laughed right smart at Will. Will says, "You'uns needn't to laugh. Hit'll be your turn tomor', Tom."

So they fixed up what vittles they could and they all went back to work in the new ground.

Next day Tom got dinner, went out and blowed the horn. There come old Fire Dragaman.

"Law me!" says Tom, "Where'll I git?"

He run and scrambled under the bed. Old Fire Dragaman come on in, eat ever'thing on the table, sopped the plates, and licked out all the pots. Lit his old pipe and pulled out down the holler, the blot, smoke jest a-bilin' like smoke comin' out a chimley. Hit'uz a sight to look at.

Will and Jack come in, says, "Where's dinner at?"

"Dinner, the nation! Old Fire Dragaman come back up here. Law me! Hit'uz the beatenist thing I ever seed!"

Will says, "Where wuz you at, Tom?"

"Well I'll just tell ye," says Tom, "I'uz down under the bed."

Jack laughed, and Will and Tom says, "You jest wait about laughin', Jack. Hit'll be your time tomor'."

Next day Will and Tom went to the new ground. They got to laughin' about where Jack'd hide at when old Fire Dragaman come, Jack fixed up ever'thing for dinner, went out about twelve and blowed the horn. Looked down the wilderness, seed old Fire Dragaman a-comin'.

Jack went on back in the house, started puttin' stuff on the table. Never paid no attention to old Bluebeard, jest went right on a-fixin' dinner. Old Fire Dragaman come on in. Jack 'uz scoopin' up a mess of beans out the pot, says, "Why hello, daddy."

"Howdy, son."

"Come on in, daddy. Git you a chair. Dinner's about ready; jest stay and eat with us."

"No I thank ye. I couldn't stay."

"Hit's on the table. Come on set down."

"No. I jest stopped to light my pipe."

"Come on, daddy. Let's eat."

"No, much obliged. I got no time."

Old Fire Dragaman went to git him a coal of fire, got the biggest chunk in the fireplace, stuck it down in his old pipe and started on back. Jack took out and follered him with all the smoke a-bilin' out; watched where he went to, seed him go down a big straight hole in the ground.

Will and Tom come on to the house, seed Jack wuz gone. Will says, "I reckon that's the last of Jack. I bet ye a dollar old Fire Dragaman's done took him off and eat him. Dinner's still on the table."

So they set down and went to eatin'. Jack come on in directly. Will and Tom says, "Whare'n the world ye been, Jack? We allowed old Fire Dragaman had done eat ye up."

"I been watchin' where old Fire Dragaman went to."

"How come dinner still on the table?"

"I tried my best to git him to eat," says Jack; "He jest lit his old pipe and went on back. I follered him, seed him go in a big hole out yonder."

"You right sure ye ain't lyin', Jack?"

"Why no," says Jack. "You boys come with me and you kin see the place where he went in at. Let's us git a rope and basket so we kin go in that hole and see what's down there."

So they got 'em a big basket made out of splits, and gathered up a long rope they'd done made out of hickory bark, and Jack took 'em on down to old Fire Dragaman's den.

"Will, you the oldest," says Jack. "We'll let you go down first. If you see any danger, you shake the rope and we'll pull ye back up."

Will got in the basket, says: "You recollect now; whenever I shake that rope, you'uns pull me out in a hurry."

So they let him down. Directly the rope shook; they jerked the basket back out, says, "What'd ye see, Will?"

"Seed a big house."

Then they slapped Tom in the basket and let him down; rope shook; they hauled him up.

"What'd ye see, Tom?"

"Seed a house and the barn."

Then they got Jack in the basket, let him down. Jack got down on top of the house, let the basket slip down over the eaves, and right on down in the yard. Jack got out, went and knocked on the door. The prettiest girl Jack ever had seed come out. He started right in to courtin' her, says, "I'm goin' to git you out of here."

She says, "I got another sister in the next room yonder, prettier'n me. You git her out, too."

So Jack went on in the next room. That second girl wuz a heap prettier'n the first, and Jack went to talkin' to her and wuz a-courtin' right on. Said he'd git her out of that place.

She says, "I got another sister in the next room, prettier'n me. Don't ye want to git her out, too?"

So he went on in. Time Jack seed that 'un he knowed she 'uz the prettiest girl ever lived, so he started in right off talkin' courtin' talk to her; plumb forgot about them other two. That girl said to Jack, says, "Old Fire Dragaman'll be back here any minute now. Time he finds you here he'll start spittin' balls of fire."

So she went and opened up an old chest, took out a big sword and a box of ointment, says, "If one of them balls of fire hits ye, Jack, you rub on a little of this medicine right quick, and this here swords the only thing kin hurt old Fire Dragaman. You watch out now and kill him if ye kin."

Well, old Bluebeard come in the door directly, seed Jack, and commenced spittin' balls of fire around in there, some of 'em big as pumpkins. Jack he'uz jest a-dodgin' around tryin' to git at the old giant with that sword. Once in a while one of them fireballs would glance him but Jack rubbed on that ointment and it didn't even make a blister. Fin'lly Jack clipped him with that sword, took his head clean off.

Then Jack made that girl promise she'd marry him. So she took a red ribbon and got Jack to plait it in her hair. Then she give Jack a wishin' ring. He put it on his finger and they went on out and got them other two girls.

They wuz awful pleased. Told Jack they'uz such little bits of children when old Bluebeard ketched 'em they barely could recollect when they first come down there.

Well, Jack put the first one in the basket and shook the rope. Will and Tom hauled her up, and when they seed her they commenced fightin' right off to see which one would marry her. She told 'em, says, "I got another sister down there."

"Is she prettier'n you?" says Will. She says to him, says, "I ain't sayin'."

Will and Tom chunked the basket down in a hurry. Jack put the next girl in, shook the rope. Time Will and Tom seed her they both asked her to marry, and went to knockin' and beatin' one another over gittin' her. She stopped 'em, says, "We got one more sister down there."

"Is she prettier'n you?" says Will.

She says to him, says, "You kin see for yourself."

So they slammed the basket down, jerked that last girl out. "Law me!" says Will, "This here's the one I'm a-goin' to marry."

"Oh no you ain't!" Tom says; "you'll marry me, won't ye now?" "No," says the girl, "I've done promised to marry Jack."

"Blame Jack," says Will, "he kin jest stay in there," and he took the basket and rope, throwed 'em down the hole.

"There ain't nothin' much to eat down there," says the girl; "He'll starve to death."

"That's jest what we want him to do," says Will, and they took them girls on back up to the house.

Well, Jack eat ever'thing he could find down there, but in about three days he seed the rations wuz runnin' awful low. Then he scrapped up ever'thing there wuz left and he wuz plumb out of vittles didn't know what he would do.

In about a week Jack had commenced to git awful pore. Happened he looked at his hand, turned that ring to see how much he'd fell off, says, "I wish I wuz back home settin' in my mother's chimley corner smokin' my old chunky pipe." And next thing, there he wuz.

Jack's mother asked him how come he wuzn't up at the new ground. Jack told her that wuz jest where he wuz started.

When Jack got up there, Will and Tom wuz still a-fightin' over that youngest girl. Jack come on in the house and seed she still had that red ribbon in her hair, and she come over to him, says, "Oh Jack!"

So Jack got the youngest and Tom got the next 'un, and that throwed Will to take the oldest.

And the last time I'uz down there they'd done built 'em three pole cabins and they wuz all doin' pretty well.

HARDY HARDBACK

Tradition Bearer: Jane Gentry

Source: Carter, Isabel Gordon. "Mountain White Folk-Lore: Tales from the Southern Blue Ridge." *Journal of American Folklore* 38 (1925): 347–49.

Date: 1923

Original Source: North Carolina

National Origin: European American

"Hardy Hardback" is an American recreation of "The Helpers" (AT 513), in which Jack is rewarded for his kindness to a stranger by advice that allows him to rescue a princess from enchantment by assembling a group of extraordinary companions who help him defeat the king's witch and make his fortune. As with the other *märchen* from the southern highlands, the king's domain is localized in the region, complete with mountains, farm houses, and livestock. Jack's success results not from cleverness or luck in this tale but from kindness.

A man, an old king, he got so rich that he put out an oration that anyone that could do more than his old witch or could find anyone who could do more might have his youngest daughter and half his kingdom. So they was an old poor man and he had three sons, Jack, Will and Tom. And they decided that they'd try for a fortune. So Will he told his mother he was going over to the king's house to see if he could break the enchantment of the lady. He had to walk way long ways. His mother cooked him up a haversack full of rations.

So Will started out but if he couldn't do as much as the old king's witch could, the king would kill him, cut his head off and set it up on a pole. So when he got over to the king's house he hollered, "Hello," and the king come out and said, "What'll you have?" He said, "I come over to see if I could break the enchantment of the lady."

King says, "Now if ye can't do as much as my witch, I'll kill ye and cut your head off and set hit up on a pole."

"I know hit," says Will.

King says, "Do you think ye can hit the iron hackle as hard as my witch can?"

"Yes, bedads, I think I can."

King says, "Come, old witch," and she popped her back against that hackle and popped like a rubber ball and danced all over the floor. Will he come in and pounced agin that hackle and stove hit through his body and hit killed him and the king cut his head off and set hit up on a pole.

So then Tom decided he wanted to go. His mother said, "Oh Tom, don't go, Will was killed."

"Well, bedads I'm going anyway," says Tom.

So Tom, he starts out and meets the same little old dried up man that Will met, so he said, "Good morning, Tom."

Tom says, "Good morning."

He said, "Where ye started?"

Tom says, "None of yer business." So Tom had his haversack of rations and he tramped a long ways over to the king's house and he says, "Hello," and the king come out and says, "What'll ye have?"

Tom says, "I come over to see if I could break the enchantment of the lady."

"Well, if ye don't, I'll kill ye," says the king. "Ye know that, don't ye?"

"Yes I know hit," says Tom.

"Come in," says the king. "Can ye hit that iron hackle with your back as hard as my old witch can, or can ye find anyone who can?"

"Yes, bedads, I think I can." So the old witch come in, hit agin the iron hackle, bounced off like a rubber ball and danced all over the floor. Tom he come in, stove his back against the hackle and hit stove into his back and killed him. King cut his head off, put hit up on the pole. By that time he was a gettin' a pretty long pole full of heads.

So Jack decided he wanted to go and he got to beggin' his mother to cook up a haversack full of rations. Mother said, "Now, Jack, you're all we've got." Jack said he was a goin' anyway. But his mother wouldn't cook up a haversack full of rations so he jest took some old dried bread an' started out.

When Jack got out he met the same little dried up man. He says, "Good morning, Jack."

Jack says, "Good morning, father—good morning, uncle, ain't ye a goin' to have some breakfast with me?"

"Where ye started, Jack?"

"Well, uncle, I've started to try to make a ship sail on dry land."

"Well, you take my stick, Jack, an' go back around the way I've come to a spring. And you stir my stick in that there spring until hit turns to wine and you'll see a new tin bucket and tin cup. When ye get back here I'll have yer ship made."

So Jack went and stirred in the spring until hit turned to wine and there sat the tin bucket and he filled hit and come back and the little old man had the ship made, and they sat down and eat their bread and drank their wine. He said, "Now, Jack, you git in this ship and say, 'Sail, ship sail' and hit'll sail. Now, Jack, you take in every man that you see between here and the king's house. Now when you see a man you say, 'Hey! What's your name?' and when he tells you say, 'Come here and git in this ship and say, 'Sail, ship, sail,' and it will sail right along."

So Jack was sailing along and he looked up on the mountains and he saw a man hitting his back against the trees and knockin' 'em every which away. Jack say, "Hey! What's your name?"

"Hardy Hardback."

"Hardy Hardback? Hardy hard back I think you are, come an' get in here." So they sailed on a little ways and he saw a man out in the pasture jest a eatin' up the sheep and hogs. "Hey! What's your name?" says Jack.

"Eat Well."

"Eat Well? Eat well I think you are, come and get in here." Went on a little ways and he saw a man up the holler jest drinking up the little springs and branches. Says, "What's your name?"

"Drink Well."

"Drink Well? Drink well I think you are. Get in here."

So Drink Well got in and Jack said, "Sail, ship, sail," and it sailed right on. So went a little ways and saw a man running. He'd run a ways on one leg, then take hit up and run a while on t'other. Jack says, "Hey! What's your name?"

"Run Well."

"Run Well? Run well I think you are. Come git in here." So Run Well got in and they sailed right out; went a little further saw a man standing with a gun like he was a shootin' a hare in the skies. "Hey! What's your name?" says Jack.

"Shoot Well."

"Shoot Well? Shoot well I think you are," says Jack. "Come on git in here."

So he got in and Jack said, "Sail, ship, sail," and they sailed right out. Little further saw a man a listenin'. He'd put one hand over one ear, and one over the t'other. "Hey. What's your name?" says Jack.

"Hark Well."

"Hark Well? Hark well I think you are. Come on git in here." So Hark Well got in and Jack says, "Sail, ship, sail," and it sailed right out.

So they sailed on a little ways 'til they got to the king's house. Jack hollered, "Hello," and the king come out and says, "What will ye have?"

Jack says, "I come over to see if I could break the enchantment of the lady." "Well, if you don't, I'll kill ye."

"Yes, I know hit, "says Jack. Said, "Do you think you can hit the iron hackle as hard as my old witch can, or can ye find anyone who can?"

"Yes, bedads, I think I can." So the king called his old witch and she stabbed her back agin the iron hackle and bounced off like a rubber ball and danced all over the room. "Hardy Hardback, come in here," says Jack. Hardy Hardback come in and struck that iron hackle and stove hit through the wall, jumped off on the floor and danced all over.

King says, "Well, now do you think you can eat as much as my old witch can, or can ye find anyone who can?"

"Yes, I think I can. Come in here, Eat Well." So Eat Well come in and they assigned each a horse apiece. Eat Well jumped out and eat up his horse, and a cow or two, and a couple of sheep, and some pigs, and the old witch didn't have one horse eat up.

So they called 'em in. Said, "Well, now do you think you can drink as much as my old witch can, or can ye find anyone who can?"

"Yes, I think I can," says Jack. "Drink Well, come in here." So they assigned them a creek apiece and Drink Well jumped in and drank his up, and a spring or two, and was drinking the river up when they called 'em in.

"Well now," says the king, "can you find a man that can run as fast as my old witch can?"

"Yes, I think I can. Run Well, come in here." So they give 'em an egg shell apiece and started 'em to the ocean after an egg shell full of water. So Run Well run on to the ocean got his water and come on back and met the old witch half way.

She said, "I'm tired."

He said, "I'm tired, too."

She says, "Let's sit down and rest and not run ourselves to death for other people."

So they went up above the road a few steps to a nice grassy place and sat down and rested. She says, "Lay yer head over here and rest." She had an old jaw bone in her pocket and if she could git anybody to sleep and put that under their head they wouldn't wake up until that was knocked out. So Run Well being tired, she waited 'til he was asleep and put that jaw bone under his head. She poured his egg shell out and started on to the ocean.

Jack began to get uneasy and said, "Hark Well, hark well and see where Run Well's at."

"Jack, he's layin' asleep half way between here and the ocean with a jaw bone under his head, and he'll never wake 'til that's knocked out."

"Shoot Well, shoot well and shoot hit out," says Jack. So Shoot Well shot and knocked hit out. Run Well jumped up and picked up his egg shell and started to the ocean. When he was comin' back he ketched up to the old witch and knocked the old witch, and come on back to the king's house. And they was married 'fore the old witch got there and when I left they was rich.

HOW BRER RABBIT BRING DUST OUT OF THE ROCK

Tradition Bearer: Unavailable

Source: Backus, Emma M. "Tales of the Rabbit from Georgia Negroes." *Journal of American Folklore* 12 (1899): 113–14.

Date: 1899

Original Source: Georgia

National Origin: African American

Brer Rabbit's trick of seeming to strike dust from a rock, despite the failure of other stronger competitors, is reminiscent of the European and European American Jack Tales in which Jack uses similar slight of hand to appear to squeeze milk from a stone to intimidate giants and ogres. Unlike Jack, however, Brer Rabbit uses his deception to exploit yet another in a long line of reluctant fathers-in-law, shrugging off his ploy as just one of "his courting tricks." As Brer Rabbit once again subverts a competition designed to take him out of the running, the social message is again the triumph of brain over brawn and the flexibility of rules.

Mr. Fox, he have a mighty handsome daughter, and all the chaps was flying round her to beat all. Brer Coon, Brer Wolf, Brer Rabbit, and Brer Possum was a courting of her constant, and they all ask Brer Fox for he daughter.

Now the gal, she favor Brer Rabbit in her mind, but she don't let on who her favor is, but just snap her eyes on 'em all.

Now Ole Brer Rabbit, he ain't so mighty handsome, and he ain't no proudful man, that's sure, but somehow it 'pears like he do have a mighty taking way with the gals.

Well, when they all done ask Ole Man Fox for his daughter, he ask the gal, do she want Brer Wolf? And she toss her head and 'low Brer Wolf too bodaciously selfish; she say, "Brer Wolf's wife never get a bite of chicken breast while she live."

Then the Ole man, he ask her how she like Brer Possum. and she just giggle and 'low "Brer Possum mighty ornery leetle Ole man, and he 'longs to a low family anyhow." And Ole Man Fox, he 'low, "Dat's so for a fact," and he sound her affections for Brer Coon, but she make out Brer Coon pass all endurance. Then the Ole man he tell her Brer Rabbit done ask for her too, and she make out like she mighty took 'back, and 'low she don't want none of that lot.

Then Ole Brer Fox, he say that the gal was too much for him; but he tell the chaps to bring up the big stone hammer, and they can all try their strength on the big step rock what they use for a horse block, and the one what can pound dust out of the rock shall have the gal.

Then Brer Rabbit, he feel mighty set down on, 'cause he know all the chaps can swing the stone hammer to beat hisself, and he go off sorrowful like and set on the sand bank. He set a while and look east, and then he turn and set a while and look west, but maybe you don't know, sir, Brer Rabbit sense never come to hisself 'cepting when he look north.

When it just come to hisself what he goin' to do, he jump up and clip it off home, and he hunt up the slippers and he fill them with ashes, and Lord bless your soul, the ole chap know just what them slippers do 'bout the dust out of the rock.

Well, the next morning they was all there soon. Ole Brer Rabbit, the last one, come limping up like he mighty lame, and being so, he the last one on the land, 'cause he have last chance.

Now Brer Wolf, he take the big hammer and he fetch it down hard, and Brer Wolf mighty strong man in them days, but he ain't fetch no dust. Then Brer Coon and Brer Possum, they try, but Ole Man Fox he say, he don't see no dust, and Miss Fox she behind the window curtain and giggle, and Ole Man Fox he curl the lip and he say, "Brer Rabbit, it you turn now." Brer Wolf he look on mighty scornful, and Brer Rabbit have just all he can do to fetch up the big hammer; it so hard he just have to stand on tiptoe in he slippers, and when the hammer come down, he heels come down sish, and the dust fly so they can't see the ole chap for the dust.

But Ole Brer Rabbit, he don't count that nothing but just one of his courting tricks.

RABBIT STEALS FIRE

Tradition Bearer: Unavailable

Source: Swanton, John R. *Myths and Tales of the Southeastern Indians.* Smithsonian Institution Bureau of American Ethnology Bulletin 88. Washington, DC: U.S. Government Printing Office, 1929.

Date: 1929

Original Source: Creek

National Origin: Native American

In **myth**, fire symbolizes technology in general, and one of the common exploits of the culture hero is the theft of fire. In the overwhelming majority of cases, the bringer of fire in other narratives serves as a **trickster** figure. Although there is an innate irony in the coupling of the wily exploiter and the clever culture bearer, the combination is appropriate; innovation must deviate from the norm by definition, and who deviates better than the **trickster**? In the following **myth**, Rabbit uses his duplicity to serve humanity rather than for his own selfish ends.

All the people came together and said: "How shall we obtain fire?" It was agreed that Rabbit should try to obtain fire for the people.

He went across the great water to the east. He was received gladly, and a great dance was arranged. Then Rabbit entered the dancing circle, gaily dressed, and wearing a peculiar cap on his head into which he had stuck four sticks of rosin.

As the people danced they approached nearer and nearer the sacred fire in the center of the circle. The Rabbit also danced nearer and nearer the fire. The dancers began to bow to the sacred fire, lower and lower. Rabbit also bowed to the fire, lower and lower. Suddenly, as he bowed very low, the sticks of rosin caught fire and his head was a blaze of flame.

The people were amazed at the impious stranger who had dared to touch the sacred fire. They ran at him in anger, and away ran Rabbit, the people pursuing him. He ran to the great water and plunged in, while the people stopped on the shore.

Rabbit swam across the great water, with the flames blazing from his cap. He returned to his people, who thus obtained fire from the east.

WHITEBERRY WHITTINGTON

Tradition Bearer: Jane Gentry

Source: Carter, Isabel Gordon. "Mountain White Folk-Lore: Tales from the Southern Blue Ridge." *Journal of American Folklore* 38 (1925): 357–59.

Date: 1923

Original Source: North Carolina

National Origin: Anglo American

The present tale combines some of the traditional **motifs** associated with the **tale type** "The Girl as Helper in the Hero's Flight" (AT313), with the commonsense solutions often found in American versions of the older European *märchen*. For example, rather than the real wife magically awakening Whiteberry from an enchanted sleep (**motifs** D1971 and D2006.1.1), Whiteberry simply does not take laudanum on the third night and remains awake. The abuses suffered by the lowborn heroine of the tale at the hands of her social superiors suggests a subtext about the folk group's view of both gender and class disparity. Compare this to "Wolf of the Greenwood" (Vol. I, p. 52).

Whiteberry Whittington was a hired boy and he lived with the king, and he loved the hired girl. So he was out helpin' to kill beef one day and he got some blood on his shirt. The king's daughter she was kinda in love with him. So when he got back he says to the hired girl and the king's girl, "Whichever one washes this stain out my shirt, that's the one I'm goin' to marry." So the hired girl she washed hit out, he knowed she would, and he married her and lived with her until they had three children.

One day King's daughter says, "I washed that shirt and you said whichever one washed that stain out your shirt, that's the one you was goin' to marry."

"Yes, I did," says Whiteberry Whittington, so he left with the king's daughter.

And the hired girl she was home jest a mournin', and at last old woman come by and says, "Why are you always a grievin' and a cryin'?" The hired girl told her how her husband had left her and gone away with the king's daughter. Old woman says, "If you'll give me one of these children, I'll tell you where your husband is. But," she says, "you'll have to climb the glassy hills and wade the bloody seas to git to him."

"I don't mind that but I hate to give up one of my little children." She wasn't a aimin' to give hit up to her at all.

Old woman says, "Well, when you find your husband you kin come back and git the child." So she wouldn't give it to her and the old woman says, "Well, now listen, if you give me this child, I'll give you this beautiful fan and help you git your husband."

So she give her a child and started on her way with the two children and she traveled and traveled until she met another old woman who looked like the first one. "Oh! these two pretty children," she says. "You've jest got to give me one of them."

So the hired girl says, "No, I've already had to give one to the old witch and I can't give way nary 'nother one."

Old woman says, "You'll never find your husband if you don't give me one of them children."

Girl says, "Oh, I can't give nary 'nother child."

Old woman says, "Give me one of them children and I'll give you this pretty comb and it'll help your husband to love you and I'll help you find him."

So she give the old woman one of the children and she took the comb and started on. So she clumb the glassy hills and waded the bloody seas and went on. Traveled on for about two more days and met another old woman who says, "Oh, this pretty baby, I'm bound to have this pretty baby."

"No, I jest can't give you this baby. I've had to give the other two children to the old witches and I have to hunt my husband and I jest don't believe I could live if I had to give up this one."

The old woman says, "If you'll give me this one, I'll give you this pretty string of beads, and if you don't, you'll never find your husband and you'll never live neither."

So she took the string of beads and give the old witch the child and went on to the place her husband and the king's daughter was, and it warnt but a day or two before she saw Whiteberry Whittington, and it wasn't but a few more days 'fore she saw the king's daughter.

King's daughter says, "Oh, that pretty fan, I've got to have that pretty fan."

"No," hired girl says, "You got my man and that's enough for you."

"No, I've got to have that fan; I'll send my husband over to spend the night with you." He wasn't her husband of course because he'd married the hired girl. The king's daughter jest said that. She was anxious to git him to come over so she could tell him how the king's daughter had lied her and lied him. So she give the king's daughter the fan.

So the king's daughter went home and told him he was to go over. So he went over, he jest minded the king's daughter like he was a little brown puppy, and the king's daughter says, "You got to take this dose of laudanum because I don't want her a talkin' to you." So when he got over there, she wanted him to have some supper with her. But he said no, he was sleepy and wanted to go to bed. So she fixed the bed and he went to bed. She crawled in behind him. So she says, "I've clumb the glassy hills and waded the bloody seas, My three little babes I've give for thee. Turn over to me, my fair Whittington."

But he was jest so sound asleep he couldn't wake. So in two or three days the king's daughter happened to notice the comb.

"Oh, what'll you take for that comb; I just must have that comb."

"No, you have my man and that's enough for you."

"Say, if you'll give me that comb, I'll send him back to stay all night with you." So she give her the comb. So the king's daughter give him another dose of laudanum and he wouldn't eat no supper and all during the night she'd talk to him, but couldn't git him to wake enough to speak to. She'd say, "I've clumb the glassy hills and waded the bloody seas, my three little babes I've give for thee. Turn over to me, Whiteberry Whittington."

He'd never move.

So in two or three days the king's daughter saw her beads. "Oh, I'm jest bound to have them beads."

"No, you got my man, you got my fan, you got my comb. I'm jest not goin' to let you have these beads."

"I'll let my man come and stay all night with you if you'll jest let me have them beads." So she let her have the beads. So that night when she give the lau-danum to Whiteberry Whittington, he jest spit hit down in his boot and went on over. So she told him what a hard time she'd had to git to him, how she had had to give up her children. She told him that the king's daughter lied to him and that she was the one that washed the blood out.

So he went back to the king's daughter and says, "You jest lied me and I'm goin' back with my wife, kill the old witches and git my children." So he took his wife and they went on back and stopped at every house and killed the old witch and took the children and when I left there, they was rich and livin' happy.

OLD FOSTER

Tradition Bearer: Jane Gentry

Source: Carter, Isabel Gordon. "Mountain White Folk-Lore: Tales from the Southern Blue Ridge." *Journal of American Folklore* 38 (1925): 361–63.

Date: 1923

Original Source: North Carolina

National Origin: Anglo American

The following narrative, with its historical setting and plausible, if gory, events, could easily pass as a **legend**. This tale of Mr. Foster, a serial mur-derer and cannibal, and his apparently reluctant accomplice, Jack, is a North Carolina **variant** of a folktale with an international distribution, "The Robber Bridegroom" (AT955).

They use to be an old man, he lived way over in the forest by hisself, and all he lived on was he caught women and boiled 'em in front of the fire and eat 'em. Now the way my mother told me, he'd go into the villages and tell 'em this and that and get 'em to come out and catch 'em and jest boil they breasts. That's what she told me, and then I've heard hit that he jest eat 'em. Well, they was a beautiful stout woman, he liked 'em the best (he'd a been right after me and your mother) so every day he'd come over to this woman's house and he'd tell her to please come over to see his house.

"Why, Mr. Foster, I can't find the way."

"Yes, you can. I'll take a spool of red silk thread out of my pocket and I'll start windin' hit on the bushes and hit'll carry ye straight to my house." So she promised him one day she'd come. So she got her dinner over one day and she started. So she follered the red silk thread and went on over to his house. When she got there, there was a poor little old boy sittin' over the fire a boilin' meat. And he says, "Laws, Aunt,"—she uz his aunt—"what er you doin' here? Foster kills every woman uz comes here. You leave here jest as quick as you can."

She started to jump out the door and she saw Foster a comin' with two young women, one under each arm. So she run back and says, "Jack, honey, what'll I do, I see him a cumin'?"

"Jump in that old closet under the stair and I'll lock you in," says Jack.

So she jumped in and Jack locked her in. So Foster come in and he was jest talkin' and a laughin' with those two girls and tellin' the most tales, and he was goin' to taken 'em over to a corn shuckin' next day. Foster says, "Come on in and have supper with me." So Jack put up some boiled meat and water. That's all they had. As soon as the girls stepped in and seed the circumstance and seed their time had come their countenance fell. Foster says, "You better come in and eat, maybe the last chance you'll ever have." Girls both jumped up and started to run. Foster jumps up and ketched 'em, and gets his tomihawk and starts up stairs with 'em. Stairs was shaky and rattly, and as they went up one of the girls wretched her hand back and caught hold of a step and Foster jest took his tomi-hawk and hacked her hand off. Hit drapped into whar she was. She laid on in there until next day after Foster went out then Jack let her out.

She jest walked over to where the corn shuckin' was. When she got there Foster was there. She didn't know how to git Foster destroyed. The people thought these people got out in the forest and the wild animals would ketch 'em. So she says, "I dreamt an awful dream last night. I dreamed I lived close to Foster's house and he was always a wantin' me to come to his house."

Foster says, "Well, that ain't so, and hit shan't be so, and God forbid hit ever should be so."

She went right on, "And I dreamt he put out a red thread and I follered hit to his house and there uz Jack broilin' women's breasts in front the fire."

Foster says, "Well, that ain't so, and hit shan't be so, and God forbid hit ever should be so."

She went right on, "And he says, 'What er you doin' here? Foster kills every woman as comes here.'"

Foster says, "Well, that ain't so, and hit shan't be so, and God forbid hit ever should be so."

She went right on, "And I seed Foster a-comin' with two girls. And when they git thar the girls their hearts failed 'em and Foster ketched 'em and gets his tomihawk and starts upstairs with 'em."

Foster says, "Well, that ain't so, and hit shan't be so, and God forbid hit ever should be so."

She went right on, "The stairs was shaky and rattly and as they went up, one of the girls wretched her hand back and caught hold of a step and Foster jest took his tomihawk and hacked her hand off."

Foster says, "Well, that ain't so, and hit shan't be so, and God forbid hit ever should be so."

She says, "Hit is so, and hit shall be so and here I've got the hand to show."

And they knowed the two girls was missin' and they knowed hit was so, so they lynched Foster and then they went and got Jack and bound him out.

THE POWERS THAT BE: SACRED TALES

WHY THE SPIDER NEVER GOT IN THE ARK

Tradition Bearer: Unknown

Source: Backus, Emma M. "Animal Tales from North Carolina." *Journal of American Folklore* 11 (1898): 285–86.

Date: 1898

Original Source: North Carolina

National Origin: African American

The Biblical version of Noah and the flood identifies the rainbow as God's pledge that water would not be used again to destroy humanity. This oral narrative notes the presence of another sort of sign—the spider. This tale—with its God of the mountain, plagues and famine, and people celebrating Satan with a sinful frolic—incorporates **motifs** from the Hebrew exodus from Egypt which, according to Biblical history, occurred after the flood. Therefore, the spider was not on the ark but was created by the Old Testament God who used a giant spider as an instrument to punish human wickedness. The instrument of divine justice was allowed to live on in diminished form as a warning for potential sinners.

The spider ain't one of the sure 'nough creeping things what was in the ark, bless your soul no, Miss, that he ain't; the spider am on this here earth just as a 'minder what we be fetch back to, if we don't walk with the Lord Jesus.

In the long time back, the black man he have no Lord Jesus, he only have the great God of the mountain; and the black man he mighty big sinner, and the great God, he just 'bliged to hold the sinner in, and sometimes he have to make a instrument.

Well, Miss, one year the peoples was mighty gone away; I can't just tell you all the sins they done commit, 'cause I's mighty old, and I've seen a heap of trouble, and when I done hear the old folks tell it I was just a chap, but the great God he send the fever, and he make all the crops burn up on the face of the earth, and he do heap more works, and ever what I just disremembers; I've seen a heap of trouble, Miss, but they hard-headed and rebelling, they just go on after Satan. And the great God, he have to make a instrument, and he do it this here way. The great feast time was come, the sacred feast when they all know they have to bring the offerings to the great God; but old Satan, he 'suade them to have it a dance feast; and the great God, he knew what a worsting in they mind, so in the night, before he make a instrument, he make a great spider, more big than that church over there, Miss, and before daybreak that spider done spin a web more than a mile; it take in all the feast ground, but it so fine no sinner man could see it; and when they go up to the sinful frolic, that web it just take them in, and they go round and round on it, till they come to the great spider's mouth, and he swallow them up, the last one of them. After that the spider, he get smaller and smaller, till these here times he just a little chap, what the Lord just suffer to go about for a 'minder, but he was never in the ark, Lord bless you, no, Miss.

THE SPANISH MOSS

Tradition Bearer: Unavailable

Source: Backus, Emma M., and Ethel Hatton Leitner. "Negro Tales from Georgia." *Journal of American Folklore* 25 (1912): 135–36.

Date: 1912

Original Source: Georgia

National Origin: African American

This moral tale of the origin of Spanish moss (Tillandsia useneoides), a plant that hangs from trees in gray threadlike clusters and grows throughout the South, carries a warning that a bargain with Death is usually no bargain at all. The protagonist's fear of death leads to a worse fate.

Long time ago there was a powerful wicked man. He was that sinful, that Death he don't have the heart to cut him off in his sins, 'cepten' he give him a warning. So one day Death he appear to the wicked man, and he tell him how that day week he goin' come for him. The wicked man he that frightened, he get on his knees and beg Death to let him live a little longer. The wicked man he take on, and he beg, 'til Death he promise he won't come for him 'til he give him one more warning.

Well, the years go by, but the wicked man he grow more wicked; and one day Death he appear to him again, and Death he tell the wicked man how that day week he goin' come for him; but the wicked man he more frightened than what he was before; and he get on his knees, the wicked man do, and beg Death to let him live a little longer; and Death he promise the wicked man how before he come for him he goin' send him a token what he can see or what he can hear.

Well, the years go by; and the wicked man he get a powerful old man; he deaf and blind, and he jest drag hisself about. One day Death he done come for the wicked man once more, but the wicked man he say how Death done promise him he won't come for him 'til he send him a token what he can see or hear; and Death he say he done send a token what he can see. Then the wicked man he say how he can't see no token, 'cause he say how he done blind. Then Death he say how he done send a token what he can hear. But the wicked man he say how he plum deaf, and he say how he can't hear no token; and he beg Death that hard to let him live, that Death he get plum outdone with the wicked man, and Death he jest go off and leave him to hisself.

And the wicked man he jest wander about the woods, and his children all die, and his friends all die. Still he jest wander about the woods. He blind, and he can't see; and he deaf, and he can't hear. He that blind he can't see to find no food; and he that deaf he never know when anybody try to speak to him. And the wicked man he done perish away 'til he jest a shadow with long hair. His hair it grow longer and longer, and it blow in the wind; and still he can't die, 'cause Death he done pass him by.

So he here to wander and blow about in the woods, and he perish away' til all you can see is his powerful long hair blowing all 'bout the trees; and his hair it done blow about the trees 'til it done grow fast, and now you-all folks done calls it Spanish Moss.

HELLHOUND COMES FOR A DRUNKARD

Tradition Bearer: Zenobia Brown

Source: Williams, Ellis. "Interview of Zenobia Brown." American Life Histories: Manuscripts from the Federal Writers' Project, 1936–1940. Manuscript Division, Library of Congress. 20 October 2005. http://memory.loc.gov/ammem/wpaintro/wpahome.html.

Date: 1938

Original Source: North Carolina

National Origin: African American

This **personal experience narrative** carries messages about the wages of sin and the punishment of a neglectful spouse. In African American tradition the most famous Hellhound is undoubtedly the one that is featured in the song "Hellhound on my Trail" by Mississippi blues **legend** Robert Johnson (1911–1938).

In a little hamlet outside of Wilmington, North Carolina, about twenty years ago I had an experience which I hope shall never be mine again and which will remain with me to the end of time.

It concerned my stepfather, a man of about fifty-five, and who was up to that time an extraordinarily heavy drinker who denied himself of many comforts in order that his rapacious greed for drink could be satisfied.

My mother, a woman then of about fifty, was a very kindly and devout soul whose mature years were spent in the varied activities of the church and home where she labored unceasingly to keep body and soul together. Oft-times I would see her on her bended knees praying for my dad to do right and change his bad ways. She would talk to him continuously but her preachments always went unheeded. In her every talk she would warn that the devil would get him if he continued, but he always dismissed her lightly with a wave of the hand.

It was on a Sunday morning that Martin started on one of his sprees, running it well into the night. He arrived home around midnight in an almost helpless condition and had to be put to bed. He was hardly in bed more than an hour when my mother, attracted by an unusual noise in the room, proceeded to investigate the sounds which sounded like a combination of grumbling and moaning.

As we entered the room we found Martin crawling on his all fours groaning and moaning with the bed covers around him and going towards a locked door that led to the porch that opened upon a running brook. As we endeavored to get him back in bed we beheld out of nowhere a huge animal with a dog-like appearance and with eyes the size of saucers standing inside the door. We stood petrified as Martin crawled twice towards the object still moaning and groaning. The third time he started towards the object my mother screamed and grabbed him by the foot. Her action seemed to have broken the spell and the object disappeared. The screams brought neighbors to the house who assisted in putting him back in bed.

From that instant Martin was very sick and remained in bed until he died. He was never able to recall the incident. Were it not true that my mother witnessed the happenings, and discussed it with me over a period of years, I would have sworn it was an optical illusion.

SOL LOCKHEART'S CALL

Tradition Bearer: Sol Lockheart

Source: Steiner, Roland. "Sol Lockheart's Call." *Journal of American Folklore* 48 (1900): 67–70.

Date: 1900

Original Source: Georgia

National Origin: African American

The following **personal experience narrative** is classified in the Protestant religion as "testimony," which is the reporting of one's religious experience as a means of affirming one's faith or of converting others to belief. In this case, Sol Lockheart, a licensed (as distinct from fully ordained) minister recounts his call to the Christian ministry, an occupation that he pursued part-time while employed taking care of stock for collector Roland Steiner. During the course of his call, he is struck blind and receives a vision from Christ—an experience reminiscent of many elements of the Apostle Paul's call to preach while on the road to Damascus (Acts 9:1–9). Lockheart's notion that man is influenced by both a good and bad conscience recalls Braziel Robinson's two spirits ("Possessed of Two Spirits," p. 167). Unlike Robinson, Sol Lockheart rejects the belief in conjuring and hoodoo, although he is reported in Steiner's gloss of this narrative to be a traditional healer who uses magico-religious techniques.

When a man starts to pray, he has a conscience to tell him when and where; then he has at the same time a conscience to tell him not to go and pray. The first is a good spirit, the last is a bad spirit. Maybe you may be lying in bed at midnight, eating breakfast or dinner, or between meals. The good spirit may say, "Go in the swamp to pray," night or day. If you follow the good one, you will receive good; if the bad one, you will get nothing.

I have to work out and find the difference between the two spirits. I felt sometimes like obeying the good spirit and sometimes the bad, and I continued to live to obey it better, and was one morning, just at daylight, called out by it into a gully; and when I got there and sat down, I lost my sight, and I heard a voice at my head saying: "When a child learns to read it don't forget for seventy-five or eighty years; write and send your mistress word and give her thanks for teaching your lips to pray, and tell her to get right, if she ain't right"; and then there rose a dead head before me, with rotten teeth; the head seemed all torn up, a terrible sight; the sight made me sick and blind for three days.

A woman in the presence of me said, "Give me a pipe of tobacco"; another one said, "You don't use tobacco, just use at it" [i.e., "you don't use very much tobacco"]; a voice said, "Go and set you out a tobacco plant, and let it grow to about one and a half feet, and there is a little worm on the plant." And he showed me the plant, a pretty green plant, and I never saw as pretty a tobacco plant—"the worm eats it and lives on it. Methodists live by the power of God, the Baptists live off of grace; go and tell all the Methodists they are wrong."

Three days after that I was in the field ploughing, a sunshiny morning; there came a west wind as a fire and lifted me up, and showed me a ladder from the northwest, that passed right along by me, about two miles from me; the voice told me to go to it and be baptized. I saw the church, and in it twelve people, and in the pulpit a colored man preaching. I could see half his body; the twelve people were in front of him, and I saw myself sitting behind him in the pulpit, and by that spirit and that sign I was showed I was called to preach. The end of the ladder at the church was light and bright; the end away from the church ran up into the sky and was dark; if it had a been bright I would have seen into heaven.

I told my experience in April eleven years ago, and was baptized the third Sunday in May. As my experience I told the three deacons and our minister what I had seen and heard. When they carried me to the water I lost my sight again, got into the water about waist deep; my breath left me; a voice spoke at my right ear, "Brother Lockheart, I baptize you." I was sick all the time from the time I saw the head till I was baptized.

Tuesday night, after I was baptized, I fell from my chair dead, and when I fell back a cloud passed over me darker than any black night, and from that I got well; that night was the best night's rest I ever had.

Two days after that I was ploughing in the field, turned my mule round and sat on my plough-stock; a voice spoke in midday, "What makes me Black?" The skin and hair shows it; if you look upon a hill and see two black men standing, you say there stands two Blacks; if you see two white men, you say there stands two white men; that is to show the difference between the two, skin and hair. I saw the master and servant walk out one day; the master got snake-bit, but by the help of God he got well, and he found the servant, the black man, knew the snake was there before it bit him, but would not tell him. The master would never like the servant no more for not telling him.

The servant wants the master to tell him the terror that is in death and hell, but he won't tell him on account of the snake. Now you can see clearly to pull the mote out of your brother's eye.

Two days after that I saw the heavens open and a white cloud come out about the size of a man's hand; it spread to the size of a table-cloth, closed to the size of a man's hand again, then again spread out to the size of a table-cloth and then closed out of sight, like a door closing in the heavens: then the next day, early in the morning, I saw the spirit of God, like a bird, like a rain-crow in shape, but the color of a dove: it had wide wings; as it passed by on the right side, it burnt inside of me like a flame of fire, and run me nearly crazy for about five minutes, and then I was all right again. About a week after that I was walking along from the field, when the horn blew for dinner. I walked right up to a coffin on two little benches; it was painted a dark red, and on each side were silver handles, and when I first saw it I was badly frightened and stopped and looked in it, till when I got quiet, it was empty, but lined, with a pillow at the head. When I got over my fear a voice spoke at the head of the coffin and said, "Your body shall lie in that and rest in the shade," and then, as soon as the voice ceased speaking, the coffin disappeared, and then I began preaching.

About a year after I was called, I went on a journey preaching. I walked all the way for about forty miles. I walked, for the commandment says you must not use your critter on the Sabbath day. When I was coming home, I felt great pain, as if someone was driving nails in me. It was nine o'clock Saturday morning. Sunday morning about the same time, I saw in the road before me the likeness of a man, clothed in a long white gown; he turned my mind round, just like a wheel turning round. The next day, at the same time, I saw the same spirit again, who said to me, "You have a purple gown made like mine." The spirit looked like a young white man, clean-faced; his hair was kinder straw-colored, and hung down to his shoulders. For three days he kept after me till I had one made, and on a Friday I felt something in my shoes. I couldn't keep them on, until Saturday evening, and then a voice spoke and said, "Take off those shoes and go to Cermonia church to-morrow barefoot and preach." I now preach like the Apostles, with my purple gown on and barefoot, at my own church, Mt. Pleasant, near Grovetown, Georgia.

One night I prayed to the Lord to let me visit Heaven, and then fell into a deep sleep, and then I began a journey up in the sky. I soon came to a fine building, and it was paled round with white palings. I walked up in front of the gate; the gate was shut. I looked through the gate, and saw a white man standing in the door of the house. The house was built round, of white stone, and the house was full of windows, as high as I could see. I could not see to the top of the house. All the windows were full of little children. I didn't see any grown folks there I expect, what I see and know in this world, they are powerful scarce up there in Heaven.

WHERE DID ADAM HIDE?

Tradition Bearer: Unavailable

Source: Smiley, Portia. "Folk-Lore from Virginia, South Carolina, Georgia, Alabama, and Florida." *Journal of American Folklore* 32 (1919): 371–72.

Date: 1919

Original Source: Georgia

National Origin: African American

The following joke plays three stock characters from American regional folklore against each other: the preacher, the drunkard, and the beleaguered wife. The comic misunderstanding of conversations due to rural backwardness is a common **motif**.

De preacher went out to see an ol' woman who lived out so far, never did get to church. He asked if she heard 'bout Jesus, 'bout how he died.

"Is he dead? I didn' know he was dead. You wouldn' know yourself, bein' back here in de woods. An' I don' take de paper."

De preacher said he would come next week to catechize them. Nex' week she sent de ol' man, Adam, to de store to buy molasses. Adam took the money and bought some liquor. She sent de boy to de neighbor, Sister Clarinda, to borrow some 'lasses. Sister Clarindy didn't have but a cupful, so she let her have dat. She made de molasses pone (flat cake made with cornmeal). Adam came in drunk. She put him under de bed. Tol' him to stay dere. She didn't want de preacher to see him.

So after dinner de preacher got his catechism out an' ask some questions. "De Lord made Adam firstest, den he made Eve lastest. Put them together. One day de Lord came an' called, 'Adam!' He called again, 'O Adam!' De Lord got mad, an' hollered, 'You Adam!' *Now,* where did Adam hide when de Lord call um?"

De ol' woman said, "Somebody been tellin' you somet'in'."

"Now, my sister, dis is de catechism."

"Ain't somebody been tellin' you somet'in'?"

"I don' know, my sister. Dis here was de catechism. Adam was in de garden. Adam hide. Now, I'm askin' you dis question, 'Where did Adam hide when de Lord call?'" De ol' woman put her head under de bed an' call, "You, Adam, come f'om under dat bed! Come on out! De preacher done know all 'bout you. You come out from there!"

POSSESSED OF TWO SPIRITS

Tradition Bearer: Braziel Robinson

Source: Steiner, Roland. "Braziel Robinson Possessed of Two Spirits." *Journal of American Folklore* 13 (1900): 226–28.

167

Date: 1900

Original Source: Georgia

National Origin: African American

In terms of structure, "Possessed of Two Spirits" is best classified as a **personal experience narrative**. In terms of function, this first-person account of an individual experience serves as a **belief tale** because it exemplifies and reinforces the narrator's belief in the powers of conjuration (supernatural manipulation) possessed by root doctors (spiritual practitioners from African American tradition). The overall system mastered by conjuremen or root doctors has been labeled hoodoo, and these experts are often referred to as "two-headed doctors" in tribute to their cognizance of both the natural and supernatural world. The present narrative contains references to both culturally specific beliefs (the power of graveyard dirt, sometimes called "goofer dust," to affect the living) and more universal folk beliefs (the powers of second sight conferred by being "born with the caul," a delivery in which the birth sac is draped over the newborn's face). Typically, the more tightly structured of Robinson's narratives (such as his being conjured in May 1898) are framed by affirmations and descriptions of belief in the supernatural.

I am not a preacher, but a member of the church, but I can make a few remarks in church, I have a seat in conference, I can see spirits, I have two spirits, one that prowls around, and one that stays in my body. The reason I have two spirits is because I was born with a double caul. People can see spirits if they are born with one caul, but nobody can have two spirits unless they are born with a double caul, very few people have two spirits. I was walking along and met a strange spirit, and then I heard a stick crack behind me and turned round and heard my prowling spirit tell the strange spirit it was me, not to bother me, and then the strange spirit went away and left me alone. My two spirits are good spirits, and have power over evil spirits, and unless my mind is evil, can keep me from harm. If my mind is evil my two spirits try to win me, if I won't listen to them, then they leave me and make room for evil spirits and then I'm lost forever, mine have never left me, and they won't if I can help it, as I shall try to keep in the path."

Here he took the quid of tobacco out of his mouth, and rolling it in his hand for a few minutes, resumed:

"Spirits are around about all the time, dogs and horses can see them as well as people, they don't walk on the ground, I see them all the time, but I never speak to one unless he speaks to me first, I just walk along as if I saw nothing, you must never speak first to a spirit. When he speaks to me and I speak back I always cross myself, and if it is a good spirit, it tells me something to help me, if it is a bad spirit, it disappears, it can't stand the cross. Sometimes two or more spirits are together, but they are either all good, or all bad spirits, they don't mix like people on earth, good and bad together.

"Good spirits have more power than bad spirits, but they can't help the evil spirits from doing us harm. We were all born to have trouble, and only God can protect us. Sometimes the good spirits let the evil spirits try to make you fall, but I won't listen to the evil spirits.

"When a person sees a spirit, he can tell whether it is a good spirit or a bad spirit by the color, good spirits are always white, and bad spirits are always black. When a person sees a bad spirit, it sometimes looks like a black man with no head, and then changes into a black cat, dog, or hog, or cow, sometimes the cow has only one horn and it stands out between the eyes. I never saw them change into a black bird; a man told me he saw one in the shape of a black owl; but I have seen good spirits change into white doves, but never saw one in shape of a cat, have seen them in the shape of men and children, some with wings and some without, then I have seen them look like a mist or a small white cloud. When a person is sick and meets good. spirits near enough to feel the air from their bodies, or wings, he generally gets well. Anyone can feel a spirit passing by, though only a few can see it. I've seen a great many together at one time, but that was generally about dusk. I never saw them flying two or three along together. Good and bad spirits fly, but a bad spirit can't fly away up high in the air, he is obleeged [obliged] to stay close to the ground. If a person follows a bad spirit, it will lead him into all kinds of bad places, in ditches, briers. A bad spirit is obleeged to stay in the body where it was born, all the time. If one has two spirits, the one outside wanders about, it is not always with you. If it is near and sees any danger, it comes and tells the spirit inside of you, so it can keep you from harm. Sometimes it can't, for the danger is greater than any spirit can ward off, then one's got to look higher.

"I've heard spirits talk to themselves, they talk in a whisper like, sometimes you can tell what they're saying, and sometimes you can't. I don't think the spirit in the body has to suffer for the sins of the body it is in, as it is always telling you to do right. I can't tell, some things are hidden from us.

"People born with a caul generally live to be old. The caul is always buried in a graveyard.

"Children born with a caul talk sooner than other children, and have lot more sense.

"I was conjured in May 1898, while hoeing cotton, I took off my shoes and hoed two rows, then I felt strange, my feet begun to swell, and then my legs, and then, I couldn't walk. I had to stop and go home. Just as I stepped in the house I felt the terriblest pain in my jints [joints], I sat down and thought, and then looked in my shoes, I found some yaller [yellow] dirt, and knew it was graveyard dirt, then I knew I was conjured, I then hunted about to find if there was any conjure in the house and found a bag under my doorstep. I opened the bag and found, some small roots about an inch long, some black hair, a piece of snake skin, and some graveyard dirt, dark-yaller, right off some coffin. I took the bag and dug a hole in the public road in front of my house, and buried it with the dirt out of my shoes, and threw some red pepper all around the house. I didn't get any better, and went and saw a root-doctor, who told me he could take off the conjure, he gave me a cup of tea to drink and biled [boiled] up something and put it in a jug to wash my feet and legs with, but it ain't done me much good, he ain't got enough power, I am gwine [going] to see one in Augusta, who has great power, and can tell me who conjured me. They say root-doctors have power over spirits, who will tell them who does the conjuring; they ginerally [sic] uses yerbs [herbs] gathered on the changes of the moon, and must be got at night. People git conjur[e] from the root-doctors and one root-doctor often works against another, the one that has the most power does the work.

"People gits most conjured by giving them snake's heads, lizards, and scorpions, dried and beat up into powder and putting it in the food or water they drink, and then they gits full of the varmints; I saw a root-doctor cut out of a man's leg a lizard and a grasshopper, and then he got well. Some conjur ain't to kill, but to make a person sick or make him have pain, and then conjur is put on the ground in the path where the person to be conjured goes, it is put down on a young moon, a growing moon, so the conjur will rise up and grow, so the person stepping over it will git conjured. Sometimes they roll it up in a ball and tie it to a string and hang it from a limb, so the person to be conjured, coming by, touches the ball, and the work's done, and he gits conjured in the part that strikes the ball, the ball is small and tied by a thread so a person can't see it. There are many ways to conjur, I knew a man that was conjured by putting graveyard dirt under his house in small piles and it almost killed him, and his wife. The dirt made holes in the ground, for it will always go back as deep as you got it, it goes down to where it naturally belongs.

"Only root-doctors can git the graveyard dirt, they know what kind to git and when, the hants [haunts, i.e., ghosts] won't let everybody git it, they must git it thro' some kind of spell, for the graveyard dirt works trouble 'til it gits back inter [into] the ground, and then wears off. It must git down to the same depth it was took from, that is as deep as the coffin lid was from the surface of the ground."

MILLER'S WITCH WIFE

Tradition Bearer: Unavailable

Source: Porter, J. Hampden. "Notes on the Folk-Lore of the Mountain Whites of the Alleghenies." *Journal of American Folklore* 7 (1894): 115.

Date: 1894

Original Source: Georgia

National Origin: Anglo American

The belief in the witch's ability to transform into the shape of another creature by literally taking on the skin of an animal or by using other means of ritual transformation is widely held. An equally familiar **motif** in stories of supernatural transformation is the exposure of the shapeshifter by means of a mutilation that has occurred when he or she was in altered form and persists after the return to human shape.

Mr. H owned a mill among the Smoky Mountains in Georgia. Three of his millers died successively of some obscure disease that the doctors could not diagnose. All these men were unmarried, and lived in the mill itself. Their illnesses were brief, and it was observed that when attacked they all vainly attempted to make some communication to their friends. This it was supposed had reference to the mysterious cause that hurried them to the grave.

People began at once to feel a dread of these premises, and particularly of a long, low room off the entrance, in which these unfortunate men sat of an evening and slept. Nobody could be induced to take the place made vacant, and

171

it seemed as if the establishment was to be abandoned, when one of the neigh
bors who lived a short distance down the stream volunteered to run the mill. He
ground his axe, and came the same evening. While kindling a fire on the hearth
a brindled cat glided out of the chimney, and without exciting any special atten
tion on his part at this time, ensconced herself in a dark corner near the door. He
soon had a cheerful blaze, and sat down by a table in front of it to read his Bible

But as time passed a feeling of uneasiness, of which he was conscious from
the first, grew upon him, and gradually deepened into a kind of horror. It was
utterly unconnected with any definite apprehension, or sense of real danger
Then the cat got up and wailed at the door, clawing to be let out. She rubbed
against his legs, and looked up at him. Instantly an awful half-recognition o:
those eyes shot through his brain, and leaping up he seized the axe and struck
at her, cutting off one foot.

With a wild woman's scream the creature darted up the chimney and disap
peared, while he, thoroughly unnerved, hastened home, and found his wife
bleeding to death from a severed hand.

PHOEBE WARD, WITCH

Tradition Bearer: Unavailable

Source: Cross, Tom Peete. "Folk-Lore from the Southern States." *Journal of American Folklore* 22 (1909): 254–55.

Date: 1909

Original Source: North Carolina

National Origin: Anglo American

The fear of the night hag (the witch who comes in the night) is a terror
that crosses cultures and regional boundaries. The following **legend**
cycle alludes to many of the widely held beliefs about this supernatural
figure, including her need to remove her skin, her ability to slip through
tiny openings, and the ways of repelling her attacks.

The early years of Phoebe Ward, witch, are shrouded in mystery. It is known that she was a woman of bad morals. No one seemed to know anything of her past. She was an old, old woman when this account begins.

"Phoebe Ward had no fixed home. She lived here and there, first at one place and then at another in Northampton County, North Carolina. She stayed in a hut or any shelter whatsoever that was granted her.

"She made her living by begging from place to place. Most people were afraid to refuse her, lest she should apply her witchcraft to them. When she found a house at which people were particularly kind to her, there she stopped and abused their kindness. Hence the people resorted to a number of methods to keep her away. For instance, when they saw her coming, they would stick pins point-up into the chair-bottoms, and then offer her one of these chairs. It is said that she could always tell when the chair was thus fixed, and would never sit in it. Also, they would throw red pepper into the fire, and Phoebe would leave as soon as she smelled it burning.

"Among her arts it is said that she could ride persons at night (the same as nightmares), that she could ride horses at night, and that when the mane was tangled in the morning it was because the witch had made stirrups of the plaits. She was said to be able to go through key-holes, and to be able to make a horse jump across a river as if it were a ditch. She was credited with possessing a sort of grease which she could apply, and then slip out of her skin and go out on her night rambles, and on her return get back again. It is said that once she was making a little bull jump across the river, and as she said, 'Through thick, through thin; 'way over in the hagerleen,' the animal rose and started. When he was about half way over, she said, 'That was a damn'd good jump,' and down the bull came into the river. (The witch is not to speak while she is crossing.)

"To keep the witch away people nailed horse-shoes with the toe up over the stable-doors. To keep her from riding persons at night, they hung up sieves over the door. The witch would have to go through all the meshes before she could enter, and by the time she could get through, it would be day, and she would be caught.

"Phoebe came near meeting a tragic death before her allotted time was out. One night several men of the neighborhood gathered around a brandy-barrel. As the liquor flowed, their spirits rose, and they were on the lookout for some fun.

"They went over to where Phoebe was staying and found her asleep. Thinking she was dead, they shrouded her, and proceeded to hold the wake. They were soon back at their demijohns, and while they were standing in one corner of the room drinking, there came a cracked, weak voice from the other corner, where the supposed corpse was lying out, 'Give me a little; it's mighty cold out here.'

"They all fled but one, Uncle Bennie, and he was too drunk to move. When things became quiet and Phoebe repeated her request, he said, 'Hush, you damn'd b——h, I'm goin' to bury you in the mornin'.'

"The others were afraid to return that night, but did so the next morning, and found Bennie and Phoebe sitting before the fire, contented, warm, and drinking brandy.

"After this Phoebe lived several years, making her livelihood by begging. Her last days were as mysterious as her early life had been."

A BEWITCHED CHURNING

Tradition Bearer: Mr. Howard

Source: Wiltse, Henry M. "In the Southern Field of Folk-Lore." *Journal of American Folklore* 13 (1900): 210–11.

Date: 1900

Original Source: Tennessee

National Origin: Anglo American

This **legend** embedded within a **personal experience narrative** gives the account of the narrator's being compelled to sign the book of witches. He alleges that he acquired an ability to manipulate others and recalls being ridden by witches to nocturnal gatherings. The latter is a **variant** of the "night hag" belief discussed in the introduction to "The Witch and the Boiler" (p. 178).

I was working for a man," he said, "whose wife was regarded as a witch. One day I saw her put a very small quantity of milk into the churn and go to churning. There was not over a teacupful, or such a matter, of it. But after a while I saw her put some white powder into it. She got a big lot of butter. I noticed where she put the powder, and the first chance that I got I stole some of it and went home.

"I asked mother to let me have some milk. She thought I wanted it to drink, and gave it to me. But I put it in the churn, put in some of the powder, and I got more butter than she usually got from a whole churn full of milk.

"On my way back to the farm where I worked I met a very small, dark-haired, red-complected man, that I had never seen before. He said to me, 'You have used some of my material, and now you must put your name in my book.'

"I asked him what he meant, and he said I had made butter with his material, and I'd got to put my name down in his book. I hated like the mischief to do it, but was afraid of him, and decided to do what he said. So, following his directions, I scratched my arm until the blood came, and with it I wrote my name in a little book which he handed to me. He then went away, seeming to feel satisfied, and I have never seen him since."

The old man told Mr. Howard that the witches had several times turned him into a horse and had ridden him off to their night frolics.

He could remember distinctly looking at himself and thinking with pride what a fine horse he was.

He said that on one of these occasions they rode him through a lot of brier-bushes, and the next morning his hands were full of briers.

He also claimed to have learned the secrets of witchcraft, and declared that he could do anything with Mr. Howard that he pleased by simply thinking it, and offered to demonstrate his ability to do so by practical experiments.

THE RAVEN MOCKER

Tradition Bearer: Unavailable

Source: Mooney, James. "Myths of the Cherokee." Pages 401–3 in *Nineteenth Annual Report of the Bureau of American Ethnology 1897–1898, Part I.* Washington, DC: U.S. Government Printing Office, 1900.

Date: 1898

Original Source: Cherokee
National Origin: Native American

In traditional Cherokee theories of disease causation and cure, death is due to a personal attack, which may come from a nonhuman supernatural source or from a human agent such as a witch. The witch, in general, carries out his or her mischief under cover of darkness; therefore, the Cherokee term for witch translates as "night-goer." In his analysis of Cherokee sacred formulas, James Mooney discusses ravens as agents who never fail to take disease away from the afflicted individual and hide these afflictions in mountain crevices at the cardinal points on the Cherokee compass.

Of all the Cherokee wizards or witches the most dreaded is the Raven Mocker, the one that robs the dying man of life. They are of either sex and there is no sure way to know one, though they usually look withered and old, because they have added so many lives to their own.

At night, when someone is sick or dying in the settlement, the Raven Mocker goes to the place to take the life. He flies through the air in fiery shape with arms outstretched like wings, and sparks trailing behind, and a rushing sound like the noise of a strong wind. Every little while as he flies he makes a cry like the cry of a raven when it "dives" in the air—not like the common raven cry—and those who hear are afraid, because they know that some man's life will soon go out. When the Raven Mocker comes to the house he finds others of his kind waiting there, and unless there is a doctor on guard who knows bow to drive them away they go inside, all invisible, and frighten and torment the sick man until they kill him. Sometimes to do this they even lift him from the bed and throw him on the floor, but his friends who are with him think he is only struggling for breath.

After the witches kill him they take out his heart and eat it, and so add to their own lives as many days or years as they have taken from his. No one in the room can see them, and there is no sear where they take out the heart, but yet there is no heart left in the body. Only one who has the right medicine can recognize a Raven Mocker, and if such a man stays in the room with the sick person these witches are afraid to come in, and retreat as soon as they see him, because when one of them is recognized in his right shape he must die within seven days. There was once a man who had this medicine and used to hunt for Raven Mockers, and killed several. When the friends of a dying person know that there is no more hope they always try to have one of these medicine men stay in the house and watch the body until it is buried, because after burial the witches do not steal the heart.

The other witches are jealous of the Raven Mockers and afraid to come into the same house with one. Once a man who had the witch medicine was watching by a sick man and saw these other witches outside trying to get in. All at once they heard a Raven Mocker cry overhead and the others scattered "like a flock of pigeons when the hawk swoops." When at last a Raven Mocker dies these other witches sometimes take revenge by digging up the body and abusing it.

The following is told on the reservation as an actual happening:

A young man had been out on a hunting trip and was on his way home when night came on while he was still a long distance from the settlement. He knew of a house not far off the trail where an old man and his wife lived, so he turned in that direction to look for a place to sleep until morning. When he got to the house there was nobody in it. He looked into the sweatlodge and found no one there either. He thought maybe they had gone after water, and so stretched himself out in the farther corner to sleep. Very soon he heard a raven cry outside, and in a little while afterwards the old man came into the sweat lodge and sat down by the fire without noticing the young man, who kept still in the dark corner. Soon there was another raven cry outside, and the old man said to himself, "Now my wife is coming," and sure enough in a little while the old woman came in and sat down by her husband. Then the young man knew they were Raven Mockers and he was frightened and kept very quiet.

Said the old man to his wife, "Well, what luck did you have?" "None," said the old woman, "there were too many doctors watching. What luck did you have?" "I got what I went for," said the old man, "there is no reason to fail, but you never have luck. Take this and cook it and lets have something to eat." She fixed the fire and then the young man smelled meat roasting and thought it smelled sweeter than any meat he had ever tasted. He peeped out from one eye, and it looked like a man's heart roasting on a stick.

Suddenly the old woman said to her husband, "Who is over in the corner?" "Nobody," said the old man. "Yes, there is," said the old woman, "I hear him snoring," and she stirred the fire until it blazed and lighted up the whole place, and there was the young man lying in the corner. He kept quiet and pretended to be asleep. The old man made a noise at the fire to wake him, but still he pretended to sleep. Then the old man came over and shook him, and he sat up and rubbed his eyes as if he had been asleep all the time.

Now it was near daylight and the old woman was out in the other house getting breakfast ready, but the hunter could hear her crying to herself. "Why is your wife crying?" he asked the old man. "Oh, she has lost some of her friends lately and feels lonesome," said her husband; but the young man knew that she was crying because he had heard them talking.

177

When they came out to breakfast the old man put a bowl of corn mush before him and said, "This is all we have—we have had no meat for a long time." After breakfast the young man started on again, but when he had gone a little way the old man ran after him with a fine piece of beadwork and gave it to him saying, "Take this, and don't tell anybody what you heard last night, because my wife and I are always quarreling that way." The young man took the piece, but when he came to the first creek he threw it into the water and then went on to the settlement. There he told the whole story, and a party of warriors started back with him to kill the Raven Mockers. When they reached the place it was seven days after the first night. They found the old man and his wife lying dead in the house, so they set fire to it and burned it and the witches together.

THE WITCH AND THE BOILER

Tradition Bearer: Unavailable

Source: Porter, J. Hampden. "Notes on the Folk-Lore of the Mountain Whites of the Alleghenies." *Journal of American Folklore* 7 (1894): 116–17.

Date: 1894

Original Source: Tennessee

National Origin: Anglo American

The **legend** of "The Witch and the Boiler" illustrates common practices attributed to witches and to those who attempt to combat their negative influences. One of the witch's means of revenge in this narrative is "dancing" on the chest of her victim. In the literature on supernatural assault, this is called being "ridden" (attacked) by a "night hag" or simply "hagging." These attacks are accompanied by paralysis and a feeling of an oppressive weight bearing down on the chest of the victim. The principles of "sympathetic magic" (the concept that phenomena can be made to influence each other at a distance by means of the proper magical rituals) are seen in the measures taken by the witch doctor, who used the organs of a sheep who was killed by supernatural assault to affect the agent of that attack. At the root of this diagnosis and cure is the principle of contagion: objects that have once been in contact continue to influence each other.

An animal killed by witchcraft should be burnt, partly because that is the best and most effectual way of destroying things that are infected, and also for the reason that in more than one way this may be made to affect the witch; she can be fascinated or punished. One of the parties implicated related the effects of fire in the case of a Tennessean sorceress who had done much harm.

An incredulous and stupid person, such as exists in every community, borrowed a boiler from her and refused to return it. Then she came every night and danced on him till he nearly fainted. There was no doubt about this, because she permitted herself to be seen. Each day, also, one of his sheep reared up, gave two or three jumps, and fell dead. At length the "witch doctor" was called in, and he, being a pious man and a member of the church, advised his patient to try the effect of honesty and give back the boiler. This he did, but the witch laughed at him, and things went on as before. It was now evident that her machinations were prompted by malice, and not resorted to from a sense of justice, so the doctor directed him to eviscerate the next sheep that died, to do this alone, and in perfect silence. Moreover, on no account to lend or give away any article, however trifling its value, until the effect of his charm had been fully tried. Having taken out the lungs and heart, they were to be carried home, the kitchen cleared, and these organs laid upon a bed of live embers. While procuring them, the witch's granddaughter, "a right smart shoot of a girl, training for a witch herself," saw what he was doing as she passed through his field, and, anticipating the result, ran home, saying that her "Granny" would shortly be ill.

Such was indeed the case, for no sooner had the sheep's vitals been placed upon the coals than her shrieks alarmed the neighborhood. A crowd gathered that seems to have had some inkling of what was going on, for a committee of women inspected the sufferer by force, and found her breast completely charred. The spell was broken before fatal consequences ensued, and from that time the persecutions and losses which had persisted so long came to an end.

A BEWITCHED GUN

Tradition Bearer: William T. Howard

Source: Wiltse, Henry M. "In the Southern Field of Folk-Lore." *Journal of American Folklore* 13 (1900): 209–10.

Date: 1900

Original Source: Mr. Massengale, Tennessee

National Origin: Anglo American

This account of the removal of a negative influence from a bewitched rifle provides supplemental information about the role of the witch doctor in the southern highlands. The **legend** provides an additional example of the intimate connection between a bewitched object and the source of the bewitchment, as discussed in the introduction to "The Witch and the Boiler" (p. 178).

M r.., was reared in the Cumberland Mountains. I know him as a reliabl man. He writes that some years since, while collecting for a sewing machine company, he passed three days at the home of a M Massengale who was then about eighty years of age, but was as physically and mentally vigorous as most men in middle life. He was a strong believer in witch craft, and some of the stories which he related Mr. Howard has given me in the old gentleman's own language, as nearly as he can recall it.

"For many years," said he, "I made my living by hunting, and many deer, bea turkeys, and all sorts of varmints to be found in these mountings, have I killed.

"I was considered a powerful good shot with a rifle, and that I certainly was

"One morning, howsom'ever, I went out, and the first thing I knew I had a fine shot at a big deer, which was standing stock-still, broadside toward me. raised my gun, took good aim, and expected of course to drop him dead in hi tracks. But I missed him, point blank. He made a few jumps and then stood stock still until I had wasted three shots on him, and hadn't cut a hair. Then he ran off

"This sort of thing went on for several days. I had lots of powerful fine clos shots, but couldn't hit a thing.

"I told my wife that there was something awful wrong, either with me o with the gun. She told me I had better go to the witch-doctor, as it was likel my gun was bewitched.

"I went to the witch-doctor, who told me to go into the woods near a cer tain house, pick out a tree, and name it after the woman who lived there. H said she was a witch, and had bewitched my gun. He said after I had named the tree as he directed I must shoot at it, and listen to see if there was any noise made at the house—for if I hit the tree the witch would be hurt, and then m gun would be all right.

"I did as he said, and at the first crack of the gun I heard the woman cry out as if she had been hit instead of the tree. I went to the tree and found that i was hit. From that time on my gun was as good as ever, and my shooting was as reliable as it had ever been."

THE BELL WITCH

Tradition Bearer: Unavailable

Source: Hudson, Arthur Palmer, and Pete Kyle McCarter. "The Bell Witch of Tennessee and Mississippi: A Folk Legend." *Journal of American Folklore* 47 (1934): 46–58.

Date: 1934

Original Source: Mississippi

National Origin: European American

This extended version of the **legend** of one of the South's most famous hauntings depicts a ghost who shares the qualities of the night hag described elsewhere in this collection (see, for example, "Phoebe Ward, Witch" p. 172): "something cold and heavy had been sitting on her breast, sucking her breath and pressing the life out of her." Throughout the narrative the old female slave proves to be a living compendium of supernatural lore.

Back in the days before the War there lived somewhere in old North Carolina a man by the name of John Bell. Bell was a planter and was well-fixed. He had a good-sized plantation and a dozen slaves of field-hand age, and mules and cows and hogs a-plenty. His family was made up of his wife, a daughter thirteen or fourteen years old they say was mighty pretty, and two or three young-uns that don't figure much in this story. Until he hired him an overseer, Bell got along fine.

The overseer was a Simon Legree sort of fellow, always at sixes and sevens with other folks, and especially with the slaves. He didn't even mind jawing (arguing) with his boss. They say Mr. Bell was half a mind to fire the scoundrel and hire another one. But he tended to his business. He had a way with the women-folks. Some say he had an eye open for Mary, the daughter. And Mrs.

Bell stood up for him. So he stayed on for a good while, and the longer he stayed the uppityer he got. Whenever he and Bell had a row—and their rows got bigger and bitterer—the overseer went out and blacksnaked three or four slaves, for they were the only critters in the shape of man that he could abuse without a comeback. He was the worst kind of a bully, and a man of high temper, in fact, a regular overseer of the kind you hear about in Yankee stories.

Mr. Bell had a tall temper too, and the men did not spend a lot of time patting each other on the back and bragging about each other's good points. A stand-up fight was bound to come off.

It did. Some say it was about the way the overseer had beat up one of the slaves. Some say it was about something Mr. Bell heard and saw from behind a cotton-house one day when Mary rode through the field where the overseer was working a gang of slaves. Bell went away blowing smoke from his pistol barrel, and mumbling something about white trash. The overseer didn't go away at all.

Of course Bell was brought into court, but he plead self-defense, and the jury let him off. He went home, hired him another overseer, and allowed that everything was settled. But the truth was that everything was now plumb unsettled.

That year and the next and the next the crops on the Bell place were an out-and-out failure: bumblebee cotton and scraggly tobacco and nubbin corn. His mules died of colic or some strange disease like it. His cows and hogs got sick of something the horse-doctors couldn't cure. He had to sell his slaves one by one, all except an old woman. Finally he went broke. He got what he could for his land—lock, stock, and barrel—and moved with his family to Tennessee. They say that where he settled down the town of Bell, Tennessee, was named for him. Anyway, he bought him a house and a patch of land near the home of old Andy Jackson, who had knocked off from being President and was living in a big house called The Hermitage.

Not long after the move to Tennessee, strange things began to happen in the Bell home. The children got into the habit of tumbling, or being tumbled, out of bed at least once a week, and of waking up every morning with every stitch of the bed-clothes snatched off and their hair all tangled and mussed up. Now for young-uns to tumble out of bed and to wake up in the morning with their heads uncombed is a mighty strange thing, and the Bells realized it. The children couldn't explain this carrying-on, for they were always asleep till they hit the floor; and it was a peculiar fact that they were never tumbled out while awake.

The old slave woman told them it was the ha'nt ("haunt," ghost) of the overseer Mr. Bell had killed that was pestering the children. She was as superstitious as any other slave, and she said she had always felt jubous about what the ha'nt of a man like the overseer would do. But she had spunk, and one day she allowed she would find out whether she was right by spending the night under the young-uns' bed.

In the middle of the night Mr. and Mrs. Bell were fetched out of their bed by a squall like a panther's. When they lit a lamp and ran into the room, they found the old slave woman sprawled in the middle of the floor, dripping cold sweat like an ash-hopper (receptacle for ashes from a wood-burning stove), her face gray-blue as sugar-cane peeling, and her eyes like saucers in a dish-pan. She was stiff-jointed and tongue-tied. When they got her sitting up and her tongue loosened, she screeched: "Hit's him! Hit's him! 'Fore Gawd, hit's him! Hit peenched me all over, stuck pins in me, snatched de keenks outen ma haiuh, an' whup me, bawd Gawd, how hit whup me, whup me limber an' whup me stiff, whup me jes' lack him. Ain't gwine back dauh no mo', ain't gwine back dauh no mo'."

The Bells were so scared they told some of the neighbors. Old Andy Jackson heard about it and decided to ride over. He didn't take any stock in ha'nts, and as he rode through the gate he spoke his mind out loud about tarnation fools that believed slave tales about them. He hadn't got the words out of his mouth before something whaled him over the head and skipped his hat twenty or thirty yards back down the road. Old Andy didn't say any more. He motioned his slave boy to hand him his hat, and he went away from there.

It seems like the Witch could get hungry like folks, and was satisfied with folks' grub. But it had to be the best. One day the old slave woman came tearing into the front room where Mrs. Bell was quilting and said the Witch was back in the kitchen drinking up all the sweet milk.

Mrs. Bell was scared and said the old woman was lying.

"Come see fo' yo'se'f, missus. Come see fo' yo'se'f. Ah was back dauh a-mixin' up de biscuit, an' Ah retched ovah to git a cup o' miu'k, an' fo' Gawd, de cup was in de middle o' de auh, an' de miu'k was a-runnin' rat outen hit—an' hit wa'n't gwine nowheah, missus—hit wa'n't gwine nowheah. Jes' run outen de cup, an' den Ah couldn' see hit no mo'."

"You're just seeing things," said Mrs. Bell.

"Jes' whut Ah ain' doin'—ain' seein' de miu'k. Go on back in de kitchen efen you don' believe hit. Go on back dauh an' look fo' yo'se'f.... No, ma'am, Ah hain' gwine back in dat place. No, ma'am, dat ha'nt kin guzzle an' bile up all de miu'k de cows evah give 'fo' Ah raise mah finger to stop hit."

Mrs. Bell went back into the kitchen and looked. There was a cup there that had had milk in it, and the milk was gone, sure as shootin'. She was now as scared as the old slave woman, and sent right away for her husband to come out of the field.

They couldn't figure out how a ghost could drink milk, or what becomes of the milk if he does. Does the milk dry up into the ghost of itself? If not, where does it go when the ghost swallows it? Ghosts can't be seen. At least, this one couldn't. They could see through where it was. If they could see through it, why couldn't they see the milk as plain when it was inside the ghost as when it was outside? The old slave woman said the milk was running out of the cup, but it "wa'n't gwine nowheah."

An old Holy Roller preacher from down in Tallahatchie bottom who rode over to talk about it argued that if the old woman's tale was so, milk must be of a higher class than folks. When it turns into the soul of itself, it leaves nothing behind; but folks leave behind a corpse that must be covered up with dirt right away. Folks argued about it on front galleries in the summer time and around the fire in winter—but they didn't argue about it on the Bells' front gallery or by the Bells' fire. And the preachers preached about it at camp meetings.

But the Witch didn't let up on the Bells' grub. No one ever saw it; but lots of times some member of the family would see something to eat dive out of the cupboard or pop out of the safe. The Witch's favorite was cream, and he got to skimming it from every pan in the spring-house. The Bells were never able to get any butter from the churning.

Mr. Bell might have stood for having his young-uns' rest disturbed and his old slave woman all tore up this way, but he couldn't stand for letting the ghost eat him out of house and home. So he called the family together and allowed he would move again—this time to Mississippi, where land was rich and cheap.

Mrs. Bell raised up. "Pa," said she, "it seems like to me we have been gettin' along tolerable well here. I don't see any use moving away. What would be to keep the Witch from following us down there?"

"Nothing in the world," spoke up a hide-bottomed chair from a corner of the room. "I'll follow you wherever you go," the Chair went on. "And I'll tell you what: if you stay on here, I won't bother you much; but if you go traipsing off to Mississippi—well, you'll wish you hadn't."

Mr. Bell was scared and bothered, but he studied a while and screwed up his courage enough to ask the Witch why he couldn't live where he pleased. But there was no answer. He asked some more questions. But the Chair had lapsed into the habit of silence that chairs have.

Mary, Mr. Bell's daughter, was now old enough to argue with the old folks about things. She was pretty as a spotted puppy, they say, and had lots of spunk and took after her pa. She sided with him. Girls always like to be moving. So when the family got over its scare about the Chair they argued back and forth. But finally Mrs. Bell and what they remembered about the Witch got the upper hand. Mr. Bell and Mary gave up the idea of moving to Mississippi—for a while anyway.

And for a while the Witch eased up on them. It even did some good turns. One day Mr. Bell was talking of visiting a family across the creek where he had heard everybody was sick. "I have just come from there," said a Voice from the eight-day clock, and went on to tell how well everybody was and what everybody was doing. Later Mr. Bell met up with a member of the family and learned that everything the Witch said was so.

Maybe because she had taken sides with him in the argument about going to Mississippi, the Witch was partial to Mrs. Bell. The old slave woman said the ha'nt sided with her because she had stood up for the overseer when Mr. Bell wanted to fire him in North Carolina.

One Christmas time the family was invited to a taffy-pulling. Mrs. Bell was sick and couldn't go. They talked about whether they ought to go off and leave their mammy feeling poorly. Mr. Bell was invited too, and they needed him to do the driving; so Mary and the children begged him to take them. Mrs. Bell told them to go ahead, she didn't need them and could make out all right. So they all piled into the wagon and started.

But before they got far one of the wagon wheels flew off and let the axle down into the road with a bump. It looked like a common accident, and the old man climbed down and put the wheel back on the axle and stuck the linchpin in. He looked at all the other linchpins and saw they were on all right. Before long another wheel flew off. They looked on the ground for the linchpin but couldn't find it there. Mr. Bell whittled a new one, and when he went to put the wheel back on he found the old one in place. He fixed the wheel and drove off again, telling all of the children to watch all of the wheels. Soon they saw something like a streak of moonshine dart around the wagon, and all four wheels flew off, and the wagon dropped kersplash into a mud-hole. They put them back on, turned round, and drove back home, going quiet and easy, like sitting on eggs.

When they got there, they found their mammy sitting up by the Christmas tree eating a plate of fresh strawberries, and feeling lots better.

Other pranks were laid to the Witch. Often when the old man and the boys would go to the stable to catch the horses and mules for the day's plowing or a trip to town, the critters would back their ears and rare and kick and stomp like hornets or yellow-jackets were after them. Some morning they would be puny as chickens with the pip, and caked with sweat and mud, and their manes and tails tangled in witch-locks. The neighbors said that off and on they met an unbridled and barebacked horse, and the horse would stop, and something on his back that they couldn't see would talk to them—but not long—they had business the other way.

Maybe because Mary had sided with her pa against her mammy and the Witch, the Witch was harder on her after the argument than on anybody else. She would wake up in the middle of the night, screaming and crying that something cold and heavy had been sitting on her breast, sucking her breath and pressing the life out of her.

One time she was getting ready to go to a play-party. Some of the young sprouts were waiting for her in the front room. While she was combing her long, black hair, it suddenly was full of cuckleburs. She tugged and pulled and broke the comb to untangle it, and when she couldn't, she leaned on the bureau and cried.

"I put them in your hair," said the Witch from the looking-glass. "You've got no business going to the party. Stay here with me. I can say sweet things to you."

She screamed, and the young fellows rushed in the room, and when she told them about the Voice they shot at the glass with their pistols. But the glass didn't break. And the Witch caught every bullet and pitched it into their vest pockets and laughed. So they called it a draw and went out of there. And Mary stayed at home.

Mary was now mighty near grown. She had turned out to be a beautiful woman. She had lots of beaux. But whenever one of them screwed himself up to the point of popping the question he always found that the words stuck in his throat and his face and ears burned. For young fellows these were strange signs. But it was always that way. And none of them seemed to be able to ask Mary the question. They laid it on the Witch, and finally quit hitching their horses to the Bell fence.

All but one. His name was Gardner. He was a catch for any girl, smart as a briar, good-looking, easy-going and open-hearted, and the owner of rich bottom land, a passel of slaves, and a home as big as the courthouse, with columns as tall and white. He got all wrapped up in Mary, and they say Mary was leaning to him.

The way of the Witch with him was different, more businesslike. Maybe it was because the Witch realized this was the man Mary was setting her heart on. One night when Gardner was walking up the row of cedars in the Bell yard to see Mary, something he couldn't see reached out from a big cedar and touched him on the shoulder, and a voice said, "Wait a minute."

Gardner was afraid to wait, but he was more afraid to run. So he waited.

"You might as well understand, here and now, that you are not going to have Mary Bell."

"Why not?" Gardner asked.

"You might have guessed from all that's happened round here. I'm in love with her myself. It's going to be hard to get her consent, and it may be harder to get the old man's. But she's not going to marry you. I'll see to that. If you open your mouth about it tonight, you'll be dead as a door-nail before morning."

Gardner studied a while and said, "If you'd only come out like a man."

The cedar tree stepped out and snatched his hat off and stomped it.

"Well, I reckon I'll have to lay off for a while," says Gardner. "But I do love her, and I'd go to the end of the world for...."

"Well, you don't have to go that far, and it wouldn't do you any good if you did, and if you love her the only way you can keep her out of hell is to get out yourself. If you keep on hanging round here, I'll make it hell for you. Now this is how far you go. Pack up your traps and get out of the country, hide and hair. Go any place you think the Bells won't hear tell of you—and go before breakfast. If you slip out quiet without raising any rookus I'll never pester you again. What's more, on the day you get married I'll give you a pair of new boots you'll be proud of all your life."

Gardner couldn't see why the Witch's promise of a pair of wedding boots was in the same class as the threat of death before breakfast, but he didn't split hairs, and he didn't argue any more. He picked up his hat, sneaked back to his horse, and rode off.

He never said or wrote a thing to the Bells about what had happened, part because he was scared, but more because he was ashamed of being scared. He left the neighborhood before sunup and moved to the western part of the state. He got somebody else to sell out for him. They say the town of Gardner, where he settled, was named after him when he got old and respected.

After he had been there a while he fell in love with a girl and got engaged to her. And they say that when he was dressing for the wedding he couldn't find his boots. He looked high and low, every place a pair of boots was liable to be and lots of places where they couldn't possibly be, but no boots could he find.

He was about to give up and go to his wedding in his sock feet, when a Voice told him to crawl out from under the bed and look in the bed. And there between the sheets he found a pair of shiny new boots. He put them on and went his way rejoicing and thinking of how well a ghost kept his word, and wondering if the boots would ever wear out and if they were like the Seven-League boots he had read about in old McGuffey.

But they looked like natural boots. He told some of his friends how he had got them. They thought he was a liar. But they had to own up they were wrong.

One day Gardner's house-boy made a mistake and carried them instead of another pair to a cobbler. The cobbler said they were in perfect shape, that they were not made by mortal hands, and that the soles were sewed on in a way that no man or man-made machine could have stitched them. And there is a lady in this neighborhood who has seen the boots.

While Gardner's mind was getting mossed over about Mary, Mr. Bell decided again to move to Mississippi. It looked like his move from North Carolina was jumping from the frying pan into the fire, but he figured maybe the skillet wouldn't be any hotter. Gardner's break-up with Mary and Mary not marrying hung heavy on his mind. Mrs. Bell raised up again, telling him about rolling stones. And the Witch horned in. By this time the family got used to the Witch and would talk free with him, but respectful.

Every time the question came up there was a row between Mr. Bell and Mary on one side and Mrs. Bell and the Witch on the other. The old slave woman told Mr. Bell the ha'nt didn't want him to move because he was afraid of witch hunters in Mississippi. She said there were powerful ones down there.

And so one winter after the crops had petered out on him again, he sold his place dirt cheap. But the old slave woman told him to wait till spring to start. She said Easter was early that year and there would be plenty of time to pitch a crop. Good Friday would be a good day to leave, she said, for the ha'nt would have to go back to his grave and stay three days under the ground and would be puny-like several days more. While he was in good working order he could be in two or three places at once and be in any of them in the bat of an eye, but then he would have to lie low, and that would give them plenty of start.

So Mr. Bell early on Good Friday stacked his furniture and duds in a couple of wagons, climbed into the front one with Mary, put the old slave woman and his biggest boy into the hind one, and told Mrs. Bell, "Git in with old Patsy if you're a-comin', and don't forgit the young-uns."

And that was the way the Bell family came to Mississippi. Mr. Bell bought him a little place in Panola County, ten miles east of Batesville on the Oxford road. He was all ready to begin life over again without supernatural interference.

But the Witch made a quick come-back, not before the family got there, but before they moved into their new home.

When Mr. Bell first got to Batesville, or Panola as they called it then, he left the family there and went out to look at the land he aimed to buy. When he got a place that suited him, he went back to town for his family and stuff. There was some sort of hitch, and the wagons did not get started till late in the evening.

As the wagons moved slowly out of town, dark clouds began to roll up in the south and west, and before they had gone three miles the storm broke. Dark came on earlier than usual, for the clouds hid the sun. The rain beat down on the wagon covers. Every now and then the lightning flashes lit up the swaying trees on each side of the road, the draggle-tailed horses, and the road itself, a long, muddy creek, and then it was dark as a stack of black cats. The folks all stopped talking. There was nothing to listen to but the beating rain and the thunder and the suck of the horses' feet and the wheels in the mud.

All at once the hind wagon, with the family in it, slid to the side of the road and sunk into the mud up to the bed. Mr. Bell saw it in a lightning flash and came back. It couldn't be moved; the horses had no foothold, and the wheels were in too deep. The fix they were in wasn't dangerous, but it was mighty uncomfortable.

And then the Witch took a hand. "If you'll go back to your wagon and stop your cussin'," said the empty dark beside the wagon, "I'll get you out. Hump it back to your wagon now—light a shuck!"

Mr. Bell waded back and crawled in.

And then the horses and the wagon and the furniture and the family and the dog under the wagon and the calf tied behind and everything else but the mud on the wheels riz up about eight feet high and floated down the road till they were just behind the front wagon, and then they settled down easy and went on home without any trouble.

The family got settled down in their two-story double-loghouse amongst the cedars on the Oxford road.

A few nights later, the Witch spoke up from one of the andirons and told Mr. and Mrs. Bell he was in love with Mary. He said he wanted to marry her. Mr. Bell was shocked and surprised. He explained, respectful but emphatic like, that he could never dream of letting a daughter of his marry a ghost, not even so noble a ghost like the one he was talking with.

"I got a claim on you, John Bell," said the Witch. "I got a claim on you and on yours. I got a claim." And his voice was deep and hollow-like.

This was a point Mr. Bell maybe didn't want to hear any more about. So he said, "Have you spoken to Mary?"

"No, not spoken."

"Well, how do you know she would have you?"

"I don't. But I haven't got any reason to believe she wouldn't love me. She's never seen me. She doesn't know whether she would or not. Maybe she would consider it an honor to be married to a ghost. Not many girls are, you know. Why, it would make her famous."

"I don't want any daughter of mine getting famous that way. And besides, what if you were to have children? What in the world do you reckon they'd be like? Like you or her? Maybe half good human meat and bone, and the other half sight unseen. Or maybe they'd be the vanishin' kind and goin' round here

189

and raisin' hell invisible. Do you think I want a passel of soap-suds young-uns floatin' round here and poppin' up into puffs of wind every time I p'inted to the stovewood pile or sprouts on a ditch bank? Not on your life. I reckon plain flesh and blood's good enough for Mary."

"But, John Bell, I love Mary. And remember. Remember."

"So do I, and that's why I'm not a-goin' to let you marry her. Why, when she got old and hard-favored I reckon you'd quit her for some young hussy. You could do it easy enough. Mary'd have a hard time keepin' up with a stack of wind and a voice, and I'd have a hard time trackin' down and shootin' a low-down, no-count dust devil. When Mary marries, she marries a man that's solid and alive in body."

"I gather, John Bell, that you're opposed to me courting your daughter. But she's the one to say, and I'm going to talk to her about it. You'll be my father-in-law yet, or you'll be a-mourning, a-mourning."

"But what kind of wedding would it be like?" Mrs. Bell put in. "Think of it. Mary standing in front of the preacher and the preacher saying, 'Do you take this woman?' to a vase of flowers. And the ring floating down to Mary from the hanging-lamp maybe, or rising up from under a bench. I won't stand for it. I've stood for a lot of things, and you can't say I haven't been a friend to you. But I won't stand for Mary being a laughing-stock and disgrace to the family."

"If we're a-goin' to add to this family," Mr. Bell took up, "we're a-goin' to be able to see what we're addin'. I don't even know what shape you've got, if any."

"Oh, I can give you some idea what shape I have. I'll let you shake hands with me. But you must promise not to squeeze. We're very delicate, especially when we touch folks. Here, hold out your hand, and I'll put mine in it."

Mr. Bell held out his hand, felt something, and grabbed it. It was, he said later, the hand of a new-born baby—soft and crinkly and warm and just about the size of a new-born baby's hand.

"How big are you all over?" he asked.

"I can't tell you that."

"Well, there's one other thing I want to know. How do you get into this house any time you want to when every window and door is locked and barred? Do you ooze through the walls?"

"No. It's a lot easier than that. If you'll watch the corner of the ceiling up there, you'll see."

And all the rest of his life Mr. Bell swore to trustworthy witnesses that he saw the corner of the ceiling raised a good three feet and then let down again, all without the slightest racket.

"Do you mean to tell me that anything with a hand like that can h'ist the top off of the house that a-way?"

"Sure," came the answer. "But about Mary. I'm going to talk to her right off."

"Don't," said Mr. Bell. "Do you want to drive her crazy?"

But the meeting was over, for there was no answer. And the fire had died down, and the andiron looked glum.

The story is kind of skimpy here. Nobody seems to know what the Witch said to Mary or what Mary said to the Witch.

But the family noticed next day that she was drooping and wasn't minding what was going on around her. For days she wandered about the house and up and down the yard under the gloomy old cedars, like somebody sleep-walking. And the color left her face, and deep in her wide-open black eyes was a far-away look, like she was trying to see something that ought to be but wasn't there. Every day she got up later and went to bed earlier.

And finally there came a day when she didn't get up at all. In the evening a screech-owl hollered in a cedar right by the gallery.

That night her fever was high, and by midnight she was raving. "We've put off seein' a doctor too long," said Mrs. Bell.

"The roads like they are, it'll take me two hours goin' and him and me two hours comin'," said Mr. Bell. "It'll be might' nigh daylight before we get back. But I reckon you're right, and I'll go as quick as I can saddle a horse."

"No use," said a Voice. "All the doctors and medicines in the world won't cure her. But if you want one, I'll get him, and get him a lot quicker than you can."

The doctor got there just as the old eight-day clock struck one. "I heard somebody hollering at my window about midnight, telling me to come out here right away. When I got to the door, nobody was there; but I thought I'd better come anyway." He was a young doctor just starting out. "Say, what kind of road overseer and gang do you fellows have out this way? Last time I came over this road, about Christmas, it was the worst I ever saw. Why, I picked up a Stetson hat in the middle of a mud-hole near the four-mile board, and by George there was a man under it. 'You're in the middle of a bad fix, old man,' I said. 'Hell,' he said, 'that ain't nothin' to the fix this mule's in under me.' I had to lift up my feet half the way to keep them from dragging in the mud by the horse's belly. But to-night my horse skimmed over it in an hour. Well, who's sick out here?"

"It's her mind and nerves," he told them after he had questioned them and examined Mary. "I won't conceal from you, she's in pretty bad shape. And medicine won't do her any good. You've just got to be gentle and careful with her. Humor her and be patient with her. I'll give her something to put her to sleep when she gets like this. Watch her close and don't let her get lonesome. She's young and strong and ought to come round in time."

But she never did. For a month she lay there on the bed, looking at nothing and yet straining to see something. Something too far off. At night her pa and ma took turns sitting up. They didn't want the neighbors in. They called the doctor back a few times, but he shook his head and said he couldn't do any more. So they would watch and wait, wanting to do something, but helpless.

One night her ma was sitting there, holding Mary's hand and stroking the dark hair back from her forehead. Suddenly Mary pushed her mother away and sat up and looked across the foot of the bed, as if somebody was standing there.

"Mamma," she whispered, "Mamma.... I see him.... at last.... And I think.... I think.... I'm going.... to love him."

And she died with the only expression of happiness they had seen on her face in months.

Some folks have tried to explain Mary's strange death. A few say the Witch tortured her continually and kept her in such constant terror that her mind was affected. Others have heard that a school teacher ventriloquist that was jealous of Gardner played tricks on her and the family, and then when she wouldn't have him tormented and frightened her to death. Some believe she was in love with the overseer from the first, and then when he was killed she was in love with the Witch and didn't want to live because she knew she would never be happy with him until she too became a ghost.

But she died, just the same. And they say that on the day of the funeral, when the coffin was carried from the house to a wagon a great black bird flew down from the sky and hung in the air just above the wagon.

And around its neck was a bell that tolled in the mournfullest tone ever heard by the ear of man. And when the funeral procession began to move, the great bird floated just in front of it all the way to the grave-yard and circled round and round the grave during the burial, the bell tolling all the while. And when the mound was rounded up, the bird swung high up in the air and flew away to the west and finally became just a little speck above the treetops and disappeared. But long after it was gone the mourning notes of the bell floated back to those who stood and watched.

AVENGING GHOSTS

Tradition Bearer: Unavailable

Source: Porter, J. Hampden. "Notes on the Folk-Lore of the Mountain Whites of the Alleghenies." *Journal of American Folklore* 7 (1894): 110–11.

Date: 1894

Original Source: West Virginia

National Origin: Anglo American

The following supernatural **legends** represent the belief in revenants, deceased persons who appear to the living after death. Belief in revenants is closely linked to the belief systems of the community and their messages concerning not only death but ethics and the appropriate behavior and social roles of community members. It is believed that the appearance of revenants is the result of an unfulfilled duty either on the part of the deceased or the community of the living. In the cases below, the revenants seek the justice that was denied them in life.

Sometimes an apparition comes on a mission of justice; at others, ghosts revisit "the glimpses of the moon," inspired with the desire for vengeance.

Before the separation of West Virginia from the mother State, Colonel murdered one of his slave women with aggravated circumstances of cruelty. The crime could not be proved against him, and his act remained unpunished by law. But when investigation was at an end, and it became evident that nothing would be done, a white dog made its appearance upon the estate. Numbers saw it, and knew it for a specter by its vanishing while in full view. This goblin brute hunted the man to death. It followed and went before him, came into his room, haunted the guilty being night and day, until he pined away, and, having made a confession, died.

* * *

A miser, whose ruined house still stands, disappeared and was never seen again.

Two single women, living in a poor way in the neighborhood, suddenly came into possession of money, concerning which they gave an improbable account. Inquiry was made, but it came to naught.

The dead man's ghost, however, headless and bleeding, walked upon the hill where their cottage stood. It passed along the garden fence between sunset and dark, and the elder of these murderesses was soon literally frightened to death.

Her companion lived longer and suffered more. She wasted away, said one of the many persons from whom I heard this tale, "till nothing of her was left but a little pile of bones." Then death came, and it took four strong men to lift the coffin in which her body was enclosed. The hidden money was there.

* * *

A headless horseman rides upon the road near Indian Fort, in the foothills of Cumberland Mountain. His story is unknown, and this phantom's wanderings are apparently objectless. Nevertheless he is ill to meet, for this brings misfortune, and those who have seen it had reason to regret their encounter.

THE RICH GHOST

Tradition Bearer: Unavailable

Source: Bunter, Rosa. "Ghosts as Guardians of Hidden Treasure." *Journal of American Folklore* 12 (1899): 64–65

Date: 1899

Original Source: *Southern Workman* and *Hampton School Record*, March 1898.

National Origin: African American

A gloss appended to the original source of this tale asserts that, "If [a ghost is] met with courage, he rewards those who speak to him, as he is in many cases the guardian of concealed treasure." The pale ghost of this narrative manifests a solicitous concern for a living relative and rewards the female protagonist for her help in fulfilling his mission. The belief in the power of reading a Bible verse backward is more commonly associated with evil forms of conjuration rather than exorcisms of this sort, however.

Once upon a time, in a lonely little house upon a hill, there lived a man and his wife. The husband worked down in the town all day, and the wife worked at home alone. Every day, at noon, when the clock was striking twelve, she was startled by the pale, ghost-like figure of a man that stood in the doorway and watched her. She was very much frightened, and told her husband that she could not stay in that house any longer. But they were very poor, and the rent was cheaper than they could find elsewhere.

While the husband was looking for another house, the preacher came to see the wife. She told him about the pale-faced ghost that continually watched her. The preacher told her to sit down before her looking-glass with her back to the door and read a certain passage from the Bible backward. Then she must turn her chair around, look the ghost in the face and ask him, "What do you want here?"

The very next day she did as she was told. At first her voice trembled and she did not think that she could finish, but strength came to her and she read it. Then she turned upon the ghost and asked him the question. His face was frightful to look upon, but he told her to take her hoe and follow him. He led her to a lonely spot and rolled away a large stone and commanded her to dig. She dug until she was exhausted and the hoe fell from her hand. He jerked it up and dug until she had regained her strength. Then she commenced to dig again and at last struck something hard. He commanded her to stop, then stooped down and with wonderful strength drew up a large earthen pot. Upon taking off the cover, she saw, by the dim light of the setting sun, gold and silver coins in great abundance. The ghost told her to go home and tear the plastering from off the western corner of her little one-room house, and she would find a package of letters. From these she must get his brother's address and send him half of the hidden treasure. The other half was for herself.

She did as she was told. The pale-faced ghost was never seen again, and she was made a rich woman and they lived happily ever afterward.

RETURN OF THE GHOST WIFE

Tradition Bearer: Unavailable

Source: Porter, J. Hampden. "Notes on the Folk-Lore of the Mountain Whites of the Alleghenies." *Journal of American Folklore* 7 (1894): 109.

Date: 1894

Original Source: West Virginia

National Origin: Anglo American

The revenants who appeared in the **legends** titled "Avenging Ghosts" (p. 192) were victims of violent crimes who had returned to pursue justice. The appearance of revenants, therefore, is the result of an unfulfilled duty either on the part of the deceased or the community of the living. In this case, the community of the living (in the person of the ghost's widowed husband and his new wife) neglected its obligations (the violation of an oath not to remarry) to the dead person (the deceased wife) after death.

M iss F, who was not born on Christmas week, and therefore had no natural power of seeing spirits, related the apparition of her brother's first wife. This lady was devotedly attached to her husband, and when in the last stage of consumption could not die until he made an oath to remain single for the remainder of his life.

Not long after he perjured himself, but the peace of that household was gone. Ever after there was "a sense of something moving to and fro" upon them all. His sister, in common with the rest, heard the sighs and sobs of the disconsolate ghost, she saw her dim figure floating through the dusk, and was chilled to the heart by its icy atmosphere as the spirit went by in passages or upon the stairs.

RIDERS PURSUED BY GHOSTS

Tradition Bearer: Unavailable

Source: Porter, J. Hampden. "Notes on the Folk-Lore of the Mountain Whites of the Alleghenies." *Journal of American Folklore* 7 (1894): 110.

Date: 1894

Original Source: West Virginia

National Origin: Anglo American

The following two **legends** provide no explanation for the supernatural assaults they recount, beyond the fact that the road by Crackwhip

Furnace is "haunted." The black bear that screams in a human voice suggests the shape-shifting witch **motif** seen in "Miller's Witch Wife" (p. 171). The inability of a malevolent supernatural creature to cross running water is a common folk belief in the southern highlands as well as other European American traditions.

Mr. B, going home one night by Crackwhip Furnace, then abandoned, beheld the likeness of a black bear in front, but it screamed horribly at him with a human voice. His horse was terrified, and when the thing came nearer and screamed again, he rode for his life. Half a mile away from the spot this same dreadful cry sounded in his ears shriller and more appalling than before.

* * *

Mr. C, riding on the same road one dark autumnal evening, suddenly found his mare attacked by an invisible adversary. Blows were struck at her head, but the animal, though snorting, plunging, and rearing in terror, could not stir from the place; something met it at every turn. The rider tried to pray, but in vain. He was able to think the words, yet not to utter them. In his extremity the name of God at last burst from his lips. At once the horse sprang forward, and clasping its neck the pair dashed down hill into a brook. Whatever it was that beset them could not follow across flowing water, but a shriek that shook his heart swept by him as he fled.

THE MYSTERIOUS DEER

Tradition Bearer: A. S. Wiltse

Source: Wiltse, Henry M. "In the Southern Field of Folk-Lore." *Journal of American Folklore* 13 (1900): 211.

Date: 1900

Original Source: Tennessee

National Origin: Anglo American

The following **legend** operates as a **belief tale** intended to substantiate the existence of a white deer that displayed an uncanny ability to avoid death, screamed with the voice of a human being, and had the ability to exact supernatural revenge on a hunter who had wounded it.

There is quite a prevalent belief among mountaineers in the existence of a mysterious deer, of which they stand in no inconsiderable awe. I have heard of a hunter in upper East Tennessee, who claims to have shot at this deer, or one of these deer, under a misapprehension. The bullet came back and lodged in his own leg, and he shows the scar in apparent confidence that the evidence is conclusive.

Dr. A. S. Wiltse, who has for many years practiced his profession in the Cumberland Mountains, and who takes a deep interest in the mountain people and their peculiarities, writes me this version of the deer **myth**, secured from a celebrated hunter named Jackson Howard. The language of the original relator is reproduced as nearly as practicable:

"El Moore is a good hunter, and a splendid good shot, too. But he gat into a streak o' mighty ornery luck one time jes' on account of one of them thar white deer. He tole me all about hit with 'is own lips, an' El is a mighty truthful man.

"He said he war out a' huntin' one mornin', an' he come onter a white deer, an' hit war not more 'n fifteen er twenty feet from him.

"He fired at hit, but never touch a hair. That deer jes' stood still until he'd a-wasted seven or eight shots on hit. Then hit run off, an' he tried his gun on a spot in a tree, an' the bullet went straight to their mark.

"He got his dander up then, an' laid for that white deer, an' he wasted a powerful lot more ammunition on hit, until fin'ly 'e plugged hit in the shoulder.

"But he was mighty sorry for that, right then an' for a long time afterwards. He said hit made the sorrowfulest noise 'at he ever heard in all of his life. An' from that day twelvemonth hit war impossible for El ter kill any kind of deer whatsomever. He could kill other kinds of varmints all right enough, but kill a deer he couldn't."

THE BRIDE OF THE EVIL ONE

Tradition Bearer: An African American gardener known as "Old William"

Source: Cooke, Elizabeth Johnston. "English Folk-Tales in America. The Bride of the Evil One." *Journal of American Folklore* 12 (1899): 126–30.

Date: 1899

Original Source: Louisiana

National Origin: African American

This tale of the demon lover who comes to claim the rich, beautiful, and heretofore inaccessible Maritta warns of the dangers of avarice. This narrative plot is distributed cross-culturally. "The Demon Lover" (also known as "James Harris" and "The House Carpenter") presents the plot in the form of a British ballad. The **motifs** of the closing test of the Devil's questions and the Obstacle Flight enjoy a similar popularity. Localization of what is undoubtedly an old tale is seen in Satan's breakfast of buckwheat cakes and his spending his days in his blacksmith shop overseeing "his hands" at work.

In former times there lived, on a great plantation far out in the country, the richest and most beautiful lady in the world. Her name was Maritta, and she was beloved by all who knew her, especially so by her parents, with whom she dwelt.

She was so rich that one could not count her wealth in many days; and her home was a palace, filled with rare things from all quarters of the globe. Rich hangings of damask and tapestry adorned the walls, and massive and wonderfully carved furniture filled the rooms. Instead of gilt, as is usual in splendid mansions, the mirrors and pictures were framed in gold, silver, and even precious stones. Then, the dining-table was a wonder to behold—glittering with costly glass and golden service. The lady Maritta always ate from a jeweled platter with a golden spoon; and her rooms were filled with wondrous vases, containing delicious spices and rare perfumes of many kinds.

Half the brave and daring fine gentlemen of her country had sought her hand in marriage; but her parents always declared that each was not rich enough. So loath were her parents to give her up, that they finally said she should never marry unless she could view her suitor ten thousand miles down the road.

Now, as roads in general are not straight for so great a distance, to say nothing of one's eyesight, the poor lady was quite in despair, and had almost decided to remain a spinster.

199

At last the Evil One, seeing the covetousness of this old couple, procured for himself an equipage of great magnificence, and went a-wooing. His coach was made of beaten gold, so ablaze with precious stones that the sun seemed mean in comparison with it. Maritta beheld it thirty thousand miles off, and all the household were called out to view it; for such a wonder had never been seen in that part of the world. But so great was the Evil One's power for conjuring that he was a very short time in arriving. He drove up to the door with so grand a dash and clatter and style that Maritta thought she had never beheld as princely a personage. When he had alighted most gracefully, uncovering [removing his hat] and bowing to the mother and father, he knelt at the feet of Maritta, kissed her hand, and turning to her astonished parents, asked the hand of their daughter in marriage. So pleased were they all with his appearance that the wedding was hastened that very day. After the marriage compact was completed Maritta bade adieu to her proud parents; and tripping lightly into his coach, they drove away with great effect.

Then they journeyed and journeyed, and every fine house or plantation which they approached, Maritta would exclaim, "Is that your home, my dear?"

"No, darling," he would reply with a knowing smile, "my house is another cut to [different from] that." Still they journeyed, and just as Maritta was beginning to feel *very* weary they approached a great hill, from which was issuing a cloud of black smoke, and she could perceive an enormous hole in the side of the hill, which appeared like the entrance to a tunnel. The horses were now prancing and chafing at the bits in a most terrifying manner; and Maritta thought she saw flames coming from out their nostrils. just as she was catching her breath to ask the meaning of it all, the coach and party plunged suddenly into the mouth of the yawning crater, and they sank down, down into that place which is called Torment. The poor trembling lady went into a swoon, and knew nothing more until she awoke in the House of Satan. But she did not yet know that it was the Evil One whom she had married, nor that, worse still, he was already a married man when she had made his acquaintance. Neither did she know that the frightful old crone was his other wife. Satan's manner had also undergone a decided change; and he, who had been so charming a lover, was now a blustering, insolent master. Lifting his voice until it shook the house, as when it thunders, he stormed around, beating the old hag, killing her uncanny black cat, and raising a tumult generally. Then, ordering the hag to cook him some buckwheat cakes for breakfast, he stamped out of the house, towards his blacksmith shop, to see how his hands were doing their work. While the wretched young wife sat in her parlor, looking very mournful and lovely, wiping her eyes and feeling greatly mystified, the old hag was turning her cakes on the griddle and growing more and more jealous of this beautiful new wife who was to take her place. Finally she left the cakes and came and stood by Maritta. "My child," quoth she, "my dear daughter, have you married that man?"

"Yes, dame," replied the pretty Maritta.

"Well, my child," said she, "you have married nothing but the Devil." At this the wretched young wife uttered a scream and would have swooned again, except that the hag grasped her by the arm, and putting a rough horny hand over Maritta's mouth, said in a low and surly voice, near her ear: "Hist! Should he hear you, he will kill us both! Only do my bidding, and keep a quiet tongue, and I will show you how to make your escape." At this Maritta sat up quite straight, and said in trembling tones: "Good dame, prithee tell me, and I will obey, and when I am free, I will send you five millions of dollars."

But the forlorn hag only shook her head, replying: "Money I ask not, for it is of no use to such as I; but listen well."

Then seating herself on the floor at the feet of Maritta, her black hair hanging in tangles about her sharp ugly face, like so many serpents, she continued in this wise: "He has two roosters who are his spies, and you must give them a bushel of corn to pacify them—but I shall steal the corn for you. He also has two oxen; one is as swift of foot as the wind can blow; the other can only travel half as fast. You will have to choose the last, as the swift one is too well guarded for us to reach him. The slower one is tethered just outside the door. Come!" she cried to Maritta, who would have held back, "a faint heart will only dwell in Torment."

At this thought the poor Maritta roused herself, and summoned all her strength. Her hair had now fallen loose and she was all in tears. But she mounted quickly, looking over her shoulder, to see if he was coming even then. "But dame," cried she, "will he not overtake me, if his ox is so much more fleet of foot than mine?"

"Hold your slippery tongue," replied the hag, "and mark my words. Here is a reticule [a drawstring bag] to hang at your side; this is a brickbat which I put in the bottom, and on that I place a turkey egg and a goose egg. When you feel the hot steam coming near you, drop the brickbat—for he will soon return, and missing you, will start on your chase, mounted on the ox. As he approaches near, you will feel the heat of his breath like hot steam. When you drop the brickbat a wall will spring up from the earth to the sky; and the Devil cannot pass it until he tears down every brick, and throws it out of sight. When you feel the hot steam again, drop the turkey egg, and there will come a river; and when he reaches this river he cannot cross over until his ox drinks all the water. Do the same with the goose egg, and a river will again flow behind you, thus giving you more time in which to reach home. Now off with you, and Devil take you, if you don't hold on tight and keep up your spirits. But, hark ye, if he catches you, I will poison you when you come back. At this terrible threat the lovely Maritta was so frightened that she forgot to thank the old hag or say good-by. In the twinkling of an eye the weird-looking creature had raised her mighty arm, and gurgling out a frightful laugh, she lashed the ox with a huge whip.

Away he sped, verily as fleet as the wind, with the beautiful lady clinging on, her arms wound around his neck, and her soft face buried in his shaggy hair. Onward they floated, above the earth, it seemed to Maritta, over hills and plains, through brake and swamp. Just as the lady began to rejoice at being set free, for it seemed a kind ox, and, after all, it was not so *very* hard to hold on, as she glided along, she heard a piercing shriek behind her; and suddenly a burning hot steam seemed to envelop her. Thinking of the brickbat, in an instant she snatched it from the reticule—almost breaking the eggs in her haste—and flung it behind her, nearly suffocated with the heat. Then she turned to look and lo! A great dark wall shut the awful sight from her gaze.

Onward, onward they sped, as she urged the ox by kind words, stroking his great neck with her delicate white hands. After they had traversed a great distance, Maritta began to think of home and the loved ones, when her reveries were broken by a gaunt black hand clutching at her hair over the back of the ox; and again she felt the intense heat. Too terrified to put her hand in the reticule, she gave it a shake, and the turkey egg fell to the ground. On the instant water was flowing all about her, cooling the air and quite reviving her. Then a harsh voice fell upon her ear, crying: "Drink, drink, I tell you; mighty hard on you, but you must drink!"

Soon the river was left far behind, and again Maritta aroused herself as she began to notice many familiar landmarks, which told that she was nearing home. After urging the ox on at a great rate for many more miles, she dropped the goose egg, in order to give herself ample time, although as yet she had not again felt the approach of her fiendish husband.

At length the welcome sight of her own broad fields greeted her anxious and weary eyes; and soon her dear home arose upon the horizon. With a few more strides the wonderful ox halted at her own very door, and she fell from his back more dead than alive. For some moments she was unable to rise and embrace her alarmed parents, who had seen her approach.

They had only had time to retire into the house, when Satan rode up to the steps. Throwing himself from the ox, he banged for admittance, in a vastly different manner from that of his first visit. But the father confronted him, and he had to content himself with talking to Maritta over her father's shoulders, while the poor lady was cowering in a corner of the room clinging to her mother. However, the touch of loving parental arms soon reassured her, and she demanded of Satan what he wished further. "I have," replied his Satanic majesty, "three questions to propound to you; and if not properly answered, I shall take you by force again to my realms." Then placing his feet wide apart, with head thrown back, one arm akimbo on his hip, and snapping the fingers of his other hand, he sang in an impudent, swaggering manner:

> What is whiter than any snow?
> What is whiter than any snow?
> Who fell in the colley well?

The gentle Maritta lifted her soft eyes, and raising her sweet voice sang in a pure and tender strain:

> Heaven is whiter than any snow,
> Heaven is whiter than any snow,
> Who fell in the colley well?

"Yes, ma'am," replied Satan, rather taken aback. "That's right." Then he continued:

> What is deeper than any well?
> What is deeper than any well?
> Who fell in the colley well?

Maritta replied in the same strain:

> Hell is deeper than any well,
> Hell is deeper than any well,
> Who fell in the colley well?

Again the Evil One took up his strain:

> What is greener than any grass?
> What is greener than any grass?
> Who fell in the colley well?

Maritta lifted her voice a third time:

Poison is greener than any grass,
Poison is greener than any grass,
Who fell in the colley well?

Greatly confounded at her answers, the Evil One stamped his feet in such a manner that smoke and sparks flew upward, and an odor of sulphur filled the room. Then turning on his heels be cried to the mother that he had left a note under the doorsteps with the Devil's own riddle on it.

A thousand or more acres of green corn grew about the house; and the Devil, pulling it all up by the roots, carried it in his hands, tore the roof off the mansion, and raising a fearful storm, disappeared in it. When the storm had abated, the mountains around about were all leveled to the ground. After the panic caused by his wonderful conjuring had subsided, the mother bethought herself of the note, and when found it read as follows:

Nine little white blocks into a pen,
One little red block rolled over them.

None could guess it save Maritta, who said it meant the teeth and tongue.

THE CHOSEN SUITOR: THE FORBIDDEN ROOM

Tradition Bearer: Julius Jenkins

Source: Parsons, Elsie Clews. Pages 47–48 in *Folk-Lore of the Sea Islands, South Carolina.* Memoirs of the American Folklore Society 16. New York: American Folklore Society, 1923.

Date: 1923

Original Source: South Carolina
National Origin: African American

The following tale presents a "John" character who differs from the African American John or Jack seen in other tales in this collection. The John of "The Chosen Suitor" is a "little boy witch" with a supernatural ability to see the intentions of his sister's suitors. Rather than seeking his help, the sister forces him to hide when the King comes courting. John's claims that the King is the Devil in disguise are met with physical abuse. Roger Abrahams, in his book *African American Folktales* (22–24), explains the power of this **stock character** by attributing to him the power that comes from living between customary categories as is the case with **trickster**. When he rescues his sister, the little witch boy uses his power to help them escape the Devil by turning ordinary objects into obstacles to impede pursuit (a folktale **motif** commonly called the "obstacle flight"). The act results in raised social status for little John. This tale shares with others in the collection the dangers inherent in judging by surface appearances only. Variants of this tale (AT312C, "Devil's Bride Rescued by Brother") are found both along the southern coast of the United States and throughout the Caribbean. (Compare the tale to the Caribbean "The Chosen Suitor," p. 277). The original Gullah rendering of this tale appears in the appendix to this volume (p. 311).

An' he [John] had a sister. An' dis king was payin' dis boy sister address [courting his sister]. Dis little boy was a witch, could tell whether his sister goin' to get a good husban' o' not. So when dis man come, his sister always put dis boy underneat' de step, an' put him to bed. So den dis little boy wake up an' tell his sister, "Sister, you married to de Devil." Sister slap him aroun' an' kick him, wouldn' listen de boy.

So, sure enough, he [she] married de man against de boy. Man carry his sister from there an' carry her to his house, little over t'irty or forty miles. So, after carryin' dis woman many nights an' many days, dis boy know exactly how dis man was treatin' his sister. One day de man han' his wife seven key. An' he had seven room in de house. But he show him [her] de room, an' say, "Use de six room; but de seven room don' use it, don' go in dat room!"

So one day his wife say to herself, "I got all de key. I wan' to see what is in dat room." He husban' been 'bout twenty-five mile from there when she said dat. She wen' into de room, open de room. When she open de room, was nothin' but de wife dis man married, de skeleton hung up in de room. Dis one fall down, faint, right to de do', Less dan half an hour she come to her sense. He lock de do' back. Gone, set down, take her as the room. Husban' drive up to de do' at de time, an' tell um, "Dis night you will be in dat room." Forty mile from her broder den. So her broder know dat his sister have a fast' horse. An' he took seven needle with him. He started fo' his sister den. He reached his sister's place 'bout four o'clock. Sister was to put to deat' at firs' dark.

When he see dat his broder-in-law come, he welcome him like any broder-in-law do, like not'in' goin' to be done. Dis king ask him what his horse eat? He tol' him, "I feed my horse wid cotton-seed." Dis king den had to go half a mile from dis house to his nex' neighbor to get cotton-seed for his broder-in-law horse.

When he gone, he tell his sister, "Sister, take not'in', jump in de buggy!" Dey had fo'ty miles to go.

When he get a half a mile from de house, he han' his sister dese seven needle. He said, "Sister, he done hitch up his horse, he comin' after us." Drop one o' de needle, an' it become a swamp across de road. De king drive until he come to de swamp. He had to turn back home an' get a grubbin'-hoe an' axe to cut t'rough there.

All dat time John was goin' wid his sister. De king was a witch himself. He cut um so quick, he was on dem again. He [she] drop anoder needle. Den it become a ocean across de road. He had to sup [sip] up all dat water befo' he could star' again.

When dey was one mile of John house where his sister live, he tell his sister t'row all de needle out his han'. Dey become an ocean. Dey cross de oder side den. He drive down here. When he get to de ocean, he had to stop, couldn' get any furder.

John an' his sister arrive his of cabin where de king carry her from. An' dis sister gave de broder what she used to kick about lovin' praise. An' John save his sister life.

THE HAUNTED HOUSE

Tradition Bearer: Unavailable

Source: Fauset, Arthur Huff. "Negro Folk Tales from the South (Alabama, Mississippi, Louisiana)." *Journal of American Folklore* 40 (1927): 258–59.

Date: 1925

Original Source: Alabama

National Origin: African American

Preacher, often a **stock character** in African American folktales, is tested in this comic narrative and is shown to be less than perfect. Armed with his Bible and his religious faith, he takes on the ghosts haunting a house and learns that "Patience" is not always a virtue.

Bout a preacher.

So was a haunted house. Could nobody stay in it. Everybody go in there, the hants [ghost] run them out. So the preacher says, "I believe I'll go in that house. Ain't no hants kin run me out." So he takes his grip, a hymn book an' a Bible, an' he went in the house. An' so he got in the bed an' he locked the door before he got in bed. He turned his head over against the wall. The door came open with a slam-bam.

So he turned over, look over at the door. So he sees a ghost looked just like a cat settin' up in a chair with his front paws up. So the man turned his head back to the wall. So after he turned his head back, the door opened again, slam. He was just tremblin' in bed. Second spirit what come in asked the other what he was waitin' for.

The first spirit said, "Patience." So they just went to rockin' in the chair. When the man turned his head again the door opened and slammed again, and another spirit walked in.

The spirit said, "What you waitin' for?" The other spirits said, "Patience." So all these of 'em went to rockin'. Man was so skeered in bed, he didn't see no way to git out. They was settin' between him an' the door. So they couldn't skeer him out.

The big one said, "What-are-you-waitin'-on?"

One of them said, "He-just-havin'-fits-in-the-bed."

The other one said, "Let's start now." So the man jumped out of bed clean over their heads an' ran out the door.

So when he got out he looked back at 'em and said, "Tell Patience. I been an' gone."

RACE WITH A GHOST

Tradition Bearer: Joseph Madden

Source: Hubert, Levi. "Interview of Joseph Madden." *American Life Histories: Manuscripts from the Federal Writers' Project, 1936–1940.* Manuscript Division, Library of Congress. 12 October 2005. http://memory.loc.gov/ammem/wpaintro/wpahome.html.

Date: 1938

Original Source: Unavailable

National Origin: African American

The following joke depicts the powers of fear of the supernatural to make one of the characters forget the infirmities of age when confronted by a ghost. Given that the tale is set in the South, told by an African American who has migrated to New York, and that the older of the two protagonists is the more obviously frightened, the tale may represent a rejection of what the narrator considers the superstitions of the South. In any case, the grandson rejects all filial duties in an effort to save himself. Along the way he outruns a rabbit, perhaps an unconscious allusion to the notoriously elusive anthropomorphized Rabbit of other African American folktales.

A youth, agile, strong and supple, was walking along a country road, accompanied by his aged grandfather, almost incapacitated by the infirmities of age and compelled to hobble along in an uncertain fashion, assisted by a cane and the firm arm of the grandson.

The two were compelled to make frequent halts by the wayside and although they had started their journey while the sun was still high, yet the pauses which the old man requested had stretched their trip until the afternoon sun had long before hidden itself behind the towering pines in the western hills.

On one of their pauses they seated themselves on a stone which lay beside the road, and there the old man rested and attempted to catch his breath and fight off the overpowering fatigue which further impeded his slow progress.

They had no sooner seated themselves than a ghostly figure also seated himself beside them.

"There don't seem to be but three of us here tonight," commented the addition to the group.

One quick look and the young fellow got to his feet and saw that a cemetery skirted the road at that point.

"Yea, but there ain't gonna be but the two of you in a minute," so off he went, disregarding his grandfather's plea not to be left behind. As the grandson ran down the road, he surprised a rabbit hurrying along. "Git outta the way, rabbit, and let somebody run as kin run."

The distance covered by the running youngster was a little over five miles, and he did it in double-quick time. But, just as he reached home and tried to close the door after him, he felt someone pushing against it and heard his grandfather say, "Don't slam the door in your poor old grandpappy's face, son."

THE GHOST OF ALEX

Tradition Bearer: Eldora Scott Maples

Source: Mosley, Ruby. "Interview of Eldora Scott Maples." *American Life Histories: Manuscripts from the Federal Writers' Project, 1936–1940.* Manuscript Division, Library of Congress. 12 October 2005. http://memory.loc.gov/ammem/wpaintro/wpahome.html.

Date: 1938

Original Source: Missouri

National Origin: European American

The **legend** of "The Ghost of Alex," actually a series of interrelated legends, is an example of family folklore. Although the narratives are performed for outsiders, the primary audience for and focus of the tales is the Scott family. The fact that the narratives began as **personal experience narratives** recounted by Billy Scott and eventually developed into **legends** transmitted by his daughter and, presumably, other members of the family speaks not only to the belief in Alex but to the family's sense of shared identity and history. Among other messages conveyed by the following tale is the sense that there is a continuity of the deceased with the living; the former care about the living and may intervene at important junctures in their lives.

My father, Billy Scott, was born in Joplin, Missouri, where he lived most of his life.

When my father was twelve years of age he heard a strange tap, tap one night as he lay in bed that sounded as if water was dripping from the top of the house down to a feather mattress. The tap, tap come repeatedly through a duration of a year or more before he recognized that some message was trying to be revealed. The tap, tap, tap, appeared so frequently that they soon ceased to be taps but were an insistent stream, then stopped when the usual tap, tap, tap, began as before. While in that lone room in the stillness of the night with blared eyes the constant tap, tap, never varying from sound except by frequency, my father decided that the visitor was a ghost.

Many times the entire family searched for the ghastly specter but it was never physically located even though one could hear the sound. One time Grandmother Scott said, "Billy, someone's spirit has come to watch over you." It did through the remaining years. My father had tried every way plausible to locate some physical cause of the tapper, although his efforts were in vain. One lonely, quiet night he was listening to the insistent tapping when he decided to talk to his spiritual companion, the question came up as to how he might receive an answer. Finally the two decided to work out a code as: two taps for yes, and one tap for no. Thus the conversation began. Of course father wanted to know who the tapper was and if he was either of his favorite generals, Hannibal or Napoleon; the answer came with one tap which meant no. He asked about several other celebrities and found the tapper to be Alexander the Great, therefore he was and is until this day, called Alex by the Scott generation. He is known by the entire family and is recognized by advice at intervals, which proves helpful in many instances.

My father was almost a genius in regard to Latin, Greek and French languages; also a lover of history, therefore he had an understanding of theosophy that would be meaningless to the ordinary person.

I will relate several of Alex's theurgies which saved my father's life several times. Alex reported the death of my mother's first born; a son's life saved when a war ship was blown up. I could name minor incidents reported by Alex that would fill a book.

Father, just an ordinary boy at 17 years of age, went over to a boy friend's to play a little game of poker, lost his money and started home. The vicinity of Joplin was sparsely populated and the wooded section made a very desirable place for a riff-raff of robbers to harbor as there was money in "them there hills," of the new mining town, as it is today in the oil boom towns. Father was a little shaky as he had to cross a little ravine. The paths were connected by a foot log crossing the stream, a big tree spread her branches in every direction, one going directly over the path. When father came near the tree he was frightened out of his wits by hand clutches on his trembling shoulders. He wheeled around to recognize his assailant when he found himself alone. He grabbed a stick and searched the underbrush on either side of the path for his assailant but found no one. He gave up with disgust and turned homeward. As he got back to the big tree he discovered a huge panther sitting on the limb of the tree that extended over the trail. He retraced his tracks, whistled to his boy friends, they brought the dogs and gave chase but the panther disappeared. Father went home and stretched out for a good night's sleep, when the tap, tap, met his ears. He asked Alex if he had saved him from the panther and his answer was two taps, which meant yes. Alex vanished and didn't bother any more that night. In case father didn't recognize Alex's presence, he was gently touched on the shoulder or an arm.

One night Alex was tapping and father was so tired and sleepy he said, "Go away Alex, I'm too tired to talk with you tonight," Alex continued the tap, tap indefinately [sic] until he became so tiresome that father said, "Get out of here, you damned son-o-a-b." At these words father was struck on the head by a magic blow of a streak of blind lightning which left him unconscious for hours. The next morning he was so weak that he could hardly get out of the bed of cold sweat. His headache lasted several days and he never refused to recognize Alex [again?]. Alex was silent for several months. Father would call on him and pray that he would return and he did.

Alex saved father again, when working in a lead and zinc mine at Joplin. Father's ears were trained to catch Alex's taps instantly, as they were unexpected warnings which were often urgent. On this occasion they struck an especially rich vein of lead and zinc. The miners were enthusiastically working to obtain as much ore as possible. Father heard a tap, tap, on his shovel handle and felt the light brush of a magic hand on his shoulder. He felt Alex's presence, looked up in time to see thousands of tons of dirt caving in when he shouted, "My God, men, get out of the way!" They all dashed down the tunnel where they were saved again. Alex came tapping that night and father thanked him for his warning. The shaft of a mine was dug straight down as a well or cellar, then the vein of zinc or lead was traced and its course was followed as far as the wealth was obtainable. The whole set-up was similar to a large house with a hallway leading to each room. My father and his partner were forty feet below the surface, digging zinc. One that far under the ground never knew what was happening on top. The railroads in the mine were always graveled which caused a grinding sound when walked upon. My father and his partner heard footsteps come to the turn and stop. His co-worker said, "I heard someone coming, Billy." Then dad answered, "I thought I heard someone too." They walked around the bend and saw no one. When they resumed their work, footsteps were heard again. They knew that they could see anyone that entered the mine, from the place they worked. The footsteps were heard for the third time and dad felt the light brush of someone's hand on his shoulder. "Let's get out of here! Something must be wrong," cried [D]ad. "I'm coming, I won't stay where hants walk," replied the partner. They rushed out to the drift in the shaft and before they arrived in the shaft they were met by the water that was waist deep and still flowing in torrents. Dad's partner couldn't swim a lick but he helped him to get a hold on the pump. Father rang the bell but no answer came; no bucket was let down to them. The engineer was asleep on the job—I will explain that the engineer's job was to keep the water pumped out of the mine. The pump was run by steam as there was no electricity in those days; when the fire died out the pump stopped and the engineer slept on, even though the partner was almost exhausted, dad pulled him up the forty foot ladder to safety. Again Alex had saved his life. The workers on top only smiled when dad and his partner related how Alex had saved them, but the partner thanked God for the warning.

Father and mother were as elated over their first born as any ordinary new parents, no other child was ever so perfectly sweet. Father was making good money and sent mother on a ten days' visit with relatives to show the new offspring. Everyone was well and happy. When they had been gone four or five days Alex came to my father in the mines and gave his tap, tap, on the shovel handle. His first thoughts were of mother and baby. He asked Alex if it was his wife. He tapped once, meaning no. A lump came in his throat as he knew it must be the baby. When he hesitated to ask about the baby, Alex kept knocking. Then he asked, "Is it my baby?" Alex tapped twice. He asked if it was sick. Alex tapped once. With a weak body and trembling voice he asked if baby was dead, when the answer was two sad taps on the shovel handle. At these taps father dropped his shovel and went home and waited for a message from mother, which came stating that baby was dead. Alex was a true and faithful spiritual companion that guided the Scott family in many tragical hours.

When Bob's ship went down, Alex comforted the family. My brother, Bob, did service in the World War, his duty was fireman on the W.P.A. San Diego, the largest ship convoy at that time. Father was at his usual task when Alex, true to his watchfulness throughout the many years, come to warn dad about the boy. Naturally in those trying times of war when Alex kept his insistent knocking, dad's thoughts turned to Bob. As [on?] so many occasions he was reluctant to ask this time if his visit concerned Bob. Finally he secured enough courage to force the words from his lips. Alex's answer was tap, tap, meaning yes. He asked, "Is Bob dead?" and waited restlessly for the answer. Relief surged through him and tears came in his eyes as Alex gave one joyous tap, no. Father shouted, "Bob is alive! Bob is alive!" That was all that mattered at that time. Father came running home, telling us that Bob was alive, and found us with broken hearts, grieving over Bob's death as we had read in the Fort Worth Record where the bottom was blown out of Bob's ship on the morning of July 19, 1918. Mother's faith in Alex at that time fell to nothing as she stated, "Alex's hind end is full of blue mud, Bob can't be alive." Later news came that Bob was alive. All belief in Alex was strengthened and the family lived under the guidance of Alex. The Dr. on the ship was a German spy and his communications with friends set the trap to blow the ship up fifty miles from New York, near Fire Island.

Thus through the years, Alex warned my father of death and he passed the news on to mother, whose faith was built up enough that she prepared for the departure which came as predicted.

Alex comes to Bob and me now but neither of us talk to him. I cannot encourage such a character as it worries me to think of him and if he revealed more I would certainly believe every tap which would cause me to live a life of unrest. Therefore, Alex is regarded as a sacred mystery that runs in the bones of the Scott family. When he taps we know that something is going to happen, good or bad. We never question Alex's theurgy and receive the tragedies as God sends them.

THE SPIRIT DEFENDERS OF NÏKWÄSÏ'

Source: Mooney, James. "Myths of the Cherokee." Pages 336–37 in *Nineteenth Annual Report of the Bureau of American Ethnology 1897–1898, Part I.* Washington, DC: U.S. Government Printing Office, 1900.

Date: 1898

Original Source: Cherokee

National Origin: Native American

In Cherokee belief, the Nûñnë'hï ("the immortals") were a spirit race who lived much as humans did. They were invisible except when they wanted to be seen. In traditional narrative, they are depicted as benevolent protectors of the Cherokee.

Long ago a powerful unknown tribe invaded the country from the south east, killing people and destroying settlements wherever they went. No leader could stand against them, and in a little while they had wasted all the lower settlements and advanced into the mountains. The warriors of the old town of Nïkwäsï', on the head of Little Tennessee, gathered their wives and chil dren into the townhouse and kept scouts constantly on the lookout for the pres ence of danger. One morning just before daybreak the spies saw the enemy approaching and at once gave the alarm. The Nïkwäsï' men seized their arms and rushed out to meet the attack, but after a long, hard fight they found them selves overpowered and began to retreat, when suddenly a stranger stood among them and shouted to the chief to call off his men and he himself would drive back the enemy. From the dress and language of the stranger the Nïkwäsï' peo ple thought him a chief who had come with reinforcements from the Overhill settlements in Tennessee. They fell back along the trail, and as they came near the townhouse they saw a great company of warriors coming out from the side of the mound as through an open doorway. Then they knew that their friends were the Nûññë'hï, the Immortals, although no one had ever heard before that they lived under Nïkwäsï' mound.

The Nûññë'hï poured out by hundreds, armed and painted for the fight and the most curious thing about it all was that they became invisible as soon as they were fairly outside of the settlement, so that although the enemy saw the glancing arrow or the rushing tomahawk, and felt the stroke, he could not see who sent it. Before such invisible foes the invaders soon had to retreat, going first south along the ridge to where it joins the main ridge which separates the French Broad from the Tuckasegee, and then turning with it to the northeast. As they retreated they tried to shield themselves behind rocks and trees, but the Nûññë'hï arrows went around the rocks and killed them from the other side and they could find no hiding place. All along the ridge they fell, until when they reached the head of Tuckasegee not more than half a dozen were left alive and in despair they sat down and cried out for mercy.

Ever since then the Cherokee have called the place Dayûlsûñ'yï, "Where they cried." Then the Nûññë'hï chief told them they had deserved their punish ment for attacking a peaceful tribe, and he spared their lives and told them to go home and take the news to their people. This was the Indian custom, always to spare a few to carry back the news of defeat. They went home toward the north and the Nûññë'hï went back to the mound.

And they are still there, because, in the last war, when a strong party of Federal troops came to surprise a handful of Confederates posted there they saw so many soldiers guarding the town that they were afraid and went away without making an attack.

*   *   *

There is another story, that once while all the warriors of a certain town were off on a hunt, or at a dance in another settlement, one old man was chopping wood on the side of the ridge when suddenly a party of the enemy came upon him—Shawano, Seneca, or some other tribe. Throwing his hatchet at the nearest one, he turned and ran for the house to get his gun and make the best defense that he might. On coming out at once with the gun he was surprised to find a large body of strange warriors driving back the enemy. It was no time for questions, and taking his place with the others, they fought hard until the enemy was pressed back up the creek and finally broke and retreated across the mountain.

When it was over and there was time to breathe again, the old man turned to thank his new friends, but found that he was alone—they had disappeared as though the mountain had swallowed them. Then he knew that they were the Nûñnë'hï, who had come to help their friends, the Cherokee.

THE POWERS THAT BE: SECULAR TALES

JIM JOHNS AND THE TIGER

Tradition Bearer: Sam Chesser

Source: Harper, Francis. "Tales of the Okefinoke." *American Speech* 1 (1926): 410–11.

Date: ca. 1914

Original Source: Georgia

National Origin: European American

The following **personal legend** warns of the dangers of the surrounding environment, in this case a swamp at the border of Georgia and Florida where even the most experienced locals can find themselves in peril at any moment. The protagonist is a model for imitation by learning from the potentially fatal incident.

In the old days Black Jack Island was a virgin wilderness of longleaf pine, miles in area. It was a particularly favored hunting-ground and the scene of many a stirring adventure. The "Tiger" of this story, and of Okefinokee speech in general, is the Florida Cougar (*Felix coryi*), which has lingered in the swamp fastnesses almost, if not quite, to the present day.

Sam Chesser, the elder brother of Allen, was also given to reviving old memories during his occasional visits to camp.

"Did my buddy ever tell you of the Tiger that Jim Johns run into over on Black Jack? The three of us wuz over there on a big hunt. We carried Jim along with us. We trained 'im up, an' he become a good hunter.

"Allen wuz off some'eres, an' Jim an me made a sets fer Deer. Then Jim wanted ter go fire-lightin' on that night, but I wuz worried out an' stayed in camp. So Jim went down the island with 'is lantern. The woods is right open there, with palmetto bushes about that high [indicating a height of about three feet]. Wal, Jim seed a yearlin' fawn or two, their eyes shinin' in the light. Then when 'e got closer, he seed some big eyes a-shinin', right down in the grass. He thought it 'u a Coon er somethin', an' moved on up. Finally he saw two big eyes a-blazin', an' 'is head an' breast a-shinin' in the light. I heerd 'is shot, an' in jest a few minutes Jim 'uz back in camp, a-rattlin' the dishes, though he'd ben quite a piece off."

"Jim had knocked 'is shanks all up on stumps an' logs," interpolated Tom Chesser, who was listening with enjoyment to his father's tale.

"I sat right up then," the old man continued, "an' says: 'Why, whut's the matter, Jim?'"

"Sam," 'e says, "I come jest as near to gittin' Tiger-catched as a man ever could. He 'uz shore a big un."

"I reckon it 'uz a Tiger all right."

At that my own curiosity got the better of me. "Why, didn't he kill it?"

"No, sir."

"Didn't he go back the next morning to see if he'd hit it?"

"No, sir. An' 'e didn't go fire-lightin' no more, neither."

WHEN MR. TERRAPIN WENT RIDING ON THE CLOUDS

Tradition Bearer: Unavailable

Source: Backus, Emma M. "Animal Tales from North Carolina." *Journal of American Folklore* 11 (1898): 285–86.

Date: 1898

Original Source: North Carolina

National Origin: African American

In small traditional communities in which regular face-to-face interaction is the order of the day, gossipers, backbiters, and similar malcontents are likely to receive "rough justice" to preserve the social order. The best outcome of such scenarios is realized in this tale in which the grumbling Mr. Terrapin gets his wish, regrets it, and reforms.

Have they done tell you 'bout ole Mr. Grumble Terrapin? Well, one day ole Brer Terrapin was mighty bad, and making up a poor mouth, and a-grumbling and a-fussing, 'cause he have to creep on the ground. When he meet Brer Rabbit, he grumble 'cause he can't run like Brer Rabbit, an' when he meet Brer Buzzard he grumble 'cause he can't fly in the clouds like Brer Buzzard, and so grumble, grumble, constant.

Well, the folkses stand it till they nigh 'bout wore out, and so they 'gree amongst theyselves, the folkses did, and they 'gree how they goin' take Brer Terrapin up in the clouds and drop him.

So one day, when Brer Terrapin grumble to Miss Crow he can't fly in the clouds, Miss Crow she say, she did, "Brer Terrapin, go get on my back, and I give you a ride in the clouds." So Brer Terrapin, he mighty set up in he mind, and he get on Miss Crow's back, and they sail off fine, and they sails this here way, and they sails that there way. Brer Terrapin, he look down on all he friends, and he feel that proudful he don't take no noticement when they take off they hats to hisself.

But presently Miss Crow she get tired, and so she say, old Miss Crow did, "This here just as high as I can go, Brer Terrapin, but here come Brer Buzzard; he can fly heap higher than what I can, Brer Buzzard can, and you just get on his back, and he sail you heap higher."

So Brer Terrapin, he get on Brer Buzzard back, and they sail up higher and higher, till Brer Terrapin can't make out he friends when they take off they hats to hisself, and he say that the bestest day of his life, Brer Terrapin do, and they sails over the woods, and they sails over the waters.

Then Brer Buzzard, he get broke down a-toting Brer Terrapin, and he 'low: "This here just as high as I can go, Brer Terrapin, but there come Miss Hawk; she can go a heap higher than what I can," and Miss Hawk she say she be delighted to take Brer Terrapin to ride, that just what Miss Hawk done tell Brer Terrapin.

So Brer Terrapin, he get on Miss Hawk's back, and they go higher and higher, and Brer Terrapin he 'joy it fine, and he say to hisself, "I'se getting up in the clouds now, sure 'nough."

But directly here come King Eagle, and he say, "Oho, Brer Terrapin, you don't call this here sailing. Oho, Sis Hawk, if you goin' sail Brer Terrapin, why don't you take him up where he can get a sight?" But Miss Hawk, she 'bliged to 'low that just as high as she can go.

Then King Eagle say, "Well, just get on my back, and get a sure 'nough ride." So Brer Terrapin, he get on King Eagle's back, and they go up and up, till old Brer Terrapin he get skeered, and he beg King Eagle to get down; but King Eagle, he just laugh and sail higher and higher, till old Brer Terrapin say to his self he wish he never study 'bout flying in the clouds, and he say, Brer Terrapin did: "Oh please, King Eagle, take me down; I that skeered, I'se 'bout to drop," and he fault hisself cause he was such a grumbling fool, and he say to hisself, if he ever get on he own foots once more, he never grumble 'cause he can't fly in the clouds, but King Eagle, he just make like he goin' up higher and higher, and poor old Brer Terrapin, he dat skeered, he can't hold on much more, and he 'bout lose he hold.

Just den he think how he got a spool of thread in he pocket, what Miss Terrapin done send him to fetch home from the store that day, and he tie the end to King Eagle's leg, unbeknownst to him, Brer Terrapin did, and then he drop de spool, and he take hold of the thread, and hold it fast in he hands, and he slip down to the ground, and you never hear old Brer Terrapin grumble 'cause he can't run or fly, 'cause the old man he done fly that here day to satisfy hisself that he did, sure's you're born, he did fly that there day.

ARE YOU MAN?

Tradition Bearer: "Pappy" Jackson

Source: Fauset, Arthur Huff. "Negro Folk Tales from the South (Alabama, Mississippi, Louisiana)." *Journal of American Folklore* 40 (1927): 243.

Date: 1925

Original Source: Louisiana

National Origin: African American

The most obvious social message in this tale is the admonition to follow the advice of one's elders. The narrative further warns that being assured of one's own strength and status may lead to destruction. Rabbit, though a relatively minor character in this story, plays the pivotal role of the **trickster** who overcomes strength with wit—and a more powerful accomplice.

An old lion lied over on his death bed. He told his son, "Son, meet everything on earth but man. You'll be all right so long as you meet everything on earth but man."

So the son listened to the words of his father for a while. So the older he got the more ambitious he became.

He runs up on Rabbit one day an' said to him, "Are you man?"

Rabbit was scared out o' his wits an' said, "I'm nothin' but a poor cottontail; by God, dogs, cats, everything runs me."

So Lion ran off. He met a donkey. He run up on Donkey an' knocked him down. He said to him, "Are you man?" Donkey said, "No, I'm not man. Children n' everything comes along an' knocks me about."

So Lion runs up on 'nother rabbit. He wanted know from him was he man. Rabbit said, "No, I ain't nothin' but a rabbit. But I can show you man; you want to see man?" Lion says, "Yes." Rabbit says, "Well, 'bout an' hour from now you will see him." So Lion says, "All right."

So Rabbit ran off an' met a man. He said, "There's a bad animal out here to meet you. He's the king of the world. He wants to see who is man, he is so great."

So the man was layin' behind a big oak tree. He had a double barrel rifle. He said to Rabbit, "Now let's see if he is around."

Rabbit said, "Yes, he's just aroun' the corner. Don't fail to sting him." So he went an' called Lion.

The man fired a shot at him an' he fell. He got up an' the man fired another shot; he fell again. He got up again an' the man fired another shot. This time the lion fell an' did not get up.

He said, "Ah, Rabbit, you're the one who led me to my slaughter. By God, you did me nothin'. I promised I pay you. It's painin' now. Ah, it's a bad thing to be disobedient. If I had listened to my father I would still be living and happy."

THE GREASE GIRL

Tradition Bearer: Unavailable

Source: Fortier, Alcee. "Louisianian Nursery-Tales." *Journal of American Folklore* 1 (1888) 140–42.

Date: 1888

Original Source: Louisiana

National Origin: French American

"The Grease Girl" bears the traits of the European *märchen* or magic tale by virtue of its aristocratic personnel, romance between a prince and a commoner, and the device of the animal helper for the heroine. The plot resolution differs drastically from the *märchen*'s usual triumph and elevation of the protagonist. At the heart of this tale is a message best summed up by the collector when the Grease Girl is rejected by the prince: "Such is the inconstancy of man."

There was once a lady who had four daughters. They were so pretty that everybody wanted to marry them. They were called La Graisse [grease], Depomme [apple], Banane [banana], and Pacane [pecan]. La Graisse was the prettiest, but she never went out in the sun, because they were afraid that she would melt. La Graisse used to go out every day in a beautiful golden carriage. The son of the king saw her every day, but La Graisse was so pretty and the carriage shone so much that it dazzled his eyes, and he had to rub them in order to be able to see. The king's son was in love with La Graisse. He ran to the mother to ask her to let him marry her; but the mother, who knew that La Graisse was the prettiest of her daughters, wanted to marry the others first.

She called Depomme: "Depomme oh! Orimomo, orimomo!" Depomme came, but the gentleman looked at her well, and said that it was not the one he wanted; she would spoil too quickly.

The mother called: "Banane oh! Orimomo, orimomo!" Banane came. The gentleman did not want her; she would rot too quickly.

The mother called: "Pacane oh! Orimomo, orimomo!" Pacane came. The gentleman said Pacane would become rancid. At last the mother called: "La

Graisse oh! Orimomo, orimomo!" La Graisse came. As soon as he saw her he took her, and led her to his beautiful house and married her.

The king's son went hunting every day. While he was not there, the servants tormented La Graisse. She was afraid to tell her husband, and she did all they wanted. One day the cook told her that she did not want to cook the dinner; that La Graisse had to do it herself. Poor La Graisse! She cried and cried, but they forced her to stay by the fire. But she was melting and melting. In the end, there was nothing but La Graisse [grease] everywhere; the kitchen was full of it.

The little bird of La Graisse saw that. It dipped its wings into the grease; it flew in the wood to the gentleman; it flapped its wings in his face. The gentleman saw the grease which was on the wings; he thought of his dear La Graisse; he galloped home; he found his wife all melted on the floor. He was so sorry that he picked up all the grease and put it in an old bath-tub, and when the grease was cold it became a woman again. But she was never as pretty as before; for the earth had mixed with the grease, and she was all yellow and dirty. Her husband did not love her any more, and sent her back to her mother.

ALL DRESSED UP AND NO PLACE TO GO

Tradition Bearer:

Source: Fauset, Arthur Huff. "Negro Folk Tales from the South (Alabama, Mississippi, Louisiana)." *Journal of American Folklore* 40 (1927): 268.

Date: 1925

Original Source: Mississippi

National Origin: African American

This ethnic joke represents the "Pat and Mike" cycle that proved popular among not only African Americans but various other American groups in the late nineteenth and early twentieth centuries. Despite the ironic fate of the arrogant Mike of this narrative, he does not fulfill the **numskull** stereotype of similar Irish jokes. For example, compare this tale to "The Irishman and the Pumpkin" (p. 73) and "The Sea Tick and the Irishman" (p. 74).

Pat and Mike were arguin' one afternoon on the sidewalk. Mike said to Pat "What's all this talk about heaven an' hell? I don't believe there is no heaven. I don't believe there is no hell. I don't believe any of that stuff. Why should a person worry about that?"

Pat went home that afternoon an' overloaded his stomach. Pretty soon he died of indigestion.

Mike came over the next day to see his friend lyin' in the coffin. All the people were sittin' there. Mike began to laugh.

People wondered at the wake, an' pretty soon somebody asked him, "What's the trouble?"

Mike said, "Oh, nothin', only yesterday I an' my friend Pat was talkin' on the corner of heaven an' hell, an' he told me that there was neither heaven nor neither hell, an' there was no need to make preparations for either place, an' the part that tickled me was to see Pat lyin' out all dressed up an' no place to go."

THE TALKING EGGS

Tradition Bearer: Unavailable

Source: Fortier, Alcee. "Louisianian Nursery-Tales." *Journal of American Folklore* 1 (1888) 142–45.

Date: 1888

Original Source: Louisiana

National Origin: French American

The following Creole folktale, a **variant** of "The Kind and the Unkind Girls" (AT480), develops the typical *märchen* plot in which the protagonist Blanche is in miserable circumstances at the mercy of her mother and her self-indulgent sister Rose. After meeting a supernatural helper disguised as a beggar who follows her to her home through a gamut of extraordinary events and creatures, Blanche is rewarded for being kind and trusting. The punishment meted out to Rose when she tries to follow Blanche's path without mending her foul disposition gives this tale the moral impact commonly associated with the *märchen*. Folklorist Alcee Fortier contends that the tale is based on a French model.

There was once a lady who had two daughters; they were called Rose and Blanche. Rose was bad, and Blanche was good; but the mother liked Rose better, although she was bad, because she was her very picture. She would compel Blanche to do all the work, while Rose was seated in her rocking-chair.

One day she sent Blanche to the well to get some water in a bucket. When Blanche arrived at the well, she saw an old woman, who said to her: "Pray, my little one, give me some water; I am very thirsty."

"Yes, aunt," said Blanche, "here is some water"; and Blanche rinsed her bucket, and gave her good fresh water to drink.

"Thank you, my child, you are a good girl; God will bless you."

A few days after, the mother was so bad to Blanche that she ran away into the woods. She cried, and knew not where to go, because she was afraid to return home. She saw the same old woman, who was walking in front of her.

"Ah! My child, why are you crying? What hurts you?"

"Ah, aunt, mamma has beaten me, and I am afraid to return to the cabin."

"Well, my child, come with me; I will give you supper and a bed; but you must promise me not to laugh at anything which you will see."

She took Blanche's hand, and they began to walk in the wood. As they advanced, the bushes of thorns opened before them, and closed behind their backs. A little farther on, Blanche saw two axes, which were fighting; she found that very strange, but she said nothing. They walked farther, and behold! it was two arms which were fighting; a little farther, two legs; at last, she saw two heads which were fighting, and which said: "Blanche, good-morning, my child; God will help you."

At last they arrived at the cabin of the old woman, who said to Blanche: "Make some fire, my child, to cook the supper"; and she sat down near the fire-place, and took off her head. She placed it on her knees, and began to louse herself. Blanche found that very strange; she was afraid, but she said nothing. The old woman put back her head in its place, and gave Blanche a large bone to put on the fire for their supper. Blanche put the bone in the pot. Lo! in a moment the pot was full of good meat.

She gave Blanche a grain of rice to pound with the pestle, and thereupon the mortar became full of rice. After they had taken their supper, the old woman said to Blanche: "Pray, my child, scratch my back." Blanche scratched her back, but her hand was all cut, because the old woman's back was covered with broken glass. When she saw that Blanche's hand was bleeding, she only blew on it and the hand was cured.

When Blanche got up the next morning, the old woman said to her: "You must go home now, but as you are a good girl I want to make you a present of the talking eggs. Go to the chicken-house; all the eggs which say 'Take me,' you must take them; all those which will say 'Do not take me,' you must not take. When you will be on the road, throw the eggs behind your back to break them."

As Blanche walked, she broke the eggs. Many pretty things came out of those eggs. It was now diamonds, now gold, a beautiful carriage, beautiful dresses. When she arrived at her mother's, she had so many fine things that the house was full of them. Therefore her mother was very glad to see her. The next day, she said to Rose: "You must go to the woods to look for this same old woman; you must have fine dresses like Blanche."

Rose went to the woods, and she met the old woman, who told her to come to her cabin; but when she saw the axes, the arms, the legs, the heads, fighting and the old woman taking off her head to louse herself, she began to laugh and to ridicule everything she saw. Therefore the old woman said: "Ah! My child you are not a good girl; God will punish you."

The next day she said to Rose: "I don't want to send you back with nothing: go to the chicken-house, and take the eggs which say 'Do not take me.'"

Rose went to the chicken-house. All the eggs began to say: "Take me," "Don't take me"; "Take me," "Don't take me." Rose was so bad that she said: "Ah, yes, you say 'Don't take me,' but you are precisely those I want." She took all the eggs which said "Don't take me," and she went away with them.

As she walked, she broke the eggs, and there came out a quantity of snakes, toads, frogs, which began to run after her. There were even a quantity of whips, which whipped her. Rose ran and shrieked. She arrived at her mother's so tired that she was not able to speak. When her mother saw all the beasts and the whips which were chasing her, she was so angry that she sent her away like a dog, and told her to go to live in the woods.

YOUR HORSE STAYS OUTSIDE

Tradition Bearer: Unavailable

Source: Fauset, Arthur Huff. "Negro Folk Tales from the South (Alabama, Mississippi, Louisiana)." *Journal of American Folklore* 40 (1927): 274–75.

Date: 1925

Original Source: Mississippi

National Origin: African American

This protest tale comments on the social conditions that began under the plantation system and continued into the post-Civil War Jim Crow era by projecting racism into the afterlife. As the plot of the tale runs, even the staunch abolitionist Horace Greeley (1811–1872), who had been the founding editor of the *New York Tribune*, a Congressman, and a U.S. Presidential candidate, could not desegregate Heaven. Choosing to disguise Brother Abraham Jasper as Greeley's horse offers additional commentary on the status of African Americans as perceived by the narrator.

Ol' Brother Abraham Jasper he died. Well, he went to heaven as they say. When he got there they wouldn't admit him. Old Salt [Saint] Peter wouldn't let him in.

Ol' Abraham said, "Well, things ain't here like I thought they was. I'm goin' back." So he met Ol' Brother Horace Greeley goin' to the same place he comin' from. Greeley said to him, "Well, hello Brother Jasper, where you been?"

Brother Jasper said, "I just been to heaven."

"Well, what you comin' back for?"

Brother Jasper said, "Well, ol' Brother Salt Peter wouldn't let me in."

Brother Horace Greeley said, "Well now, that's too bad. Now I'm gonna work a plan to git you in. Well now, you just let me get on your back an' when I get there I'll let on you're my horse an' we'll both get inside the gates."

So Brother Horace Greeley rode on Brother Jasper's back. When they got to the gates of [Heaven] Salt Peter said, "Whoa there, who's there?"

"Brother Horace Greeley."

Ol' Salt Peter said, "Is you ridin' or walkin'?"

Brother Horace Greeley said, "Ridin' on a horse."

Ol' Salt Peter said, "Hitch your horse outside an' come on in."

THE CARIBBEAN

ORIGINS

ADAM AND EVE

Tradition Bearer: Richard Barrett

Source: Hurston, Zora Neale. "Dance Songs and Tales from the Bahamas." *Journal of American Folklore* 43 (1930): 300–301.

Date: 1929–1930

Original Source: Nassau, Bahamas

National Origin: African American

The following **myth** offers an alternative look at the concept of original sin through an episode of adultery between Eve and the Devil and the subsequent marriage of Cain to a gorilla.

The reason the world is so wicked is because the first child born in the world was a bastard. Cain was a bastard child. He was the son of the Devil.

One day Adam was working out in the field and the Devil turned himself into a good-looking man and come to see Eve. He had been wanting to get up to her for a long time. So he showed Eve this deep point about everything and got Eve all excited about this apple tree.

So they went out under the apple tree and Eve parted with what she didn't know she had. She bit Satan on the neck and shoulder. They was under the tree and that's why people make love under trees today.

So he knowed there was going to be some hereafter to the thing, so he put her up to get Adam into it, too. So soon as Adam come home Eve started in on him and kept on till he got mixed up in it.

Next day Eve had on a pretty calico dress and Adam was dressed, too, when God come and drove them off. Adam blamed Eve because he knowed something was wrong—but he didn't know what.

Way after, Adam and Eve often quarreled about how she come to know what she knowed. Adam would ask her: "Did Satan do with you as I do?"

She would say: "Naw, honey, didn't I tell you he just *told* me about it, and I told you just as he told me."

"But, Eve, I can't understand why you didn't call me to talk with him and let him tell me instead of you lying about with him all the afternoon like you did."

That is the way they used to fuss about Satan. So when Cain was born Adam saw he looked just like Satan and not a bit like him, and they fussed some more; but Eve stuck to her point and Adam had to shut up. When Abel was born he compared the children, and there wasn't no comparison between them.

So that is why Cain hated Abel, because they was not whole brothers. And that is why God wouldn't accept Cain's sacrifice—because he was the Devil's son. And that is why he accepted Abel's sacrifice—because he was Adam's son.

So when Cain killed Abel he fled away and married a gorilla. So all of the people in the world come from Cain and that gorilla. That is how the animal got into us. That's how come those old patriarchs used to live so long. They was close to the gorilla and strong. That's why old Methusaleh lived nine hundred sixty-nine years—he was just full of that old gorilla blood.

As time goes on that old animal blood works out and leaves the human blood. That is why they say we are growing weaker and wiser.

BROTHER RABBIT AN' BROTHER TAR-BABY

Tradition Bearer: Unavailable

Source: Edwards, Charles L. "Some Tales from Bahama Folk-Lore." *Journal of American Folklore* 4 (1891): 50–51.

Date: 1891

Original Source: Green Turtle Cay, Bahamas
National Origin: African American

This tale enjoys a general popularity due to a widely read version, "The Wonderful Tar-Baby Story," by Joel Chandler Harris; the twentieth-century Walt Disney print and film versions; and a wide oral distribution as well (see in this collection "The Wine, the Farm, the Princess, and the Tarbaby," "The Tar Baby," and "The Rabbit and the Frenchman"). The tale of "The Tarbaby and the Rabbit" (AT175), usually coupled with the "Briar-patch Punishment for Rabbit" (AT1310), enjoys world-wide distribution, with versions found in South and East Asia, Africa, and Europe, as well as the western hemisphere. The **formulaic** opening marker, "Once it was a time a very good time/De monkey chewed tobacco an' 'e spit white lime," is equivalent to the familiar "Once upon a time" of the *märchen*. As is common in African American tradition, Rabbit is a **trickster** figure living by his wits, outsmarting stronger beings, and overcoming superior numbers to achieve his ends. Given the position in which the African bondsperson was placed in the New World context, Rabbit's antics may serve not only as comic catharsis but also as models for emulation under social oppression. In this version, Rabbit plays out both his strengths (cleverness and audacity) and weaknesses (selfishness and impulsiveness) in his effort to obtain the necessities of life at the expense of others' labor. Nevertheless, Rabbit plays a common role of tricksters in transforming the world, taking vengeance on the other animals by forcing them from their initial anthropomorphic lifestyle and condemning them to run wild in the bush.

Once it was a time, a very good time,
De monkey chewed tobacco an' 'e spit white lime.

So dis day Brother Rabbit, Brother Bouki (hyena), Brother Tiger, Brother Lizard, Brother Elephant, Brother Goat, Brother Sheep, Brother Rat, Brother Cricket; all o' de creatures, all kind, so now dey say, "Brother Rabbit, you goin' help dig well?" Brother Rabbit say, "No!"

Dey say, "When you wan' water, how you goin' manage?"

'E say, "Get it an' drink it."

Dey say, "Brother Rabbit, you goin' help cut field?"

Brother Rabbit say, "No!"

Dey say, "When you're hungry, ho' you goin' manage?"

"Get it an' eat it." So all of 'em gone to work. Dey went; dey dig well first. Nex' dey cut field.

Now dis day Brother Rabbit come. Dey leave Brother Lizard home to mind de well. So now Brother Rabbit say, "Brother Lizard, you wan' to see who can make de mostest noise in de trash?"

Brother Lizard say, "Yes!"

Brother Rabbit say, "You go in dat big heap o' trash dere an' I go in dat over dere" (Brother Rabbit did wan' to get his water now). Brother Lizard gone in de trash; 'e kick up. While 'e was makin' noise in de trash, Brother Rabbit dip 'e bucket full o' water. He's gone!

So no' when Brother Elephant come, an' all de other animals come out of de field, Brother Elephant say, "Brother Lizard, did you let Brother Rabbit come here today an' take dat water?"

Brother Lizard say, "I couldn't help it!" 'e say, "'E tell me to go in de trash to see who could make the mostest noise."

Now de nex' day dey leave Brother Bouki home to mind de well.

Now Brother Rabbit come. 'E say, "Brother Bouki, you wan' to see who can run de fastes'?"

Brother Bouki say, "Yes."

'E say, "You go dat side, an' le' me go dis side." Good! Brother Bouki break off; 'e gone a runnin'. Soon as Brother Bouki git out o' sight Brother Rabbit dip 'e bucket; 'e gone.

So no' when Brother Elephant and the rest of 'em come dey say, "Brother Bouki, you let Brother Rabbit come 'ere again today and take our water?"

'E say, "'E tell me to have a race to see who could run de fastes', an' soon's I git a little ways 'e take de water an' gone."

So Brother Elephant say, "I know how to ketch him!"

All of 'em went to de pine yard. Dey make one big tar-baby. Dey stick 'im up to de well.

Brother Rabbit come. 'E say, "Hun! Dey leave my dear home to min' de well today." Brother Rabbit say, "Come, my dear, le' me kiss you!" Soon as 'e kiss 'er his lip stick fas'. Brother Rabbit say, "Mind you better le' go"; 'e say, "You see dis biggy, biggy hand here"; 'e say, "If I slap you wid dat I kill you." No' when Brother Rabbit fire, *so*, 'e han' stick. Brother Rabbit say, "Min' you better le' go

ne"; 'e say, "You see dis biggy, biggy han' here; if I slap you wid dat I kill you."
Soon as Brother Rabbit slap wid de other han', *so*, 'e stick. Brother Rabbit say,
"You see dis biggy, biggy foot here? My pa'," say, "'f I kick anybody wid my biggy,
biggy foot I kill 'em." Soon as 'e fire his foot, *so*, it stick. Brother Rabbit say,
"Min' you better le' go me." Good! soon as 'e fire his foot, *so*, it stick. Now
Brother Rabbit jus' was hangin'; hangin' on de tar-baby.

Brother Bouki come runnin' out firs'. 'E say, "Ha! We got 'im today! We got
'im today!" 'e gone back to de field; 'e tell Brother Elephant; 'e say, "Ha! Brother
Elephant; we got 'im today!"

Then all of 'em gone out now dey ketch Brother Rabbit. Now dey did wan'
to kill Brother Rabbit; dey didn't know where to t'row 'im. Brother Rabbit say,
"'f you t'row me in de sea" (you know 'f dey had t'row Brother Rabbit in de sea,
dey'd a kill 'im), Brother Rabbit say, "'f you t'row me in de sea you won't hurt
me a bit." Brother Rabbit say, "'f you t'row me in de fine grass, you kill me an'
all my family."

Dey take Brother Rabbit. Dey t'row 'im in de fine grass. Brother Rabbit
jump up; 'e put off a runnin'. So now Brother Rabbit say, "Hey! Ketch me 'f you
could." All of 'em went away now.

Now one day dey [the other animals] was all sittin' down eatin'. Dey had
one big house; de house was full o' all kinds o' animals. Brother Rabbit gone; 'e
git up on top de house; 'e make one big hole in de roof o' de house. Brother
Rabbit sing out, "Now, John Fire, go out!" Brother Rabbit let go a barrel o' mud;
let it run right down inside de house. When 'e let go de barrel o' mud, *so*, everyone of 'em take to de bush, right wild; gone right over in de bush. Brother
Rabbit make all of 'em went wild; till dis day you see all de animals wild.

E bo ban, my story's en',
If you don't believe my story's true,
Ask my captain an' my crew.

NANCY AND THE HONEY TREE

Tradition Bearer: George W. Edwards

Source: Johnson, John H. "Folk-Lore from Antigua, British West Indies." *Journal of American Folklore* 34 (1921): 51–52.

Date: 1921

Original Source: Green Bay, Antigua

National Origin: African American

This tale of the **trickster** Anansi (Nancy in this version) is a popular one in the West Indies. The narrative portrays Anansi as both **trickster** and dupe when he matches wits with Monkey. Supernatural elements include the speaking tree, the transformation of Nancy, and the power of the word "Wheelum," which causes the tree to wheel around and throw its victims. In a Jamaican **variant** collected by Martha Warren Beckwith in 1924, the word is "Fling-a-mile" rather than "Wheelum."

While Nancy was goin' on dis day, he see dis tree. Come up to dis tree, an say, "Ah! Dis a pretty little tree. Dis honey tree is a pretty little tree."

De tree say dat he mus' call 'em "Wheelum." Nancy laugh, an' say dat it was a honey tree. Dat he not need to call it "wheelum." Den Nancy get up in dat tree, an' start to suck de honey. He suck till he get all de honey what he want. Den he got stuck when he go to pull off from de tree. He twist, but he can't loose himself. Nancy start to beg. Say, "Please, Mr. Honey-Tree, don' catch me! Leave me go, please, Mr. Honey-Tree!"

Honey-Tree say, "My name not Honey-Tree. My name Wheelum." Nancy say, "Alright, Mr. Wheelum! Dat all right! Please let me go, Mr. Wheelum!"

When Nancy say "Wheelum," de tree start to spin. Dat tree wheel an' wheel When it have him goin' round so, yap it loose him. Nancy was put at a distance by dis tree. He land, an' pick hisself well hurted by dis tree call "Wheelum."

Now Nancy come, an' all prepare to fool some a dese other animals wid dis tree. Soon he see Bro' Cow comin'. Bro' Cow he a stupid one, an' Nancy pick him quick. Say, "O Bro' Cow! Ah done find one very sweet tree."

Bro' Cow say, "Where dis tree? Show me it!"

An' Nancy carry him to where dis tree was. When he got him dere, he tell him dat he mus' suck, an' he will get all de honey dat he can eat. Bro' Cow did suck. When he finish, he not able to loose hisself. He cry, an' tell Bro' Nancy to help get him off. Nancy laughin' for fair now. Cow beg de tree to let he go. De tree say it name Wheelum. Den when Cow say "Wheelum," de tree t'row him also at a distance. An' he was hurted too. Bro' Nancy have all dis sport. He fool some dese other animals wid dis same honey tree. By an' by he see Bro' Monkey. Now, Bro' Monkey was in dis tree, an' see all dat Nancy do. He come down, an' pass to where Nancy was. Nancy greet him. Say, "Well, Bro' Monkey, jus' de man I like to see. Jus' de man. Bro', dere is a honey tree dat has so sweet t'ing; an' I going to carry you dere, bro'." De monkey was willin', an' Nancy took him.

Dey come to dis tree. Nancy tell Monkey dat he must suck. Monkey answer dat he will not suck till Nancy firs' suck. Nancy say, "What matter, bro'? Dat is sweet dere. You go. I have finish my suck. What matter you? Not want dat sweet 'ing dere! Come on, Bro' Monkey! Suck from dis tree!" But Monkey refuse to suck till Nancy go firs' to suck. No matter what Nancy say, he still will not suck firs'. After dis, Nancy go to de tree, an' whisper, "Ah goin' suck firs', Bro' Honey-Tree, but don' hol' me! Hear, Bro' Honey-Tree, don' hol' me!"

De honey tree answer dat it will not hol' him. Den Nancy say, "Alright, Bro' Monkey! I going suck firs'. We going get full of dis honey."

Nancy went, an' he suck. But Monkey did not suck. De tree hol' him; an' no matter what he say, de tree not loose him. Monkey had in dis time gone to a distance. Here he put up a tall spike. Dese spike were jus' where de tree was growin'. Monkey tell Nancy dat he going tell de tree wheelum.

Nancy say, "No!" Monkey he in all kind of glee an' jump 'round. Nancy he keep beggin' dat tree please let he go. Dis de tree would not do. Nancy say, "Please don' hol' me, Bro' Honey-Tree! Please let me go, Bro' Honey-Tree!"

Tree say, "My name not Honey-Tree. My name Wheelum."

Den Bro' Monkey shout, "Wheelum, wheelum, wheelum!" An' de tree turn an' commence to spin about. De tree wheel an' wheel. Yap de tree let Nancy go, an' he land upon dis spike. Nancy he turn to spider, an' run in de cassy tree.

> I went through Miss Havercomb alley,
> An' I see a lead was bendin';
> So da lead ben',
> So da story en'.

BROTHER ELEPHANT AND BROTHER WHALE

Tradition Bearer: Unavailable

Source: Edwards, Charles L. Page 65 in *Bahama Songs and Stories*. Memoirs of the American Folklore Society 3. New York: American Folklore Society, 1895.

Date: 1895

Original Source: Green Turtle Cay, Bahamas

National Origin: African American

"Brother Elephant and Brother Whale," a **variant** of "Deceptive Tug-of-war" (AT291), is distributed in the West Indies, the American South, and African South America. Brother Rabbit (B'Rabby) indulges in his pastime of stirring up trouble by issuing false challenges that pit unwitting competitors against each other. Along the way, there is another object lesson concerning the power of brain over brawn.

Once it was a time, a very good time,
De monkey chewed tobacco an' 'e spit white lime.

Now dis day Brother Rabbit was walkin' 'long de shore. 'E see Brother Whale. 'E say, "Brother Whale!"

Brother Whale say, "Hey!"

Brother Rabbit, "Brother Whale, I bet I could pull you on de shore!"

Brother Whale, "You can't!"

Brother Rabbit say, "I bet you t'ree t'ousan' dollar!"

Whale say, "All right!" 'E gone.

'E meet Brother Elephant. 'E say, "Brother Elephant," 'e say, "I bet I could pull you in de sea!"

Brother Elephant say, "Me!" 'E say, "Dey ain't any man in de worl' can pull me in de sea!"

Brother Rabbit, "I'll try it to-morrow at twelve o'clock."

'E gone an' get a heap o' rope. 'E say, "Now today we'll try."

'E tie one end of the rope aroun' Brother Whale's neck, and den 'e tie one end aroun' Brother Elephant's neck. 'E say, "When you hear me say, set taut, you mus' set taut."

'E say, "Pull away!"

When Brother Whale pull, 'e pull Brother Elephant in de surf o' de sea. 'E say, "You think dis little Brother Rabbit doin' all o' dat!"

When Brother Elephant pull it, 'e pull Brother Whale in de surf o' de sea. Brother Whale catch underneath one shelf o' de rock, and Brother Elephant catch to one big tree. Den de two of 'em pull so heavy de rope broke.

Brother Whale went in de ocean and Brother Elephant went way over in de pine-yard. Das why you see Brother Whale in de ocean today and das why you see Brother Elephant over in de pine bushes today.

> E bo ban, my story's en',
> If you don't believe my story's true,
> Ask my captain an' my crew.

WHY RABBIT HAS A SHORT TAIL

Tradition Bearer: George W. Edwards

Source: Johnson, John H. "Folk-Lore from Antigua, British West Indies." *Journal of American Folklore* 34 (1921): 49–50.

Date: 1921

Original Source: George W. Edwards, Green Bay, Antigua

National Origin: African American

In this tale of the master **trickster** tricked, Rabbit seems a particularly easy dupe. The narrative resembles "The Tail-fisher" (AT2). In the classic model, however, Bear or Wolf is tricked into using his tail to fish through a hole in the ice. The ice freezes around the tail, and when the tail-fisher is compelled to escape, the originally long tail is bobbed. Caribbean environmental factors obviously require a modification of this plot.

Dis was how dis come, Rabbit once have a tail long like dem other an'-mals. Not short all de time.

On dis occasion Rabbit was goin' about, an' he was hot. Dis was summer, an' everyt'ing was hot. Rabbit he had run all over, was feelin' warm. By a' by he come to where Bro' Barracuda was. When Bro' Rabbit come near to de water Bro' Barracuda speak to him. Say, "Why is it dat you so warm, Bro' Rabbit?"

Rabbit tell him dat is so warm 'round here, an' dat he been runnin' all 'bout. He not able to stay cool.

Den Bro' Barracuda fool Rabbit. An' Rabbit is a smart one. Bro' Barracuda say, "Bro' Rabbit, I will tell you which way you can get cool." Rabbit he glad for dat, an' ask de Barracuda to please do dis. Bro' Barracuda say dat Rabbit must come up to dis piece of wood what is over de water, an' let he tail hang down into de water. "In dis way, Bro' Rabbit, de cool from de water will go up from you' tail, an' you will not be warm."

Rabbit not against dis, an' he come. Now, when Rabbit come up to dis piece a wood, he drop his tail to de water. Den Bro' Barracuda sneak up to Rabbit tail an' he bit it off.

Dat how Barracuda fool Rabbit, an' is why Rabbit has dat short tail.

Finish.

PLAYING MOURNER

Tradition Bearer: George W. Edwards

Source: Johnson, John H. "Folk-Lore from Antigua, British West Indies." *Journal of American Folklore* 34 (1921): 61–62.

Date: 1921

Original Source: George W. Edwards, Green Bay, Antigua

National Origin: African American

The theft of food by a **trickster** is a common folktale **motif**. This tale of rat's betrayal of his friend cat closely resembles "Theft of Butter (Honey) by Playing Godfather" (AT15). Variants of AT15 are found elsewhere in this collection (see "Playing Godfather," p. 64). The following narrative departs from AT15, however, in its omission of the concluding **motif** of pinning the food theft on the victim (see "How Brer Fox Dream He Eat Brer 'Possum" p. 83). "Playing Mourner" concludes instead with justice for the offender, which serves to explain the origin of the enmity between cats and rats.

Pussy and Rat was great friends. Dey was all de time in each other company. On dis occasion Pussy learn dat his father is dead. Rat cry an' tell him dat he sorry. Pussy is sick at dis. Dese two prepare to go to de wake. Pussy not feelin' well. Rat pretend dat he is sick too. Dey both had a big barrel of rice. Before dey go to de wake, dey is goin' to cook dis rice. Dey cook it.

When de wake is over, dey will come for de rice. Both put a big cover over dis rice. De rice was finish. Also dey was to take somet'ing for dis wake. Dey had a tambourine, a triangle, an' a fiddle-bow. Dey prepare dese to take. At de wake dey will have dese. Pussy say, "Come, Bro' Rat! Me father dead. We goin' to de wake now."

"Dat is all right," Rat tell him. An' dey went. When dey gone some ways, Rat say, "Ah, Bro' Pussy! me forget de tambourine. Goin' back to get it." Pussy tell him he mus' hurry. He father dead, an' de wake done commence.

Rat went back. He hop in de kettle an' eat some of de rice. Now he come again. Dey went on. Pussy cryin' 'cause he father dead. Rat he cry too. Dey have de tambourine. Rat stop here. Say, "Ah, Bro' Pussy! we done forget de triangle. Can't go widout de triangle."

"Bro' Rat, how go off widout de triangle? We need dem t'ings for to have at de wake."

Rat tol' him dat is "you' father," an' he will go back for de triangle. Bro' Pussy consent, an' Rat went back to their house. When he get back again, he jump in de kettle wid de rice. Eat full. Now he come, an' dey go on. Pussy cryin' an' Rat bawlin'. Pussy say, "Step up dere, Bro' Rat! We is behin' for de wake now. My father mus' need for me to get to de wake."

Dey almos' dere. Rat stop. Say, "What happen to de fiddle-bow? You has de fiddle-bow?" Pussy has not it. He excite dat dey no have de fiddle-bow.

Rat tell him dat is all right, an' dat he goin' get it. "You' father dead, and me goin' bring back dat fiddle-bow. You is wait here. Jus' wait at dis point for me. I goin' back." An' Pussy let Rat go back.

Rat get back, an' he clean de pot. Not any rice in it. In dis time Pussy start to t'ink dat Rat fool him. An' he come back.

When he is dere, he not see nothin'. Look around, Bro' Rat not in sight. He move all round, can't find he friend. By an' by he hear sound: "Chip, chip, chip, chip, chip, chip, chip, chip!"

Dis sound is at de kettle. Soft, Pussy move to it. He creep up to it. Hear, "Chip, chip, chip, chip, chip!" Now he know where was Bro' Rat. De cover is on de pot. Bro' Pussy get to de cover. Jump on it. Cry, "Well, Bro' Rat, I's got you at it. So you is in dere. I goin' kill you, Bro' Rat." Rat beg him not to kill 'im. Say, "Please don' kill me, Bro' Pussy! Do anyt'ing to me, but please don' kill me!" Bro' Pussy insist dat he was goin' kill him. Rat beg dat he don't. Say he must not kill 'em. Den Pussy agree not to kill him, an' open de top.

Rat hop out. Pussy jump on him. Den John Cowrie (cat) lift him. He toss him. He let him go, den catch him. He beat him. He t'row him. He pounce on him. Beat him, but he did not kill him. He do dis till Rat was dead. But he did not kill him. He played him till he dead. Dat is why cat play wid de rat dat dey caught.

COCK'S BREAKFAST

Tradition Bearer: Richard Morgan

Source: Beckwith, Martha Warren. Page 61 in *Jamaica Anansi Stories*. Memoirs of the American Folklore Society 17. New York: American Folklore Society, 1924.

Date: 1924

Original Source: Santa Cruz Mountains, Jamaica

National Origin: African American

The tale of "Cock's Breakfast" casts Cockroach in the role of the **trickster**. In fact, Martha Warren Beckwith suggests in *Jamaica Anansi Stories* (1924) a comparison between Cockroach and the more famous African and African American **trickster** Anansi (260). Cockroach is featured in similar tales in Caribbean tradition. The present narrative is built on **motif** A2494.5.18, "Enmity of Fowl and Cockroach."

One day Cockroach said to Cock, "Brother Cock, get little breakfas', so I will come an' have breakfas' wid you." Cock said yes. Cockroach come, Cockroach eat. When he done 'e said, "Brother Cock, when you know time my breakfas' ready, come."

Cock said, "How mus' I know?"

Cockroach said, "I will gi' you a sign. When you hear I make noise, don' come; but when you hear I stay still in de yard you mus' come."

When Cock go, he didn't fin' Cockroach. Cock return back to his yard. Secon' day, Cockroach come an' say, "Oh, Brother Cock! after I lef' you here, I got pain all over my skin so I go an' lie down, I couldn't look a t'ing; but t'-day you can come."

Cock do de same, go to de yard, didn't fin' him, return back. When he got halfway, he hear in Cockroach house,

> "Ring a ting ting,
> Me know fool for fool!"

Cock take time, tip on him toe. An' go long to one gourd, he hear cockroach in de gourd. An' Cock take him beak, lick him out de gourd. Cockroach run out. Cock pick him up an' swaller him.

So from dat day, not a cockroach walk a fowl yard anymore.

THE ORIGIN OF WOMAN

Tradition Bearer: Harry Murray

Source: Bates, William C. "Creole Folk-Lore from Jamaica II: Nancy Stories." *Journal of American Folklore* 9 (1896): 124–25.

Date: 1896

Original Source: Jamaica

National Origin: African American

The following "origin" tale, embedded within an argument between a husband and wife, does not serve as an explanation like the **myth** that it parodies; rather, it is an example of a comic **anecdote** turning on an alleged gender difference based on a flawed act of creation. See the appendix to this volume for the unedited version of this narrative.

A discussion arose between black Lizzie and her husband upon the origin of man. Harry laid it down for an axiom that he was made from the dust of the earth, because the minister said so.

"I make out o' dust fe' sartin."

To him, according to the story, Lizzie replied: "Me no make out o' none dirt." Then Harry: "Ef you don' make out o' dirt, wha' you make out o'? You make out o' dirt, yes!"

"I don't make out o' notin' o' de skin."

"Den wha' you make out o'? You mus' make out o' some golden thing or another, den?"

"I don' make out o' no golden thing, an' I don' make out o' none dirt. I make out o' bone."

"Make out o' wha'?"

"Bone!"

"Bone?"

"Yes, bone to be sho'."

"Wha' kin' o' bone?"

"Rib's bone! You na hea' minista' say so?"

"Well, I don' know what to say 'bout dat; I don' like to say dat wha' minista' say not de truth; but I mean fe' say, when minista' read 'bout dat rib's bone, him must mean white woman, because dem white, so de bone white. Ef you make de same, you' skin would a been white."

"Cho," said Lizzie, "ef you had opened your ears instead of sleeping, you would a hea' de minsta' say de skin notin', but de blood, da de thing, because in de book say, dat white-o, brown-o, black-o, all make de same blood; you eba' see white blood an' black blood?"

"Look you," said Harry, "It you know how me Uncle Jame use to say woman came in dis worl'?"

"Cho, no bother me."

"Never min', I going tell you. Dem make two men; de first one he made very well; but when dem make de other one, it's kinda spoil. Den as dem look upon it, so it began to jump about, and shake him head, and do all kind o' stupid thing, like a how woman goes on. Den one o' dem hold him, say, 'Wha' kind o' thing you?' Den de oder say: 'Cho, him no use, him can' talk.' Every day him was like a dummy, till one day dem hol' him so, examine him tongue, den dem see de tongue tie; dem take a razor, cut it. As dem cut it so, bam! De thing mouth begin to fly, dem couldn't stop it. Dem say: 'Well, dem sorry dey ever cut de tongue.' From dat time, it make you hear dem say: 'ef you wan' woman to be good, give her 'tump o' tongue (stump of tongue, a tongue-tie).'"

Heroes, Heroines, Tricksters, and Fools

THE BRAVE TAILOR

Variant A

Tradition Bearer: Samuel Carrington

Source: Parsons, Elsie Clews. "Barbados Folklore." *Journal of American Folklore* 38 (1925): 272–74.

Date: 1925

Original Source: Barbados

National Origin: African American

In the first Caribbean **variant** of "The Brave Tailor" (AT1640), Mr. Tailor accomplishes the task of taming a bear—a challenge issued by the queen for those wishing to win her daughter's hand—by the use of his wits rather than by luck (as is the case in some European **variants**). When the mother and daughter later turn on him, his wits and boldness continue to save him, until he gives in to greed. In the much shorter **Variant** B, words are the only weapons the tailor needs to remain in control.

Oncet it was a tailor. He was sittin' down eatin' some rotten cheese. The fly begin to humbug him. So wid dat he fired a slap and he killed seven. He says, "Ah, I am a tailor by name and a tailor by trade. I fired a nice slap and I killed seven, and if I had a fired a little harder, I'd a killed seventy-seven."

Write it on his belt and walk about wid the belt. Wid dat the queen saw him and widdat large number he killed. She had a bear to tame. She tol' him if he was to tame dat bear dat she would give him her daughter. Wid dat she tol' him she would give him fifty horse guard to go widhim when he go to tame this bear. He said he don't wish de horse guard, he'll go his own self.

Got him some walnuts and he fill his pocket and he got him some rock stones and he fill his pocket, too. Soon de bear see him, he got his fiddle and de bear begin to dance.

> Diddle diddle, diddle diddle
> He diddle do, he dance, he dance.

After he dance de bear begin to get hungry, which Mr. Tailor was hungry too, so he out wid few of dese walnuts and begin to eat. He fling a few to de bear and he begin to eat too. Fling some mix up with the rock stones. Broke out ev'y one his teeth, dese rock stones did. So as he got dose out he begin to play again.

> High diddle, high dooddle
> High diddle do.

He begin to dance. He got close him, he out with his scissors and cut off his smellers. After he cut his smellers off, he took his scissors and he clip his nails, all his nails, his paws. Got on the back of him and he ride him all over the pen.

Came down and told dem he tamed de bear. Went wid de many horse guard to the queen, he went to the pen and got on him and ride him. Ev'y person den could ride him. Well, they came back. Got married to de daughter.

After dat, one day ridin' out de horse flung him down. Tol' his wife dat she'd have his pants to mend. She cried, didn' knowin' dat she would have to do dat. Now dey want him destroy', the mother did.

The queen tol' him dat she had three giants to behead and dis Mr. Tailor was to tek 'em, otherwise Mr. Tailor was to be behead. She tol' him she would send horse guard with him. He says he didn' need dem.

He was out in de forest in a great large place by himself den. Mr. Tailor went on and whils' he gone on, he got plenty of stones and pebbles and put in his pocket. He reached dere at night and he seen de light, and dere was a large tree in front of de buildin', and he got up in de tree, and whils' de giants was playin' and droppin' to sleep, he was out wid his stones and fired through the window and hit one.

He that got hit told the other, "Man, stop it! Let me get ma rest!" Wid dat he went back to sleep, and he struck him again. "If you struck me again, man, the two of us will fight." Wid dat he went back and he struck him again.

De two-head giant and de three-head giant cot (caught) hold to fight den. De three-head giant cut off de two-head giant head. After dat de three-head giant felt so lonely now, so sorry, he fell asleep.

Mr. Tailor den come down off the tree, took the sword and chop de three-head giant one off. He carried it home to de queen. So den all dese men got afear' of him, see what he can do, all de queen horse guard.

Wid dat he used to pass ev'y mornin', see a little fellow, he goes about, hears dese queen horse guard goin' to come for him at night. Mr. Tailor gives de little boy a couple of coppers ev'y mornin' and ev'y mornin' little boy told what was goin' to do.

And when dey was goin' to send seventy-five horse guard for him he kep' awake. When dey came he cried out, "I am a tailor by name, I am a tailor by trade, I fired a nice slap, I killed seven, and if I had fired a little harder, I had killed seventy-seven."

They star' back, gone back, says de horse star' back, horse couldn't stan' the voice of him.

Nex' mornin' little boy says, "Dey sent seventy-five for you, tonight goin' to send a hundred for you." Says all right, gives little boy a couple of coppers.

Soon as one hundred was come, said, "Come on, I killed de two-head giant and I killed de three-head giant, and I fired a nice slap."

And de hundred start back. Wid dat dey went back and said, "Ah, Mr. Tailor can't be took in, it's no use worryin' wid him."

Wid dat it come on nex' mornin' he didn' give little boy anythin'. Little boy went to de queen and said if she was to make him and his family happy, he would behead Mr. Tailor. Queen has arrange upon to make him and family happy. Got a sharp sword and come along nex' mornin'.

(Mr. Tailor) says, "Little boy, anythin'?"

Says, "No, sir." Boy had a sharp sword. Soon as he did, he step behind and took his head clean off. Got on de horse and took up his head and carried to de queen, and so he and his family was happy from dat. Dat was de las' end of Mr. Tailor.

Variant B

Tradition Bearer: Pedro Smith

Source: Parsons, Elsie Clews. "Barbados Folklore." *Journal of American Folklore* 38 (1925): 272–74.

Date: 1925

Original Source: Barbados

National Origin: African American

Tailor was sittin' in his tailor shop one day, when de woman pass' sayin', "Get your sponge." De tailor bought a piece for a penny, placed it on his table. When de flies got on, he caught at his belt and killed seven of the flies with one blow. Then he wrote on his belt, "What a mighty man am I to kill seven at one blow."

The king heard about it and asked him if he would marry his daughter so as to protect her. But one night he talked in his sleep, saying it was only seven flies he had killed, instead of seven men. The princess told her father and placed some soldiers behind the door to kill him. He got up in de night, and said, "I killed seven men with one blow and what about you couple of men standin' behind the door?" At that de soldiers run and the tailor and his wife lived happily after.

NANCY FOOLS HIS WIFE

Tradition Bearer: George W. Edwards

Source: Johnson, John H. "Folk-Lore from Antigua, British West Indies." *Journal of American Folklore* 34 (1921): 49–50.

Date: 1921

Original Source: Green Bay, Antigua

National Origin: African American

Nancy (Anansi) turns tragedy to selfish triumph by claiming to his wife that his arm was lost not as punishment for a crime but in a work accident. His use of disguise to deceive his wife out of her only possessions suggests the **trickster**'s common ploy of "shapeshifting."

Dis Nancy was real smart. He have wife too, an' a son name Little Toukouma. On one day when Nancy was out stealin', he get his arm caught, an' it was cut off. Some man stuff he was stealin' when de arm get caught, an' it take off. Dis arm got take jus' at de elbow. When Nancy come home, his wife say, "Ah, Nancy! How you get your arm cut off?"

Nancy say he been to a mill workin', when it caught his arm an' tear it off. He say dat it took all his arm. Dey was sorry fer Nancy, an' he don' do nothin' now. He eat all dat he could get. An' when da wife she gone, Nancy take all de food from de little Toukouma. Dis boy would be dere wid de food, an' Nancy would come to him. Say, "Gi' me dat food, or ah show you me stump." Den de boy go shoutin', for he afraid to have Nancy show him de stump a his arm. While he cryin', de wife come, an' say Nancy refuse to admit dat he show de boy de stump.

Dis day come when Nancy want to get all de food what his wife got. Now, de woman had two pigs and a field of yams. Nancy try to t'ink how he could get dese. Each day she go to feed de pigs an' work de yams. Nancy make up his mind dat he must get dem. On dis day Nancy he stay in de bed. Make out dat he sick. Say, "Wife, me so sick! O wife! Me too sick. Me too sick." De woman tell him dat he must go to de doctor. Nancy say, "Ah, wife, me too sick. Me can't go, wife. Me too sick, wife." He roll an' toss about, an' de woman t'ink he about to die. Nancy tell her, "Wife, you go get de doctor! Wife, me too sick. You go!" She t'ink dat her husban' was really sick, an' she start fer de doctor. When she gone, Nancy up from de bed an' take another road, so dat he come out in front of where de woman is goin'.

When Nancy get dere [to meet her on the road], he have another kind a coat, so dat de woman not able to know he her own husban'. She come along. Nancy come out. Say to her, "Whar you goin', Mrs. Anancy?" She tell him dat her husban' so sick. Dat he look like he goin' to die. She goin' to get de doctor to come. He tell her dat she is doin' de right, an' dat she must be sure to get de doctor for him.

So she went. Nancy take by different road, and he come to de place where de doctor live. When de woman come, he take bearing like he de doctor. She come to dis place.

Say, "O doctor! Nancy is too sick. Me 'fraid he will die. Me here to bring you to him."

Den Nancy say to her. She not know who he was. All time t'ink dat dis was de doctor. "Well, Mrs. Anancy, dat is too bad. Dis is what you try to make you' husban' better. You has two pigs an' a field a yams. If you kill dem pigs an' cook 'em up wid jus' de hair off, also cook up de yam wid dem, dat will cure you' husban'."

Dese pigs an' de field a yam was all dat dis woman had. But she fool. De doctor say dat no matter what Nancy say, she mus' give him dese t'ings, or he will die. She got home. Nancy was dere now in bed. Groanin' like he was goin' to die. Ask her what de doctor tell her. She say dat de doctor say she mus' kill a pig wid only de hair off, an' cook wid de yams.

Nancy say, "Don' do it, wife! Don' kill you' pig! Me not satisfy you kill de pig." He foolin' her now, an' she was sure to kill dem. So she have one pig kill, an' did as de doctor tol' her. When she bring de pig an' yams to Nancy, he eat it all.

On de next day she ask him how he feel. He say, "O wife! Me sure to die. Me too sick." Den she tol' him dat she was goin' to kill de other pig. Nancy say, "No!" But she sure dat only way to save Nancy, an' she did it.

She bring de food. Nancy eat every bit a dis, an' not give his wife an' Little Toukouma any. Dat's de way Nancy fool his wife.

Finish.

ANNANCY AND THE YAM HILLS

Tradition Bearer: Unavailable

Source: Smith, Pamela Coleman. "Two Negro Stories from Jamaica." *Journal of American Folklore* 9 (1896): 278.

Date: 1896

Original Source: Kingston, Jamaica

National Origin: African American

"Annancy and the Yam Hills" shows the Caribbean and African **trickster** in a typical attempt to satisfy his own needs at his neighbor's expense. In a gloss on a **variant** of this tale, Martha Warren Beckwith claims that the story turns on a belief that it is "unlucky to reveal to others a marvel one has seen oneself, or to repeat certain taboo words" (1924, 254). In any case Annancy, rather than being constrained by the witch queen's tyranny, finds a way to subvert it, at least temporarily. The concluding maxim concerning the penalty for greed is a common way of ending Annancy tales in some Caribbean traditions.

One time Annancy lived in a country where de Queen's name was Five, an' she was a witch; an' she says whoever say "five" was to fall down dead.

It was very hungry times, an' so Annancy go build himself a little house by de side of de river. An' him make five yam hills. An' when anybody come to get water at de river he call dem an' say: "I beg you tell me how many yam hills I have here. I can't count whoever well." So den dey would come in an' say, "One, two, three, four, *five!*" an' fall down dead. Then Annancy take dem an' corn dem in his barrel [preserved dem in brine] an' eat dem, an' so he live in hungry times—in plenty.

So time go on, an' one day Guinea fowl come dat way, an' Annancy say: "Beg you, Missus, tell me how many yam hills have I here." So Guinea fowl go an' sit on hill an' say: "One, two, three, four, an' de one I am sittin' on!"

"Cho!" say Annancy; "you don't count it right!" An' Guinea fowl move to another yam hill an' say: "Yes, one, two, three, four, an' de one I am sittin' on."

"He! You don't count right at all!"

"How you count, den?"

"Why dis way," say Annancy: "One, two, three, four, FIVE!" an' he fell down dead, an' Guinea fowl eat him up!

Dis story show dat "Greedy choke puppy."

SEEKING TROUBLE

Variant A

Tradition Bearer: Samuel Carrington

Source: Parsons, Elsie Clews. "Barbados Folklore." *Journal of American Folklore* 38 (1925): 267–68.

Date: 1925

Original Source: Barbados

National Origin: African American

In this first **variant**, Nancy (Anancy), the most notorious of the Caribbean **tricksters**, appears to manipulate others for no other reason than to stir up trouble—and perhaps to make a meal out of his friend Rabbit. The contests of Anancy or Rabbit using their wits versus the strength of Tiger and Wild Hog are common in Caribbean tradition. Strangely, **Variant** B substitutes Tiger for the Anancy figure. In all three versions of the tale, however, Rabbit proves clever enough to escape the menu, even when pitted against Anancy.

It was a rabbit once. He was a tailor. He says he never know trouble, but Nancy tol' him to follow him, "Get a bag and come on with me."

So, dey went in de wood and dey find de tiger young ones. Nancy put his one in de bag whole, make like he was a-tearin' of it to pieces. Ber Rabbit tore up his one in pieces. Ber Nancy tell Ber Rabbit, "Let us go now."

On der journey dey met Ber Tiger. Ber Nancy says, "Ber Tiger, I ha' been in de wood, and find yer young ones, so I ha' brought dem for yer."

The reply to Ber Nancy, de tiger tell him, "I thank you, Ber Nancy."

He says, "Empty dem out de bag for me." Ber Nancy beat out his, skipping about. He says, "Ber Rabbit, you empty out yours now."

When Ber Rabbit empty out, his only was tore in pieces. Ragin' and foamin' tiger made for Ber Rabbit ter catch him. Ber Rabbit was off runnin'. When he got to a crack Ber Tiger was taking hold of him.

Down in de crack he went. Ber Tiger leave Ber Nancy in charge of him now, went in de wood for Wil' Hawg to dig him out. Ber Rabbit says, "Ber Nancy, I was an ol' man about eighty, I never knows trouble." Ber Rabbit ask Ber Nancy to release him. He says, "No, I could not do dat, man, I am leave in charge of you."

He says, "Do, release me, dis is trouble."

He says, "No, man." He says, "I put you in trouble and I am going to take you out of trouble." He says, "When Ber Wil' Hawg come, he will dig you out and Ber Tiger and he will destroy you. But by I put you in trouble, I will release you again. While Ber Hawg a diggin' for you, you scratch back de mould into his eyes, he'll come to me to blow it out. I will blow the first stuff out his eyes, though the next time he'll ha' to apply to Ber Tiger."

He done so, asked him to blow it, he blow it. When he come Ber Tiger, he afraid of Ber Tiger, but he did ask him to blow it out, and de water jump in Ber Tiger mouth outer Wil' Hawg eyes. He start at him to run him down.

Ber Nancy says, "Ber Rabbit, dis yer chance, cut for yer han'."

With dat Ber Nancy turn back, he says, "Man, you left him the first time to watch him, but not dis time." He says, "If I had a couple of wil' hawg, I couldn' ha' trust to dat."

Ber Tiger den had a ball, invite all of de high fellows, tell dem to invite Ber Rabbit, too. Ber Rabbit says when Ber Tiger die he will go to de funeral.

Went back and told Ber Tiger to invite Mr. Tie-low, Mr. No-wag and other official to come to encourage Mr. Rabbit to come to de funeral. "And I will catch him and we'll ha' a nice dinner off of him."

Funeral take place at three o'clock. Ber Rabbit appear hisself. Soon as he come he begin to brush his feet. "Come in, Ber Rabbit," he says.

"I don't like to come in a man drawing-room, my feet is dirty, you know." He says, "When he die did he give a large blow (i.e., did he break wind)?"

"No, he did not give a large blow when he died."

He says, "Well, I never know a man die and never blow yet."

He stepped back and he told Ber Tiger, he said, "I never knowed a dead man blowed yet."

Variant B

Tradition Bearer: Louise Lavinia Barrow

Source: Parsons, Elsie Clews. "Barbados Folklore." *Journal of American Folklore* 38 (1925): 268.

Date: 1925

Original Source: Barbados

National Origin: African American

Oncet it was a rabbit, a wil' hawg and a tiger. De tiger strip de wil' hawg young one in half.

De wil' hawg meet up wid de rabbit and say, "Ber Rabbit, ye see my young one?" He said, "Go 'long out dere, I got one here in my bag. Go 'long out dere!"

Ber Tiger got de oder wil' hawg young one rip up in half. De Tiger tell de rabbit to jump down in de hole and when de hawg come, to take up a handful of gravel and throw in his face and blin' him.

De rabbit did do so, and when de wil' hawg beg de tiger to blow it out of his eyes, he say he would not.

He said, "Do, God bless you, blow it out of my eyes for me."

And jus' as Tiger blew out of Wil' Hawg eyes, he taste de saliva. "Man, you are sweet enough, why I think of you flesh much sweeter (than rabbit's)."

He make a snatch den at de tiger and de tiger make an escape and get away from him.

An' dat wa' de end.

Variant C: The Give-away

Tradition Bearer: Louise Lavinia Barrow

Source: Parsons, Elsie Clews. "Barbados Folklore." *Journal of American Folklore* 38 (1925): 268.

Date: 1925

Original Source: Barbados

National Origin: African American

De meaning to dat is de rabbit an' de tiger was good frien's. De rabbit provoke de tiger and den de tiger get his frien's an' arrange ter kill de rabbit.

De tiger and de wil' hawg was good frien's. Summon up his frien's den to eat de rabbit. De tiger sen' to de rabbit, sayin' de wil' hawg was dead, so as to get de chance to eat him [rabbit.] An' when de rabbit get to de do', he wouldn't go inside, he stay outside. De tiger say, "Frien' come in, your frien' has dead."

De rabbit den ask de tiger if de wil' hawg did pass de wind when he die, an' he say no.

De rabbit say den, "Mus' touch him, and if he pass de wind, he dead." He did touch him and he pass de win'. He say, "Impossible for a dead man to pass de win'." An' he say good mornin' and he was gone.

BROTHER RABBIT, BROTHER BOOKY, AND BROTHER COW

Variant A

Tradition Bearer: Unavailable

Source: Edwards, Charles L. "Some Tales from Bahama Folk-Lore." *Journal of American Folklore* 4 (1891): 50–51.

Date: 1891

Original Source: Green Turtle Cay, Bahamas

National Origin: African American

In the usual pairing of Rabbit and Booky (spelled variously as Bouqui, Bouki, Bookie), Booky plays the foil to Rabbit and serves as the butt of all his jokes. In this tale, however, Bouki imitates Rabbit, tries his hand at being a con man, triumphs over his targets, and wins Rabbit's praise. In **Variant** B, the would-be **trickster** is not so lucky.

Once it was a time, a very good time,
De monkey chewed tobacco an' 'e spit white lime.

Now dis day it was Brother Rabbit an' Brother Booky. The wind was blowin'; dey did n' have nuthin' to eat; dey could n' ketch no fish. Dey was travelin' along to see if dey could n' find something to eat. An' now when Brother Rabbit look 'e see one big cow; 'e gone to de cow.

Den 'e take his hand an' spank on de cow bottom. 'E say, "Open, Kabendye, open!" When de cow bottom open Brother Rabbit jump in with his knife an' his pan. 'E cut his pan full o' meat. Brother Rabbit say, "Open, Kabendye, open!" an' de cow bottom open an' Brother Rabbit jump out.

Good! Now Brother Rabbit was goin' home; his pan full o' meat. Brother Booky see Brother Rabbit; say, "Brother Rabbit, where you get all dat meat?" Brother Booky say, "'F you don' tell me where you get all dat meat I goin' tell!"

Brother Rabbit say, "Go right down dere where you see one big cow."

Brother Booky say, "Hall right!"

Brother Rabbit say," When you get dere you must take your han' an' spank hard on de cow bottom an' say, "Open, Kabendye, open!" Brother Rabbit say, "Soon as dey open you must jump in." Den 'e say, "You see one big t'ing inside dere; you must n' cut dat!" Brother Rabbit say, "Mind, 'f you cut dat de cow goin' to fall down dead."

Brother Booky gone. When 'e got dere 'e take his hand; 'e spank on de cow bottom an' 'e say, "Open, Kabendye, open." Den 'e jump in. Brother Booky cut, 'e cut, 'e cut his hand full! Brother Booky wan' satisfied; 'e went an' 'e cut de cow heart; de cow fall down; Bran', 'e dead! Den Brother Booky say, "Open, Kabendye, open!" After 'e foun' de cow bottom could n' open, 'e went inside de cow mouth. Nex' mornin', when de people come to feed 'im, dey found de cow dead.

Now dey begin to clean de cow; skin 'im. After dey done clean 'im dey cut 'im open; dey take out all his guts. Brother Booky was inside de maw; swell up. De woman say, "Cut dat big t'ing open. See what in dere!" After dat dey went to cut it open; den Brother Booky jump 'way yonder. Dey did n' see 'im.

Brother Booky say, "See what you t'row on me. Ma jus' sent me down here to buy fresh beef, den you go t'row all dis nasty stuff on me!"

De people say, "Hush, don' cry, we give you half o' de cow!"

Brother Booky say, "I don' want no half!" 'E say, "I goin' to carry you to jail!"

Den de man say, "No, Brother Booky, we give you half o' de cow!" De man goin' t'row another stinkin' pan o' water an' blood out. Brother Booky jump 'way yonder [in order to be splashed by the water and blood]. De man t'row it on Brother Booky.

Den Brother Booky say, "Now I ain' goin' to stop; I goin' carry you right to de jail!"

De man say, "Hush, Brother Booky, don' cry, I goin' give you half o' de cow!" Anyhow, dey give Brother Booky half o' de cow. Brother Booky take it on his shoulder; 'e gone.

When 'e look 'e see Brother Rabbit.

Brother Rabbit say, "Hey, where you get all o' dat meat?"

Brother Booky say, "I went down dere; I cut dat big, big t'ing in de cow, an' de cow fall down dead." Den 'e say, "When de people come in de mornin' to kill de cow," 'e say, "I was inside de cow; when dey cut dat big t'ing I jump 'way yonder; I say, "See what you t'row 'pon me!" 'E say, "Den dey give me half o' de cow."

Brother Rabbit say, "Dat's de way to do!"

> E bo ban, my story's en',
> If you don't believe my story's true,
> Ask my captain an' my crew.

Variant B: In the Cow's Belly

Tradition Bearer: Unavailable

Source: Johnson, John H. "Folk-Lore from Antigua, British West Indies." *Journal of American Folklore* 34 (1921): 54.

Date: 1921

Original Source: Antigua

National Origin: African American

Once was a time when dere was not much to eat. Nancy he went out, an' come to a cow. He gwine jump in dis cow. He say, "Open, Toukouma, open!" An de cow open behin'. He went in.

In dere he cut off all de flesh he want. He fill da sacks he got. Den he say da same, an' cow open. He went home wid de flesh.

Toukouma had a little datter. Send dis datter to get fire. Chil' see dat Nancy was cookin'. Don' know what it is. She wanted to know. Every fire dat she got, she put it out. She put out all de fire he gi' her. An' de chil' got a bit a de meat. De bit which she get, one strand stick in her teeth. Goin' home she grin' her teeth to her fader. An' he went to Nancy to know where he could get dis flesh. Nancy tol' him about de same cow.

Unknowing to Nancy, Toukouma went to dis cow. He get in dis cow da same way. Toukouma greedy, cut out de main guts. De cow fall, an' he not able to get out. De owner, seein' dat he cow dead an' de big bump in de belly, wondered what is it. Dey cut dis open, an' find it is Toukouma. He receive a beating, an' t'row away de meat from him.

THE SPERRIT HOUSE

Tradition Bearer: Merle Woods

Source: Hurston, Zora Neale. "Dance Songs and Tales from the Bahamas." *Journal of American Folklore* 43 (1930): 306–7.

Date: 1929–1930

Original Source: Nassau, Bahamas

National Origin: African American

The pairing of Rabbit and Bookie (Hyena) is common not only in the Caribbean (as in "Brother Rabbit, Brother Booky, and Brother Cow," p. 255) but also in other traditions sharing regions with African-descended cultures. The Louisiana Cajun tales "On Horseback" (p. 61) and "The Wine, the Farm, the Princess, and the Tarbaby" (p. 49) also rely on the **stock characters** Rabbit (Lapin) and Bouqui. "The Sperrit House" paints a typical portrait of Bookie as a blundering, greedy character. In the following narrative, rather than Bookie serving as the foil for Rabbit, Rabbit simply provides the means for Bookie to get in trouble. Rabbit, in fact, proves the more sensible of the two, but he cannot influence Bookie to exercise the same good judgment. The rhymed opening and closing of the tale follow a familiar Caribbean formula.

Once upon a time was a good old time.
Monkey chew tobacco and spit white lime.

Now it was Brer Bookie and Brer Rabbit used to go out stealing. Go to de sperrit (spirit) house and this night Brer Bookie see Brer Rabbit coming down wid a dray (low, heavy horse cart without sides used for hauling) load of things. Brer Bookie say: "Brer Rabbit, where you get all these good things from?" He scratch he head.

Brer Rabbit tell him: "From de sperrit house and tomorrow morning at six o'clock I will take you get something, too."

Bookie wake up at five o'clock and say to Brer Rabbit: "Six o'clock now time to go. Six o'clock now time to go."

Rabbit say: "Naw, it ain't six o'clock yet."

So Bookie catch a big fire in de yard to say daylight come. Rabbit say: "No, mon, daylight ain't come yet."

So when six o'clock come, Brer Rabbit put on his clothes and both of them went till they come to de sperrit house. When they come there Rabbit say: "My house come down so low."

And de house come down and they went in and Brer Bookie say: "Mon, good food in here, good food in here. I will cook a pot of peas and rice."

And he did and both of them sit down and eat. And when it was time for them to go, Brer Bookie didn't went. He say: "Mon, I got to stay and eat."

And Brer Rabbit went out and said: "My house, my house, go up so high." And de house went up.

And when it was time for de sperrits to come, they said: "My house, my house, come down so low." And they went in and said: "Someone has been in here."

They begin to cook peas and rice and salt, but when it was finish de sperrit give his little girl a pan full and she went by de bed to sit down and eat. Bookie had done hid under de bed from de sperrits.

Bookie say to her: "Gimme some, gimme some." And he beg and beg all from her. And she went and ask her father for more and de father give it to her, and he eat all dat from de little girl. And she went and ask for more and her father say: "Your gut must be as a barrel, eh?"

After Bookie done eat all dat from her, she say: "I got two, papa. One on top de bed and one underneath de bed."

Then de sperrit get a sea rod and beat him—Bookie—wid it. All de time de house going up, going up, and he t'row him out and broke Bookie neck.

> Biddy, biddy bend,
> My story is end.
> Turn loose de rooster.

BALE OF COTTON OR BAG OF SALT

Tradition Bearer: Unavailable

Source: Parsons, Elsie Clews. "Barbados Folklore." *Journal of American Folklore* 38 (1925): 276.

Date: 1925

Original Source: Barbados

National Origin: African American

The following joke articulates the intergroup strife between Jamaica and Barbados from the Barbadian perspective. The Barbadian, apparently relying on the Jamaican to make an inappropriate choice, allows the other to choose between two burdens to carry to Heaven. The choices suggest greed on the Jamaican's part, owing to his choice of the larger, more valuable but ultimately less portable of the two items. This results in the Barbadian having the last laugh from Heaven as the Jamaican remains tied to earth by an unwise choice. This brief narrative, therefore, combines both the attributes of an ethnic joke and a moral tale.

A little joke a man was giving me one time about a Jamaican and a Barbadian. All told him they was going to Heaven. So they had two things to carry along, a bale of cotton, and a bag of salt. The Jamaican says, "Barbadian, choose first.

The Barbadian says, "No, Jamaican, you choose first."

The Jamaican went for the bale of cotton, the Barbadian ran for the bag of salt. Before they start now the rain came down and the salt giff (melt away), and the Barbadian went up light.

The Jamaican never get there, the cotton was too heavy.

MR. HARD TIME

Tradition Bearer: George W. Edwards

Source: Johnson, John H. "Folk-Lore from Antigua, British West Indies." *Journal of American Folklore* 34 (1921): 81–82.

Date: 1921

Original Source: Green Bay, Antigua
National Origin: African American

The foolish misunderstandings of a husband's orders to his wife lead first to disaster then to wealth in this **variant** of "Guarding the Door" (AT1653A).

You see, it was like dis. A man was goin' out one day, an' he took his money an' give it to his wife, an' tell her to keep it for hard time. At da same time, you know, he had owed a man by da name of Mr. Hard Time

His wife misunderstand him, an' pay it all to Mr. Hard Time. When da husban' come home, she tol' him, "Mr. Hard Time was here, an' I pay him all da money you gave."

You can picture dat man feelin', for it was all da money he had. Man got rouse', an' start to quarrel with his wife. Den he tol' her to close de door an' follow him. Instead of she closin' de door, she lift up de door an' put it on her shoulder.

An dey went travelin' through a wood. Whiles' dey was goin' on, you know, dey saw all kinds of food under a tree, an' dey sat down an' was ready to eat some of what was dere. In da meantime dey heard a set of robbers comin', an' both clambered up in da tree. Dis woman climb da tree with dis heavy door on her back, too. Well, da robbers come an' form a circle under da tree. Dey bring in all dere gold, an' had it under dis tree. Well, da robbers didn't see dem. Den da woman said de door was hurtin' her shoulders, an' she were goin' to t'row it; an' her husban' tell her not to do it, da robbers see it an' kill dem. An' she 'rowed it down. Da robbers got scared, an' said, "Da Lord has sent us vengeance in an earthquake." 'Cause dat door came crashin' down. So dey run an' make anodar camp.

Dere was a little boy with dem. Dey sent him back to see what had become of da gold. Da little boy came along whistlin'. Da man tol' him dat's not da way to whistle—come, an' he'll show him how to whistle like a man. He tell him to long out [stick out] his tongue an' let him scrape it. Da man did scrape a little of da boy's tongue, an' he whistle a little clearer. Den he ask him, "Don't you see you whistle clearer?"

Da boy say, "Yes," an' ask him to scrape a little more. Da boy long out his tongue, an' da man cut off a piece of his tongue.

At dat da boy run back to da robbers, goin', "Ma, ma, ma, ma, ma, ma!" talkin' like a man who is dumb. At dat da robbers got scared an' start to run too, an' dey run in da sea an' all over. Some turn shark, some turn whale, some turn ballyho [a fish], some turn turtle—dey turn all different kind a animal. During dis time da man an' woman took to carry home da gold. Dey brought back a wagon an' carry away da rest of da stuff.

An' I, da storyteller, got some of dat money, an' became rich myself.

And I went through Miss Havercomb alley,
An' I see a lead was bendin';
So de lead ben',
So de story en'.

JOHN THE FOOL AND JOHN THE SMART

Tradition Bearer: Unavailable

Source: Comhaire-Sylvain, Suzanne. "Creole Tales from Haiti." *Journal of American Folklore* 50 (1937): 274–81.

Date: 1930

Original Source: Haiti

National Origin: African American

"John the Fool and John the Smart" represents one of the more complex tales in the current collection. Burdened with a well-intentioned but foolish brother, John the Smart is dragged along in the wake of John the Fool's foolish antics and impulsive choices, from the killing of their mother with boiling bath water (**motif** K1462) through confrontations with devils in groups and in single combat to winning the hand of a princess—all due to John the Fool's miscues. Ti-Malice and Buki are well-known folktale characters; Ti-Malice is the true **trickster**, whereas Buki (compare to "Bouqui and Lapin: The Smokehouse," p. 108) is the genuine fool. In this narrative, John the Fool unwittingly combines attributes of both.

Voila! There was a very old woman who had twin boys, one was called John the Fool, the other John the Smart. John the Fool used to stay at home with his mother to watch the shop, John the Smart used to go to the market.

One day John the Smart was sick, he sent his brother. John the Fool asked for a lot of money for all the purchases he thought necessary. His mother gave him a large quantity of two-cob coins, amounting to three gourdes. He set forth.

"Thus, if I meet some beggars, I shall have enough money to give them." This idea in his head, before turning the crossroad he thought he had heard one. He did not turn back but looked aside and saw his shadow walking behind him.

"Very well, you may go, here are two cobs!"

He threw away two cobs and walked on. At another crossroad he again saw his shadow.

"I am in a hurry, dear, I cannot stay. Here are two cobs, take it all the same!" He threw away the money and went on. Each time he had this thought he looked aside and saw his shadow.

"What a lot of beggars! It is a procession! Why do these people walk like that behind me? Maybe my brother told them I had some money."

When he had only two gourdins more, he told the shadow:

"Friend, I have already given away all my money, go to my home to get some more."

The shadow still followed him.

"How stubborn this man is!"

John the Fool turned round angrily, the shadow disappeared. "When a man knows how to speak with people. I am a superman!"

When he reached the market he thought his brother had asked for spinach. They sold him a small bundle for ten cobs. He chided: "Thieves! You have me pay ten cobs for a tiny bundle of weeds. I do not want it. Keep your thing!"

He entered a small shop where they sold tafia. He asked for ten cobs. They poured it in his bottle. The liquid reached the height of two spread fingers. The man was dissatisfied.

"How stupid I would be to stay here and lose my money! Madam, I am not asking for alms, I am buying, take back your thing and return my money."

The merchant protested shouting, John the Fool shouted back. He had the woman take back her tafia to get his bottle. Disgusted he went away. On the roadside he saw wild spinach, he plucked it and filled his bottle in the river.

When he reached home John the Smart asked: "Where are the goods I asked you to buy?"

"These people are thieves. They thought they could deceive me. They sold for spinach a handful of weeds and wanted me to pay quite a sum for it. If you want weeds, here are some, gratis! They gave me two fingers of tafia for ten cobs, I left it to them, here is God's tafia gratis! I had forgotten the other errands..."

"Where is my money?"

"Your money? As soon as I had passed the door a lot of beggars set to walk behind me, I gave them the whole money. There is two gourdins left, take them!"

"John the Fool, my poor brother! I am obliged to go to town, you will stay here to give mother her bath. Don't forget, a lukewarm bath!"

Now the old lady was paralysed, she could watch the shop but one had to help her to get dressed, to eat, to walk, she could not even blow her nose alone. John the Fool put water on the fire, he had his mother sit at the bottom of the bath and threw a boilerful of hot water upon her. The old lady died without a word.

"How pleased mother is with her bath! Look at her laugh, she cannot close her mouth. Let me give you your pipe!"

He did not wait for an answer and thrust the old woman's pipe down into her throat.

"When you want to get out, call me to help you!"

He sat down at the doorsill and forgot the mother. When John the Smart came back he told him: "My dear! How happy the old lady is about her bath! She laughed so much that her mouth remained opened. I gave her her pipe."

John the Smart, who knew his brother, felt uncomfortable and ran into the house.

"Mother, Mother!"

He came nearer: "John the Fool, the old woman is dead, you have killed our mother!" John the Fool burst into shrieks (if I may say so without lacking respect for the audience).

"Don't cry, poor brother, it is not your fault, God has made you this way, I ought not to forget that."

They made the funeral and sold the house to get some money: John the Smart wanted to travel. He gathered all his clothes in a big bundle and put all his money in a silk handkerchief which he placed in the middle of the bundle. John the Fool took his game cock, his razor and a calabash of water. While walking John the Smart said: "I have forgotten my pot!"

Now if you are looking for an obliging man and do not take John the Fool you will not find any. He darted homeward and came back with a door on his back.

"What do you want me to do with that?"

"Did you not ask for your door?"

"How foolish! Take the door back where it belongs, it will hinder our walking."

"No! I will not make this journey another time!"

They walked a great deal. Night came. They saw a big wood and as they were afraid of beasts and of bad people they climbed up a tree. This tree was a very large kapok tree; they sat in a fork, John the Fool pulled up the door and held it upright in the branches. He put the cock in the pocket of his jacket and the calabash in the pocket of his trousers. They slept.

In the middle of the night they heard some noise and got up. (Under the tree) they saw a big trestle table with cloth, silver-plate and all kinds of good things to eat or drink. In a corner there were four big bags well tied up. A great quantity of small devils were frolicking around the table. How they were frolicking!

John the Smart said: ("I want some wine!) I am thirsty for wine."

"I do not have any, here is water!"

John the Fool passed the calabash. He took it awkwardly, the water fell on the tablecloth of the devils. They laughed merrily. "Here is the dew! Our business is blessed!"

All of them got up, they began to dance and to sing and made a large ring around the table. John the Fool wanted to see everything but the table prevented it.

"I will let it fall!"

"Look out! Watch out for your life, these people will strangle you."

"Have you forgotten my razor?"

He dropped the door! It fell in the middle of the table, put out the lamp of the devils and crashed the glassware and china.

"Earthquake, earthquake!" The devils vanished away. John the Fool came down with his brother and they lighted a candle. John the Smart examined the bags, found them filled with money and put one into his bundle. John the Fool sat beside the table and ate till full. While he was eating, one of the devils came back. These devils were big-headed dwarfs of the size of a ten-year-old child with a long beard. The dwarf gazed for a long time. John the Fool shaved his beard with his razor. The devil laughed. John the Fool shaved half his beard and asked him:

"Do you want to shave? At your service. But before that I want to know only one thing, let me see the string of your tongue, open your mouth!"

The devil opened his mouth. John the Fool severed his tongue. The devil howled and ran to his people.

"What is the matter? Where is our money?"

"Tru-ru-ru-ru-ru!"

He showed them his maimed tongue. They sent another devil. Now John the Fool was eating in the dark with his brother, the lamp had remained on the table; when the devil arrived they saw him while he could not see them, they jumped on him and severed his tongue. John the Smart said: "Let us take all the bags and go away!"

"They are too heavy. My dear! I don't want to get sick!" They left.

They walked and walked. They reached a town where they did not see anybody. All the houses and shops were brightly lighted, there were lamps and candles everywhere but no man or animal was in sight.

As they stared at this, a calabash rolled near them. John the Fool touched his brother: "Take care of your feet!" Another calabash came to meet the first, there was a conversation. The brothers stayed on the side of the hilly road. Calabashes appeared tumbling down the slope, they came into collision, they gathered and whispered. The brothers did not understand a word.

Then a calabash marched up to John the Fool: "You are foreigners?"

"Yes, Mrs. Calabash. But, tell me, is there anything else than calabashes? did not see anybody. How can a calabash speak?"

"Shut up, child! We are men like you but we are obliged to live in cal abashes, the master of the town is a frightful devil. For six months we have been in the night, because fearing robbers he has hidden the key of daylight in the middle of his heart. If he were to find you here walking like a man surely he would eat you! Here are two empty calabashes, get in!"

John the Smart was a man who did not like to get into trouble. He asked "How can we manage? We are too big."

"Look at this hole! Put the point of your foot into it, the whole foot will pass, push a little, the whole leg will pass, your body will reduce, it will grow smaller and smaller, push on, it will slip to the bottom of the calabash."

Smart did as he was told, these people were right, he disappeared into the hole. The Fool stood alone.

"Get into your house!"

"I, never! I am not a coward, the devil may kill me. I will not creep into a calabash. You are all dastards! All the men I have seen in the town let only one devil rule them (this way)? You consent to lose the daylight and live like beasts what did I say? Worse than beasts, there are walking beasts, as for you, you can only roll. No, gentlemen, I will stay upright, if I die I will die like a man, not like a beast!"

At this moment, John the Fool's cock crowed: "Ko-kee-yoo-koo! Ko-kee-yoo-koo!"

The devil had given orders to kill all cocks, the crowd vanished. "This man is crazy! If the Master believes we are his accomplices he will kill us!"

The cock felt it was four o'clock, as he did not see the sun, he crowed again. "Ko-kee-yoo-koo!"

From very far a confused roar was heard in answer:

"I have told the day it would break no more.
I have told the day it would break no more.
Either on this side or on the other.
I have told the day it would break no more!"

"Aha!" John the Fool also sang:

"I tell the day it must break anew.
I tell the day it must break anew.

Either on this side or on the other.
I tell the day it must break anew!"

The devil's song was coming nearer and nearer, and always louder.

"I have told the day it would break no more.
I have told the day it would break no more
Either on this side or on the other.
I have told the day it would break no more!"

John the Fool swelled his whole body, he shouted so as to cover the voice of the devil.

"I tell the day it must break anew.
I tell the day it must break anew.
Either on this side or on the other.
I tell the day it must break anew!"

The devil appeared: he was taller than this house, when he sang everything shook.

"I have told the day it would break no more.
I have told the day it would break no more.
Either on this side or on the other.
I have told the day it would break no more!"

John the Fool prepared his razor.

"I tell the day it must break anew.
I tell the day it must break anew.
Either on this side or on the other.
I tell the day it must break anew!"

They fought relentlessly. John the Fool goaded him with his razor, he cut him, he carved him, he did not leave to the devil time enough to breathe. The devil was tired. The Fool plunged the razor into his temple, the devil cried and died. The Fool hurled him on the ground and opened his heart, he found a small box with a tiny lock in which the key was hung. He turned the key and the sun shone, it was daylight.

During the time all these things were happening, John the Smart was talking merrily with the people (in the calabashes). They told him there was a king who ruled the country (before) the devil came and stole the key of daylight. The king was greatly offended, but he was afraid to fight the devil, so he promised that the man who would bring back the key would marry his legitimate daughter. John the Smart approached his brother.

"Hand me the key, I want to see something!"

"Here it is!"

John the Fool did not look at him, he was lecturing the crowd. "Gentlemen, come out of your calabashes, don't be afraid, you are men anew. I am your chief, my brother is your lieutenant. Where has he gone? John the Smart, John the Smart!"

The Smart was far away. With his money he had hired a horse and rushed to the Palace. The guards stopped him.

"Tell the king I have come to him with news of his key."

The king came.

"What do you know?"

He held his tongue and handed the key.

"Where is the box?"

"Good Lord! I was galloping so fast that the box has dropped."

"Don't take it so to heart, that's nothing. I will have another one made, only the key was indispensable. Now tell me how you managed to kill this big devil."

John the Smart sat down. Everything the Fool had done he said it was himself. The king was glad, he called his children and his wife, introduced Monsieur and betrothed him to the girl.

John the Fool was looking for his brother. He left his money and his commanding position to walk and search. He stopped everybody he met to ask if they had not seen the other one.

"John the Smart is like Ti-Malice, he cannot be dead. I must find him!"

One day he was overtired, he sat down in a crossroad to eat a cassava soaked in cane syrup. He heard two women talking: "My dear, what a beautiful wedding it will be! These people have prepared such a quantity of food!"

John the Fool listened more carefully, his mouth watered. He understood it was the king's daughter who was to marry the man who had killed the devil, the same man who had caused the day to break. He felt unable to realize how this could be done:

"I am the man they are talking about! I don't want to be married to somebody I do not know, to a girl I have never seen, she may be hunchbacked! I don't want, I do not want that at all! I am going to the king!"

He reached the Palace. The guards stopped him. "No trespassing. What do you want?"

"I want to speak to the king."

"Have you an appointment? What have you to tell him?"

"Is that your business? What insolence! You don't want me to come in, very well I will call the king from here."

The fellow began to shout: "King, king! They oppose my entering here, come out to meet me! King, kiing!"

The soldiers tried to silence him, the more they tried, the more he shouted. The king appeared at the window.

"Let him speak. You, what do you want?"

"King, I heard everybody announce the wedding of your daughter with the man who had killed the devil who kept day from breaking. King, I am this man and I have come to tell you not to be in such a hurry. How could I want your daughter, I don't know her!"

"This man is mad!"

"You are the mad man! Listen, king, here is your box!"

"How did you lose the key?"

"It was never lost, I lent it to my brother who wanted to see how it was made."

John the Fool did not look like a liar. The king understood there was some deceit in the whole thing. He sent for his (future) son-in-law who came in splendidly dressed. John the Fool rushed to his neck:

"Where were you! I thought you were lost. What fine clothes, dear, how elegant!"

"When will you stop with your bad manners? You have crumpled my jacket so it looks chawed by an ox."

The king asked them very severely: "Now, gentlemen, explain to me what I see. You wanted to fool me!"

John the Smart was ashamed but the Fool told the old man: "Is it your business, king? You have your key and you have your box. You had promised your daughter to the man who would bring back the key, he did it, give him your daughter, I will not be jealous!"

The Fool came a little nearer: "You had never spoken of the box, I have brought your box, you cannot leave me without compensation, do you have something for me?"

"Listen! Both of you are twins, is it not true? You look so much alike. I will appoint you general, I have other daughters..."

"Ach, king! Ambition kills the rat. When I passed through the yard I smelt all kinds of good flavours, my heart was thrilled. Would you care to appoint me your kitchen inspector?"

"Oh my! Buki is Buki."

ANANSI AND THE LADY IN THE WELL

Tradition Bearer: Unavailable

Source: Trowbridge, Ada Wilson. "Negro Customs and Folk-Stories of Jamaica." *Journal of American Folklore* 9 (1896): 283–84.

Date: 1896

Original Source: Jamaica

National Origin: African American

Anansi, often simply called "Nancy" in Jamaican tradition, plays out the ambiguities of tricksters cross-culturally. While identified with a large, black spider found throughout the islands, in the "Nancy tales" he may take on human form along with his human attributes. Often turning his guile to selfish and even sadistic ends, in the tale of "Anansi and the Lady in the Well," he acts as a compassionate intermediary between an abused wife and her neglected child. Although his motivations remain unknowable, the same figure who, in "Nancy Fools His Wife," reveals himself to be an abusive father and an exploitive spouse intervenes to help the victims of an abusive and exploitive male figure.

Once it was a time when there was a good queen. An' she have husban' an' one pretty baby. An' she have one little pet dog, who go trot, trot, all 'bout de house after her.

Now de husban' he t'ink nothin' at all of him wife, an' he say to himse'f. "I put dat queen down de ole well, and den I get another mo' beau'ful queen." Den he do dis same t'ing what he t'ink in him ole black heart.

Now de queen she fall way down to de bottom of de well an' she can't scramble out no way, an' jus' sit all de day and cry fu' her baby. By an' by Nancy he come scrape, scrape, crup, crup, down de side de well an' say: "Howdy! W'at fo' you cry, me lady?"

De queen say: "Howdy, Nancy! Me cry fo' me baby."

"Jus' jump on me back," say Nancy, "an' I fetch you' out dat well."

He take de queen on him back and go scrape, scrape, crup, crup, up de side de well. Den he say: "Now run! Wash de baby, an' me fetch you down de well again befo' your husban' catch you."

Den she run to de door an' sing:

> O-pen de do', my lit-tle dog-gie!

An' de little dog sing:

> Yes, fo' certain, my fair la-dy!

Den she sing 'gain:

> Fetch the baby, my lit-tle dog-gie!

An' de little dog sing:

> Yes, fo' certain, my fair la-dy!

An' so till all de t'ings fetched* an' de baby all wash, dress, an' sleep so sweet. Den she run back to Nancy an' he take her on him back an' go scrape, scrape, crup, crup, back down de well 'gain.

An' ev'ry day Nancy come dis way and say: "Howdy, me lady!" and take de queen on him back an' fetch her out de well, an' she wash an' dress dat baby till him grow big boy.

*In telling this story the narrator will often sing for each article of the baby's toilette, and sing the reply of the dog, in the simple measures given above.

MAGIC FLIGHT

Tradition Bearer: Fred Gill

Source: Parsons, Elsie Clews. "Barbados Folklore." *Journal of American Folklore* 38 (1925): 275.

Date: 1925

Original Source: Barbados

National Origin: African American

The following **ordinary folktale** is a brief version of the internationally distributed "The Girl as Helper in the Hero's Flight" (AT313). In this tale the male hero plays a subordinate role to his female benefactor, who helps him escape from bondage to her father by cleverness and magic.

Once 'pon a time and a very long time.

A young feller and a giant played dice. The giant told the boy, if he wanted, he would give him his daughter and make him rich. But if he won the boy would have to undertake great tasks.

The giant succeeded in winning from the boy, took the boy to his home and told him to cut down a large tree. As soon as he had cut the tree, the tree sprung up again, and the giant's daughter gave the boy an ax which cut down the tree at one blow.

The giant then gave him another job. Cut down the hill. The more he cut, the higher the hill grew. The giant's daughter gave him a drill which struck the hill down with one blow.

The girl told the boy she would get him away from the place. Said her father had three horses, one which could go sixty miles an hour, another fifty, the last one, forty. She took the one that goes sixty, and gave the boy the one that goes fifty and left the other one for her father. They started up.

As soon as they passed a great forest the father shouted, "How did you pass through?"

The girl said, "I eat and my horse eat, too."

The father and his horse eat so much that they could scarcely move. As soon as the girl and the boy had passed a river, the father shouted out, "How did you get through?"

The girl said, "I drink and my horse drank, too."

The father and his horse drank until their bowels were burst, and the girl and the boy were married and lived happily after that.

> I jump on a wire and the wire ben',
> That's the way the story end.

THE THREE SONS

Tradition Bearer: Merle Woods

Source: Hurston, Zora Neale. "Dance Songs and Tales from the Bahamas." *Journal of American Folklore* 43 (1930): 307–9.

Date: 1929–1930

Original Source: Nassau, Bahamas

National Origin: African American

This classic Old World **ordinary folktale** ("The Table, the Ass, and the Stick," AT563) can be found in the present collection in both this Caribbean **variant** and the Mid-Atlantic **variant** "Tablecloth, Donkey, and Club" (Vol. I, p. 279). This **tale type** begins with a child cast out due to stupidity; in the Bahamian **variant**, however, three sons are cast out because of the lies told by a talking goat. Further, this tale is developed according to another common European formula, the trials of three brothers. This constitutes an important structural difference between both the usual structure of AT563 and the Mid-Atlantic **variant**.

Once upon a time was a good old time,
Monkey chew tobacco and spit white lime.

There was a man. He had three sons. One day he send de eldest out into de woods to feed de goat. And de son looked for de greenest place to feed de goat. And when he was ready to go home he asked de goat have he had sufficient and de goat said, "I had enough till I hardly can pull."

When de goat went home, de father asked de son if he give de goat a plenty of food. And de son said: "Yes, I have give it plenty."

And de father asked de goat had he have enough and de goat said: "I hadn't hardly anything." So he beat that son out and drove him away.

And de next day he sent de other son wid de goat and de son looked for de greenest place to feed de goat. And when he was going home he asked de goat if he had sufficient and de goat said: "I had enough till I hardly could pull."

When de son went home de father asked if he give de goat plenty and he said: "I have give him enough till he said he hardly could pull."

De father asked de goat if he had sufficient and he said: "I had hardly anything." And he beat that son and he stoned him away.

De next day he sent de last son and when de son went he looked for de best spot he could find. And when he was going home he asked de goat if he had sufficient and de goat said de same as he told de other two.

When he got home de father asked de son, who said: "I gave de goat plenty so he hardly could pull."

And when he asked de goat he said he hardly had anything. So he stoned that son out.

And de next day de father went and he looked for de best place and when he was coming home he asked de goat if he had sufficient and de goat said: "I had enough till I hardly could pull." And when he get home he asked de goat had he had enough and de goat said: "I hadn't hardly anything."

So he said: "You was de cause of my three sons not being here today," and he killed de goat and sent it away. And de eldest son was coming home then, and de man who he was working wid give him a table. And he said, "This is not an ordinary table. Just as you say 'Table be covered' de table will have all kind of nice food on it."

When he come that night he stopped at de restaurant and then he begin to eat. He say to de landlord: "I could get better food than all of you all." Just as he say "Table be covered" de daintiest food come on and everybody wanted some, and he give everybody some. And after he lodged there that night, while he was asleep de landlord stole away his table and put his table there and when he wake up that morning, he didn't notice this table. He just take it up and went on and when he get home he told his father he have got a table can be covered wid de best food. Just as I say: "Table be covered" de best food come on. So he called all de neighbors around and people was saying: "We won't have to eat no dinner at home then." So he said: "Table be covered," and nothing come on de table. He was shame and de people had to went back without anything.

And de father said: "I have to take up my needle and thread again."

Next day de other son come. And when he was leaving his master give him a donkey and he told him: "This is not an ordinary donkey. Soon as you say 'brickle-a-brick,' piles of gold will come."

So he came to de same restaurant. When he get his food he give de man a piece of gold he asked de boy where he get it. And he didn't say anything. He went outside and said "brickle-a-brick" and piles of gold came on de tablecloth.

And de landlord was peeping through a hole and he saw him, and after that he tied his donkey and that night he went to bed. While he was 'sleep de land-lord went and stole his donkey and put his donkey in place. And next morning he didn't notice de donkey.

He went home and told his father about his donkey and he called all de neighbors around. When de neighbors came he said "brickle-a-brick" and de donkey didn't do anything. And he was so shame and he wrote to de youngest brother and telling him what de landlord had stole from de two brothers.

So when de last son was leaving his master give a stick in de sack. He said: "This is not an ordinary stick. Just as you say 'Stick out de sack,' it will jump out and beat up your enemies."

And when he come de landlord was watching this bag. When he went to bed he played sleep.

De landlord went and take de bag away and de boy get up and say "stick out de sack" and de stick jumped out and beat up de man. He had to plead for mercy. De boy say: "Stick in de bag, if you promise to give me de two things you stole from my brothers I'll have mercy on you." And he promise him that he will give back de table and de donkey. And he give it to him.

And he went home wid all to his father and brothers and de father said: "At last I will put down my needle and thread."

Biddy, biddy, biddy, my story is ended.
I let go Dorothy and hold you.

THE POWERS THAT BE: SACRED TALES

THE CHOSEN SUITOR

Tradition Bearer: George W. Edwards

Source: Johnson, John H. "Folk-Lore from Antigua, British West Indies." *Journal of American Folklore* 34 (1921): 62–63.

Date: 1921

Original Source: George W. Edwards, Green Bay, Antigua

National Origin: African American

The story of a young woman's marriage to an animal (boar, snake, and bull, among others) in human disguise is a common West Indian tale. The young woman's savior is most often her brother, and this is the case in "The Chosen Suitor" (p. 277), a tale from the southern United States. The boy is despised because of some physical affliction—in this tale he has leprosy, in others the affliction is yaws, a clubfoot, or an infestation of vermin. Despite the loathing of others, he is an "ol' witch boy" who is able to perceive the suitor's disguise and compel him to reveal himself. Commentators are in general agreement that this tale is of African origin.

Dere's a woman had one daughter an' one son. Dis boy coco-bay (leprosy) boy, an' he was an ol' witch too. Dis woman wouldn't allow da girl to court anybody, you know. So one day Bro' Boar-Hog came dere, properly dressed same as any gentleman. When he want to drop off his clothes, he had a song to sing.

Da day when dis Bro' Boar-Hog come to see da daughter, da son tell his mother, "Ma, don' let sister marry to dis man, for he's a boar-hog!" Da mother drive him off, an' say dat he was rude. She say dat dis man was a gentleman.

He tol' da mother, "All right! You will see." One day da mother give him some food to carry to dis man, all tied up nicely on a tray. When da boy reach to da yard, he got behind a tree. While he got behind da tree, he see dis boar-hog rootin' up de ground. An' dis boar-hog root all de ground, like ten men with forks. Dis boy stay behind da tree an' see all he do. When da boy see him, he wait a little; den da boy say, "Ahem!"

Boar-Hog jump around; he start to say,

> "Indiana, Indiana, um, um!
> Indiana, Indiana, um, um!
> Indiana, Indiana, um, um!"

Dat caused his clothes to jump right on him accordin' as he sing da song. He step out, put his two hands in his pocket, an' say, "Boy, see how I plough up dis land!" He boast about da work he do on da field. Den he say to da boy, "How long you come?"

Boy say, "Just come." He took da food an' carry it in da house, an' tell da boy all right, he can go home. Da boy didn't go home. He got behind de tree again. When Bro' Boar-Hog t'ought da boy gone, he had a long trough, an' he dump all de food in da trough. He t'row a bucket a water in too. Den, when he done, he start to say,

> "Indiana, Indiana, um, um!
> Indiana, Indiana, um, um!
> Indiana, Indiana, um, um!"

An' all his clothes drop off. He went in da trough. All dat time da boy watchin' him, you know.

Boy start for home now, an' tell his mother all what he see. Da grandfather tell him all right, dey'll catch him. De daughter an' mother didn't believe, but da grandfather believed.

So dat same afternoon dis Bro' Boar-Hog came to da house all dressed up in frock-coat. As he come in da house, he start talkin' an' laughin' wid da mother an' daughter. During dis time da ol' man had his gun prepare. Little boy take up his fife an' start to play da same song:

"Indiana, Indiana, um, um!
Indiana, Indiana, um, um!
Indiana, Indiana, um, um!"

Bro' Boar-Hog say, "What vulgar song dat boy singin'!" He start to movin'. He not able to keep still, 'cause his tail comin' out fast. Quick he say, "Stop it, stop it! Let's go out for a walk! Let's go out for a walk! I can't stay here."

So dey all went out, da daughter, da mother, an' da grandfather. After dey was goin' on, dey was talkin' when Bro' Boar-Hog look back, he see da boy was comin'. He say, "Where dat boy goin', where he goin'? Turn him back. I don't want to be in his company." So da grandfather tol' him let da boy alone, let him go for a walk too. Grandfather say, "Play, boy! Play, boy!" Da boy start,

"Indiana, Indiana, um, um!
Indiana, Indiana, um, um!
Indiana, Indiana, um, um!"

His beaver [hat] drop off. Den he play on again da same song: his coat drop, his shirt drop. All drop save his pant.

Da ol' man tell him, "Play, boy! Play, play, play!" An' his pant drop off. Dey see his long tail show, an' he start to run. Da ol' man point da gun at him an' shoot him dead.

"An' I went through Miss Havercomb alley,
An' I see a lead was bending;
So da lead ben',
So da story en'.""

THE BIG WORM

Tradition Bearer: Unavailable

Source: Edwards, Charles L. Pages 72–73 in *Bahama Songs and Stories*. Memoirs of the American Folklore Society 3. New York: American Folklore Society, 1895.

Date: 1895

Original Source: Green Turtle Cay, Bahamas

National Origin: African American

"The Big Worm" is a member of the class of stories known in the Bahamas as "old story." These stories are, at their cores, of African rather than European origin. See the appendix to this volume (p. 301) for the original version of this tale.

Once it was a time, a very good time,
De monkey chewed tobacco an' 'e spit white lime.

So once there was a man; he had two sons; dey did n' have no fire. All dey had to eat was raw potatoes. Now de man send dis boy to look for fire. De boy walk; he walk; he walk till 'e saw smoke rising. When 'e gone 'e get to dat fire.

When 'e get there, he saw a worm was full o' fire. De boy say, "Dimme some fan!" (Give me some fire).

De worm say, "'T ain', 't ain' none; jus' enough for me." De worm say, "Come in little closer." *Good!* Soon as de boy wen' a little closer, when 'e went to reach de fire de worm swallow 'im down.

Den de boy wen' down, right down, down inside de worm till 'e stop. De boy met whole lot o' people what de worm did swallow.

So now de man tell de other son, "I wonder where my son gone?"

De other son say, "Pa, I goin' look for him." 'e walk, 'e walk, 'e walk till 'e come to this big worm, what had de fire in his mouth. So now de boy went to de worm. De boy say, "Dimme some fan!"

De worm say, "Keelie o' fire" (Come and get fire).

De boy say, "*Do i en e* [untranslated, perhaps a retention from an African language], dimme some fan?"

De worm say, "Come a little closer." De worm say, "Time for Joe come" (Time to go home). De worm say, "Keelie o' fire."

When de boy wen' to get de fire *so*, de worm swallow him down. De boy wen'; 'e wen' down; 'e wen' down, till 'e met 'e brother.

Now de boy father say, "My two sons gone an' I might as well gone too." De man take 'e lan' (lance); it fairly glisten, it so sharp. When 'e get there where de worm was wid de fire in he mouth, de man say, "Dimme some fan?"

De worm say, "You too do fur me!" (You're too much for me). De worm say, "Keelie o' fire."

When de man wen' to get de fire, *so*, de worm wen' to swallow him. De man take he' lan'; as 'e was goin' down 'e cut de worm; 'e cut de worm till 'e cut de worm right open an' all de people come, an' dat was a big city right there.

> E bo ban, my story's en',
> If you don't believe my story's true,
> Ask my captain an' my crew.

THE NIGHT BEAUTY

Tradition Bearer: Unnamed twenty-year-old Haitian woman

Source: Comhaire-Sylvain, Suzanne. "Creole Tales from Haiti." *Journal of American Folklore* 50 (1937): 215–17.

Date: 1930

Original Source: Baconoir (Nippes), Haiti

National Origin: African American

"The Night Beauty" is a Haitian Creole version of "The Singing Bone" (AT780). The plot is based on the spirit of a murder victim calling out for justice through a bone (as in this case), other remains, or an instrument made from the victim's body (see "Under the Green Old Oak Tree," p. 283, for a **variant** from the Anglo-phonic West Indies). The type is found in poetic as well as prose versions.

Now there was a girl. She was so pretty that they called her the Night Beauty. Brothers and sisters, all of them were jealous, they would have liked her to die but nobody knew it. They shut the lady in the house all day long:

"You get sick easily; better to work double in the field than to sit up with somebody with fever."

When there was a dance or a wake in the neighbourhood, those people went on:

"But look at the face of the person who would like to go out! The part under your eyes is blackish. Either Mayotte or Sonson will stay with you. Don't cry, we will tell you all that happens."

Well! One day when she was sitting very quietly, her elbow on the window, gazing at the frolics of the butterflies, the King's child happened to pass nearby. What a pretty girl! His heart jumped.

He came again in the afternoon, he entered the house, he spoke with the people. The next day he did the same, he could not go away; he lingered in the house of these people. This love was a wonderful love!

He sent to the Night Beauty a bouquet of flowers as high as this [gesture to show the height], made only of roses. Now the eldest brother, the most jealous one, waited till his mother had gone with all the children, he hurled the flowers on the ground, he stamped, he trampled upon them and strangled the girl. When he had finished, he carried the corpse very far away and after sunset he dug her grave in a cornfield.

In the evening when the King's child came, he found everybody in tears. "What has happened?"

"We do not see the Night Beauty, we do not know where she is!"

They searched very thoroughly, by day, by night, nothing! Three years passed away.

The King's child married another girl, but for all that he did not forget the Night Beauty. He gave some money to her people. They bought land. Now the cornfield was included in the land they had bought.

One day of duty service [collective cooperative labor] they were digging to plant, a small bone leaped from a hole and fell on the road. The younger sister of Beauty was passing.

> Pass by, dear sister of mine, pass by.
> Then pass by, dear sister of mine.
> Pass by, dear sister of mine, pass by.
> Then pass by, dear sister of mine.
> Oh yes! the Night Beauty has been killed
> Because of a bunch of roses.

The girl was frightened, she ran to look for her mother and her elder brother. As soon as the woman appeared, the bone took it up:

Pass by, dear mother of mine, pass by.
Then pass by, dear mother of mine.
Pass by, dear mother of mine, pass by.
Then pass by, dear mother of mine.
Oh yes! the Night Beauty has been killed
Because of a bunch of roses!

She passed by. The brother stopped for a moment.

Pass by, criminal, pass by.
Then pass by, criminal.
Pass by, criminal, pass by.
Then pass by, criminal.
O yes! you have killed the Night Beauty
Because of a bunch of roses!

He stopped up his ears so as not to hear. He ran very far away. He went through the town like a *flonde* [very swift fish]; still running, he reached the country, the hills, he ran on; [another] town, he ran on, more hills. When he felt himself dying he stopped a little, then resumed his race. One day when thunder was roaring he lost himself in the woods.

The mother went back home, but the thought of her daughter's death did not leave her mind, it gnawed her continuously. It was not yet one month after the bone had sung [when] they brought the woman [mother] to the cemetery.

UNDER THE GREEN OLD OAK TREE

Tradition Bearer: George W. Edwards

Source: Johnson, John H. "Folk-Lore from Antigua, British West Indies." *Journal of American Folklore* 34 (1921): 62–63.

Date: 1921

Original Source: Green Bay, Antigua
National Origin: African American

"Under the Green Old Oak Tree" offers another **variant** of "The Singing Bone" (AT780) **tale type** discussed in the introduction to "The Night

Beauty" (p. 281). The following version is of interest for at least two reasons. This **variant** is much closer to the "classic" plot; the bone is crafted into a musical instrument prior to making its accusation. Second, the current rendering bears more of the marks of oral transmission, whereas "The Night Beauty" reads like a literary reworking of this **tale type**.

Dis a nice little story. Der woman had two chil'ren. One was a boy, an' der oder was a girl. De fader a dese chil'ren die. Moder decide to marry again. She marry to anoder man.

Each day dese chil'ren did go to de mountain to get flowers. Dey went on dis day. Girl had a better bucket den what de broder got. Dey cumin' wid de flowers. On his way home, de boy stop wid de gal. He t'inkin' some evil plan. Want dis bucket which was his sister. She would not consent to gi' him dis bucket. He t'ink it best to kill der sister. He kill de sister. He kill dis girl near to a big oak tree. An' he hide her dere. After he kill her, he go home. Can't give no account a he sister. Dey all went to search for de girl, but none can find her.

Der broder stay home. Month gone.

Shepherd-boy dat is comin' down de mountain meet [finds] a big bone like a flute. He pick dis bone under dat same tree. He took up de bone an' play. Comin' home wid de flock, he play on de bone. It play a sweet tune:

"My broder has killed me in de woods, an' den he buryth me.
My broder has killed me in de woods, an' den he buryth me
Under de green of oak tree, an' den he buryth me."

Dat's all it could play. It play sweet, you know. Comin' home, all dat hear dis tune beg de boy for a play on it. He give dem a play.

Now he way down de mountain. Mos' to where de moder is livin'. He meet de moder. She ask him for a play. He give her a play. As quick as she play, t'ing say,

"My dear moder, my dear moder, it my dead bone you play.
My dear moder, my dear moder, it my dead bone you play."

She drop an' faint, but never die. All de people was lookin' for de girl. Dis broder meet de boy. He ask him for a play. Take de bone an' start. T'ing say,

"My broder, it is you dat has killed me.
My broder, it is you dat has killed me."

An' dere he faints an' dies.
Dat is de end a da green of oak tree.

THE OLD WOMAN AND HER CHILD

Tradition Bearer: Merle Woods

Source: Hurston, Zora Neale. "Dance Songs and Tales from the Bahamas." *Journal of American Folklore* 43 (1930): 303–4.

Date: 1929–1930

Original Source: Nassau, Bahamas

National Origin: African American

This tale, like "The Night Beauty" (p. 281) and "Under the Green Old Oak Tree" (p. 283), offers another **variant** of "The Singing Bone" **tale type**. Unlike the more common motive for murder in the usual variants of the tale (sibling rivalry), "The Old Woman and Her Child" constructs a chilling scenario of a mother testing her child's kindness to a stranger and rewarding that kindness with death.

Once there was an old woman who had a little girl. One day she was sending her out with some fig. She said to the little girl: "Don't give anybody a fig."
"All right, mama." Then she went on her way. "Nice fig to sell."
Her mama came to her in a form of an old woman. "Do, child, give me a fig."
"Mama say that I must not give anybody a fig."
"Do give me if only five fig."
"Mama say that I must not give anybody a fig."
She give the old woman five fig and when she went home her mama asked her if she give anybody a fig.

"Mama, I did not give anybody a fig." She said, "I give an old woman fig."

She send the little girl out for the hatchet and lay the child neck over the butcher block and chop the child neck off and put it under the pepper tree. And when the father came home he asked for the little girl.

His wife said that she send her out and her husband went to the pepper tree and begin to pick pepper.

"Do, my father, don't pull my hair for mama has kill me for one fig."

The father call his wife and asked her where is the little girl and she said: "I send she out pick on pepper."

When she pick the pepper the child said: "Do, my mama, don't pull my hair for you has kill me for five little fig."

Then the husband send his wife for the butcher block and hatchet and chop off her head and put it in the oven and burn it.

Bid bid biddy
My story is end.

RESCUED FROM THE LOUPS GAROUS BY LOA SAINT JAMES

Tradition Bearer: Termeus Joseph

Source: Simpson, George E. "Loup Garou and Loa Tales from Northern Haiti." *Journal of American Folklore* 55 (1942): 222–23.

Date: 1942

Original Source: Haiti

National Origin: African American

Loup garou literally translates as "werewolf." This term was borrowed from the French, but the concept of loup garou in African-descended Caribbean traditions typically does not entail transformation into a wolf. The Haitian version of the loup garou is a shapeshifter that is capable of removing its skin and assuming any shape necessary to accomplish its goals. In this context, Saint James is synonymous with the powerful loa or lwa (supernatural figure), Ogoun. Among other attributes, Ogoun is a lwa who deals with warfare and may remove obstacles from the path of the faithful.

A woman went to Bahon to attend the burial service of her brother. After the service she told her husband that she was going to her home in Grande Riviere. He protested, but she said that she had a good horse, and that she was not afraid to go alone.

She started from Bahon about one o'clock in the morning, and after traveling a short distance she heard someone say, "Now I am going to maltreat you, as you have maltreated me." Then she heard the voice of her brother who had been captured by the loups garous.

Evil spirits took her and her brother to their camp, where the chief of the loups garous first offered them kola and cooked maize, and then passed judgment upon them. "You may kill them now," he said.

A loup garou stepped forward and thrust a knife into her brother's neck. He fell to the ground, and when the loup garou struck him and kicked him he became a bull. They intended to kill the woman, too, but she was a faithful servant of Saint James, and he saved her from the fate of her brother.

A ZANGE DISGUISES AS A SNAKE

Tradition Bearer: Bertrand Velbrun

Source: Simpson, George E. "Loup Garou and Loa Tales from Northern Haiti." *Journal of American Folklore* 55 (1942): 224–25.

Date: 1942

Original Source: Haiti

National Origin: African American

George Eaton Simpson, in his introductory remarks to the following **legend**, asserts that zange is a synonym for loa (also "lwa"), a supernatural being of the Haitian vodun religion. The snake is important to vodun; for example, Danballah, one of the major lwa, is represented as a snake. According to another source, the zange is actually the anj (also "ange") that returns to the "ancestral waters" (the spiritual realm or realm of ancestral spirits), and this is the meaning of "the capital of the Zanges under the water." In this realm the zange/anj is judged in the afterlife as the judge hears the case of the peasant and the disguised zange.

Every Friday for seven weeks a peasant saw a big snake lying at the entrance to his courtyard. The peasant was afraid to enter his yard while the snake was there. Finally he took a cane and struck the snake on its kidneys, but he did not kill it and the snake ran away.

The next night the man dreamed that two soldiers came to his house and arrested him. A few minutes later he found himself in a large pond and was drowned. Within a short time he was in Ville-au-Camp, the capital of the Zanges under the water. This country seemed very mysterious to him, and he noticed that everyone was busy.

He soon found himself in the courthouse where a judge sat listening to some cases. A man who seemed to be sick was sitting in one corner of the courtroom. The judge announced a decision, called the next case, and the man who seemed to be sick got up and came before the judge. He spoke these words: "Your honor, I went for seven Fridays to visit this farmer," and he pointed to the peasant who had struck the big snake. "Last Friday he became very angry and struck me on the kidneys without cause and thus brought on my disease. I demand justice."

The judge asked the peasant to reply to this charge and the man said, "Your Honor, every Friday when I tried to enter my yard I found a very formidable snake at my gate, and I was too frightened to enter when it was there. Last Friday I was forced to defend myself, but I had no way of knowing that the big snake was a zange. Your Honor, I did not intend to commit a crime and I am sure that you will give me my freedom."

The judge called the plaintiff and said to him: "Is it true that you changed yourself into a big snake to frighten him and to stop him when he wanted to come into his house?" "Yes, Your Honor, but I was simply joking."

The judge said to him: "You are a wretched man. This farmer was right in defending himself because you are a very ugly snake. You shall be thrown in prison." Two guards stepped up and arrested the Zange and took him away to prison.

Then the judge said to the peasant: "We are sorry that a very bad Zange caused you this great inconvenience. You are now free and I shall see to it that you are returned safely to your home." The soldiers then escorted the peasant to his house. The peasant awoke, but he was still afraid.

A LOUP GAROU DISGUISES AS A BEGGAR

Tradition Bearer: Ulysse Marius

Source: Simpson, George E. "Loup Garou and Loa Tales from Northern Haiti." *Journal of American Folklore* 55 (1942): 221–22.

Date: 1942

Original Source: Haiti

National Origin: African American

The following **legend** opens with the familiar feature of a powerful bene-factor disguised as a helpless beggar. Although the disguised beggar and his followers are called loups garous, their role in the narrative seems more like the sanpwels (literally "without skins," due to their reputa-tions for removing their skins before changing their physical forms). According to some sources, the sanpwels, unlike the loups garous who threaten the social order, are an organization with supernatural sanction to punish improper behavior within the community and extend its pro-tection to the just and the kind.

Sometimes one meets a poor man who begs along the road, but who is really the chief of the *loups garous*. There is such a man, who seems to be poor and sick, living in Plaisance.

One evening a woman merchant from Cape Haitian told him she wished to return home that night. He told her that it was very dangerous for anyone to travel at night because the night does not belong to the living.

He said: "The day is for the living, but the night is full of mysteries. However, if you wish to travel to the Cape tonight, I can give you the proper authorization." He then handed her a goblet and said: "If you should meet some loups garous who ask for your authorization show them this goblet, and they will leave you alone."

The woman took the poor man's gift and thanked him. A few hours later she started to walk to the Cape, but about ten o'clock she met five men who acted very strangely and said to her: "It is not permissible for a woman to travel alone at night. Where is your authorization?"

The traveler showed them the goblet given to her by the old man. The men bowed respectfully and let her pass.

Later she met a group of ten men and one of them said: "Who gave you the right to travel alone at night? I must stop you."

Another said: "Before stopping this woman we had better ask her something about her authorization."

The woman produced the goblet again and the man who had intended to stop her said: "You are a great person. You have a powerful friend."

The woman continued for some time unmolested. As she approached a crossroads she encountered a large group of at least one hundred persons who were singing. One man stopped her and said: "I must take you to the great chief. You are too bold. You should not be traveling alone at night."

The woman was conducted to the chief who wore very expensive clothes and looked like a king. He said to her, "Who gave you the right to travel alone at night? The night is not yours. You have the day and that is enough. Where is your authorization?" The woman again showed the goblet and the chief smiled and said: "Your authorization is good. You may continue your journey."

The following week the woman merchant returned to Plaisance and saw the poor man begging in the market. He said to her: "My friend, I am very glad to see you. What have you brought me from the Cape?"

The woman gave him some money, some syrup, some codfish, a loaf of bread and a ring. The poor man said to her: "I see that you are a good person, that you are grateful, and I am very glad. Did you recognize me the other night?"

The woman replied that she had not recognized him. "During my journey I met several groups of persons who demanded my authorization. Each time I showed them your goblet and they immediately freed me."

The beggar answered, "I was the chief before whom you were brought."

THE POWERS THAT BE: SECULAR TALES

THE SOLOMON CYCLE

Tradition Bearer: Richard Barrett

Source: Hurston, Zora Neale. "Dance Songs and Tales from the Bahamas." *Journal of American Folklore* 43 (1930): 301–3.

Date: 1929–1930

Original Source: Nassau, Bahamas

National Origin: African American

Tales of this type, which improvise on and extrapolate from preexisting religious narratives, may be said to constitute a "folk Bible" that accompanies the written text. The focus of the "Solomon Cycle," in spite of its source, is about the secular rather than the sacred qualities of Solomon. The tradition bearer Richard Barrett, who also performed "Adam and Eve" (p. 231) for folklorist Zora Neale Hurston, seems to specialize such semimythic tales.

Variant A

Do you know why Solomon said, "Vanity of vanities; all is vanity and a vexation of spirit"? Well, you see, Solomon married up thousands of women. They say them folks way back didn't have no sense, but Solomon was the wisest man that ever lived.

He had a room in that gold palace with a glass ceiling in it. Whenever one of his new wives would be brought to him, before he would see her he would sit and talk with her awhile in that room over the glass floor. If she looked to suit him, he would excuse himself and make out he had some business out in the yard. Then he would go into that room with the glass ceiling and look up at the girl sitting upstairs.

Well, after he had done married hundred of girls he got a little old. He wasn't so old in years, but he was all tired out.

Then here comes the Queen of Sheba to visit him. She was very beautiful and everything, and Solomon took her right up to the room and entertained for a while. Then he went downstairs and peeped up. She was beautiful every way he looked at her, but he realized his constitution was wore away.

Then Solomon took off his crown and dashed it against the wall and said: "All is vanity and a vexation of spirit."

Variant B

When the Queen of Sheba visited Solomon she fell in love with him right away, but he talked very slow. So she said to him: "King Solomon, I want something."

He said: "You can have anything you want, even to half of my kingdom. What is it you want?"

She says: "I want some water to drink."

Old Solomon called a man and told him to bring her some water in a golden goblet.

She said: "No, I don't want no water out of no golden goblet. I want a drink of living water, and I don't want no water out of no well; I don't want no water out of no lake; I don't want no water out of no river, nor no stream, nor no pump. But I am thirsty, I want a drink!"

So Solomon called one of his men and told him to take his fastest race horse and put him on the track and to take a basin with him and to run that horse until he sweat that bowl full of sweat.

After a while the man come back with the bowl of horse-sweat and Solomon put it in a golden bowl and handed it to Sheba to drink.

She throwed it on the ground and told him: "I heard that you was a very wise man, but you don't know how to quench thirst."

So she went on home.

Variant C

When the Queen of Sheba come to Solomon he loved her as soon as he saw her, but she acted so indifferent he didn't know how to get up to her.

So you know he was a very wise man, so he thought up a scheme. So he told her: "Now, Queen of Sheba, you mustn't steal nothing while you are here in my kingdom. If you do, I will punish you in any way I want to. You will have to do anything I say."

She said: "Oh no, I don't steal."

So he give her a great banquet, and everything was salty. He didn't have a drop of drinking water nowhere. There was a fountain out on the lawn and that was the only water to be found around the palace.

After the dinner was over, Solomon run out and hid in the bushes close to the fountain and waited.

Pretty soon the Queen sneaked up to the fountain and got a drink of water.

Soon as she got through, Solomon rose up and said: "Unh hunk, Queen of Sheba, I told you not to steal and here you are stealing my water."

He called the servants and had her took right into the palace. She was in his power then.

DE STORY OF DE MAN AND SIX POACHED EGGS

Tradition Bearer: Unavailable

Source: Smith, Pamela Coleman. "Two Negro Stories from Jamaica." *Journal of American Folklore* 9 (1896): 278.

Date: 1896

Original Source: Kingston, Jamaica

National Origin: African Caribbean

The following tale is derived from an English source, "The Witty Exploits of Mr. George Buchanan, the King's Fool." Buchanan, although he survives in folk narrative as a "fool" in the Elizabethan tradition, was known as a social reformer and served as a tutor to James VI of Scotland as well as an advisor. See the southern highlands tale "The King and Old George Buchanan" (p. 132) for another example.

O nce a man go travelin' an' he get hungry, so he stop at a tavern an' order somethin' to eat, so dey bring him six poached eggs. He eat dem, but he did not have any money, so he say he would come back an' pay. In six years—or maybe it was more—he come back an' pay sixpence for de eggs. But den de tavern keeper say dat if he had not eaten de six poached eggs dey might have been chickens, an' den de chickens would have grown up an' hatch more chickens, an' dey more—an' more—an' more—an' tell de man he must pay six pounds instead of sixpence. An' de man say he would not.

So dey go to de judge. An' while dey was conversin' a boy come in with a bundle under his arm. An' de judge say: "What you got in de bundle?" an' de boy say, "Parch'peas," say, "What you goin' do with dem?" "Plant dem, sir!" "Hi," say de judge, "You can't plant parch'peas, dey won't grow!" "Well, sir, an' poached eggs won't hatch!" So dey dismiss de man an' he never pay a penny!

Dis story show dat you mus' never count you' eggs before dey hatch!

EDUCATION FOR A CARPENTER'S SON

Tradition Bearer: J. B. Cineas' great-grandmother

Source: Simpson, George E., and J. B. Cineas. "Folk Tales of Haitian Heroes." *Journal of American Folklore* 54 (1941): 179.

Date: 1941

Original Source: Haiti

National Origin: African American

Henri Christophe (1767–1820) was a Haitian military leader and statesman who participated in the Haitian Revolution of 1791 and rose to the rank of general. He eventually became president of Haiti and, on making Haiti a kingdom in 1811, ruled as Henri I. Regarded as tyrannical by his opposition, he also was noted for his dedication to education. Both qualities are combined in the following **legend**.

One day the King [Henri Christophe] stopped at a carpenter shop in Quartier-Morin, admired the man's work and complimented him on it. As he was about to leave he noticed a young apprentice who seemed to be indifferent about his tasks. "Who is this young boy?"

"King, he is my son. I am teaching him the carpenter's trade."

"That is very well but he is too young yet. He should be in school. If he knew how to read and write he would surpass you and become a good artisan. I have established schools. Why don't you send this boy to school?"

"King, I am not ready yet. I am preparing his clothes."

"That is not a good reason. He can go to school as he is. I shall give you eight days to put your son in school."

After the King had left the peasant said to himself, "You are King and therefore rich. I have only this boy to help me."

The following week the King returned to the carpenter shop. Surprised, the man said, "King, my little boy had malaria and the tailor has not finished his clothes." "I shall allow you a fortnight because of the illness and the tailor," said the King, who was boiling inwardly with anger.

The carpenter said to himself, "Oh, this troublesome man! Why does he think he can make my son go to school? He should tend to his own business."

When at the end of two weeks he saw the King's procession approaching he was terrified. With bulging eyes and broken voice he threw himself at the feet of Christophe, "King! King! The little boy..."

"I understand. It is easy to see that you are an abnormal man. Your ears are not placed as other men's are but seem to be located on your rear. It is too bad. Gentlemen, do your duty. Diable canaille!" Four men seized the obstinate carpenter and by giving him a good beating put his ears in place, and the child went to school.

DAYDAY AGASTIN

Tradition Bearer: Unnamed Informant from Sault du Baril, Haiti

Source: Comhaire-Sylvain, Suzanne. "Creole Tales from Haiti." *Journal of American Folklore* 50 (1937): 247.

Date: 1937 (collected 1930)

Original Source: Haiti
National Origin: African American

Overtly, the tale of "Dayday Agastin" presents a narrative on infidelity and revenge. The female protagonist is at the mercy of a persistent young stranger and a domineering husband. The fact that she gives in to the stranger's request to sleep with her so easily may be interpreted as a comment on how lightly she takes her wedding vows. On the other hand, charms and spells are commonly framed as chants, rhymes, or songs, and the stranger's seduction is cast in song. As a result, Dayday Agastin may be seen as an innocent victim rather than an adulteress.

There was a beautiful young woman who lived all alone with her husband in a small house in the mountains. There were no neighbours, only fields in this place. Now, the man went to town to arrange a land business; he told the woman he would be away three days, to be careful, and not to open the door to anybody after sunset. Nowadays people are robbers, moreover they are too pert. The man went away.

He had not been away for two hours when the woman was in need of wood to light a fire. She went to her wood pile which was put away in the kitchen, the wood was used up. "What a bore for me! My husband is gone, I have nobody to cut wood for me!"

She went toward the main road to see if she could find somebody to cut wood for her. She waited very long. When the sun began to go down, she saw a young man coming along the road.

"Good morning, Madam!"

"Do you want a small, well-paid job? Come and cut my wood."

"Where?"

"Walk along a little with me!"

The man came and accepted the work, but he had not given ten ax strokes when the trunk cracked. It fell on the foot of the man and wounded it severely. He sang:

> Dayday Agastin who called me
> Who called me to cut wood
> Wood has cut my foot!
> Oh! Dayday Agastin
> Give me the thing so that I may go
> You don't see that the wood has cut my foot!

Dayday Agastin gave him his pay so that he could go away. The man was not able to walk. He advanced the good foot, he stumbled, he advanced the wounded foot, he fell down. How it ached! The man asked her to stay for the night in the yard.

"You may. Here is a mat to lie down."

The sun set, the woman ate, she gave the man broth, then she closed her door to sleep.

She had hardly put her head on her pillow when the song took up:

> Dayday Agastin who called me
> Who called me to cut wood
> Wood has cut my foot!
> Oh! Dayday Agastin
> Give me the thing so that I may go
> You don't see that the wood has cut my foot!

"What is the matter with this man to complain like that? What do you want? You took your money already! Speak!"

"That's nothing, Madam, I have a shooting pain in the foot, I cannot sleep in the night dew, that is why I was singing that song."

"Put your mat inside the doorsill and shut up! I want to sleep." He stopped a little. When he saw that the lady was asleep, he resumed:

> Dayday Agastin who called me
> Who called me to cut wood
> Wood has cut my foot!
> Oh! Dayday Agastin
> Give me the thing so that I may go

297

You don't see that the wood has cut my foot!

"What is your purpose, Sir, did I not tell you that I wanted to sleep? What is the thing I would have to give you?"

"Let me come into your bed, I will tell you which thing."

Dayday Agastin told him to come. She gave him what he wanted and the man let her sleep. Four o'clock struck, they were asleep, five o'clock, they were asleep.

Now, the master of the house, the husband of Dayday Agastin, had begun to settle his business, he saw it would be too long, he entrusted it to a friend and went back to the hills the same day, so that his wife should not stay alone very long in the house: there are so many wicked people!

He arrived very early in the morning. He saw the door open, he came in and saw Dayday Agastin lying in bed with a young man, he went for his gun and aimed, they were still asleep, he fired three times.

Then he came back to town. He left the two dead bodies in the bed.

THE GIRL AND THE FISH

Tradition Bearer: Unavailable

Source: Edwards, Charles L. "Some Tales from Bahama Folk-Lore: Fairy Stories." *Journal of American Folklore* 4 (1891): 247.

Date: 1891

Original Source: Green Turtle Cay, Bahamas

National Origin: African American

Collector Charles Edwards notes that catching the tiny fish that gather in old conch shells is a common pastime for children in the Bahamas. Martha Warren Beckwith, in her discussion of this **tale type** that she labels "The Fish Lover," notes that it is common in Jamaica and distributed widely in the West Indies in her 1924 book *Jamaica Anansi Stories*. The theme—that violations of the natural order cannot be tolerated—is in some ways reminiscent of "The Chosen Suitor" (p. 277). This tale, of course, lacks the supernatural elements of "Suitor."

This day this girl wen' down to de sea for salt water. She catch one little fish out de conch shell. She name 'im Choncho-wally. She put 'im in de well. Ev'ry morning she use to put some of her breakfas' in de bucket an' carry to de fish; an' some of her dinner, an' some of her supper. She feed 'im till 'e get a big fish.

This mornin', when she wen' to carry de breakfas' for 'im, she sing:

> "Conch-o, Conch-o-wall-y
> Don't you wan' to mar-ry me,
> My daddy short-tail."

'E comes up an' she feed 'im. Den she let 'im go down. When she wen' home, de boy say, "Pa, sister got somet'in' inside de well."

Den de nex' day she come; bring vittles again for 'im. De man say to de boy, "You go behin' de tree an' listen to what she goin' sing." De gal sing:

> "Conch-o, Conch-o-wall-y
> Don't you wan' to mar-ry me,
> My daddy short-tail."

Huh! De boy catch it [hears her song]; 'e gone; tell 'e pa. De boy say, "Pa, sister say, 'Conch-o, Conch-o-wally,' etc. De man go; 'e took 'e grange [fish spear], 'e sing, "Conch-o, Conch-o-wally," etc. De fish come up; 'e strike 'im. 'E carry 'im home an' they had some for dinner. De gal say, "I bet you this nice fish!"

Den de gal took some in de bucket to carry to de fish. Den when de gal wen' to de well to call de fish, she sing,

> "Conch-o, Conch-o-wall-y
> Don't you wan' to mar-ry me,
> My daddy short-tail."

She sing again,

> "Conch-o, Conch-o-wall-y
> Don't you wan' to mar-ry me,
> My daddy short-tail."

She ain' hear no fish, an' she ain' see none. She sing again,

> "Conch-o, Conch-o-wall-y
> Don't you wan' to mar-ry me,
> My daddy short-tail."

She begin to cry now,

> "Conch-o, Conch-o-wall-y
> Don't you wan' to mar-ry me,
> My daddy short-tail."

Den she wen' home to de house, behin' de house, an' she cry 'erself to death.

> E bo ban, my story's en',
> If you don't believe my story's true,
> Ask my captain an' my crew.

Appendix: Original Versions

THE SOUTH

Ol' Rabbit an' de Dawg He Stole

Tradition Bearer: Unavailable

Source: Owen, Mary A. "Ol' Rabbit an' de Dawg He Stole." *Journal of American Folklore* 9 (1890): 135–38.

Date: 1890

Original Source: Missouri

National Origin: African American

In de good ole times, Ole Rabbit he wuzzen' scrouge none by de nabuz. Hit wuz miles ter de cornder ob enny un ob ums fiel'.

Atter wiles, Mistah Injun an' he folkses sot um up er sottlemint, but dat ain' nuttin, kase deco Injun folks wuz alluz a-perawdin' eroun' an' a-ketchin up dey plundah, an' a-movin' it hyeah an' yondah.

Bimeby, dough, de wite men come 'long a-choppin' down de trees an' a-diggin' up de yeath. Den all de crittuz pack dey go-ter-meetin' close in er piller-case an' git ready ter staht, kase dey know dat Mistah Wite Man come foh ter stay, an' he ain' one o' de kine dat wanter sleep free two in de bed an' dey ain' ne'er.

Dat is all on um cep Ole Chuffy Rabbit an' de Squirl fambly sot out. Dey two 'low dey gwine ter tough hit out while longah.

Wat pester Ole Chuffy mo' den all de res' wuz dat wite man's dawg. Hit wuzzen' lak dem Injun dawgs, dat's a-scatterin' roun' de kyentry ter day an' in de pot ter morrer. Hit wuz one o' dem shahpnose houn'-dawgs dat hunt all day an' howl all night. Hit wuz es still ez er fox on er tucky-hunt fum de mawnin' twell cannel-light, but des wait twell de sun go down an' de moon come up an'—oh Lawd! Ah, oo-oo-oo, wow, ow, ow! Ah oo-oo-oo, wow, ow, ow! Ah oo-oo-oo, wow, ow, ow! Heah hit go fum mos' sun-down ter mos' sun-up, an' dat wuz de mos' aggervaxines' soun' dat de Ole Boy e'er putt in de thote ob er libin crittur. Hit des' stractid Ole Rabbit. He flounce roun' in de bed lak er cat-fish on de hook. He groan an' he grunt, an' he tuhn an' be roll, an' he des kyarn' git no good res'. He bin un o' de smoove torkin' kine gin'ly, but dat houn' mek 'im cuss twell ole Miss Rabbit she bleege ter roll de bed-kivuz roun' huh yeahs, she dat scannelize.

"Wy doan' yo' git outen de baid an' tuhn yo' shoe wid de bottom-side up an' set yo' bar foot onter hit?" she say. "Dat mek enny dawg stop he yowlin'."

"Well! Ain' I done hit forty-leben time?" say Ole Man Rabbit des a-fumin' an' a-snortin'. "Ain' I bin a-hoppin' in an' out de baid all de lib-long night? Cose hit stop um foh er half er jiff an' den hit chune up ergin 'foh I des kin git de baid wahm unner me."

Ah oo-oo-oo, wow, ow, ow! Ah oo-oo-oo, wow, ow, OW! Dat ole houn' fetch er yowl dat far mek de man in de moon blink.

"Cuss dat ole dawg! Cuss um say I! Wy doan' dat ole fool dat own um stuff er cawn-cob down he frote, ur chop um inter sassige-meat?" sez Ole Rabbit, sez 'e. "I gin up on de sleepin' queschun ter night," sez 'e, "but I lay I ain' 'sturb lak dis in my res' termorrer," sez 'e.

Wid dat he bounce out on de flo' an' haul on he britches an' light 'er toller-dip; an' he tek dat toller-dip in he han' an' he go pokin' roun' mungs de shadders lak he a-huntin' foh sumpin'.

Scratch, scratch! scuffle, scuffle! he go in de cor

nderz ob de cubbered.

Ah oo-oo-oo! wow, ow, ow! go de houn' outside.

Scratch, scratch! scuffle, scuffle! Ah oo-oo-oo! wow, ow, ow! Scratch, scratch! scuffle, scuffle! Ah oo-oo-oo! wow, ow, ow!

An' so dey keep hit up, twell ole Miss Rabbit des ez mad at one ez turr. "Wot is yo' doin', Mistah Rabbit?" she say agin an' 'gin; but Ole Chuff ain' satify 'er bout dat.

Treckly, dough, wen he git thu an' blow out de cannel an' de day gunter broke, she bin nodiss dat he step sorter lop-side. "Wat is de mattah, Mistah

Rabbit?" she ax. "Is yo' run er brier inter yo' foot?" "No," sez 'e, mighty shawt, "I ain' got no brier in my foot dat I knows un, but I gotter brier in my mine 'bout de size ob er snipe-bill, of I ain' mistookened."

At dat she let fly er swam o' queschins, but he des grin dry an' say—

"Ax me no queschins an' I tell yo' no lies. Doan' bodder me, ole ooman (old woman, wife). I ain' feel berry strong in de haid dis mawnin', an' I mought hatter anser queschins wid my fist of I gits pestered."

Dat shet 'er up, in cose, an' she sot in ter gittin' brekfus. Putty soon she holler out, "Who bin techin' de braid? Somebody bin a-cuttin' de braid! I lay I gotter trounce deco greedy chilluns foh dat. Pear lak I kyarn' set down nuttin' dese days but dey gotter muss in hit! I gwine ter cut me er big hick'ry lim' dis mawnin' an' see of I kyarn' lick some mannuz inter de whole kit an' bilin' un um! In de meanwiles o' gittin' dat lim' I gwine ter smack de jaws ob de whole crowd." "No yo' ain'," sez Ole Rabbit, sez 'e. "Des lef dem young uns o' mine 'lone. Dey ain' done nuttin. I cut dat braid, an' I got dat braid, an' I ain' gwine ter gin 'er up."

Putty soon ole Miss Rabbit sing out ergin. "Who bin cuttin' de bakin (bacon) fat?" sez she, "an' cuttin' hit crookid too," sez she. "I lay I des leaf de brekfus an' set out 'n' git dat lim' right now," sez she.

"No, yo' woan'," sez Ole Rabbit, sez 'e. "I ain' gwine ter hab de sense w'ale outen dem young uns o' mine. I tuck dat fat an' I got dat fat, an' of I haggle de slice dat my look out," sez 'e. "I paid foh hit, an' I gwine ter cut hit wid de saw ur de scissuz, of I feel lak hit," sez 'e.

Wid dat he git up an' walk off, lim-petty-limp.

Miss Rabbit ain' see no mo' un 'im twell sundown. Den he come in lookin' mighty tuckahd out, but des a-grinnin' lak er bake skunk. He sot down he did, an' et lak he bin holler clar to he toes, but he woan' say nuttin. Wen he git thu he sorter stretch hissef an' say, "I gwine ter go ter baid. I gotter heap o' sleep ter mek up, an' I lay no dawg ain' gwine ter 'sturb my res' dis night."

An' dey doan'. Dey wuzzen' er soun', an' Miss Rabbit mek er gret miration at dat in huh min', but she ain' got nobody ter tork hit unter twell de nex' mawnin', wen Ole Rabbit git up ez gay an' sassy ez er yeahlin'. Den 'e hab de big tale ter tell, an' dis wuz wut he tell 'er:

Wen he wuz a-foolin' in de cubberd he git 'im er piece o' braid, an' he tie dat on he foot. Den he cut 'im er slice o' bakin, an' he putt dat on top de braid. Den he slip on he shoe an' he staht out. Dat he do kase he gwine ter fix 'im some shoe-braid foh feed ter dat dawg, kase of yo' wah braid in yo' shoe an' den gin hit unter er dawg, an he eat hit, dat dawg yo'n. He gwine ter foller yo' ter de eens o' de yeath, dat he am. De bakin he put on ter gin dat braid er good tase, an' ter fool de folks wut see 'im, kase he gwineter let on lak he run er brier in he foot an' tuck 'n' putt on dat bakin foh ter dror out de so'ness an' kip 'im fum a-gettin' de lock-jaw.

Well, he tromp roun' twell de wite man go ter de fiel', an' den he sorter slip up easy-like, an' he fling dat shoe-braid afront o' dat Ole houn'-dawg. Hit gulf hit down in des one swaller. Yo' know dem houn'-dawgs des alluz bin hongry sence de minnit dey wuz bawn, an' yo' kyarn' fill um up no mo' 'n of dey got holes in um de same ez er cullendah.

De minnit dat shoe-braid bin swaller, dat Ole houn'-dawg des natchelly hone atter Ole Rabbit. He tuck out atter 'im thu' de bresh so swif' dat hit sorter skeer Ole Chuffy. He was des a-studyin' 'bout a-leadin' dat houn' ter de crik, an' a-tyin' a rock roun' he neck an' a-drownin' um, but dis hyeah turrible hurry 'sprize 'im so dat he des run lak de Ole Boy wuz a-tryin' ter ketch 'im. Hyeah dey had hit! Up hill an' down holler, crost de fiel' an' roun' de stump, obah an' undah, roun' an' roun', ketch of yo' kin an' foller of yo' kyarn'. O suz, dat wuz er race!

No tellin' how hit mought er come out of Ole Rab hedn' run crost an Injun man wid er bow an' arrer.

De Injun gun ter fit de arrer ter de string foh ter shoot dat Chuffy Rabbit, wen he holler out loud ez he c'd holler foh de shawtness ob he bref—

"Oh! hole on, Mistah Injun Man, hole on er minnit. I'm a-fetchin' yo' er present," sez 'e, "er mighty nice present," sez 'e.

"Wut yo' fetch?" sez de Injun Man, kine o' spishis-lak. "Hit's er dawg," sez Ole Rabbit, a-wuhkin he yeahs an' a-flinchin' he nose, kase he hyeah dat dawg a-cracklin' thu' de bresh, "a mighty nice fat dawg, Mistah Injun Man. I hyeah tell dat yo' ole ooman wuz po'ly, an' I wuz a-brungin' dis hyeah houn'-dawg sost yo' c'd mek er stchew outen um," sez 'e. "I'd a-fotch um ready cook," sez 'e, "but my ole ooman des nowurz 'long o' yo'n in de mekin' o' stchews," sez 'e. "I wuz foh fetchin' er string o' inguns foh seas'nin an' den I doan' know of yo' lak um wid inguns," sez 'e.

De Injun suttinly wuz tickle wid dat lallygag, but he doan' say much. He des sorter grunt an' look todes de bresh.

"Dat um! dat my houn'-dawg a-comin'!" say Ole Rabbit a-flinchin' mo' an' mo' ez de cracklin' come a-nighah. "Yo' bettah shoot um, des ez 'e bonce outen de bresh, kase dat er mon'sus shy dawg, mon'sus shy! He woan' foller nobody but me, an' I kyarn' go 'long home wid yo' an' tek um, kase Ise lame. Las' night I c'd'n sleep my lef' ban' hine foot huht so, an' now I got um tie up in bakin fat. Shoot um right hyeah, Mistah Injun! Dat de bes' an' de safes', mon!"

Des dat minnit out jump de dawg, an'—zim!—Mistah Injun des shoot um an' pin um to de groun'.

Den Ole Man Rabbit mop de sweat offen he face an' lope off home, leas' dat de tale he tell de fambly, an' of tain' true nobody ain' a-'nyin' hit dese days, an' ez he say ter he ole ooman, bit er good laughin' tale ter day, but twuz mon'sus solemncholly yistiddy.

Sence dat time all de houn'-dawgs is sholy cunjer, kase of dey kech er gimpse ob er rabbit tail out dey putt atter hit.

Allen Chesser's Initiation: The Bear Fight

Tradition Bearer: Allen Chesser

Source: Harper, Francis. "Tales of the Okefinoke." *American Speech* 1 (1926): 409–10.

Date: ca. 1914

Original Source: Georgia

National Origin: European American

Now I'll tell yet erbout that Bear fight, of yer'll git yer book.

"I must tell yet how come we come ter go. I wuz a boy, I reckon ten er twelve yurs old, an' the other boys 'uz older. I 'uz off with muh bow an' arrer some'eres, an' they went off an' lef' me; tuk the gun an' the dogs.

"They lef' one gun, an' hit wuz an of flint-an'-steel. As true a shootin' gun as I ever shot, too. I taken that gun, an' went ter Hurst Islant. Wal, when I walked out on the islant, I didn't haf ter look, there wuz the Bear *right there*. An' I, yet know, could 'a' killed with all ease ef I had a mind ter—ef I'd had the sense I have now—but I thought I had ter be right close on ter 'im.

"An' while I wuz a-slippin' ter git close-ter ter 'im, he jumped up a tree. He went erbout two jumps up the tree (I could hear 'is paws hit the tree), an' slung 'is haid off on each side, *thisaway* an' *thataway,* an' then 'e come down. He tuk 'is time, an' went noselin' erbout, feedin' on pa'meeter buds. An' 'e drifted off in the bay, an' me erlong after 'im, tryin' ter git a chance ter shoot. Pokin' erlong an' feedin' erlong. As fur as he went, I went. An' I got, I reckon, in erbout ten steps er 'im. Lost all muh good chances ter kill 'im out on the islant, an' had 'im there in that bay. I couldn't see nothin' er 'im but 'is haid. When I decided ter shoot (I got a notion ter shoot then), I aimed through the bushes ter strike 'is body, an' I shot. Uv cose, them kind er ball is easy turned. An' uv cose I missed 'im clair—never teched 'im. So I stood still, an' so did the Bear. An' 'e stood there, I reckon, somep'n like a quarter er a minute, somep'n like a few breaths. An' 'e commenced grumblin', growlin'; I could hear 'im jest as plain, in 'is manner. An' the notion struck me, I had *better git out er that bay*. So I went, an' I went in a hurry, too. I didn't look fer a Bear er nothin', only fer a way ter git out er that bay, *quick*. I got out ter the islant. The islant wuz burnt off, an' the grass 'uz only erbout that high [stretching out his hand a foot above the ground]; looked prooty an' green. So I went out erbout, I reckon, seventy-five yards on the islant. The notion struck me I better load muh gun. An' I sot muh gun down jest like that [butt touching the ground, barrel at a slant], an' I wuz a-pourin' muh charge er powder in. An' I raised muh haid an' looked back ter see of I could see any-thing er the Bear; an' shore enough he come right on muh trail. So I pulled out muh knife an' opened it, an' stuck it in the ground right down beside me, so of I come in close contact, I'd have a chance ter use it. So I kep' on loadin' then jest as fast as I could (kep' the balls aroun' loose in muh pocket), an' a-lookin' fer the Bear, an' he kep' a-comin', too.

"So there 'uz an ol' log that had fell, lyin' jest like that, an' 'e come ter the top er the log (some of rotten limbs), an' he 'uz a-gnawin' on them limbs, pop-pin' the limbs an' throwin' the bark off'n 'em."

"Wha'd he do that for?" I ventured to ask.

"He 'uz mad. He walked jest like a billy goat (you've seen 'em when they're mad—feel bigitty), an' 'e had 'is yurs hugged right close ter 'is haid, jest *that-away*, an' I wuz settin' erbout four er five steps frum the stump er that tree. An' 'e got through gnawin' there (at the other end er the log). He raised 'is haid up, jest looked right at me, jest as straight as he could do it. An' 'e grinned. An' I could see 'is teeth a-shinin', jest as prooty an' white. Didn't open 'is mouth, jest there with 'is yurs laid back.

"He started ter walk then, right aside er the log, till 'e got ter the stump. An' then 'e put in ter gnaw on it, jest like 'e had on the top, an' jest like 'e'd be gnawin' on me in a minute, I thought, an' me a-loadin' all that time. I 'uz erbout done loadin' then. I'd turned the gun down then ter put the primin' in the pan. Wal, I 'uz down on muh knees. I jest squatted down thataway. I tuk delib'rate aim at 'im, too, an' shot. I knowed it had ter be a dead shot, er me ketched one er nuther. *Spang* said the rifle, an' at the crack er the gun the Bear dashed. An' I riz an' tuk right after 'im. Now there wuz a chase, shore as you're livin'. Wal, it 'uz erbout a hunderd yards, I reckon, ter the swamp on the other side. I made a brave run that far. I thought I'd see 'im fall any minute, an' I wanted ter see that sight.

"So when 'e landed inter the bushes, I stopped. I reckon I 'uz erbout thirty steps behind 'im. The next thing occurred ter my mind 'uz ter git out er that place. So I went an' got muh knife an' muh gun-stick. An' I had a bay, I reckon, erbout three-quarters uv a mile through, an' the water erbout up ter hyere [indicating his waist-line] on me. So yer better know I 'uz makin' all the railroad time I could.

"Now all this [that follows] is imagination, I know it wuzn't so, but I'm goin' ter tell yer. I could hear that Bear come a-sousin' right in behind me.

"So that's erbout all uv it. I come back home. That's jest erbout how near I come ter gittin' Bear-ketched. The next stump he'd 'a' gnawed on, I reckon 'u'd 'a' ben me.

"I've had lots uv contests with Bears an' Alligators an' things, but that's erbout as near as I ever come ter gittin' Bear-ketched.

"It tuk me frum erbout one o'clock in the day ter erbout sundown.

"When the Bear 'uz up that tree, it 'uz only erbout sixty yards; I could 'a' broke a ten-cent piece on 'im—a dollar anyhow. Them kind er guns shore shot true.

"That 'uz my initiation, an' it 'uz a prooty bad un, too. Like George Stokes said that time he got ketched in the storm, with the timber fallin' all erbout 'im, I wouldn't 'a' given ten cents fer muh chances."

Mr. Deer's My Riding Horse

Tradition Bearer: Unavailable

Source: Johnston, Mrs. William Preston. "Two Negro Folktales." *Journal of American Folklore* 9 (1896): 196–98.

Date: 1896

Original Source: Louisiana

National Origin: African American

Now, children, I'm tired tellin' you every even' 'bout Mr. Rabbit and the Tar-Baby over and over agin; I'll see of I can't 'member a story Mammy used ter tell 'bout "Mr. Deer's my riding horse."

Well, onct upon a time, when Mr. Rabbit was young and frisky, he went a courting Miss Fox, who lived way far back in the thick woods. Mr. Fox an' his family was very skeery, an' they very seldom come outer the wood 'cep' for a little walk in the clearin' near the big house, sometimes when the moon shine bright; so they did n' know many people 'sides Mr. Rabbit and Mr. Deer. Mr. Deer he had his eyes set on Miss Fox, too. But he din' suspicion Mr. Rabbit was a lookin' that way, but kep' on being jus' as frenly with Mr. Rabbit as he ever been.

One day Mr. Rabbit call on Miss Fox, and wile they was tawkin, Miss Fox she tells him what a fine gentleman she thinks Mr. Deer is. Mr. Rabbit jes threw back his head and he laf and he laf.

"What you laffin 'bout?" Miss Fox says; and Mr. Rabbit he jes laf on an' wone tell her, an' Miss Fox she jes kep' on pestering Mr. Rabbit to tell her what he's laffin 'bout, an' at las' Mr. Rabbit stop laffin an' say, "Miss Fox, you bear me witness I did n' want to tell you, but you jes made me. Miss Fox, you call Mr. Deer a fine gentleman; Miss Fox, Mr. Deer is my riding horse!"

Miss Fox she nearly fell over in a faintin' fit, and she say she done bleve it, and she will not till Mr. Rabbit give her the proof.

An' Mr. Rabbit he says, "Will you bleve it of you sees me riding pass yo' do'?" and Miss Fox says she will, and she wone have nothin' to do with Mr. Deer if the story is true.

Now, Mr. Rabbit is ben fixing up a plan for some time to git Mr. Deer outer his way; so he says good even' to Miss Fox, and clips it off to Mr. Deer's house, and Mr. Rabbit he so frenly with Mr. Deer he done suspec' nothin'.

Presently Mr. Rabbit jes fall over double in his cheer and groan and moan, and Mr. Deer he says, "What's the matter, Mr. Rabbit, is you sick?" But Mr. Rabbit he jes groan; then Mr. Rabbit fall off the cheer and roll on the floor, and Mr. Deer says, "What ails you, Mr. Rabbit, is you sick?"

And Mr. Rabbit he jes groans out, "Oh, Mr. Deer, I'm dying; take me home, take me home."

An' Mr. Deer he's mighty kinehearted, and he says, "Get up on my back, and I'll tote you home"; but Mr. Rabbit says, "Oh, Mr. Deer, I'm so sick, I can't set on your back 'less you put a saddle on."

So Mr. Deer put on a saddle. Mr. Rabbit says, "I can't steady myself 'less you put my feets in the stirrups." So he put his feets in the stirrups.

"Oh, Mr. Deer, I can't hold on 'less you put on a bridle." So he put on a bridle. "Oh, Mr. Deer, I done feel all right 'less I had a whip in my hand." So Mr. Deer puts the whip in his hand. "Now I'm ready, Mr. Deer," says Mr. Rabbit, "but go mighty easy, for I'm likely to die any minute. Please take the short cut through the wood, Mr. Deer, so I kin get home soon."

So Mr. Deer took the short cut, an' forgot that it took him pass Miss Fox's house. Jes' as he 'membered it, an' was 'bout to turn back, Mr. Rabbit, who had slipped a pair of spurs on unbeknownst to him, stuck 'em into his sides, and at the same time laid the whip on so that po' Mr. Deer was crazy with the pain, and ran as fas' as his legs could carry him right by where Miss Fox was standin' on the gallery, and Mr. Rabbit a standin' up in his stirrups and hollerin', "Didn't I tell you Mr. Deer was my riding horse!"

But after a while Miss Fox she found out 'bout Mr. Rabbit's trick on Mr. Deer, and she wouldn't have nothin' more to do with him.

Incriminating the Other Fellow

Tradition Bearer: Unavailable

Source: Smiley, Portia. "Folk-Lore from Virginia, South Carolina, Georgia, Alabama, and Florida." *Journal of American Folklore* 32 (1919): 366–67.

Date: 1919

Original Source: South Carolina

National Origin: African American

Miss Kingdeer of Coon Swamp had two da'ghters, and Brer Wolf and Brer Rabbit was in love with the young Miss Kingdeer. Young Miss Kingdeer 'lowed she loved Brer Rabbit better than she did Brer Wolf. Brer Wolf he got jealous, and say he's goin' to git even with Brer Rabbit by killing Miss Kingdeer's goat, 'kase she say anybody who'd kill that goat, her father would horn 'im. So Brer Rabbit and Brer Wolf went to call on Miss Kingdeer; and when dey was gwine back home, Brer Wolf said to Brer Rabbit, "Ye must 'scuse me for not going home all de way wid you, 'kase I promised to call on Brer 'Possum wife, who is mighty sick." Brer Rabbit 'lowed, "I'd go along wid you, but I'm mighty feeble myself to-night." So Brer Wolf left Brer Rabbit, an' went back in the field an' kill Miss Kingdeer's goat. Next day he went callin' on Miss Kingdeer to see what dey'd say, like he know nothin' about it. "Good-mornin', Miss Kingdeer!" says Brer Wolf, "how's your ma?"—"She's between de gate-posts an' de hinges dis mornin', Brer Wolf, how is you?"—"Well, I'm kinder hucckumso."—"Brer Wolf, has you hearn about our goat? Someone killed her last night." Brer Wolf he made out he's so 'stonished. "Miss Kingdeer, I think I know who killed dat dere goat, nobody but Brer Rabbit, 'kase I saw him pream-blin' a-cross de field after he left de house last night!" Miss Kingdeer is very sorry 'cause she loved Brer Rabbit an' didn't want Brer Rabbit killed. "I don't t'ink he'd do dat, 'kase he done loved dat goat," says she. "Well, I'd make him tell you himself dat he killed dat goat." An' he went, an' he went 'round to Brer Rabbit's house. "Mornin', Brer Rabbit! how is you today?"—"Kinder po'ly, Brer Wolf, kinder po'ly. How's you?"—"Well, I'm between de hawk an' de break-down, ain't much myself today. Brer Rabbit, I got a scheme on foot; I thought we'd ser-enade de girls to-night. I done told dem what a good bass-singer you is; we'll practise de song. I'll play de fiddle, and den we'll go under de window an' sing, an' den de ladies 'll come out an' invite us in!" Brer Rabbit agreed, an' same night dey went up to Miss Kingdeer's house an' stood under de window. Brer Numphit (Wolf) chumin de fiddle—plum, plum, plum! chan, chan, chan!

> Brer Rab—bit is a trick—y man, and ev—ery—bod—y know.
> Did you kill Miss King—deer's goat and ev—ery—bod—y know?
> Yes, yes, yes, yes, yes, yes, yes, and ev—ery—bod—y know.

Chorus.

> Rio Brer Rab—bit, Pop—eyed rab—bit,
> Buck—eye rab—bit,

"Ladies," said Brer Wolf, "I told you Brer Rabbit killed Miss Kingdeer's goat, 'kase he done tell you." Den Brer Rabbit threw up his hands, an' said, "Brer Numphy got this game up on me, 'kase he's jealous!" Miss Kingdeer says she didn't believe Brer Rabbit killed de goat, and Brer Wolf is de fox dat is de finder, an' he's done killed dat goat, an' she called for her pa. Den Brer Numphit licked out an' tore down de road at such a rate, you couldn't see him running for de sand. Miss Kingdeer an' Brer Rabbit got so tickled, dey had to hold deir sides to keep from poppin'. Brer Wolf is runnin' yet from Kingdeer.

Where Did Adam Hide?

Tradition Bearer: Unavailable

Source: Smiley, Portia. "Folk-Lore from Virginia, South Carolina, Georgia, Alabama, and Florida." *Journal of American Folklore* 32 (1919): 371–72.

Date: 1919

Original Source: Georgia

National Origin: African American

De preacher went out to see an ol' woman who lived out so far, never did get to chu'ch. Asked if she heard 'bout Jesus, 'bout how he died. "Is he dead? I didn' know he was dead. You wouldn' know yourself, bein' back here in de woods. An' I don' take de paper."

De preacher said he would come next week to catechize um. Nex' week sent de ol' man to de store to buy molasses. Adam took the money and bought some liquor. Sent de boy to de neighbor, Sister Clarinda, to borrow some 'lasses. Sister

Clarindy did have but a cupful, so she let her have dat. Made de molasses pone. Adam came in drunk. She put him under de bed. Tol' him to stay dere.

Didn't want de preacher to see him. So after dinner de preacher got his catechism out an' ask some questions. "De Lord made Adam fustes', den he made Eve lastes'. Put um togeder. One day de Lord came an' called, 'Adam!' He called again, 'O Adam!' De Lord got mad, an' hollered, 'You Adam!' *Now*, where did Adam hide when de Lord call um?"

De ol' woman said, "Some-body been tellin' you somet'in'."

"Now, my sister, dis is de catechizum."

"Ain't somebody been tellin' you somet'in'?" "I don' know, my sister. Dis here was de catechizum. Adam was in de gyarden. Adam hide. Now, I'm askin' you dis question, Where did Adam hide when de Lord call?" De ol' woman put her head under de bed an' call, "You, Adam, come f'om under dat bed! Come on out! De preacher done know all 'bout 'um. You come out dah!"

The Chosen Suitor: The Forbidden Room

Tradition Bearer: Julius Jenkins

Source: Parsons, Elsie Clews. Pages 47–48 in *Folk-Lore of the Sea Islands, South Carolina*. Memoirs of the American Folklore Society 16. New York: American Folklore Society, 1923.

Date: 1923

Original Source: South Carolina

National Origin: African American

I's a boy name John. An' he had a sister. An' dis king was payin' dis boy sister address. Dis little boy was a witch, could tell whe' his sister goin' to get a good husban' o' not. So when dis man come, his sister always put dis boy underneat' de step, an' put him to bed. So den dis little boy wake up an' tell his sister, "Sister, you married to de Debil." Sister slap him aroun' an' kick him, wouldn' listen de boy. So, sure enough, he [she] married de man against de boy. Man kyarry his sister from dere an' kyarry him to his house, little over t'irty or forty miles. So, after kyarrin' dis woman summuch nights an' summuch days, dis boy know exaxly how dis man was treatin' his sister. One day de man han' his wife sewen key. An' he had sewen room in de house. But he show him [her] de room, an' say, "Use de six room; but de seven room don' use it, don' go in dat room!" So one day his wife say to heself, "I got all de key. I wan' to see what is in dat room." He husban' been 'bout twenty-five mile from dere when he [she] said dat. He [she] wen' into de room, open de room. When he open de room, was nothin' but de wife dis man married, de skeleton hung up in de room. Dis one fall down, faint, right to de do'. Less dan half an hour he come to his sense. He lock de do' back. Gone, set down. Husban' drive up to de do' at de time, an' tell um, "Dis night you will be in dat room." Forty mile from his [her] broder den. So his broder know dat his sister have a fas' horse. An' he took sewen needle wid him. He started fo' his sister den. He ritched his sister's place 'bout fo' o'clock. Sister was to put to deat' at fus' dark. When he see dat his broder-in-law come, he welcome him like any broder-in-law do, like not'in' goin' to be done. Dis king ask him what his horse eat? He tol' him, "I feed my horse wid cotton-seed." Dis king den had to go half a mile from dis house to his nex' neighbor to get cotton-seed for his broder-in-law horse. When he gone, he tell his sister, "Sister, take not'in', jump in de buggy!" Dey had fo'ty miles to go. When he get a half a mile from de house, he han' his sister dese sewen needle. He said, "Sister, he done hitch up his horse, he comin' after us." Drop one o' de needle, an' it become a swamp across de road. De king drive until he come to de swamp. He had to tu'n back home an' get a grubbin'-hoe an' axe to cut t'rough dere. All dat time John was goin' wid his sister. De king was a witch himself. He cut um so quick, he was on dem again. He [she] drop anoder needle. Den it become a ocean across de road. He had to sup up all dat water befo' he could star' again. When dey was one mile of John house where his sister live, he tell his sister t'row all de needle out his han'. Dey become an ocean. Dey cross de oder side den. He drive down here. When he get to de ocean, he had to stop, couldn' get any furder. John an' his sister 'rive his ol' cabin whey de king kyarry him [her] from. An' dis sister gave de broder what he [she] used to kick about lovin' praise. An' John save his sister life.

La Graisse [The Grease Girl]

Tradition Bearer: Unavailable

Source: Fortier, Alcee. "Louisianian Nursery-Tales." *Journal of American Folklore* 1 (1888): 140–42.

Date: 1888

Original Source: Louisiana

National Origin: French American

Yavé eune madame ki té gagnin cate filles. Yé té si joli, ké tout moune té oulé marié aver yé. Yé té pelé yé: La Graisse, Dépomme, Banane, et Pacane. La Graisse té pli joli, mais lé to jamin sorti dans soleil pasqué yé té pér lé va fonne. La Graisse to sorti tou les jou dans eune bel carosse en or. Fi léroi té oua li tou les jou, mais La Graisse té si joli et carosse li té si apé brillé ké so zié té fait li mal; li té gagnin pou frotté yé pou oua clair. Fi léroi té limmin La Graisse: li couri chez moman la pou mandé li pou marié avec La Graisse, mais moman la ki té connin La Graisse té pli joli, lé té oulé marié les otes avant.

Li pélé Dépomme: "Dépomme oh! orimomo, orimomo!" Dépomme vini, mais michié la gardé li ben, li dit c'est pas cila là mo oulé, li sré gaté trop vite.

Moman pélé: "Banane oh! orimomo, orimomo!" Banane vini, Michié té pas oulé, li dit la connin pourri trop vite.

Moman pélé: "Pacane oh! orimomo, orimomo." Pacane vini. Michié dit pacane va vini rance.

Enfin moman pélé La Graisse: "La Graisse oh! orimomo, orimomo." La Graisse vini. Sito li oua La Graisse, li prend li et ménin li dans so bel la maison, et li marié li.

Fi léroi té couri la chasse tou les jou: pendant li té pas la, domestiques té fait la Graisse tout plein la misère. Li té pér dit so mari, et li té fait tout ça yé oulé.

Eune jou kisinière la dit, li vé pas fait dinin. I faut La Graisse fait li. Pauvre La Graisse li crié, li crié, mais yé forcé li pour resté coté di fé: mais li tapé fonne fonne. A la fin yavé pli qué La Graisse partout, la kisine la té tout plein. Piti zozo La Graisse oua ça, li trempé so zaile dans La Graisse. Li volé dans bois coté michié la, si batte so zaile dans so figuire.

Michié la oua La Graisse ki té on so zaile, li pensé so chère La Graisse, li galopé chez li, li trouvé so femme tout fonne par terre. Li té si chagrin, li ramassé tout La Graisse, et metté li dans vie baignoire, et quand La Graisse la vini fret, li to eune femme encor. Mais li té jamin si jolie com avant, pasqué la terre té mélé avé li, et li té tout jaune et sale. So mari té pli limmin li et renvoyé li coté so moman.

THE CARIBBEAN

B′ Helephant and B′ V′wale
(Brother Elephant and Brother Whale)

Tradition Bearer: Unavailable

Source: Edwards, Charles L. Page 65 in *Bahama Songs and Stories*. Memoirs of the American Folklore Society 3. New York: American Folklore Society, 1895.

Date: 1895

Original Source: Green Turtle Cay, Bahamas

National Origin: African American

Once it was a time, a very good time,
De monkey chewed tobacco an' 'e spit white lime.

Now dis day B' Rabby vwas walkin' 'long de shore. 'E see B' V'wale. 'E say, "B' V'wale!"

B' V'wale say, "Hey!"

B' Rabby, "B' V'wale, I bet I could pull you on de shore!"

B' V'wale, "You cahnt!"

B' Rabby say, "I bet you tree t'ousan' dollar!"

Vw'ale say, "Hall right!" 'e gone.

'E meet B' Helephant. 'E say, "B' Helephant," 'e say, "I bet I could pull you in de sea!"

B' Helephant say, "Me!" 'e "Dey ain't ary man in de worl' can pull me in de sea!" B' Rabby, "I'll try it to-morrow at twelve o'clock."

'E gone an' get a heap o' rope. 'E say, "Now to-day we'll try."

'E tie one rope aroun' B' V'wale's neck, and den 'e tie one aroun' B' Helephant's neck. 'E say, "Vw'en you hear me say, 'set taut,' you mus' set taut." 'E say, "Pull away!" Vw'en B' V'wale pull, 'e pull B' Helephant in de surf o' de sea. 'E say, "You t'ink dis little B' Rabby doin' all o' dat!"

W'en B' Helephant pull 't, 'e pull B' V'wale in de surf o' de sea. B' V'wale ketch underneath one shelf o' de rock, and B' Helephant ketch to one big tree. Den de two on 'em pull so heavy de rope broke.

B' V'wale went in de ocean and B' Helephant vwen' vay over in pine-yard. Das v'y you see B' V'wale in de ocean to-day, and das v'y you see B' Helephant over in de pine bushes to-day.

E bo ban, my story's en',
If you don't believe my story's true,
Hax my captain an' my crew.

The Origin of Woman

Tradition Bearer: Harry Murray

Source: Bates, William C. "Creole Folk-Lore from Jamaica II: Nancy Stories." *Journal of American Folklore* 9 (1896): 124–25.

Date: 1896

Original Source: Jamaica

National Origin: African American

A discussion arose between black Lizzie and her husband upon the origin of man. Harry laid it down for an axiom that he was made from the dust of the earth, because the minister said so. "I mek out o' dust fe' sartin." To him, according to the story, Lizzie replies: "Me no mek out o' none dirt." Then Harry: "Ef you don' mek out o' dirt, wha' you mek out o'? You mek out o' dirt, yes!" "I don't mek out o' notin' o' de kin'." "Den wha' you mek out o'? You mus' mek out o' some goolin' (golden) ting or noder, den?" "I don' mek out o' no goolin' ting, an' I don' mek out o' none dirt. I mek out o' bone." "Mek out o' wha'?" "Bone!" "Bone?" "Yes, bone to be sho'." "Wha' kin' o' bone?" "Rib's bone! You na hea' minista' say so?"

"Well, I don' know wha' fe' say 'bout dat; I don' like fe' say dat wha' minista' say not de trut'; but I mean fe' say, when minista' read 'bout dat rib's bone, him must mean buckra ooman [white woman], becasin so dem white, so de bone white. Ef you mek de same, you' 'kin would a ben white."

"Cho," said Lizzie, "ef you ben open you' ears, 'tidda da sleep, you would a hea' de minsta' say de 'kin notin', but de blood, da de ting, becasin in de book say, dat white-o, brown-o, black-o, all mek de same blood; you eba' see white blood an' black blood?" "Look you," said Harry, "It you know how me uncle Jame use fe' to say ooman came in dis worl'?"

"Cho, no boda' me." "Neba' min', I da go tell you. Dem mek two men; de fuss one mek berry well, but when dem mek de oder one, it kinda' 'poil. Den as dem look upon it, so it da jump about, and shake him head, and do all kin' o' 'tupid ting, like a how ooman hab fe' go on. Den one o' dem hol' him, say, 'Wha' kin' o' ting you?' Den de oder say: 'Cho, him no use, him can' talk.' Ebery day him da go on like a dummy, till one day dem hol' him so, 'zaman him tongue, den dem see de tongue tie; dem tek a raza', cut it. As dem cut it so, bam! de ting mout begin da fly, dem coud n' 'top it. Dem say: 'Well, dem sorry dey eber cut de tongue.' From dat time, it mek you hear dem say: 'ef you wan' ooman fe' good, gib him 'tump o' tongue'" (stump of tongue, a tongue-tie).

Seeking Trouble

Variant A

Tradition Bearer: Samuel Carrington

Source: Parsons, Elsie Clews. "Barbados Folklore." *Journal of American Folklore* 38 (1925): 267–68.

Date: 1925

Original Source: Barbados

National Origin: African American

It was a rabbit oncet. He was a tailor. He says he never know trouble, but Nancy tol' him to follow him, "Get a bag and come on with me." So be, dey went in de wood and dey find de tiyger young ones. Nancy put his one in de bag whole, make like he was atearin' of it to pieces. Ber Rabbit tore up his one in pieces. Ber Nancy tell Ber Rabbit, "Let us go now." On der journey dey met Ber Tiyger. Ber Nancy says, "Ber Tiyger, I have been in de wood, and find yer young ones, so I have brought dem for yer." The reply to Ber Nancy, de tiyger tell him, "I thank you, Ber Nancy." He says, "Empty dem out de bag for me." Ber Nancy beat out his, skipping about. He says, "Ber Rabbit, you empty out yours now." When Ber Rabbit empty out, his only was tore in pieces. Wid de frome (?) and de splunge the tiyger made for Ber Rabbit ter ketch him. Ber Rabbit was off runnin'. When he got to a crack Ber Tiyger was taking hold of him. Down in de crack he went. Ber Tiyger leave Ber Nancy in charge of him now, went in de wood for Wil' Hawg to dig him out. Ber Rabbit says, "Ber Nancy, I was an ol' man about eighty, I never knows trouble." Ber Rabbit ask Ber Nancy to release him. He says, "No, I could not do dat, man, I am leave in charge of you." He says, "Do, release me, dis is trouble." He says, "No, man." He says, "I put you in trouble and I am going to take you out of trouble." He says, "When Ber Wil' Hawg come, he will dig you out and Ber Tiyger and he will destroy you. But by I put you in trouble, I will release you again. While Ber Hawg a diggin' for you, you scratch back de moul' into his eyes, he'll come to me to blow it out. I will blow the first stuff out his eyes, though the next time he'll have to apply to Ber Tiyger." He done so, axed him to blow it, he blow it. When he come Ber Tiyger, he afraid of Ber Tiyger, but he did ask him to blow it out, and de water jump in Ber Tiyger mouth outer Wil' Hawg eyes. He star' at him to run him down. Ber Nancy says, "Ber Rabbit, dis yer chance, cut for yer han'." With dat Ber Nancy turn back, he says, "Man, you left him the first time to watch him, but not dis time." He says, "If I had a couple of wil' hawg, I couldn' ha' trust to dat." Ber Tiyger den had ball, invite all of de high fellows, tell dem to invite Ber Rabbit, too. Ber Rabbit says when Ber Tiyger die he will go to de funeral. Went back and told Ber Tiyger to invite Mr. Tie-low, Mr. No-wag and other official to come to encourage Mr. Rabbit to come to de funeral. "And I will ketch him and we'll have a nice dinner off of him." Funeral take place at three o'clock. Ber Rabbit appear hisself. Soon as he come he begin to brush his feet. "Come in, Ber

Rabbit," he says. "I don't like to come in a man drawing-room, my feet is dirty, you know." He says, "When he die did he give a large blow?"—"No, he did not give a large blow when he died." He says, "Well, I never know a man die and never blow yit." He stepped back and he told Ber Tiyger, he said, "I never knowed a dead man blowed yet."

Variant B

Tradition Bearer: Louise Lavinia Barrow

Source: Parsons, Elsie Clews. "Barbados Folklore." *Journal of American Folklore* 38 (1925): 268.

Date: 1925

Original Source: Barbados

National Origin: African American

Oncet it was a rabbit, a wil' hawg and a tiyger. De tiyger strip de wil' hawg young one in half. De wil' hawg meet up wid de rabbit and say, "Ber Rabbit, ye see my young one?" He said, "Go 'long out dere, I got one here in my bag. Go long out dere!" Ber Tiyger got de oder one rip up in half. De Tiyger tell de rabbit to jump down in de hole and when de hawg come, to tek up a handful of gravel and throw in his face and blin' him. De rabbit did do so, and when de wil' hawg baig de tiyger to blow hit out of his eyes, he say he would not. He said, "Do, God bless you, blow it out of my eyes for me." And jus' as Tiyger blew out of Wil' Hawg eyes, he taste de saliva. "Man, you are sweet enough, whay I think of you flesh much sweeter." He make a snatch den at de tiyger and de tiyger make an escape and get away from him. An, dat wa' de end.

Variant C

Tradition Bearer: Louise Lavinia Barrow

Source: Parsons, Elsie Clews. "Barbados Folklore." *Journal of American Folklore* 38 (1925): 268.

Date: 1925

Original Source: Barbados

National Origin: African American

De meaning to dat is de rabbit an' de tiyger was good frien's. De rabbit p'ovo' de tiyger and den de tiyger get his frien's an' arrange ter kill de rabbit. De tiyger and de wil' hawg was good frien's. Sum' up his frien's den to eat de rabbit. De tiyger sen' to de rabbit, sayin' de wil' hawg was daid, so as to get de chance to eat him [rabbit]. An' when de rabbit get to de do', he wouldn't go inside, he stay outside. De tiyger say, "Frien' come in, your frien' has daid." De rabbit den axe de tiyger if de wil' hawg did pass de wind when he die, an' he say no. De rabbit say den, "Mus' touch him, and if he pass de wind, he daid." He did touch him and he pass de win'. He say, "Impossible for a daid man to pass de win'." An' he say good mawnin' and he was gone.

De Big Worrum (The Big Worm)

Tradition Bearer: Unavailable

Source: Edwards, Charles L. Pages 72–73 in *Bahama Songs and Stories.* Memoirs of the American Folklore Society 3. New York: American Folklore Society, 1895.

Date: 1895

Original Source: Green Turtle Cay, Bahamas

National Origin: African American

Once it vwas a time, a very good time,
De monkey chewed tobacco an' 'e spit white lime.

So dis day it vwas a man; he had two sons; dey did n' have no fire. Hall dey had to heat vwas raw potatoes. Now de man sen' dis boy to look for fire. De boy vwalk; he vwalk; he vwalk till vw'en 'e look 'e see one smoke. Vw'en 'e gone 'e git to dat fire. Vw'en 'e get dere, de worrum vwas full o' fire. De boy say, "Dimme some fan!" (Give me some fire).

De worrum say, "'T ain', 't ain' none; jes' do fur me." De worrum say, "Come in little closer." *Good!* Soon as de boy vwen' a little closer, vw'en 'e vwen' to reach de fire de worrum swallow 'im down. Den de boy vwen' down, right down, down inside de worrum till 'e stop. De boy met whole lot o' people vwat de worrum did swallow.

So now de man tell de hudder son, "I wonder whey my son gone?" De hudder son say, "Pa, I goin' look fur him." 'e vwalk, 'e vwalk, 'e vwalk till 'e come to this big worrum, vw'at had de fire in his mouth. So now de boy vwen' to de worrum. De boy say, "Dimme some fan!" De worrum say, "Keelie o' fire" (Come and get fire). De boy say, *"Do i en e,* dimme some fan?" De worrum say, "Come a little closer." De worrum say, "Time for Joe come" (Time to go home). De worrum say, "Keelie o' fire." Vw'en de boy vwen' to get de fire so, de worrum swallow him down. De boy vwen'; 'e vwen' down; 'e vwen' down, till 'e met 'e brudder.

Now de boy fadder say, "My two sons gone an' I might as vwell gone too." De man take 'e lan' (lance); it fairly glisten, it so sharp. Vw'en 'e get dere whey de worrum vwas wid de fire in he mouth, de man say, "Dimme some fan?" De worrum say, "You too do fur me!" (You're too much for me). De worrum say, "Keelie o' fire." Vw'en de man vwen' to get de fire, *so*, de worrum vwen' to swallow 'im. De man take he' lan'; as 'e vwas goin' down 'e cut de worrum; 'e cut de worrum till 'e cut de worrum right open an' all de people come, an' dat vwas a big city right dere.

> E bo ban, my story's en',
> If you don't believe my story's true,
> Hax my captain an' my crew.

The Girl and the Fish

Tradition Bearer: Unavailable

Source: Edwards, Charles L. "Some Tales from Bahama Folk-Lore: Fairy Stories." *Journal of American Folklore* 4 (1891): 247.

Date: 1891

Original Source: Green Turtle Cay, Bahamas

National Origin: African American

Dis day dis girl vwen' down to de sea for salt vwatah. She ketch one little fish hout de conch shell. She name 'im Choncho-wally. She put 'im in de vwell. Ev'ry mohnen she use to put some 'er breakfas' in de bucket an' carry to de fish; an' some 'er dinner, an' some 'er supper. She feed 'im till 'e get a big fish.

Dis mohnin', vw'en she vwen' to cahy de breakfas' for 'im, she sing—

> Conch-o, Conch-o-wall—y,
> Don't you vwan' to mar-ry me,
> My deddy short-tail?

'E comes up an' she feed 'im. Den she let 'im go down. Vw'en she vwen' home, de boy say, "Pa, siste' got somet'in' inside de vwell."

Den de nex' day she come; bring vittles again for 'im. De man say to de boy, "You go behin' de tree an' listen to vw'at she goin' sing." De gal sing—

> Conch-o, Conch-o-wall—y,
> Don't you vwan' to marr-y me,
> My deddy short-tail?

Huh! De boy ketch it; 'e gone; tell 'e pa. De boy say, "Pa, sister say, 'Conch-o, Conch-o-wally,'" etc. De man go; 'e took he grange, 'e sing, "Conch-o, Conch-o-wally,"

> Don't you vwan' to marry me,
> My deddy short-tail?

De fish come hup; 'e strike 'im. 'E carry 'im home an' dey had some fur dinner. De gal say, "I bet you dis nice fish!"

Den de gal took some in de bucket to cahy to de fish. Den vw'en de gal vwen' to de vwell to call de fish, she sing, "Conch-o, Conch-o-wally,"

> Don't you vwan' to marry me,
> My deddy short-tail?

She sing again, "Conch-o, Conch-o-wally,"

> Don't you vwan' to marry me,
> My deddy short-tail?"

She ain' hear no fish, an' she ain' see none. She sing again, "Conch-o, Conch-o-wally,"

> Don't you vwan' to marry me,
> My deddy short-tail?

She begin to cry now, ""Conch-o, Conch-o-wally,"

> Don't you vwan' to marry me,
> My deddy short-tail?

Den she vwen' home to de house, behin' de house, an' she cry 'erself to death.

> E bo ban, my story's en',
> If you don't believe my story's true,
> Ask my captain an' my crew.

Glossary

anecdote: Single episode narrative, regarded as true and commonly concentrating on an individual

animal tale: Narratives told as conscious fictions in which the characters, though they speak and behave like human beings, are animals. These animal characters are commonly stock types. For example, in many Native American traditions, Coyote is regarded as an exploitive, impulsive manipulator. In African American tales, Rabbit is typecast in the same role. The tales are most often moralistic ("don't be greedy") or etiological (why the frog has no tail) in intent.

belief tales: Legends or personal experience narratives that are told with the purpose of validating a particular folk belief.

culture hero: Character in myth who finishes the work that brings technology (usually symbolized as fire), laws, religion, and other elements of culture to humans. Culture heroes may take over the business of creating order out of chaos where a Supreme Creator left off. Therefore, the culture hero serves as a secondary creator or transformer of the universe. The culture hero transforms the universe by means of gifts into a universe in which humans can live. In some myths, the culture hero cleanses the universe of those things which threaten human existence: monsters, cannibals, or meteorological phenomena.

fable: Fictional narrative ending with a didactic message that is often couched in the form of a "moral" or proverb.

family saga: Chronologically and often thematically linked collection of legends constituting the folk history of a particular family, usually over several generations. The term was coined by folklorist Mody Coggin Boatright.

formulaic: Refers to conventional elements that recur in folk narrative. Examples include clichés, structural patterns, and stock characters or situations.

framing: The act of setting apart a traditional performance from other types of activity by words, occasions of performance, or other distinguishing features.

genre: Type or category

legend: Narrative told as truth and set in the historical past, which does not depart from the present reality of the members of the group

local legend: Legends derived from and closely associated with specific places and events believed to have occurred in those locales

motif: Small element of traditional narrative content; an event, object, concept, or pattern

myth: Narratives that explain the will (or intent) and the workings (or orderly principles) of a group's major supernatural figures. Myth is set in a world which predates the present reality.

natural context: Setting, in all its elements, in which a performance would ordinarily take place.

numskull: Character who behaves in an absurdly ignorant fashion, also called "noodle."

ordinary folktale: Highly formulaic and structured fictional narrative that is popularly referred to as "fairytale" and designated by folklorists as *märchen* or "wonder tale." Term coined by folklorist Stith Thompson

personal experience narrative: First-person narrative intended as truth

personal legend: Narrative intended as truth told about a specific (usually well-known) individual

stock character: Recurrent narrative character who invariably plays a stereotyped role such as trickster or fool

tale type: Standard, recurrent folk narrative plot

tall tale: Fictional narrative often told as a first-hand experience, which gradually introduces hyperbole until it becomes so great that the audience realizes the tale is a lie

trickster: Characters who defy the limits of propriety and often gender and species. Tricksters live on the margins of their worlds by their wits and are often regarded as possessing supernatural powers. Often a mythic figure such as Coyote or Hare will function as both culture hero and trickster.

validating device: Any element occurring within a traditional narrative that is intended to convince listeners that the tale is true.

variant: Version of a standard tale type

Bibliography to Volume II

Abrahams, Roger D., ed. *African American Folktales: Stories from Black Traditions in the New World.* New York: Pantheon, 1985.

———. *The Man-of-Words in the West Indies.* Baltimore: Johns Hopkins University Press, 1983.

Ancelet, Barry Jean. "The Cajun Who Went to Harvard: Identity in the Oral Tradition of South Louisiana." *Journal of Popular Culture* 23 (1989): 101–15.

Backus, Emma M. "Animal Tales from North Carolina." *Journal of American Folklore* 11 (1898): 284–92.

———. "Folk-Tales from Georgia." *Journal of American Folklore* 13 (1900): 19–32.

———. "Tales of the Rabbit from Georgia Negroes." *Journal of American Folklore* 12 (1899): 108–15.

Backus, Emma M., and Ethel Hatton Leitner. "Negro Tales from Georgia." *Journal of American Folklore* 25 (1912): 125–36.

Bates, William C. "Creole Folk-Lore from Jamaica II: Nancy Stories." *Journal of American Folklore* 9 (1896): 121–28.

Beckwith, Martha Warren. *Jamaica Anansi Stories.* Memoirs of the American Folklore Society 17. New York: American Folklore Society, 1924.

Bowman, Earl. "Interview of William D. Naylor." American Life Histories: Manuscripts from the Federal Writers' Project, 1936–1940. Manuscript Division, Library of Congress. 12 October 2005. http://memory.loc.gov/ammem/wpaintro/wpahome.html.

Bunter, Rosa. "Ghosts as Guardians of Hidden Treasure." *Journal of American Folklore* 12 (1899): 64–65.

Carter, Isabel Gordon. "Mountain White Folk-Lore: Tales from the Southern Blue Ridge." *Journal of American Folklore* 38 (1925): 340–74.

Chase, Richard. "Jack and the Fire Dragaman." *Southern Folklore Quarterly* 5 (1941): 151–55.

———. "The Lion and the Unicorn." *Southern Folklore Quarterly* 1 (1937): 15–19.

Claudel, Calvin. "Louisiana Tales of Jean Sot and Boqui and Lapin." *Southern Folklore Quarterly* 8 (1944): 287–99.

Claudel, Calvin, and J.-M. Carrier. "Three Tales from the French Folklore of Louisiana." *Journal of American Folklore* 56 (1943): 38–44.

Comhaire-Sylvain, Suzanne. "Creole Tales from Haiti." *Journal of American Folklore* 50 (1937): 207–95.

Cooke, Elizabeth Johnston. "English Folk-Tales in America. The Bride of the Evil One." *Journal of American Folklore* 12 (1899): 126–30.

Cross, Tom Peete. "Folk-Lore from the Southern States." *Journal of American Folklore* 22 (1909): 251–55.

Dorsey, J. Owen. "Two Biloxi Tales." *Journal of American Folklore* 6 (1893): 48–50.

Douglas, Sir George. "The Witty Exploits of Mr. George Buchanan, the King's Fool." *Scottish Fairy and Folktales.* New York: A. L. Burt Company, 1901.

Dubois, Sylvie, and Barbara M. Horvath. "Creoles and Cajuns: A Portrait in Black and White." *American Speech* 78 (2003): 192–207.

Dubois, Sylvie, and Megan Melançon. "Creole Is; Creole Ain't: Diachronic and Synchronic Attitudes Toward Creole French Identity in Southern Louisiana." *Language in Society* 29 (2000): 237–58.

Edwards, Charles L. *Bahama Songs and Stories.* Memoirs of the American Folklore Society 3. New York: American Folklore Society, 1895.

———. "Some Tales from Bahama Folk-Lore." *Journal of American Folklore* 4 (1891): 47–54.

———. "Some Tales from Bahama Folk-Lore: Fairy Stories." *Journal of American Folklore* 4 (1891): 247–52.

Fauset, Arthur Huff. "Negro Folk Tales from the South (Alabama, Mississippi, Louisiana)." *Journal of American Folklore* 40 (1927): 213–303.

Fischer, David Hackett. *Albion's Seed: Four British Folkways in America.* New York: Oxford University Press, 1989.

Fortier, Alcee. "Louisianian Nursery-Tales." *Journal of American Folklore* 1 (1888): 140–45.

Harper, Francis. "Tales of the Okefinoke." *American Speech* 1 (1926): 407–20.

Hubert, Levi. "Interview of Joseph Madden." American Life Histories: Manuscripts from the Federal Writers' Project, 1936–1940. Manuscript Division, Library of Congress. 12 October 2005. http://memory.loc.gov/ammem/wpaintro/wpahome.html.

Hudson, Arthur Palmer, and Pete Kyle McCarter. "The Bell Witch of Tennessee and Mississippi: A Folk Legend." *Journal of American Folklore* 47 (1934): 46–58.

Hurston, Zora Neale. "Dance Songs and Tales from the Bahamas." *Journal of American Folklore* 43 (1930): 294–312.

"The Irishman and the Pumpkin." *Journal of American Folklore* 12 (1899): 226.

Johnson, John H. "Folk-Lore from Antigua, British West Indies." *Journal of American Folklore* 34 (1921): 40–88.

Johnston, Mrs. William Preston. "Two Negro Folktales." *Journal of American Folklore* 9 (1896): 194–98.

McNeil, W. K. *Ozark Country.* Oxford: University Press of Mississippi, 1995.

Miller, E. Joan Wilson. "Ozark Culture Region as Revealed by Traditional Materials." *Annals of the Association of American Geographers* 58 (1968): 51–77.

Mooney, James. *James Mooney's History, Myths, and Sacred Formulas of the Cherokees.* Asheville, NC: Historical Images, 1992.

———. "Myths of the Cherokees." *Journal of American Folklore* 1 (1888): 97–108.

———. "Myths of the Cherokee." *Nineteenth Annual Report of the Bureau of American Ethnology 1897–1898, Part I.* Washington, DC: U.S. Government Printing Office, 1900.

———. "The Sacred Formulas of the Cherokees." *Seventh Annual Report of the Bureau of American Ethnology.* Washington, DC: U.S. Government Printing Office, 1891.

Mosley, Ruby. "Interview of Eldora Scott Maples." American Life Histories: Manuscripts from the Federal Writers' Project, 1936–1940. Manuscript Division, Library of Congress. 12 October 2005. http://memory.loc.gov/ammem/wpaintro/wpahome.html.

Owen, Mary A. "Ol' Rabbit an' de Dawg He Stole." *Journal of American Folklore* 9 (1890): 135–38.

Parsons, Elsie Clews. "Barbados Folklore." *Journal of American Folklore* 38 (1925): 267–92.

———. *Folk-Lore of the Sea Islands, South Carolina.* Memoirs of the American Folklore Society 16. New York: American Folklore Society, 1923.

Porter, J. Hampden. "Notes on the Folk-Lore of the Mountain Whites of the Alleghenies." *Journal of American Folklore* 7 (1894): 105–17.

Rath, Richard Cullen. "Drums and Power: Ways of Creolizing Music in Coastal South Carolina and Georgia, 1730–1790." Pages 99-130 in *Creolization in the Americas*, edited by David Buisseret and Steven G. Rheinhardt. College Station: University of Texas at Arlington Press, 2000.

Ray, Marie. "Jean Sotte Stories." *Journal of American Folklore* 21 (1908): 364–65.

"The Sea Tick and the Irishman." *Journal of American Folklore* 12 (1899): 226.

Simpson, George E. "Loup Garou and Loa Tales from Northern Haiti." *Journal of American Folklore* 55 (1942): 219–27.

Simpson, George E., and J. B. Cineas. "Folk Tales of Haitian Heroes." *Journal of American Folklore* 54 (1941): 176–85.

Smiley, Portia. "Folk-Lore from Virginia, South Carolina, Georgia, Alabama, and Florida." *Journal of American Folklore* 32 (1919): 357–83.

Smith, Pamela Coleman. "Two Negro Stories from Jamaica." *Journal of American Folklore* 9 (1896): 278.

Speck, Frank G. "European Tales among the Chickasaw Indians." *Journal of American Folklore* 26 (1913): 292.

Spitzer, Nicholas R. "All Things Creole: Mout de tour le monde." *Journal of American Folklore* 116 (2003): 57–72.

Steiner, Roland. "Braziel Robinson Possessed of Two Spirits." *Journal of American Folklore* 13 (1900): 226–28.

———. "Sol Lockheart's Call." *Journal of American Folklore* 48 (1900): 67–70.

Swanton, John R. *Myths and Tales of the Southeastern Indians*. Smithsonian Institution Bureau of American Ethnology Bulletin 88. Washington, DC: U.S. Government Printing Office, 1929.

Trowbridge, Ada Wilson. "Negro Customs and Folk-Stories of Jamaica." *Journal of American Folklore* 9 (1896): 279–87.

Wiltse, Henry M. "In the Southern Field of Folk-Lore." *Journal of American Folklore* 13 (1900): 209–12.

General Bibliography

Aarne, Antti, and Stith Thompson. *The Types of the Folktale: A Classification and Bibliography.* 2nd rev. ed. Folklore Fellows Communications 184. Helsinki: Academia Scientiarum Fennica, 1964.

Aaron, Abe. "Interview of Cab Drivers." American Life Histories: Manuscripts from the Federal Writers' Project, 1936–1940. Manuscript Division, Library of Congress. 12 October 2005.
http://memory.loc.gov/ammem/wpaintro/wpahome.html.

Abrahams, Roger D., ed. *African American Folktales: Stories from Black Traditions in the New World.* New York: Pantheon, 1985.

———. *The Man-of-Words in the West Indies.* Baltimore: Johns Hopkins University Press, 1983.

Alaska Judicial Council. "Resolving Disputes Locally: A Statewide Report and Directory." Alaska Judicial Council. 9 December 2005.
http://www.ajc.state.ak.us/index.htm.

Algren, Nelson. "Interview of Davey Day." American Life Histories: Manuscripts from the Federal Writers' Project, 1936–1940. Manuscript Division, Library of Congress. 11 November 2005.
http://memory.loc.gov/ammem/wpaintro/wpahome.html.

Allen, Barbara, and Thomas Schlereth. *A Sense of Place: American Regional Cultures.* Lexington: University Press of Kentucky, 1990.

Ancelet, Barry Jean. "The Cajun Who Went to Harvard: Identity in the Oral Tradition of South Louisiana." *The Journal of Popular Culture* 23 (1989): 101–15.

Angermiller, Florence. "Interview of Jack Robert Grigsby." American Life Histories: Manuscripts from the Federal Writers' Project, 1936–1940. Manuscript Division, Library of Congress. 12 October 2005. http://memory.loc.gov/ammem/wpaintro/wpahome.html.

Bacon, A. M., and E. C. Parsons. "Folk-Lore from Elizabeth City County, Virginia." *Journal of American Folklore* 35 (1922): 250–327.

Backus, Emma M. "Animal Tales from North Carolina." *Journal of American Folklore* 11 (1898): 284–92.

———. "Folk-Tales from Georgia." *Journal of American Folklore* 13 (1900): 19–32.

———. "Tales of the Rabbit from Georgia Negroes." *Journal of American Folklore* 12 (1899): 108–15.

Backus, Emma M., and Ethel Hatton Leitner. "Negro Tales from Georgia." *Journal of American Folklore* 25 (1912): 125–36.

Baker, Ronald L. *Hoosier Folk Legends.* Bloomington: Indiana University Press, 1982.

Balilci, Asen. *The Netsilik Eskimo.* Garden City, NY: Natural History Press, 1970.

Banister, Manly Andrew C. "Interview of James E. Twadell." American Life Histories: Manuscripts from the Federal Writers' Project, 1936–1940. Manuscript Division, Library of Congress. 12 October 2005. http://memory.loc.gov/ammem/wpaintro/wpahome.html.

Barden, Thomas E., ed. *Virginia Folk Legends.* Charlottesville: University Press of Virginia, 1991.

Bates, William C. "Creole Folk-Lore from Jamaica II: Nancy Stories." *Journal of American Folklore* 9 (1896): 121–28.

Baughman, Ernest W. *Type- and Motif-Index of the Folk Tales of England and North America.* The Hague: Mouton, 1966.

Beauchamp, W. M. "Onondaga Tales." *Journal of American Folklore* 6 (1893): 173–89.

Beck, Horace. *Gluskap the Liar and Other Indian Tales.* Freeport, ME: Bond Wheelright, 1966.

Beckwith, Martha Warren. *Hawaiian Mythology.* New Haven: Yale University Press, 1940.

———. *Jamaica Anansi Stories.* New York: American Folklore Society, 1924.

"Beliefs of Southern Negroes Concerning Hags." *Journal of American Folklore* 7 (1894): 66–67.

Bergen, Fanny D. "Borrowing Trouble." *Journal of American Folklore* 11 (1898): 55–59.

———. "On the Eastern Shore." *Journal of American Folklore* 2 (1889): 295–300.

———. "Two Witch Stories." *Journal of American Folklore* 12 (1899): 68–69.

Bierhorst, John, ed. *White Deer and Other Stories Told by the Lenape*. New York: W. Morrow, 1995.

Boas, Franz. *Chinook Texts*. Smithsonian Institution Bureau of American Ethnology Bulletin 20. Washington, DC: U.S. Government Printing Office, 1894.

———. "Notes on the Eskimo of Port Clarence, Alaska." *Journal of American Folklore* 7 (1894): 205–8.

———. "Traditions of the Ts'ets'ā´ut I." *Journal of American Folklore* 9 (1896): 257–68.

———. "Traditions of the Ts'ets'ā´ut II." *Journal of American Folklore* 10 (1897): 35–48.

Boatright, Mody Coggin. *Mody Boatright, Folklorist: A Collection of Essays*. Edited by Ernest B. Speck. Austin: University of Texas Press, 1973.

Botkin, Benjamin A. *A Treasury of American Folklore: The Stories, Legends, Tall Tales, Traditions, Ballads and Songs of the American People*. New York: Crown, 1944.

———. *A Treasury of New England Folklore*. New York: Crown, 1944.

Bourke, John G. "Notes on Apache Mythology." *Journal of American Folklore* 3 (1890): 209–12.

———. "Popular Medicines, Customs and Superstitions of the Rio Grande." *Journal of American Folklore* 7 (1894): 119–46.

Bowman, Earl. "Interview of Harry Reece." American Life Histories: Manuscripts from the Federal Writers' Project, 1936–1940. Manuscript Division, Library of Congress. 12 October 2005. http://memory.loc.gov/ammem/wpaintro/wpahome.html.

———. "Interview of William D. Naylor." American Life Histories: Manuscripts from the Federal Writers' Project, 1936–1940. Manuscript Division, Library of Congress. 12 October 2005. http://memory.loc.gov/ammem/wpaintro/wpahome.html.

Brendle, Thomas R., and William S. Troxell. *Pennsylvania German Folk Tales, Legends, Once-upon-a-time Stories, Maxims, and Sayings*. Norristown: Pennsylvania German Society, 1944.

Bullock, Mrs. Walter R. "The Collection of Maryland Folklore." *Journal of American Folklore* 11 (1898): 7–16.

Bunter, Rosa. "Ghosts as Guardians of Hidden Treasure." *Journal of American Folklore* 12 (1899): 64–65.

Burrows, Elizabeth. "Eskimo Tales." *Journal of American Folklore* 39 (1926): 79–81.

Bushotter, George, and J. Owen Dorsey. "A Teton Dakota Ghost Story." *Journal of American Folklore* 1 (1888): 68–72.

Byrd, Frank. "Interview of Leroy Spriggs." American Life Histories: Manuscripts from the Federal Writers' Project, 1936–1940. Manuscript Division, Library of Congress. 12 October 2005. http://memory.loc.gov/ammem/wpaintro/wpahome.html.

Carey, George. *Maryland Folklore*. Centreville, MD: Tidewater Publishers, 1989.

Carter, Isabel Gordon. "Mountain White Folk-Lore: Tales from the Southern Blue Ridge." *Journal of American Folklore* 38 (1925): 340–74.

Chance, Norman A. *The Eskimo of North Alaska*. New York: Holt, Rinehart and Winston, 1966.

Chase, Richard. "Jack and the Fire Dragaman." *The Southern Folklore Quarterly* 5 (1941): 151–55.

———. "The Lion and the Unicorn." *The Southern Folklore Quarterly* 1 (1937): 15–19.

Claudel, Calvin. "Louisiana Tales of Jean Sot and Boqui and Lapin." *Southern Folklore Quarterly* 8 (1944): 287–99.

Claudel, Calvin, and J.-M. Carrier. "Three Tales from the French Folklore of Louisiana." *Journal of American Folklore* 56 (1943): 38–44.

Clough, Ben C. "Legends of Chappaquiddick." *Journal of American Folklore* 31 (1918): 553–54.

Comhaire-Sylvain, Suzanne. "Creole Tales from Haiti." *Journal of American Folklore* 50 (1937): 207–95.

Conant, L. "English Folktales in America: The Three Brothers and the Hag." *Journal of American Folklore* 8 (1895): 143–44.

Cooke, Elizabeth Johnston. "English Folk-Tales in America. The Bride of the Evil One." *Journal of American Folklore* 12 (1899): 126–30.

Cross, Tom Peete. "Folk-Lore from the Southern States." *Journal of American Folklore* 22 (1909): 251–55.

Currier, John McNab. "Contributions to the Folk-Lore of New England." *Journal of American Folklore* 2 (1889): 291–93.

Curtin, Jeremiah. "European Folklore in the United States." *Journal of American Folklore* 2 (1889): 56–59.

———. *Seneca Indian Myths*. New York: W.P. Dutton, 1922. Reprint, New York: Dover, 2001.

Cushing, Frank Hamilton. "A Zuni Folk-tale of the Underworld." *Journal of American Folklore* 5 (1892): 49–56.

Davis, Nita. "Interview of Bill Holcomb." American Life Histories: Manuscripts from the Federal Writers' Project, 1936–1940. Manuscript Division, Library of Congress. 12 October 2005. http://memory.loc.gov/ammem/wpaintro/wpahome.html.

———. "Interview of Dick McDonald." American Life Histories: Manuscripts from the Federal Writers' Project, 1936–1940. Manuscript Division, Library of Congress. 12 October 2005. http://memory.loc.gov/ammem/wpaintro/wpahome.html.

Deans, James. "The Doom of the Katt-a-quins: From the Aboriginal Folk-lore of Southern Alaska." *Journal of American Folklore* 5 (1892): 232–35.

Dixon, Roland B. "Achomawi and Atsugewi Tales."*Journal of American Folklore* 21 (1908): 159–77.

———. *Oceanic Mythology*. Boston: Marshall Jones, 1916.

———. "Some Coyote Stories from the Maidu Indians of California" *Journal of American Folklore* 13 (1900): 270.

Dorsey, George A. "Legend of the Teton Sioux Medicine Pipe." *Journal of American Folklore* 19 (1906): 326–29.

———. *The Mythology of the Wichita*. Norman: University of Oklahoma Press, 1995.

———. "The Two Boys Who Slew the Monsters and Became Stars." *Journal of American Folklore* 17 (1904): 153–60.

———. "Wichita Tales. 1. Origin." *Journal of American Folklore* 15 (1902): 215–39.

Dorsey, J. Owen. "Abstracts of Omaha and Ponka Myths, II." *Journal of American Folklore* 1 (1888): 204–8.

———. "Omaha Folklore Notes." *Journal of American Folklore* 1 (1888): 313–14.

———. "Two Biloxi Tales." *Journal of American Folklore* 6 (1893): 48–50.

Dorson, Richard M. *American Folklore. Chicago: University of Chicago Press*, 1959.

———. *Bloodstoppers and Bearwalkers*. Cambridge, MA: Harvard University Press, 1952.

———. *Buying the Wind: Regional Folklore in the United States*. Chicago: University of Chicago Press, 1964.

Douglas, Sir George. "The Witty Exploits of Mr. George Buchanan, the King's Fool." *Scottish Fairy and Folktales*. New York: A.L. Burt Company, 1901.

Doyle, Elizabeth. "Interview of Mollie Privett." *American Life Histories: Manuscripts from the Federal Writers' Project, 1936–1940.* Manuscript Division, Library of Congress. 12 October 2005. http://memory.loc.gov/ammem/wpaintro/wpahome.html

Dubois, Sylvie, and Barbara M. Horvath. "Creoles and Cajuns: A Portrait in Black and White." *American Speech* 78 (2003): 192–207.

Dubois, Sylvie, and Megan Melançon. "Creole Is; Creole Ain't: Diachronic and Synchronic Attitudes Toward Creole French Identity in Southern Louisiana." *Language in Society* 29 (2000): 237–58.

Edwards, Charles L. *Bahama Songs and Stories.* Memoirs of the American Folklore Society 3. New York: American Folklore Society, 1895.

———. "Some Tales from Bahama Folk-Lore." *Journal of American Folklore* 4 (1891): 47–54.

———. "Some Tales from Bahama Folk-Lore: Fairy Stories." *Journal of American Folklore* 4 (1891): 247–52.

Emery, W. M. "Interview of Jack Zurich." *American Life Histories: Manuscripts from the Federal Writers' Project, 1936–1940.* Manuscript Division, Library of Congress. 12 October 2005. http://memory.loc.gov/ammem/wpaintro/wpahome.html.

Espinosa, Aurelio. *The Folklore of Spain in the American Southwest: Traditional Spanish Folk Literature in Northern New Mexico and Southern Colorado.* Edited by J. Manuel Espinosa. Norman: University of Oklahoma Press, 1985.

———. "New Mexican Spanish Folklore." *Journal of American Folklore* 223 (1910): 345–418.

Farrand, Livingston, and Leo J. Frachtenberg. "Shasta and Athapascan Myths from Oregon." *Journal of American Folklore* 28 (1915): 207–42.

Farrer, Claire. *Thunder Rides a Black Horse: Mescalero Apaches and the Mythic Present.* 2nd ed. Prospect Heights, IL: Waveland Press, 1996.

Fauset, Arthur Huff. "Negro Folk Tales from the South (Alabama, Mississippi, Louisiana)." *Journal of American Folklore* 40 (1927): 213–303.

Fewkes, J. Walter. "A Contribution to Passamaquoddy Folklore." *Journal of American Folklore* 3 (1890): 257–80.

———. "The Destruction of the Tusayan Monsters." *Journal of American Folklore* 8 (1895): 132–37.

Fife, Austin E. "The Legend of the Three Nephites Among the Mormons." *Journal of American Folklore* 53 (1940): 1–49.

Fischer, David Hackett. *Albion's Seed: Four British Folkways in America.* New York: Oxford University Press, 1989.

Fletcher, Alice C. "Glimpses of Child-Life Among the Omaha Indians." *Journal of American Folklore* 1 (1888): 115–23.

Fornander, Abraham. *Fornander Collection of Hawaiian Antiquities and Folk-lore.* 3 vols. Honolulu: Bernice Pauahi Bishop Museum, 1916/1917–1919/1920.

Fortier, Alcee. "Louisianian Nursery-Tales." *Journal of American Folklore* 1 (1888): 140–45.

Frachtenberg, Leo J. *Coos Texts.* Columbia University Contributions to Anthropology 1. New York: Columbia University Press, 1913.

———. "Myths of the Alsea Indians of Northwestern Oregon." *International Journal of American Linguistics* 1 (1917): 64–75.

Gard, Robert E., and L. G. Sorden. *Wisconsin Lore: Antics and Anecdotes of Wisconsin People and Places.* New York: Duell, Sloan and Pearce, 1962.

Gardner, Emelyn E. "Folk-Lore from Schoharie County, New York." *Journal of American Folklore* 27 (1914): 304–25.

Gatschet, Albert S. "Oregonian Folklore." *Journal of American Folklore* 4 (1891): 139–43.

———. "Report of a Visit to Jack Wilson, the Payute Messiah." *Journal of American Folklore* 6 (1893): 108–11.

Gayton, A. H., and Stanley S. Newman. *Yokuts and Western Mono Myths.* Millwood, NY: Kraus, 1976.

Gibson, Robert O. *The Chumash.* New York: Chelsea House, 1991.

Gifford, Edward Winslow. "Western Mono Myths." *Journal of American Folklore* 36 (1923): 301–67.

Glimm, James York. *Flatlanders and Ridgerunners: Folk Tales from the Mountains of Northern Pennsylvania.* Pittsburgh: University of Pittsburgh Press, 1983.

Golder, F. A. "Aleutian Stories." *Journal of American Folklore* 18 (1905): 215–22.

Green, Archie. *Calf's Head and Union Tale: Labor Yarns at Work and Play.* Urbana: University of Illinois Press, 1996.

Grinell, George Bird. "Pawnee Mythology." *Journal of American Folkore* 6 (1893): 113–30.

Haight, Willliam C. "Interview of Charles Imus." American Life Histories: Manuscripts from the Federal Writers' Project, 1936–1940. Manuscript Division, Library of Congress. 14 October 2005. http://memory.loc.gov/ammem/wpaintro/wpahome.html.

Hale, Horatio. "Huron Folklore I: Cosmogonic Myth, The Good and Evil Minds." *Journal of American Folklore* 1 (1888): 177–83.

———. "Huron Folklore II: The Story of Tihaiha, the Sorceror." *Journal of American Folklore* 2 (1889): 249–54.

———. "Huron Folklore III: The Legend of the Thunderers." *Journal of American Folklore* 4 (1891): 189–94.

Hall, Julien A. "Negro Conjuring and Tricking." *Journal of American Folklore* 10 (1897): 241–43.

Halpert, Herbert. *Folktales and Legends from the New Jersey Pines: A Collection and a Study.* Bloomington: Indiana University Press, 1947.

———. "Pennsylvania Fairylore and Folktales." *Journal of American Folklore* 58 (1945): 130–34.

Harper, Francis. "Tales of the Okefinoke." *American Speech* 1 (1926): 407–20.

Hartman, George. "Interview of Ed Grantham." American Life Histories: Manuscripts from the Federal Writers' Project, 1936–1940. Manuscript Division, Library of Congress. 12 October 2005. http://memory.loc.gov/ammem/wpaintro/wpahome.html.

———. "Interview of E. O. Skeidler." American Life Histories: Manuscripts from the Federal Writers' Project, 1936–1940. Manuscript Division, Library of Congress. 18 October 2005. http://memory.loc.gov/ammem/wpaintro/wpahome.html.

Hayward, Silvanus. "English Folktales in America II." *Journal of American Folklore* 3 (1890): 291–95.

Henning, D. C. "Tales of the Blue Mountains in Pennsylvania." *Miners' Journal* (Pottsdam, PA), March 26, 1897.

Herrick, Mrs. R. F. "The Black Dog of the Blue Ridge." *Journal of American Folklore* 20 (1907): 151–52.

Hoffman, W. J. "Folklore of the Pennsylvania Germans III." *Journal of American Folklore* 2 (1889): 191–202.

Hubert, Levi. "Interview of Joseph Madden." American Life Histories: Manuscripts from the Federal Writers' Project, 1936–1940. Manuscript Division, Library of Congress. 12 October 2005. http://memory.loc.gov/ammem/wpaintro/wpahome.html.

———. "Interview of Mary Thomas." American Life Histories: Manuscripts from the Federal Writers' Project, 1936–1940. Manuscript Division, Library of Congress. 12 October 2005. http://memory.loc.gov/ammem/wpaintro/wpahome.html.

Hudson, Arthur Palmer, and Pete Kyle McCarter. "The Bell Witch of Tennessee and Mississippi: A Folk Legend." *Journal of American Folklore* 47 (1934): 46–58.

Hufford, David. *The Terror That Comes in the Night: An Experience-Centered Study of Supernatural Assault Traditions.* Philadelphia: University of Pennsylvania Press, 1982.

Hurston, Zora Neale. "Dance Songs and Tales from the Bahamas." *Journal of American Folklore* 43 (1930): 294–312.

"Interview of Bones Hooks." American Life Histories: Manuscripts from the Federal Writers' Project, 1936–1940. Manuscript Division, Library of Congress. 12 October 2005. http://memory.loc.gov/ammem/wpaintro/wpa-home.html.

"Interview of E. V. Batchler." American Life Histories: Manuscripts from the Federal Writers' Project, 1936–1940. Manuscript Division, Library of Congress. 12 October 2005. http://memory.loc.gov/ammem/wpaintro/wpa-home.html.

"The Irishman and the Pumpkin." *Journal of American Folklore* 12 (1899): 226.

Jack, Edward. "Maliseet Legends." *Journal of American Folklore* 8 (1895): 193–208.

James, George Wharton. "A Saboba Origin Myth." *Journal of American Folklore* 15 (1902): 36–39.

Jarreau, Lafayette, "Creole Folklore of Pointe Coupee Parish." MA thesis, Louisiana State University, 1931.

Jenks, Albert Ernest. "The Bear Maiden: An Ojibwa Folk-Tale from Lac Courte Oreille Reservation, Wisconsin." *Journal of American Folklore* 15 (1902): 33–35.Johnson, Clifton. "The Twist-Mouth Family." *Journal of American Folklore* 18 (1905): 322–23.

Johnson, John H. "Folk-Lore from Antigua, British West Indies." *Journal of American Folklore* 34 (1921): 40–88.

Johnston, Mrs. William Preston. "Two Negro Folktales." *Journal of American Folklore* 9 (1896): 194–98.

Jones, William. "Notes on the Fox Indians." *Journal of American Folklore* 24 (1911): 209–37.

Kamenskii, Annatolii. *Tlingit Indians of Alaska.* Translated and with an introduction and supplementary material by Sergei Kan. Fairbanks: University of Alaska Press, 1985.

Kawaharada, Dennis. *Ancient Oahu: Stories from Fornander & Thrum.* Honolulu: Kalamaku Press, 2001.

Kercheval, George Truman. "An Otoe and an Omaha Tale." *Journal of American Folklore* 6 (1893): 199–204.

Kittredge, George Lyman. "English Folktales in America." *Journal of American Folklore* 3 (1890): 291–95.

Knox, Robert H. "A Blackfoot Version of the Magical Flight." *Journal of American Folklore* 36 (1923): 401–3.

Kroeber, Alfred L. "Cheyenne Tales." *Journal of American Folklore* 13 (1900): 161–90.

———. *Handbook of the Indians of California.* Smithsonian Institution Bureau of American Ethnology Bulletin 78. Washington, DC: U.S. Government Printing Office, 1925.

———. "Tales of the Smith Sound Eskimo." *Journal of American Folklore* 12 (1899): 166–82.

———. "Ute Tales." *Journal of American Folklore* 14 (1901): 252–85.

Kroeber, Henriette Rothschild. "Papago Coyote Tales." *Journal of American Folklore* 22 (1909): 339–42.

Lightfoot, William E. "Regional Folkloristics." *Handbook of American Folklore.* Edited by Richard Dorson. Bloomington: Indiana University Press, 1983.

Lowie, Robert H. "Shoshonean Tales." *Journal of American Folklore* 37 (1924): 1–242.

Lummis, Charles. *Pueblo Indian Folk-Stories.* New York: Century, 1910.

Mallery, Garrick. "The Fight with the Giant Witch." *American Anthropologist* 3 (1890): 65–70.

Matthews, Washington. "A Folk-tale of the Hidatsa Indians." *The Folklore Record* 1 (1878): 136–43.

———. *Navajo Legends.* Memoirs of the American Folklore Society 5. New York: American Folklore Society, 1897.

———. "Noqoìlpi, the Gambler: A Navajo Myth." *Journal of American Folklore* 2 (1889): 89–94.

McHenry, Lawrence. "Interview of Minnie Wycloff." American Life Histories: Manuscripts from the Federal Writers' Project, 1936–1940. Manuscript Division, Library of Congress. 12 October 2005. http://memory.loc.gov/ammem/wpaintro/wpahome.html.

McMahon, William H. *Pine Barrens Legends, Lore, and Lies.* Wilmington, DE: Middle Atlantic Press, 1980.

McNeil, W. K. *Ozark Country.* Oxford: University Press of Mississippi, 1995.

Michaelis, Kate Woodbridge. "An Irish Folktale." *Journal of American Folklore* 23 (1910): 425–28.

Miller, E. Joan Wilson. "Ozark Culture Region as Revealed by Traditional Materials." *Annals of the Association of American Geographers* 58 (1968): 51–77.

Minor, Mary Willis. "How to Keep Off Witches." *Journal of American Folklore* 11 (1898): 76.

Monroe, Grace. "Interview of Middleton Robertson." American Life Histories: Manuscripts from the Federal Writers' Project, 1936–1940. Manuscript

Division, Library of Congress. 12 October 2005.
http://memory.loc.gov/ammem/wpaintro/wpahome.html.

Mooney, James. *James Mooney's History, Myths, and Sacred Formulas of the Cherokees.* Asheville, NC: Historical Images, 1992.

———. "Myths of the Cherokees." *Journal of American Folklore* 1 (1888): 97–108.

———. "*Myths of the Cherokee.*" *Nineteenth Annual Report of the Bureau of American Ethnology 1897–1898, Part I.* Washington, DC: U.S. Government Printing Office, 1900.

———. "*The Sacred Formulas of the Cherokees.*" *Seventh Annual Report of the Bureau of American Ethnology.* Washington, DC: U.S. Government Printing Office, 1891.

Mosley, Ruby. "Interview of Eldora Scott Maples." American Life Histories: Manuscripts from the Federal Writers' Project, 1936–1940. Manuscript Division, Library of Congress. 12 October 2005.
http://memory.loc.gov/ammem/wpaintro/wpahome.html.

Newell, William Wells. "English Folktales in America I." *Journal of American Folklore* 1 (1888): 227–34.

———. "English Folk-Tales in America." *Journal of American Folklore* 2 (1889): 213–18.

———. "The Ghost Legends of the Blue Mountains in Pennsylvania." *Journal of American Folklore* 11 (1898):76–78.

———. The Ignus Fatuus, Its Character and Legendary Origin." *Journal of American Folklore* 17 (1904): 39–60.

Oswalt, Wendell H. *Bashful No Longer: An Alaskan Eskimo Ethnohistory 1778–1988.* Norman: University of Oklahoma Press, 1990.

Owen, Mary A. "Ol' Rabbit an' de Dawg He Stole." *Journal of American Folklore* 9 (1890): 135–38.

Paredes, Américo. *With His Pistol in His Hand: A Border Ballad and Its Hero.* Austin: University of Texas Press, 1958.

Parsons, Elsie Clews. "Accumulative Tales Told by Cape Verde Islanders in New England." *Journal of American Folklore* 33 (1920): 34–42.

———. "Barbados Folklore." *Journal of American Folklore* 38 (1925): 267–92.

———. *Folk-Lore of the Sea Islands, South Carolina.* Memoirs of the American Folklore Society 16. New York: American Folklore Society, 1923.

———. *Kiowa Tales.* Memoirs of the American Folklore Society 22. New York: American Folklore Society, 1929.

———. "Pueblo Indian Folk-tales, Probably of Spanish Provenience." *Journal of American Folklore* 31 (1918): 216–55.

———. "Tales from Maryland and Pennsylvania." *Journal of American Folklore* 30 (1917): 209–17.

———. "Ten Folktales from the Cape Verde Islands." *Journal of American Folklore* 30 (1917): 230–38.

———. *Tewa Tales*. Memoirs of the American Folklore Society 19. New York: American Folklore Society, 1926.

———. "A West Indian Tale." *Journal of American Folklore* 32 (1919): 442–43.

Phipps, Woody. "Interview of Robert Lindsey." American Life Histories: Manuscripts from the Federal Writers' Project, 1936–1940. Manuscript Division, Library of Congress. 12 October 2005. http://memory.loc.gov/ammem/wpaintro/wpahome.html.

Porter, J. Hampden. "Notes on the Folk-Lore of the Mountain Whites of the Alleghenies." *Journal of American Folklore* 7 (1894): 105–17.

Pound, Louise. *Nebraska Folklore*. Lincoln: University of Nebraska Press, 1959.

Powers, Stephen. "North American Indian Legends and Fables." *Folk-Lore Record* 5 (1882): 93–143. Reprinted from *Contributions to North American Ethnology. Vol. 3, Tribes of California*. Edited by Stephen Powers. Washington, D.C.: U.S. Geographical and Geological Survey Rocky Mountain Region, 1877.

Radin, Paul. "Literary Aspects of Winebago Mythology." *Journal of American Folklore* 39 (1926): 18–52.

Radin, Paul, and A. B. Reagan. "Ojibwa Myths and Tales: The Manabozho Cycle." *Journal of American Folklore* 41 (1928): 61–146

Randolph, Vance. *Hot Springs and Hell; and other Folk Jests and Anecdotes from the Ozarks*. Hatboro, PA: Folklore Associates, 1965.

Rath, Richard Cullen. "Drums and Power: Ways of Creolizing Music in Coastal South Carolina and Georgia, 1730–1790." In *Creolization in the Americas*, edited by David Buisseret and Steven G. Rheinhardt. College Station: University of Texas at Arlington Press, 2000.

Ray, Marie. "Jean Sotte Stories." *Journal of American Folklore* 21 (1908): 364–65.

Rink, H., and Franz Boas. "Eskimo Tales and Songs." *Journal of American Folklore* 2 (1889): 123–31.

Romanofsky, Fred. "Interview of Cabbies." American Life Histories: Manuscripts from the Federal Writers' Project, 1936–1940. Manuscript Division, Library of Congress. 22 October 2005. http://memory.loc.gov/ammem/wpaintro/wpahome.html.

Roth, Terry, and Sam Schwartz. "Interview of Mr. Wollman." American Life Histories: Manuscripts from the Federal Writers' Project, 1936–1940.

Manuscript Division, Library of Congress. 16 October 2005.
http://memory.loc.gov/ammem/wpaintro/wpahome.html.

Russell, Frank. "Myths of the Jicarilla Apaches." *Journal of American Folklore* 11 (1898): 253–71.

Sapir, Jean. "Yurok Tales." *Journal of American Folklore* 41 (1928): 253–61.

"The Sea Tick and the Irishman." *Journal of American Folklore* 12 (1899): 226.

Seip, Elisabeth Cloud. "Witch-Finding in Western Maryland." *Journal of American Folklore* 14 (1901): 39–44.

Sherbert, Andrew C. "Interview of George Estes." American Life Histories: Manuscripts from the Federal Writers' Project, 1936–1940. Manuscript Division, Library of Congress. 12 October 2005.
http://memory.loc.gov/ammem/wpaintro/wpahome.html.

———. "Interview of William Harry Hembree." American Life Histories: Manuscripts from the Federal Writers' Project, 1936–1940. Manuscript Division, Library of Congress. 12 October 2005.
http://memory.loc.gov/ammem/wpaintro/wpahome.html.

Showers, Susan. "Two Negro Stories Concerning the Jay." *Journal of American Folklore* 11 (1898): 74.

Shuman, Amy. "Dismantling Local Culture." *Western Folklore* 52 (1993): 345–64.

Simpson, George E. "Loup Garou and Loa Tales from Northern Haiti." *Journal of American Folklore* 55 (1942): 219–27.

Simpson, George E., and J. B. Cineas. "Folk Tales of Haitian Heroes." *Journal of American Folklore* 54 (1941): 176–85.

Skinner, Alanson. "European Folk-Tales Collected Among the Menominee Indians." *Journal of American Folklore* 26 (1913): 64–80.

Smiley, Portia. "Folk-Lore from Virginia, South Carolina, Georgia, Alabama, and Florida." *Journal of American Folklore* 32 (1919): 357–83.

Smith, Janet. "Interview of Elfego Baca." American Life Histories: Manuscripts from the Federal Writers' Project, 1936–1940. Manuscript Division, Library of Congress. 12 October 2005.
http://memory.loc.gov/ammem/wpaintro/wpahome.html.

Smith, Pamela Coleman. "Two Negro Stories from Jamaica." *Journal of American Folklore* 9 (1896): 278.

Sparkman, P. S. "Notes of California Folklore: A Luiseño Tale." *Journal of American Folklore* 21 (1908): 35–36.

Speck, Frank G. "European Folk-Tales among the Penobscot." *Journal of American Folklore* 26 (1913): 81–84.

———. "European Tales among the Chickasaw Indians." *Journal of American Folklore* 26 (1913): 292.

———. "Penobscot Transformer Tales." *International Journal of American Linguistics* 1 (1918): 187–244.

Spencer, J. "Shawnee Folk-Lore." *Journal of American Folklore* 22 (1909): 319–26.

Spitzer, Nicholas R. "All Things Creole: Mout de tour le monde." *Journal of American Folklore* 116 (2003):57–72.

St. Clair, H. H., and R. H. Lowie. "Shoshone and Comanche Tales." *Journal of American Folklore* 22 (1909): 265–82.

Steiner, Roland. "Braziel Robinson Possessed of Two Spirits." *Journal of American Folklore* 13 (1900): 226–28.

———. "Sol Lockheart's Call." *Journal of American Folklore* 48 (1900): 67–70.

Stewart, Omer C. *The Northern Paiute Bands.* Millwood, NY: Kraus, 1976.

Stirling, Matthew W. *Origin Myth of Acoma and Other Records.* Smithsonian Institution Bureau of American Ethnology Bulletin 135. Washington, DC: U.S. Government Printing Office, 1942.

Strong, William D. *University of California Publications in American Archaeology and Ethnology.* Vol. 26, *Aboriginal Society in Southern California.* Berkeley: University of California Press, 1929.

Suplee, Laura M. "The Legend of Money Cove." *Journal of American Folklore* 31 (1918): 272–73.

Suttles, Wayne, ed. *Handbook of the North American Indians.* Vol. 7, *Northwest Coast.* Washington, DC: Smithsonian Institution, 1990.

Swanton, John R. *Myths and Tales of the Southeastern Indians.* Smithsonian Institution Bureau of American Ethnology Bulletin 88. Washington, DC: U.S. Government Printing Office, 1929.

Swenson, May. "Interview of Anca Vrbooska." American Life Histories: Manuscripts from the Federal Writers' Project, 1936–1940. Manuscript Division, Library of Congress. 12 October 2005. http://memory.loc.gov/ammem/wpaintro/wpahome.html.

———. "Interview of John Rivers." American Life Histories: Manuscripts from the Federal Writers' Project, 1936–1940. Manuscript Division, Library of Congress. 12 October 2005. http://memory.loc.gov/ammem/wpaintro/wpahome.html.

Taylor, Archer. "An Old-World Tale from Minnesota." *Journal of American Folklore* 31 (1918): 555–56.

Taylor, Helen Louise, and Rebecca Wolcott. "Items from New Castle, Delaware." *Journal of American Folklore* 51 (1938): 92–94.

Tejada, Simeon. "Interview of Manuel Jesus Vasques." American Life
Histories: Manuscripts from the Federal Writers' Project, 1936–1940.
Manuscript Division, Library of Congress. 12 October 2005. http://mem-ory.loc.gov/ammem/wpaintro/wpahome.html.

Thomas, Howard. *Folklore from the Adirondack Foothills*. Prospect, NY: Prospect
Books, 1958.

Thompson, Stith. *The Motif Index of Folk Literature*. Rev. ed. 6 vols.
Bloomington: Indiana University Press, 1955–1958.

Totty, Francis. "Interview of Maurice Coates." American Life Histories:
Manuscripts from the Federal Writers' Project, 1936–1940. Manuscript
Division, Library of Congress. 12 October 2005.
http://memory.loc.gov/ammem/wpaintro/wpahome.html.

Townsend, Edward. "Interview of A. Harry Williams." American Life
Histories: Manuscripts from the Federal Writers' Project, 1936–1940.
Manuscript Division, Library of Congress. 16 October 2005.
http://memory.loc.gov/ammem/wpaintro/wpahome.html.

Trowbridge, Ada Wilson. "Negro Customs and Folk-Stories of Jamaica."
Journal of American Folklore 9 (1896): 279–87.

Walden, Wayne. "Interview of Annette Hamilton." American Life Histories:
Manuscripts from the Federal Writers' Project, 1936–1940. Manuscript
Division, Library of Congress. 16 October 2005.
http://memory.loc.gov/ammem/wpaintro/wpahome.html.

———. "Interview of Fred Roys." American Life Histories: Manuscripts from
the Federal Writers' Project, 1936–1940. Manuscript Division, Library of
Congress. 12 October 2005. http://memory.loc.gov/ammem/wpaintro/wpa-home.html.

———. "Interview of Mrs. R. Ivanoff." American Life Histories: Manuscripts
from the Federal Writers' Project, 1936–1940. Manuscript Division,
Library of Congress. 12 October 2005.
http://memory.loc.gov/ammem/wpaintro/wpahome.html.

Weigle, Martha, and Peter White. *The Lore of New Mexico*. Albuquerque:
University of New Mexico Press, 1988.

Weippiert, G. W. "Legends of Iowa." *Journal of American Folklore* 2 (1889):
287–90.

Welsch, Roger. *Shingling the Fog and Other Plains Lies*. Chicago: Swallow, 1972.

West, John O. *Mexican-American Folklore*. Little Rock, AR: August House,
1988.

Westervelt, W. D. *Hawaiian Legends of Ghosts and Ghost-Gods*. Boston: Ellis
Press, 1916.

———. *Hawaiian Legends of Old Honolulu*. Boston: G.H. Ellis Press, 1915.

———. *Hawaiian Legends of Volcanoes*. Boston: G.H. Ellis Press, 1916.

Will, George F. "No-Tongue, A Mandan Tale." *Journal of American Folklore* 26 (1913): 331–37.

———. "No-Tongue, A Mandan Tale." *Journal of American Folklore* 29 (1916): 402–6.

Williams, Ellis. "Interview of Zenobia Brown." American Life Histories: Manuscripts from the Federal Writers' Project, 1936–1940. Manuscript Division, Library of Congress. 20 October 2005. http://memory.loc.gov/ammem/wpaintro/wpahome.html.

Williams, Mentor L., ed. *Schoolcraft's Indian Legends*. East Lansing: Michigan State University Press, 1956.

Wilson, Howard Barrett. "Notes of Syrian Folk-Lore Collected in Boston." *Journal of American Folklore* 16 (1903): 133–47.

Wiltse, Henry M. "In the Southern Field of Folk-Lore." *Journal of American Folklore* 13 (1900): 209–12.

Wissler, Clark. "Some Dakota Myths I." *Journal of American Folklore* 20 (1907): 121–31.

———. "Some Dakota Myths II." *Journal of American Folklore* 20 (1907): 195–206.

"Witchcraft in New Mexico." *Journal of American Folklore* 1 (1888): 167–68.

Wrenn, Sarah B. "Interview of Annie Cason Lee." American Life Histories: Manuscripts from the Federal Writers' Project, 1936–1940. Manuscript Division, Library of Congress. 11 October 2005. http://memory.loc.gov/ammem/wpaintro/wpahome.html.

———. "Interview of Jane Lee Smith." American Life Histories: Manuscripts from the Federal Writers' Project, 1936–1940. Manuscript Division, Library of Congress. 12 October 2005. http://memory.loc.gov/ammem/wpaintro/wpahome.html.

Wrenshall, Letitia Humphreys. "Incantations and Popular Healing in Maryland and Pennsylvania." *Journal of American Folklore* 15 (1902): 268–74.

Zingerle, Ignaz and Joseph. *Kinder- und Hausmärchen*, gesammelt durch die Brüder Zingerle. Innsbruck: Verlag der Wagner'schen Buchhandlung, 1852.

Cumulative Index

Boldface numbers refer to volume numbers.

"Chef Sampson Lands Mr. Trout,"
   1:138
"Chef Watkins' Alibi," 1:139
Cherokee, 1:32–33, 1:262, 1:298,
   2:2, 2:76; belief in "the immor-
   tals," 2:213; North Carolina
   (Eastern Band), 2:2–3; ravens in
   sacred formulas, 2:176; tales,
   2:11, 2:29, 2:35, 2:101, 2:175,
   2:213
Chesser, Allen, 2:46, 2:123, 2:124,
   2:305
Chesser, Sam, 2:217
Cheyenne, 3:132, 3:179; tales,
   3:178, 3:185, 3:262, 3:361
Chickasaw, 2:2; moieties, 2:76;
   tales, 2:76
"The Chief's Daughters," 1:149,
   1:176
"The Children of the Dog," 4:51
Chinook tales, 4:43, 4:100, 4:113,
   4:127
Chipo, 3:305, 3:335
Chippewa (Ojibway) tales, 1:147
"The Chloroformed Roommate,"
   4:204
Choctaw, 2:2, 2:21, 2:76
"The Chosen Suitor," 2:205, 2:277,
   2:298
"The Chosen Suitor: The Forbidden
   Room," 2:204; original version,
   2:311
Christensen, Julian, 1:225
"Christians Charged for Reading
   Bible in Prison," 4:241
Christophe, Henri, 2:294
"Chronic Dehydration," 4:169
Chumash, 3:268

Circuses, 3:68
"Citibank Boycott," 4:271
Civil War: and Mid-Atlantic, 1:261;
   and Midwest, 1:149, 1:248; and
   Plains and Plateau, 3:132; and
   West, 3:267
Clarke, Alexander, 1:9
Clatsop, 4:43
Clayton, W. O., 1:286
"Clothing Caught in a Graveyard,"
   1:115
Coates, Maurice, 3:83
"Cock's Breakfast," 2:242
Cody, William Frederick "Buffalo
   Bill," 1:148, 243; Wild West
   Show, 3:68
Comanches (Southern Plains),
   3:132, 3:230; tales, 3:231. See
   also Shoshonean Comanches
Comic anecdotes, 4:120
"Contempt for His Torturers," 1:6,
   1:131
Cook, Captain James, 3:269
"'Coon in the Box," 2:121
Coos, 4:12; tales, 4:12, 4:55, 4:66
Corbett, James John "Gentleman
   Jim," 3:238
Coushatta/Cousatti, 2:2, 2:20
"The Cow Is Taken to the Roof to
   Graze," 1:310
"Coyote and Beaver," 4:86
"Coyote and His Sister Robin,"
   3:268, 3:367
"Coyote and Pitch," 4:84; tar baby
   similarities, 4:85
"Coyote and Raccoon," 4:82
"Coyote and the Buffalo," 3:132,
   3:228
"Coyote and the Grizzly Bears,"
   3:339–41; formulaic closing,
   3:339
"Coyote and the Old Woman," 4:73
"Coyote and the Stump-Man," 4:92
"Coyote and the Sun," 3:344
"The Coyote and the Woodpecker,"
   3:109, 3:115

"Coyote and Wolf," 3:342
"Coyote Arranges the Seasons of
   the Year," 4:20
"Coyote Creates Taboos," 4:4,
   4:127, 4:141
"Coyote Frees the Salmon," 4:25
"Coyote's Amorous Adventures,"
   4:83
"Coyote's Theft of Fire," 3:132,
   3:164, 3:173
Creation myths. See Origins
"Creation of Man," 3:274
"The Creation of the Indians,"
   3:278
Creek Confederation, 2:2, 2:21,
   2:58, 2:76, 2:105; tales, 2:59,
   2:103, 2:105, 2:151; and ties to
   African Americans, 2:105
Creole traditions, 2:3, 2:224
"The Crop Division," 1:281
"Crossing the Plains from
   Kentucky," 3:132, 3:181
Cultee, Charles, 4:43, 4:100, 4:113,
   4:127
Cultural contact, 1:262, 1:298,
   1:344, 2:5, 2:56, 3:4, 3:17, 3:77,
   3:115; among Pueblo peoples,
   3:47; Lapin/Bouqui/Rabbit examples, 2:4, 2:49, 2:101, 2:103,
   2:105
Culture heroes, 1:4, 2:20, 3:20,
   3:165, 3:189, 3:306, 4:14, 4:279;
   abilities, 1:202; characteristics,
   3:173; coyote, 4:93; divine twins,
   1:9, 1:12, 3:47, 3:59, 3:206,
   3:213; and flow of power, 3:135;
   Papa, 3:293; Prairie Falcon,
   3:268; Raven, 4:40, 4:99, 4:134;
   and technology, 2:99, 3:22; Uuyot
   (Wuyoot), 3:289; Wakea, 3:293.
   See also Trickster legends
"Curanderas and Brujas," 3:5,
   3:124–26
"Curanderas and Brujas II,"
   3:125"Cures of a Maryland
   Witch," 1:264, 1:330, 1:352

Imus, Charles, 4:156
"In Liquor," 1:303
"In the Bee Tree," 1:300
"In the Cow's Belly," 2:257
"Incriminating the Other Fellow," 2:62; original version, 2:309
Indian Removal Act (1830), 2:2
Indian Territory, 2:2, 2:105, 3:132
Inuit, 4:3, 4:5
Irish American tales: Mid-Atlantic, 1:344; Midwest, 1:194, 1:225; Northeast, 1:81, 1:91; Northwest, 4:156
"The Irishman and the Pumpkin," 1:225, 2:73, 2:223
Iroquois Confederacy, 1:4–5, 1:128, 1:164; contact with the French, 1:5; legends, 1:4; and Shawnee, 1:148
Irving, Washington, 1:122
Isleta Pueblo: moieties, 3:42; tales, 3:41, 3:47, 3:109; Tiwa, 3:42
"It Was So Cold That…," 1:147, 1:216
Ivanoff, Mrs. R., 3:238

"Jack and the Bean Pole," 1:262, 1:275
"Jack and the Bean Tree," 2:5, 2:98
"Jack and the Beanstalk," 2:6, 2:134
"Jack and the Fire Dragaman," 2:140
"Jack-O'-M-Lantern," 1:371
"Jack-O'-My-Lantern," 1:265, 1:327; original version, 1:371
"Jack the Giant Killer," 2:6, 2:79
Jackson, Henry, Jr., 1:190

Jackson, "Pappy," 2:220
Jackson, Thomas, 4:116
"Jake Strauss," 1:6, 1:115; original version, 1:368
"James Harris," 2:199
"Jane Fonda Nomination," 4:189; variant B, 4:191
"Jean Sot Feeds Cows Needles," 2:4, 2:110
Jean Sot, 2:4; stock character, 2:113
"Jean Sot Kills the Duck," 2:4, 2:111
"Jean Sot and the Cowhide," 2:113
Jeffries, James Jackson "Jim," 3:238
Jenkins, Julius, 2:204
Jenks, Albert Ernest, 1:173
"Jim Johns and the Tiger," 2:217
John and Master tales, 1:263, 1:360, 2:122, 2:126
"John Kerry's Medals," 4:166
"John the Fool and John the Smart," 2:262
Johnson, Arthur John "Jack," 3:238
Johnson, Elsie, 1:321
Johnson, Josephine, 1:306
Johnson, Robert, 1:354, 2:37, 2:162
Johnson, Sextus E., 3:241
"Joke on Jake," 3:132, 3:233
Jokes, 1:104, 1:148, 1:263, 1:357, 1:359, 2:73, 2:120, 2:167, 2:208, 4:100; articulating intergroup strife, 2:259; beleaguered wife stock character, 2:167; Boudreaux stock character, 2:119; Cajun jokes, 2:119; drunkard stock character, 2:167; ethnic, 1:225, 1:263, 1:309, 1:310, 1:312, 1:313, 1:317, 2:73, 2:74, 2:75, 2:223, 2:260, 3:233; master/slave, 1:263, 1:358, 1:360, 2:122; myth parody, 2:243; practical, 4:100; Preacher as stock character, 1:315, 2:78, 2:167, 2:206. *See also* African American jokes; John and Master tales
Joseph, Termeus, 2:286

Joshua, 4:7; tales, 4:7, 4:74, 4:86
"Judgment Day," 1:357
"Jumping into the Breeches," 1:310

Kalapuya, 4:142; tales, 4:142
"Kamapuaa on Oahu and Kauai," 3:318
"Kampuaa Legends: Legends of the Hog God," 3:312
"Kanati and Selu: The Origin of Corn and Game," 2:11,
Karok, 4:14; tales, 4:14, 4:16, 4:25
"Katrina Blunders," 4:275
"Katrina Worker Report," 4:208
Kearny, Stephen W., 3:5
"Keeping off Witches," 1:343
"Kentucky Fried Chicken Becomes KFC," 4:165
Kickapoo, 1:147, 1:149, 1:162, 1:164–65; tales, 1:188
Kidd, Captain, 1:27
"The Killing of the Dutchman," 4:94
"The Kind and the Unkind Girls," 2:224
"The King and Old George Buchanan," 2:132
Klamath Billie, 4:18, 4:28, 4:71, 4:79, 4:82, 4:83, 4:84, 4:91, 4:92, 4:96
Kroeber, A. L., 3:179, 4:37

La Foria, 3:17, 3:19, 3:22, 3:114
La Patten, 1:292
Lakota, 3:132; Ogalala (Sioux), 3:188, 3:227, 3:254; tales, 3:188
"Lazy Jack and His Calf Skin," 1:77, 2:115
"Lazy Maria," 1:97
" Legend of Sattik," 4:4, 4:140
"Legend of the Breadfruit Tree," 3:269, 3:292
"Legend of the Teton Sioux Medicine Pipe," 3:132, 3:251
"Legendary Origin of the Kickapoos," 1:149, 1:164

Mono, 3:268, 3:277; tales, 3:277, 3:306, 3:335, 3:367, 3:369

"Moon Cheese: Two Irishmen at the Well," 1:263, 1:312

Mooney, James, 2:176

Morgan, John Hunt, 1:248

Morgan, Richard, 2:242

Mormons, 3:133, 3:241

Morris, Lucy, 1:278

Moses, 1:45

Mother Corn Ceremony, 3:160

"Mother Holle," 1:97

"The Mother of All Urban Legends," 4:223

Motifs/tale types, 4:280; aimless wandering of trickster, 1:202; animal/fish allows itself to be taken, 4:4; animal motifs, 1:45, 1:55; animal spouse motif, 1:337, 2:277, 2:298; "awl elbow witches," 1:179; bargain with death, 2:161; belief tales, 1:120; brain over brawn, 2:238; cannibal figure, 2:98, 2:100, 3:173, 3:200, 4:55; Cinderella, 1:50, 3:4, 3:77; composites (examples of), 1:304; dead horse, 2:59; demon lover, 2:199; Devil's questions, 2:199; divided village (Wichita motif), 3:213; dog ghosts, 1:327; "earthdiver," 1:9, 1:151, 1:160, 3:277; Earth Mother, 1:9; evil father-in-law, 1:179; exile, 1:45; exploiting trust of romantic rival, 1:270; extraordinary birth, 1:45; "fall from grace," 2:19; "fatal deception," 1:297; girl helper in hero's flight, 1:52, 1:272; Jack tales, 2:5,

2:149; John and Master tales, 1:263; jokes, 1:148; kind and unkind, 1:73; lying, tales of, 1:91, 1:92, 3:103; magic canoe, 1:179; magic object, 1:69; magic stick beats person, 1:69; "mock plea," 1:295; numbskull stories, 1:311, 2:75, 2:121; Obstacle Flight, 2:199, 2:205, 3:255; ogres duped to fight each other, 2:79; *ordinary folktales*, 1:179; orphan and grandparents, 4:79; personal experience narratives, 1:148, 1:149; pirate legends, 1:4, 1:26; rolling skull, 1:239; rope to climb to heavens, 4:93; sacred numbers, 3:7, 3:36; shape-shifting, 1:122, 1:337, 2:86, 2:249, 2:286; "squeezing the stone," 2:79; Star Husband Type I (wish to marry a star), 4:61; stupid stories depending on a pun, 2:111; tarbaby, 2:55; task for suitors/bride as prize, 1:69; theft of butter (honey) by playing godfather, 2:64, 2:240; transformation motifs, 1:110, 3:257; trial of three brothers, 2:273; trickster greed, 1:196, 1:289, 2:106; twins, 1:9, 1:12, 2:11, 3:47, 3:52, 3:206, 3:213; two sisters, 3:8; "unfinished business," 1:324; and validating devices, 1:227; wisdom of age, 2:107, 2:221; wish to marry a star (Star Husband Type I), 1:176; witches "riding" victims, 1:110; young woman defying parent, 4:38

Mountain Chief, Walter, 3:257

"Mr. Deer's My Riding Horse," 1:290, 2:4, 2:56, 2:58; original version, 2:307

"Mr. Hard-Time," 1:310, 2:260

"Mr. Hard-times," 1:310

"Mr. Jones's Advice," 4:175

"Mr. Peacock and the Deadly Ghost," 1:328; original version, 1:376

Miss K.'s Father, 1:346

Murray, Harry, 2:243

"Muskrat's Tail," 1:149, 1:168

"My Son Ali," 1:100

"The Mysterious Deer," 2:197

Myths, 4:280; alternative look at original sin, 2:231; and legends (examples), 3:251, 3:282; memory culture vs. sacred narrative, 3:279; and primary food groups for Native Americans, 2:18; uses, 3:297; Ute, 3:173

Nakassungnaitut, 4:37

"Nancy and the Honey Tree," 2:235

Nancy, Ann, 2:33

"Nancy fools His Wife," 2:248, 2:270

Narcom, W. P., 1:301

Narrative performance, 1:41

Natchez, 2:2; tales, 2:18, 2:53

Native American cultures: in Caribbean, 2:1–2; Indian Removal Act (1830), 2:2; of Mid-Atlantic, 1:262; of Midwest, 1:147–49; of Northeast, 1:4; in Northwest, 4:3–5; in Plains and Plateau, 3:131–33; of South, 2:2; in Southwest, 3:4–5; in West, 3:268

Native American tales: Achomawi, 3:271; Acoma Pueblo, 3:7; Alabama, 2:21, 2:98, 2:100; Aleut, 4:42, 4:146, 4:148, 4:151; Alsea, 4:117; Apache, 3:17, 3:20, 3:22, 3:115; Arikara, 3:159; Biloxi, 2:54; Blackfoot, 3:257; Cherokee, 2:11, 2:29, 2:35, 2:101, 2:175, 2:213; Cheyenne, 3:178, 3:185, 3:262, 3:361; Chinook, 4:43, 4:100, 4:113, 4:127; Comanche, 3:230; Coos, 4:11, 4:55, 4:66; Creek, 2:58,

"Origin of the Bear: The Bear
   Songs," **2**:28
"The Origin of the Narwhal," **4**:34
"The Origin of the Sauks and
   Foxes," **1**:165
"The Origin of the Seasons and of
   the Mountains," **4**:27, **4**:30; similarities to Tlingit narrative, **4**:27
"Origin of the Universe," **3**:132,
   3:213
"The Origin of Vegetation," **1**:149,
   1:158
"The Origin of Woman," **2**:243;
   original version, **2**:314
Origins: tales of, **2**:25; Caribbean,
   2:231–44; Cyber Region,
   4:165–74; Mid-Atlantic,
   1:265–74; Midwest, **1**:151–71;
   Northeast, **1**:9–44; Northwest,
   4:7–49; Plains and Plateau,
   3:135–84; South, **2**:11–48;
   Southwest, **3**:7–45; West,
   3:271–96
"The Orphan and the Turkeys,"
   1:196, **1**:202
Osagiwag`. *See* Sauk
Otos, **1**:148, **1**:149; tales, **1**:149,
   1:176
"Out of Her Skin," **1**:263, **1**:334,
   1:335
"Out of Their Skins," **1**:335, **1**:341
"Outwitting the King," **1**:7, **1**:89
Ozarks, **2**:5

Pa-skin, **1**:173
Paiute: "football," **3**:327; Northern
   (Paviotso), **3**:287; Southern

(Moapa), **3**:278; tales, **3**:278,
   3:288, **3**:326, **3**:331, **3**:342
Palmer, Francis L., **1**:54
Papa, **3**:293
Papago, **3**:111; tales, **3**:111
Parsiow, Alonzo, **1**:91
Parsons, Elsie Clews, **1**:94, **1**:262,
   1:298, **1**:309, **2**:5, **3**:77
Passamoquoddy: tales, **1**:17, **1**:64
"Paul Heym, the Wizard of
   Lebanon," **1**:122
Pavawut, **3**:365
Pawnee: Skidi and Arikaras, **3**:160
"Pele and Kamapuaa," **3**:322
"Pele's Long Sleep," **3**:269, **3**:353
Pennsylvania Dutch, **1**:6
Penny, Charles, **1**:42, **1**:363
Penobscot, **1**:4, **1**:12; tales, **1**:5,
   1:16, **1**:45, **1**:61, **1**:69
People of the Red Earth. *See*
   Mesquakie (Fox)
"Perfume Mugger," **4**:199; variant B,
   4:200; variant C, **4**:201
Personal experience narrative,
   1:148, **1**:149, **1**:243, **1**:264,
   1:330, **1**:334, **1**:343, **1**:347, **2**:6,
   2:46, **2**:123, **2**:124, **2**:162, **2**:168,
   2:217, **3**:68, **3**:80, **3**:86, **3**:224,
   3:233, **3**:362, **4**:95, **4**:121, **4**:124,
   4:157, **4**:280; "testimony," **2**:163
Personal legend, **4**:280
Personal vision quests, **3**:193
Peterson, Albert, **1**:93
Phillips, Percy, **3**:251
"Phoebe Ward, Witch," **2**:172,
   2:181
Phratries, **1**:170
Pickett, William "Bill," **3**:224
Pilgrims, **1**:5
Pimona, Molly Kinsman, **3**:277,
   3:369, **3**:377
Pirate legends, **1**:4, **1**:26
Plains and Plateau: extent of, **3**:131;
   heroes/heroines/tricksters/fools,
   3:185–239; Hispanic influences,
   3:132; horses, introduction of,

3:132, **3**:179, **3**:230; Mormons,
   3:133; Native American inhabi-
   tants, **3**:131–33; origins, tales of,
   3:135–84; sacred tales of the
   supernatural, **3**:241–63
Plains people, **3**:4
"Playing Dead Twice in the Road,"
   1:263; variant A, **1**:285; variant
   B, **1**:286; variant C, **1**:286
"Playing Godfather," **1**:287, **2**:64,
   2:67, **2**:240
"Playing Mourner," **2**:64, **2**:240
Poe, Edgar Allan, **1**:27
"Poison Payphone," **4**:205
"Poison Perfume," **4**:198; variant B,
   4:199
"Poisoned Coca-Cola," **4**:269
Polish tales, **1**:131
Ponca, **1**:149
Poohegans, **1**:64–65
Porcupine, **1**:21; tale bearer, **3**:361
"Possessed of Two Spirits," **2**:164,
   2:167
"Possum and Weasel Have a Falling
   Out," **1**:288
Pow-wowing, **1**:122, **1**:264, **1**:330
Power and social stratification
   theme, **1**:41, **1**:86
"Prairie Falcon's Contest with
   Meadowlark," **3**:335, **3**:367
Pratt, **1**:359
"President Bush's IQ," **4**:255
"Priceless," **4**:188
Privett, Mollie, **3**:68
Privett, Samuel Thomas ("Booger
   Red"), **3**:4, **3**:68
"Proctor and Gamble and Liz
   Claiborne Confess to Church of
   Satan on Sally," **4**:242
Protest tales, **2**:227; and modeling
   oppression, **2**:233
"Providence Hole," **1**:148, **1**:236,
   1:238
Pueblo, **3**:4; matrilineal clans, **3**:8
"Pumpkin Sold as an Ass's Egg,"
   2:73

von Münchhausen, Baron Karl
   Friedrich Hieronymus, 3:99
Vrbooska, Anca, 1:40, 1:85, 1:132

"Wabasaiy," 1:147, 1:162, 1:193
Waí-hu-si-wa, 3:52
"Wailing Wall," 4:250
"Wait Until I Get Dry," 1:303
Wakea, 3:293
"Wal-Mart Boycott," 4:185
"Walking Skeleton," 3:369; variant
   B, 3:372; variant C, 3:377
"Wanted for Attempted Murder,"
   4:234
Ward, Monroe, 2:87, 2:140
Ward, Miles, 2:87, 2:140
"The Watcher Tricked," 1:306
Waterspirits, 1:227
Wendat (Wyandot), 1:4, 1:9
West (California and Nevada),
   3:267–69; gold rush, 3:268;
   heroes/heroines/tricksters/fools,
   3:305, 326–46; origins, tales of,
   3:271, 277–81, 287–92;
   post–Civil war pressures, 3:268;
   pre-European contact cultures,
   3:268; sacred tales of the supernatural, 3:361, 364–86; Spanish
   influence, 3:268; terrain, 3:267
West (Hawaii), 3:267, 269; extent,
   3:269;
   heroes/heroines/tricksters/fools,
   3:297, 312–26; nature gods
   ("akua"), 3:292; origins, tales of,
   3:274, 3:281, 3:284, 3:292;
   sacred tales of the supernatural,
   3:353; terrain, 3:269; ti plant,
   3:284

"When Brer Deer and Brer Terrapin
   Runned a Race," 2:92
"When Brer Frog Give a Big
   Dining," 2:106
"When Brer 'Possum Attend Miss
   Fox's House-Party," 2:64, 2:91
"When Brer Rabbit Help Brer
   Terrapin," 2:96
"When Brer Rabbit Saw Brer Dog's
   Mouth So Brer Dog Can
   Whistle," 2:40
"When Brer Rabbit Was Presidin'
   Elder," 2:77
"When Brer Wolf Have His Corn
   Shucking," 2:69
"When Mr. Pine Tree and Mr. Oak
   Tree Fall Out," 2:25
"When Mr. Terrapin Went Riding
   on the Clouds," 2:218
"When Raven Wanted to Marry
   Snowbird and Fly with the
   Geese," 4:98
"When the World Was Formed,"
   3:17
"Where Did Adam Hide," 2:166;
   original version, 2:310
"Where's Mr. McGinnis?" 1:313
White, Joseph (Mandarong), 1:36,
   1:116
"White Substance Delays Aggie
   Football Practice," 4:230
"Whiteberry Whittington," 1:52,
   2:152
"Why Frog Lives in the Water,"
   1:270
"Why Mr. Owl Can't Sing," 2:38
"Why Rabbit Has a Short Tail,"
   2:239
"Why the Deer has a Short Tail,"
   1:149, 1:170
"Why the People Tote Brer Rabbit
   Foot in their Pocket," 2:26, 2:40
"Why the Spider Never Got in the
   Ark," 2:159
"Why We Love Children," 4:172

Wichita, 3:131–32, 3:135; divided
   village motif, 3:213; tales,
   3:136–59, 3:212
"Wild Bill," 1:148, 1:243
Wild Bunch, 3:221
Wiley, Betty, 1:353
Wilkenson, Susie, 2:132
Will, George F., 3:193
Willoughby, Loneva, 1:281
Wiltse, A. S., 2:197
"The Wine, the Farm, the Princess,
   and the Tarbaby," 2:4, 2:49, 2:53,
   2:64, 2:233, 2:258
Winnebago: cosmology, 1:227; tales,
   1:188, 1:207, 1:227; War (1827),
   1:148
"Wisa'kä," 1:149, 1:159
"The Witch and the Boiler," 2:174,
   2:178, 2:180
"Witch Flights," 3:5, 3:121, 3:124
Witchcraft: punishment for, 3:125;
   vs. hoodoo, 1:348
Witches, 1:65; ability to slip out of
   their skin (cross-cultural belief),
   1:334, 4:136; "awl-elbow," 1:179;
   borrowing object of victim motif,
   1:112; cross-cultural "hag experience," 1:112; little boy witch,
   2:204; "riding" of victims motifs,
   1:110, 2:178; salt as antidote to
   evil (cross-cultural belief), 1:334;
   shape-shifting, 1:122, 2:27; transformation motifs, 1:110, 2:171;
   with two hearts (Hopi), 3:58. See
   also Brujeria; Pavawut
"Witches Discovered," 3:5, 3:122,
   3:124
"Witch's Apprentice," 1:347, 1:350
Wolf Clan, 1:128
"Wolf of the Greenwood," 1:6, 1:52,
   2:152
"The Wolf Overeats in the Cellar,"
   2:109
Wollman, Mr., 1:131
"Woman Cat," 1:338, 3:123; variant A, 1:339; variant B, 1:340

358

About the Editor

Thomas A. Green is Associate Professor of Anthropology at Texas A&M University. His many books include *Martial Arts in the Modern World* (Praeger, 2003), *Martial Arts of the World: An Encyclopedia* (2001), *Folklore: An Encyclopedia of Beliefs, Customs, Tales, Music, and Art* (1997), and *The Language of Riddles: New Perspectives* (1984).